✳✳✳ The Normal Woman

THE
NORMAL
WOMAN

Madeline Gray

Charles Scribner's Sons   New York

To My Husband,
ROBERT RUBIN,
without whom this book would not have been possible.

✳✳✳ Contents

INFANCY

1. What This Book Is For   *1*
2. A Girl-Child Is Born   2
3. Stronger Than the Male   6
4. The Gifts She's Born With   *9*

CHILDHOOD

5. She Starts to Grow and Discover Herself   *18*
6. She Gets Independence, But Experiences Shame   26
7. She Gets Initiative and Learns to Love   34
8. The Comfort of Her Thumb   *42*
9. The Word You Cannot Say   *49*
10. "But She Doesn't Eat a Thing"   *55*
11. Is It Glands?   *61*
12. She Goes to School and Learns to Work   68

PUBERTY

13. Negative, Tomboy and Difficult   *71*
14. The Mystery of the Hormones   8o
15. She Pauses and Listens   *90*

ADOLESCENCE

16. Menstruation: A Tide Rises and Falls   *101*
17. Intense Awakening   *126*

18. Full and Brimming Over   137
19. Obsessed with Her Body   149
20. Time for Decision   174

EARLY MARRIAGE

21. True Love   183
22. The Giant Step   191
23. Period of Disillusion   208
24. Birth Control: The Greatest Freedom   211
25. It's Not Always Easy to Conceive   218
26. "Doctor, Am I Pregnant?"   230

PREGNANCY AND BIRTH

27. The Pregnancy Drama: Act I   236
28. Pregnancy: Act II   254
29. Pregnancy: Act III   266
30. Intermission   275
31. The Drama of Birth: Act I   286
32. Birth: Act II   297
33. Birth: Act III   306
34. Readjustment Time   311

MATURITY

35. The Busy Years   326
36. Backaches, Face-Lifts and Such   343
37. Hand to Mouth   352
38. Another Rung of the Ladder   361
39. The Sheltering Years   377

INDEX   395

✳✳✳ The Normal Woman

✳✳✳ 1 What This Book Is For

Women in today's world love living in that world, but it's not easy. For modern medicine has caused them to think more about their bodies than at any other time in history; modern psychology more about their minds. And the net result of this thinking has been confusion. They've been bombarded with so much publicity about physical diseases like cancer, hypertension, multiple sclerosis; told so much about mental diseases like paranoia, dementia, and schizophrenia, that they sometimes begin to think they are crazy or have them all. They're not sure where normality begins and illness ends.

They notice one day, for instance, they feel sunny and ready to conquer the world; yet a few days later, for no apparent reason, they're so irritable they can hardly keep from screaming. Does this mean they need to fly to a psychiatrist because they're going out of their minds?

They notice one day, too, that their breasts are light and small and comfortable; a few days later so heavy and puffy their oldest blouse hardly fits. Does that mean they have a cancer, or what?

Or they give birth to a baby. They very much wanted that baby, and expected right in the hospital to get a rush of "radiant motherhood," a feeling of unbounded joy. They do get such a feeling for about 48 hours. They then often shift from elation to depression, and want to do nothing but cry. Is this the way a happy mother is supposed to behave?

Then, they remember how at nine they were slim and straight and upright. But around eleven they got a potbelly that seemed to come from nowhere. Yet by around thirteen the belly had disappeared as unexpectedly as it had come.

Birth mysteries. Growing-up mysteries. Day-to-day mysteries. How much of this is normal? What's a normal woman anyway?

Women worry greatly over this matter because to many women the structure and inner workings of their bodies are mysterious and frightening, and the feelings connected with their bodily changes seem unusual or abnormal. That's because they do not know their own inner workings; know that the same things that happen to them happen to other women as well.

That's what this book is for: to help women understand themselves better. Understand their inner workings and feelings as they swing along from "womb to tomb."

Help men understand them better, too. Make it clear why it's as important for men to understand women as it is for women to understand themselves. For men are born of women, are brought up and taught by women, marry and live with women, and are—every last "he-man" among them—partly female themselves.

Above all, it is to stop both men and women, when being told the title of this book, from giving a nervous laugh or wink and answering as if it were a bright new thought, "A normal woman? I always say, *is* there such a thing?"

✳✳✳ 2 A Girl-Child Is Born

A woman lies on a hospital delivery table. A man in white near the head of the table gives her a whiff of anesthesia or talks to her encouragingly. Another man sits waiting on a low stool near her feet.

Minutes pass. The woman strains and pushes. One tremendous push and a tiny head starts to emerge. The man on the stool grasps the head gently and helps ease it through the vaginal opening. After the head he eases the shoulders, then the rest of the tiny body. The woman gives a huge, trembling sigh of relief. It's happened at last—the stupendous miracle of birth.

Soon she rallies and asks the two questions new mothers usually ask: "Is it a boy or a girl, doctor?" and "Is it normal?" The doctor does not answer for a moment. He is too busy looking at the baby or giving it the smart slap on its buttocks that brings on the birth-cry.

Hearing the cry, the doctor relaxes and replies: "It's a girl and, as far as I can see, quite normal."

With this girl-child who has just been born begins our story—the story of the bundle of nerve and flesh and bone that has puzzled people since unremembered time. Puzzled them since she was created from the changing materials of an ovum and sperm, and brought into a changing world. Indeed, the very essence of her life is change. For look what has already happened to her in the few hours since she left the womb: She has travelled from a peaceful haven of dark and quiet, to a world bright with light and buzzing with sounds. She has come from a place where the temperature never varied, to a place where the temperature constantly goes up and down. From a place where she absorbed air effortlessly through the umbilical cord, to a place where she has to breathe it in through lungs. From a place where she took in food pre-digested for her by her mother, into a world where she will have to do her own digesting down a complicated digestive tract. And from floating in a bed of supporting water that shielded her from every bump and shock, to a world where bumps and shocks are a daily occurrence and where she must learn to accept her own.

But she weathered these great birth-changes; weathered them exceedingly well. A minute or two after her head struck air, she began to breathe. At the same time, a tiny valve in her heart automatically shut while her body set up a circulation of its own. In another few minutes, she began the complicated act of sucking, sucked her fingers if nothing else was available or, if put to the breast, sucked that.

She did all these things easily because she was taught by millions of years of evolution to do them. Do them because she was normal, as are 95 per cent of the babies born today.

WHAT IS NORMAL?

What did the doctor mean by the word "normal"? What, in more detail, was he trying to say?

First, he was not trying to say "average." Take, for instance, the question of weight. Parents get very excited about weight when a baby is born. If it's above seven pounds, they are proud. If it is below, they are worried. For they have somewhere gotten the idea that seven pounds is a "must" weight, and a baby must reach it on the dot.

But seven pounds is merely an average. It was arrived at by researchers who weighed thousands of babies, added up all the figures obtained, then divided them by the total number of babies weighed. The result was not a description of any one particular baby. It was merely a mathematical computation, a statistic useful only as a general guide. So no

single baby is expected to weigh that exact amount. She may be one to
two pounds below or one or two pounds above, and still be within what
is called "normal range."

This matter of normal range is most important. "Average" is usually
expressed in a single figure. "Normal range" is expressed in several
figures. If a doctor wanted to predict the normal range of weight at birth
of a baby girl, he'd say, "between six and eight pounds," or *around
seven pounds.*"

NOT PERFECT

Then by "normal" the doctor did not mean all-over perfect.

Medicine has a concept of a "perfect" heart, a "perfect" set of lungs,
a "perfect" set of teeth, but one seldom gets them all. Parents dream of
a Greta Garbo nose, or a Marilyn Monroe figure, or a Jacqueline Kennedy pair of wide-set eyes, plus the stamina of an Eleanor Roosevelt to
boot, but it almost never happens that anybody gets all of these. When
a doctor finds a girl baby who is reasonably pretty, and in reasonably
good working order, he is well content.

NOT FREE FROM PAIN

And the doctor certainly didn't mean by "normal" that the newborn
before him was a fairy princess who would glide along free from pain
and conflict. On the contrary, he knew her life would be full of pain
and conflict. He merely meant she'd be able to bear up under all the
challenges that life brings. Have the strength to meet her problems; even
find within herself the ability to turn many of her pains into pleasures
as she went along.

To be sure, her emotional balance-scale might sometimes swing up
to such high peaks and down to such low valleys she'd be afraid she
couldn't meet them. There'd be blue moments when she'd be utterly
depressed. Others when she'd be utterly lonely. Still others when the very
bother to keep alive seemed difficult, and she was sure she was good for
nothing at all.

But the difference between normal and abnormal would be this:
there would not be too many blue or depressed moments for a normal
woman, nor would they be too lasting. They'd go away in a few days as
a rule, not stay for unbroken weeks or months.

LOVE AND WORK

In short, in spite of her peaks and valleys, she'd have the ability to function. Function toward two main goals, the ability to love and the ability to work. Love and work as a part of a survivable family. Love and work toward creating . . . creating survivable children, or good books, or love poems, or a better society, or superb pies, or all of these.

This book is not about psychiatry, but it will often quote psychiatrists for the simple reason they are among the people who have given normality a lot of thought. For how can they help a mentally ill person get better if they don't know where they're trying to go? So the definition of normal as "the ability to love and the ability to work" is reported to be Freud's, although Freud freely admitted he didn't know much about women, and didn't elaborate on his definition in regard to them.

Psychologist Leon H. Saul of the University of Pennsylvania does elaborate on it. Dr. Saul says normality and abnormality are also a matter of too little or too much. Too much misery, too little happiness. For a certain amount of joy in living is a basic ingredient. When a woman has so little pleasure in life she becomes the eternal *mater dolorosa,* or martyr mother; when she sees this world mainly as a "vale of tears" and works and loves as if these were stern, hard tasks to be performed dutifully rather than with joy, she is not normal either. For unbroken human misery often turns outward in destructive aggression against society, or inward in destructive aggression against the self. The eternally unhappy person who turns his hostility against himself to the point of suicide, the withdrawn alcoholic who kills himself in a different way, the eternally miserable person who turns his hostility outward against society to the point of murder are among the most abnormal people there are.

It is men who tend much more to go to these extremes of lasting destructive aggression, destructive despair, inability to work and love, than women do. Women may moan and talk a great deal about their "sad lot," but the statistics tell the story:

125 per cent more men than women commit murder.

220 per cent more men than women commit suicide.

300 per cent more men than women become alcoholics.

PATTERN OR RULE

For the word "normal" comes from the Latin *norma,* meaning pattern or rule. And women's lives have a more stable pattern than men's. It is not a simple pattern, to be sure; it has the intricacies and variations of a fine Oriental rug.

But it's there just the same, even though, paradoxically, women get more actual setbacks than men do. Just when they think their life-paths are going straight, they twist and weave in a maddening way. But women have resources to help them meet their setbacks, to bend with the twists and weaves rather than be broken by them. And the more carefully you examine a woman's life, the more you see what these resources are. It's just not true that "you never can tell with a woman." You can tell if you know where to look.

So let's go back to the room in which our girl-child was just born, and start to do a little looking now.

✳✳✳ 3 Stronger Than the Male

Before we can learn to work and love, to be happy or create a survivable family, we have to survive ourselves. A girl-child gets a head start toward survival because she's so comparatively sound. She's sounder than a boy before birth, sounder at birth, sounder during childhood and maturity; sounder right down the line.

Look at some figures. About 130 boys are conceived to every 100 girls. But boys in the womb are so much weaker than girls that many more boys spontaneously abort, with the result that out of the 130 boys who were started, only about 106 boys are left to get born compared to 100 girls.

We have then at birth these 106 boys to 100 girls. But newborn girls are so much stronger than newborn boys that they are almost a whole month ahead in their development as far as resistance to disease is concerned, and so more boy babies die, either immediately or soon

CHARGE TO

Mr. John Patterson
Phila. Suburban Gas Co.
Box 95
Upper Darby Penna.
Spec. ofr.

X **PURCHASER**

SOLD BY	DATE	KIND OF SALE	SHOP NO.	
3	9/17	Chf	324	**6369-21**

The Normal Woman

NO CASH REFUNDS

GIFT	X'MAS	CARD	SEPARATE

MERCHANDISE TOTAL	
TAX	
HANDLING	
TOTAL	

	NO. OF ITEMS SENT	AD CODE
1		MERCH. CODE

BOOKS

RECORDS

NEW YORK, N. Y.
724 Fifth Ave. (at 57th St.)
665 Fifth Ave. (at 52nd St.)
436 Fifth Ave. (at 39th St.)
Grand Central Terminal
(412 Lexington Ave.)
Grand Central Terminal
(Vanderbilt Ave. Concourse)
14 Wall St.

MANHASSET, N. Y.
1530 Northern Blvd.

GARDEN CITY, N. Y.
1144 Franklin Ave.

SCARSDALE, N. Y.
744 White Plains Rd.

PARAMUS, N. J.
The Fashion Center

WEST HARTFORD, CONN.
Bishop's Corner

BALA-CYNWYD, PA.
105 E. City Line Ave.

BALTIMORE, MD.
6315 York Rd.

WASHINGTON, D. C.
1331 E Street, N. W.

DETROIT, MICH.
Fisher Bldg.
Penobscot Bldg.

GROSSE POINTE, MICH.
17116 Kercheval Ave.

BIRMINGHAM, MICH.
239 Pierce St.

TOLEDO, OHIO
3301 W. Central Ave.

ST. LOUIS, MO.
310 N. 8th St.
48 Maryland Plaza

CLAYTON, MO.
8131 Forsythe Blvd.

DALLAS, TEXAS
1411 Commerce St.
218 North Park Center

FORT WORTH, TEXAS
7000 Camp Bowie Blvd.

PHOENIX, ARIZ.
2460 East Camelback Rd.

NEW ORLEANS, LA.
633 Canal St.

MIAMI BEACH, FLA.
934 Lincoln Rd.

PALM BEACH, FLA.
228 Worth Ave.

BOSTON, MASS.
Associated with
The Old Corner Book Store
50 Bromfield St.

BOOKS AND RECORDS
ARE MORE THAN A GIFT
THEY ARE A COMPLIMENT

---

after birth, so that by the end of the first few months or years, there are only about 100 boys left to 100 girl infants.

True, a few extra boys do seem to get born in wartime, as people have always noticed. During or right after a war, there often are 108 boys born to 100 girls.

These extra two boys have puzzled people for a long time. Usually they have attributed them to the workings of Divine Providence, saying, "God just knows that many men are being killed, so he fixes things up so extra boys get born to make up for it."

But scientists answer that two extra boys in a hundred hardly make up for the huge number of men killed. They believe that women during wartime tend to marry younger and have their children earlier, and young women are healthier than older women. These healthier, younger women help prevent the less fit boys from aborting, so a few more get carried through to delivery date.

AS THE YEARS GO BY

But whatever the reason, girls still prove more survivable not only during the first crucial months of life, but as the years go by.

In childhood and adolescence, many more boys than girls meet with accidental deaths, mainly because girls are less restless and aggressive, and so keep out of dangerous situations more. (Boys are so comparatively restless, a good detective can tell if a boy or girl has slept in a certain bed; the boy's is much more mussed up.) Then girls are more resistant to childhood infections and fevers. And later on, the only illnesses women suffer more from than men are gall bladder trouble, or trouble connected with the reproductive system (so-called "female trouble"). Women get less heart trouble, fewer peptic ulcers, less almost everything else.

Women are more prone to disorders of the reproductive system because theirs is a more complicated reproductive system than men's. Sexually you might compare women to modern cars with power steering, power brakes, automatic shifts and air-conditioning; and men to the simple old Model Ts. In women there are so many more reproductive things that can go wrong. That is why, in the old days, so many of them died in childbirth and filled the graveyards before their time. But today, with modern obstetrics, this does not happen. Today the unnatural situation of dying while giving birth has been corrected, so we find women outliving men. We get the interesting situation of about 130 males starting the race by being conceived as against 100 females conceived, more males than females aborting so that only about 106 males to 100 females survive to delivery date, about an equal number of each surviving to maturity, and women living many years more.

The latest figures of the Metropolitan Life Insurance Company give women at birth a life-expectancy of five to seven years more than men.

OF MICE AND WOMEN

Hearing this, many men will still cry quickly: "But of course women live longer! Look at how much less they drink and smoke! Or are women under the same terrific stress that men are to make big money? Do they engage in dangerous occupations like mining, rolling hot steel, piloting planes? Do they get drafted so they must get out and fight whether they want to or not? It's the drinking and fighting and stresses that kill men ahead of women, that's what!"

Alas, these arguments don't hold up. For female mice live longer than male mice. Female moths live longer than male moths. Female houseflies live longer than male houseflies. And almost all the old fish caught in the great Bering Sea fishing-waters are female fish, since the male fish have died before.

Now male fish don't drink anything harder than water. Male houseflies don't smoke themselves into the grave. Male mice are not noted for living dangerously. And if male moths have heart attacks as a result of worrying about junior moth's college education, we have yet to hear the tale. Yet males die earlier throughout the natural world.

Since it happens universally, the cause of longer life in women must be looked for elsewhere—in their basic strength.

THE MONKS AND THE NUNS

Recently a pair of researchers decided to do a special survey on this. They looked for a group of men and women who as nearly as possible led identical lives, and found them in monks and nuns. Monks and nuns work about the same number of hours a day; they have the same lack of family or money problems; they eat and drink about alike. Yet the Sisters lived longer than the Brothers. The results duplicated those of the studies on fish, flies, mice and moths.

"The scientific explanation for longer life among females must be biological rather than social," declared *The Journal of the American Medical Society,* which reported the study. In sum, longer and healthier life for women is an advantage that doesn't come from their way of living. It's biological, or built in.

✳✳✳ 4 The Gifts She's Born With

Where does a baby girl get her biological advantages—what gifts is she born with that help her get started toward her first goal of surviving, or keeping herself alive?

We're back now in the hospital. The nurse is carrying our baby girl, a few minutes old, to the nursery—carrying that tiny, exquisite body which isn't nearly as fragile as it looks.

SHE WEIGHS LESS THAN A BOY

It is easier to carry her than it is to carry a boy. She weighs around seven pounds, or slightly less than a newborn boy, with a normal range from as little as five pounds to as high as nine.

SHE IS COMPLETE

But whatever she weighs, if she is a baby who has spent her full allotted time in the womb, she is amazingly complete.

She has all the muscles, all the body structures and all the nerve cells she will ever have. Most of these nerve cells, to be sure, are not yet connected up with each other, as only about one-fourth of the brain is developed at birth. People often wonder why a human baby can do some things at birth like kicking its feet vigorously, but not others like lifting its head. This is because the nerve cells that carry the impulses for head-lifting are not yet connected to the brain, as later they will be.

SHE CAN BREATHE

But far more important than lifting her head, the minute she is born, she can breathe. Take in the air essential to life. That's why a baby is born head first as a rule; she has to have her head out first so she can start breathing immediately.

This breathing is a remarkable achievement. Air is a brand new medium to a baby, since in the womb a baby is completely surrounded by water, and gets its oxygen through the umbilical cord, as a deep-sea diver gets oxygen through a special line to the surface.

Yet when our baby emerges, she starts breathing away like an old hand. The birth-cry that has puzzled people for centuries is a device to help her do this. Misanthropes like Schopenhauer used to try to explain the birth-cry as a cry of rage over suddenly finding oneself in a cruel, cold world. It's nothing of the sort. The cry is a survival-device that gets a baby's mouth open wide so that she can take in a big breath of air to inflate the lungs. And if a baby's face seems contorted while uttering this birth-cry, the contortions spell strain, not pain, at doing a brand new act.

A MARGIN OF SAFETY

A baby also arrives with an extra supply of oxygen in its blood that you might call a "packed lunch" or emergency ration, to tide it over in case it doesn't start breathing immediately.

Because of this emergency oxygen supply, a baby can survive for a much longer period without breathing than an older person can. A grown man or woman cannot live longer than about five minutes without breathing. In fact, irreparable damage can be done to his brain in as little as three minutes. But a baby has a far greater margin of safety. Dr. Clement A. Smith, Medical Director of the Children's Hospital of Wayne, Michigan, says that a newborn baby can survive unharmed up to fifteen minutes before taking its first independent breath. So if, as sometimes happens during the birth process, the umbilical cord becomes tangled and no air is taken in for several minutes, no damage is done. The baby not only survives, it is normal. Its packed lunch has carried it through.

Once breathing is established, however, it is far less regular in a baby than in an adult, and shows a much greater range. A baby may take as few as twenty breaths per minute, or as many as 100. Adults often get frightened because a baby seems to be "holding its breath," when it is merely breathing temporarily at a slow normal rate.

OTHER MARGINS OF SAFETY

But a baby has other margins of safety. The minute it is born, its temperature drops dramatically, yet it is prepared to cope with this, too. It does not do this as efficiently as it will a year later, when it will shiver, which will produce heat and raise its temperature. So at first it will need clothing that changes with the temperature of the room. Another margin of safety at birth is a tiny valve in its heart that automatically shuts and sets up independent circulation of the blood the minute it is born. And it starts to suck immediately—even before it has to, or before there is really any need for food. For its second "packed lunch" of its own food makes it unnecessary to have anything besides water for the first twenty-four hours at least. Yet sucking movements, which are as complicated and marvelous as breathing, are also made right after birth though no sucking was done in the womb.

SHE HAS TASTE, TOUCH AND SMELL

Why should it suck when it does get fed? What is conducive to its survival and what not?

Nature stands by and helps here as well. A newborn arrives with a surprisingly well-developed sense of smell and taste. Smell guides it toward food before it touches its lips; taste attracts it toward sweet liquids like milk, and away from liquids that are sour or spoiled. Dr. Elizabeth Hurlock of Columbia University tells of tests done on newborn babies in which small amounts of sour, salty, sweet or bitter fluids were dropped into their mouths. They made pleasant faces and swallowed vigorously when the sweet fluids hit their taste-buds; they made wry faces and spat when the bitter or sour fluids arrived. And, interestingly, they welcomed the salty fluids almost as eagerly as the sweet.

In other tests for touch, newborn babies spat out pieces of rubber nipples that had been deliberately damaged, while they sucked contentedly from nipples left smooth and whole.

ALL KEENER IN A GIRL

Most important for our story, the senses of taste, smell and touch are all keener in a girl.

Doctors have a name for the first two weeks of life, the crucial period when a baby is changing over from life within mother to life with mother, when the battle for survival is as great as it will ever be. They call these two weeks the "neonate," or change-over time.

During the neonate, a girl responds more quickly and eagerly to every sense test. Her skin, which has also dramatically changed from the skin of a creature underwater to a creature on dry land, is more sensitive. She is more irritated over wet diapers than a boy baby is, proving it by fussing for clean diapers while a boy remains nonchalant and undisturbed.

In all this a girl foreshadowing her greater awareness—a feminine awareness to everything around her and inside of her that will keep her listening with special intensity to her body's signals all her days.

LITTLE SIGHT

Oddly enough, sight is one of the senses that is least developed at birth. The newborn, whether boy or girl, sees little and sees that vaguely. Because its eyes aren't focusing yet, for the first few weeks its mother's face is merely a distant blur attached to the nearer and far more fascinating bottle or breast.

OTHER POOR EQUIPMENT

The filtering power of its intestinal tract is poor at birth too, so it cannot filter out certain complex proteins in its food, making it develop allergies sometimes that later disappear. The concentrating power of the kidneys is poor, too, so it can't concentrate its urine and must get rid of it frequently in small amounts. And its muscle-tone is hypertonic, so that it tosses about in a way that will later subside.

PAIN AND FEAR

Oddly, too, the feelings of pain and fear are little developed at birth. This is odd because pain and fear are vital for survival; no one can stay alive very long without pain and fear as warnings of danger. But a human baby has few fears because there are adults around to do the fearing for it. Also, a human baby can neither fight nor run, and of what use are fears without the ability to fight or run from that which has made one afraid?

So a baby is born fearing mainly two things—noises and falling. The noises have to be sudden or very loud, however, like the sound of a train whistle shrieking or of voices screaming. Everyday noises, like those of ordinary conversation and a radio playing, are accepted as the humdrum things they are. But a baby is very sensitive to the *tone* of different voices. In this way, it learns soon to distinguish between various people even though it does not see them clearly; to single out its mother's voice in particular, starting a tight bond with its mother that will last throughout its days.

THE STARTLE REFLEX

Doctors lump the fear of falling and of sudden noise into the "startle reflex." By this they mean that a newborn baby instinctively startles when a fall is impending, or a sudden loud noise is heard.

One test of normality in the newborn is the presence of this startle reflex. Dr. A. H. Parmalee, Professor of Pediatrics at the University of Southern California in Los Angeles, lays a baby a few hours old on a table and lets it rest there a few minutes. Then he strikes the table hard with his fist, creating both a noise and a sudden shake-up. If it is normal, it will startle by extending its arms and spreading its fingers, then bring its arms forward in an embracing movement as if trying to grab onto something for support. If it does not, he concludes it has not the sense to be frightened and has suffered brain-damage before birth.

Two Cornell University psychologists, Drs. Richard Wall and Eleanor Gibson, did other experiments with year-old babies. They wanted to see whether babies who tumble off beds do so because they don't know the danger of high places and let themselves roll to the edge by accident, or whether they know the danger and want the excitement of tumbling and being picked up. So they placed some babies on the middle of a sheet of heavy glass a few feet above a carpeted floor, using glass so that the babies could look through it and be aware of the drop below. They then tried to coax the babies to crawl toward the edge where they might tumble off.

Ninety-two per cent looked down through the glass, recognized the danger and refused to budge. Or if they did, they merely ventured near the edge, took a fast look and beat a retreat. The other 8 per cent were more foolhardy, and fell. *Life* magazine for June 15, 1959, reported the experiment with pictures, and the startled expression on those who did venture near the edge was something to see.

OTHER TESTS OF NORMALITY

In addition to testing for normality by the startle reflex, Dr. Parmalee tests the "grasping reflex" in a newborn, as well as noticing the way it sleeps.

The grasping reflex means grabbing onto anything handy and holding on. Dr. Parmalee tests it by placing one of his fingers first on the palm of the baby's hand, then under its toes, then on the ball of its foot. A normal baby should almost immediately curl hand, toes or foot over his fingers. Indeed, its grasp at birth should be as strong as it ever will be. Though a human baby does not need to hang onto the branches of a tree the way a monkey does, it still needs a strong grasp to enable it to hang onto breast or bottle during the vital act of nursing, or to hang onto its mother's neck if it is tied to its mother's back and its mother has to run.

And a normal newborn should still sleep in what Dr. Parmalee calls "the posture of comfort"—slightly curled up as it blissfully slept in the womb.

The remarkably little pain a newborn has during its first few weeks may also be because a human baby is secluded from danger. Or maybe it's just because its nerve cells aren't all connected to each other yet, especially the nerve cells that carry pain-messages to the brain. But whatever the reason, there is no question that a newborn has a minimum of pain for a while.

It is because of this undeveloped sense of pain that boy babies can be circumcised without anesthesia before they're two weeks old. They may howl because they've been startled by the unaccustomed handling, but it's not a howl of pain. The Jews discovered this centuries ago, and decreed that circumcision should be done as early as possible after birth.

And recently the papers reported the extraction of a tooth from the mouth of a newborn who, by one of those mistakes nature occasionally makes, had been born with a big front tooth which would have interfered with nursing. It let out one surprised yelp when the dentist pulled the tooth, then quieted down and gave no evidence of even a painful twinge.

Something else a newborn has little of is saliva. This is because saliva both moistens the mouth and starts digestion of solid foods. But since it lives mostly on liquids like milk, saliva is another gift that isn't needed for a while.

Later, when saliva does come in, it comes in with a rush. So a baby wastes much of it by drooling it down its bib. One fond modern mother promptly gave her child the nickname of "Spitnick" when this occurred.

HER SEX ORGANS

All of these—few fears, little pain or sight, keen smell and taste, excellent sucking ability—belong to a newborn by right of its being a person. But our newborn is more than just any kind of person. She is something special, a girl. She has gifts that are exclusively hers. Chief among these are her sex organs.

First, there are her seen, or outside, organs—her vagina, clitoris and such, the ones on which the doctor based his announcement about the sex to which she belonged. Next there are her unseen, or inner, organs—her womb, ovaries and tubes.

HER VAGINA

A baby girl's vagina is exceedingly small at birth—hardly more than a narrow slit between her thighs. But this slit is made up of several parts. Starting at the outside of the vagina, there are two large folds or outer lips. Next, there are two smaller folds or inner lips. Next there is the entrance, or vestibule, and finally the interior, or cavity.

At the front of the vagina there is also the clitoris, a tiny piece of flesh embedded in the vaginal lips and protruding from them. Sometimes at birth it protrudes enough to be quite prominent, sometimes only enough to be barely seen. The clitoris is the most sensitive part of the vagina, however, so sensitive it almost rivals the male penis in sensitivity. It also resembles the penis in shape and structure, down to the foreskin which occasionally covers it at birth and makes it look even smaller than it is.

HER HYMEN

Then across the entrance to the vagina there is the hymen. Especially the hymen! I say "especially" because this thin piece of tissue, named after the "Hymenaeus," or song sung at ancient Greek marriages as the bridal procession marched to the groom's home, has probably caused more speculation than any other part of the human body you can name.

For it's the hymen that made people for centuries sure that nature had placed it where it is for the deliberate purpose of ensuring a girl's virginity.

It was to guard the hymen also that Victorian parents refused to let a girl ride a horse cross-saddle, or a bicycle with a long bar.

It was to keep the hyman intact that made some Egyptians sew up a girl's vaginal lips at puberty, then unsew them at marriage-time.

And it's because of the hymen that many mothers today still disapprove of menstrual tampons.

Yet it's the hymen that the University of Oregon's Dr. Goodrich C. Schauffler calls a "biologically unimportant organ," since he's not sure it was put there for any reason, and its function is something nobody knows. For, as we'll see, it is perfectly normal to be born without any hymen at all, or with one already full of holes.

THE UTERUS, OVARIES AND TUBES

So much for a girl's seen female sex organs. Now for her unseen ones, her uterus, ovaries and tubes.

If you want to start a spirited argument, bring up the question: "What makes a woman a woman, her ovaries or her womb?"

On the one side will be those who argue heatedly for the womb or uterus. (Both are merely names for the same thing.) They will argue that it's the womb that lets a woman do a job no man can do—bear a child. They may also say some people think the very word "woman" comes from womb-man, or man-with-a-womb.

Those who hold out for the other side may declare that even a woman without a womb, as after a hysterectomy, is still a woman if she has her ovaries. For it's her ovaries that make her sex-hormones, and these decide the case.

Whoever wins, they will have to agree on one thing: the womb is like a pear hanging upside down. A pear because it's wide and rounded at the top, and long and narrow at the bottom, and when a girl is fully grown it's about three inches long, or the size of a ripe Bartlett pear.

It can also be compared to a pastry-bag—the kind of wide cloth bag with a narrow metal tube that is used to make fancy cookies. Because, like a pastry-bag, the womb is hollow when empty. Like a pastry-bag, it puffs up when full, then squeezes out its contents and flattens again.

And how the womb can puff up or grow, then flatten again! It can grow from a weight of two ounces in a non-pregnant woman, to a weight of two pounds at delivery-date, and from two ounces to two pounds is a lot of growth, 1600 per cent to be exact. Yet within a few weeks after delivery it flattens out to two ounces again.

As to its squeezing-power, the womb has such strong muscles that during menstruation it can squeeze out in a few days what it took several weeks to build up; during childbirth it can push and squeeze a large baby down the long length of the birth-canal.

Yet oddly enough, the womb's first job after birth is neither to grow nor to squeeze, but to shrink. At birth it weighs only a fraction of an ounce, but it gets even smaller than it was, and stays smaller throughout childhood. Then at puberty it gets its big growth-spurt and grows to the two-ounce, non-pregnant size. Why it shrinks and then grows again we shall soon see.

HER OVARIES

Thousands of eggs are a lot of eggs, but that's the amazing number that lie hidden in the ovaries of a girl-child at birth. For her ovaries are her egg warehouses, and most researchers think she's born with all the eggs she'll ever produce. But her ovaries are much more than egg warehouses. They're also makers of ovarian hormones, and it's these hormones that will basically decide if she's female or male.

The ovaries lie in the lower part of the abdomen, and they look like almonds. They're long and slender and rounded like almonds, and also about an almond's size when fully grown, though at birth they are much, much smaller. And there they lie at birth, with their thirty thousand eggs already inside of them, waiting in her abdomen for the day when their eggs will be released one at a time, as crocuses are released from bulbs, to travel down the narrow passageways between her ovaries and womb to do their part in continuing the great chain of life.

HER TUBES

Her Fallopian tubes are the narrow passageways between ovaries and womb down which the eggs will one day travel. The eggs are no larger than the period at the end of this sentence, and the tubes so incredibly narrow they will never be thicker than a lead pencil, and they are called Fallopian tubes because they were discovered by an Italian named Gabriello Fallopius in the sixteenth century.

CHARGED WITH ENERGY

So our newborn baby girl lies in her crib, bassinet or box, with all these gifts: her gift of special sex organs, her gifts of immediate breathing, sucking, digesting and eliminating. Above all, her gift of the mysterious force called energy that distinguishes life from non-life and enables her to fight to survive.

And she is exceedingly survivable. Her design has been perfected by the millions of years of trial and error we call evolution, so that everything about the design, from the growth-possibilities of her uterus, to the keenness of her senses, to the brain that directs everything, is there according to plan. A plan that will become clearer and clearer as she grows.

✳✳✳ 5 She Starts to Grow and Discover Herself

And how she grows!

The neonate period is past, she takes the proverbial deep breath and starts on the period called infancy, which lasts from age two weeks to about two years.

Within a few months her nerve cells are making better connections so her breathing becomes more regular, she swallows with more decision and chokes less. By the end of the year her intestinal filtering system is working better, too, so that her allergies decrease, and her skin becomes more resistant to irritation so she has less diaper rash, while her body begins to build its own defenses against infections, supplanting the defenses acquired from her mother which last for only about six months.

Mostly, however, she is unaware of all this. Mostly, the first year of her life is spent in blissfully eating. She eats ravenously. Next to being near to her mother, her chief satisfaction is the passive one of satisfying her enormous hunger. But captive in a crib, what else can she be but passive? And how else besides eating ravenously can she begin to grow? So, weight for weight, she eats 2½ times as much as an adult, and at the end of her first year, she has gone up to an average of 23 pounds.

EYE-HUNGER

But soon food isn't her only hunger. Soon something else is added. This is eye-hunger. As her eyes begin to focus and see better, everything around her becomes fascinating. She literally devours the world with her eyes.

Simple things like plain light suddenly become alluring. Even while still lying flat and comparatively helpless, she tries energetically to turn herself toward a window rather than away from it. And a toy hung above her crib gives her such pleasure she'll stop the most intense bout of crying just to look at it, especially if it is colored a fascinating bright orange or red.

TOUCH-HUNGER

A few weeks of eye-hunger, and touch-hunger is added. Now it isn't enough to explore an object with her eyes, she also has to explore it with her sensitive fingers and mouth. Before she is four months old, she is ravenously exploring everything this way, trying to grasp, feel and manipulate her bed-cover, her mother's face, her crib bars, anything touchable in sight.

Adults think that when a baby puts everything she can get hold of into her mouth, she is trying to eat it. Not at all. She is trying to "feel" or explore it. Kittens put everything they can into their mouths; so do puppies and other young creatures. This is because in infancy the mouth is one of the most sensitive parts of the body, with nerve-endings as keen as they ever will be, and also because in infancy the mouth has muscles far more developed than the muscles of the hand.

At birth, only the palm of the hand is well developed; the original grasping reflex involves mainly the palm. The fingers are relatively weak, and cannot manipulate objects yet. But the mouth at birth is full of grasping muscles; it has a strong tongue, strong lips and strong jaws, all of which can manipulate or shift objects around.

The strong muscle-structure of the mouth, plus its keen sensitivity, makes the mouth for a long time the foremost feeling organ an infant has. And she uses it to savor and explore everything within reach.

SHE DISCOVERS HER OWN BODY

Yet none of an infant's explorations of things compare in interest to the explorations and discoveries she makes of her own body.

It's hard to realize how important this discovery of herself is. We adults know a good deal about our bodies. We have lived with them for so long, looked at them so often in mirrors, touched them, heard them criticized or praised, that we forget a baby knows nothing of itself; that each child is born as new and ignorant of itself as a traveler in an utterly strange country is ignorant of its customs. That she has to discover her body and what it can do completely from scratch.

The first step an infant takes in self-discovery is to learn what the parts of her body are. She explores her hands and feet with her mouth, then she starts exploring herself with her eyes.

One day our girl baby happens to look down and see, for instance, her fingers. At the beginning she isn't sure they *are* her fingers; she may not distinguish between them and toys of the same shape. But soon, maybe because her fingers stay always in the same place while toys come and go, maybe because her fingers give her different sensations than toys do, soon she realizes they are part of herself.

Another day she happens to look down and see her toes; another day her wrists, another her knees. Each absorbs her, as each in turn she comes to realize are hers, and each she misses if temporarily they disappear from view.

Having begun to get a picture of herself by exploring herself with her eyes, she next begins to explore herself by touch. And since touch at birth is even keener than sight, she probably enjoys touching herself even more than looking at herself. So she touches her fingers to each other; she touches her fingers to her wrists; she touches them to her toes. And she keeps on touching with particular interest those parts of herself that stick out, and those parts of herself that turn in.

Her nose sticks out, so it interests her more than her eyes which do not. Her navel turns in, so it is more fascinating than her abdomen which is flat. And the greatest pleasure of all comes when she touches a part of herself that sticks out against a part that turns in. When with her sticking-out fingers she explores her turned-in navel, she glows for fair.

The third way she gets a picture of herself is through position. This means the position her whole body is in.

All creatures develop some ideas of position. They know if they are standing right side up or upside down, lying on their backs or stomachs, or on the right or left sides. So even while in her crib, our baby begins to notice her position and fuss if she's changed from one which makes her feel comfortable to one that does not.

THE BODY IMAGE

And these three—her eye picture, touch picture and position picture—blend into a still larger picture of her body. A picture which is the sum of them all yet somehow more, as a melody is somehow more than the separate notes of which it is composed.

This larger picture of herself is her body image, meaning her body as she is totally aware of it. She doesn't arrive at this body image quickly. Indeed, she will be building and rebuilding it all her life. But she can hardly begin to live or move without it. For there can be no movement without advance knowledge of the tools.

So before a baby can lift herself in her crib, she must know she has a back that can do the lifting. Before pulling herself up in her playpen, realize she has arms that can reach and pull. Before taking a step, realize she has feet with the power to go. Before she attempts anything at all, she must say to herself in effect: "I have a body, and I can make it obey me. See! It is my body that is moving, my body that is lifting. I am on my way."

Thus, from seeing, touching, feeling, and, finally, thinking, this conception of herself as a creature with power is gradually built.

A CHILD WITH NO BODY IMAGE

The importance of a body image that grows from a discovery of what one has to what one can do is well illustrated by the story of Anna.

Anna was the illegitimate child of an uneducated farm girl, whose father, pious to the point of fanaticism, decided she must hide her shame by keeping the baby hidden in a dark attic so it would never be seen. Maybe he hoped the child would die, maybe he didn't know what he hoped; but anyway Anna was not only hidden but tied tight from birth, first into a crib and then a chair, so she couldn't move. Moreover, her mother wasn't allowed to speak to her, merely to bring her a small amount of milk at mealtimes, then to hurry back to work.

The child lived this way alone in the dark attic until one day some neighbors heard strange, whimpering sounds. They had heard them before and been told they were nothing, but this time they insisted on searching the house. They found the child, a handful of bones and naked except for a filthy diaper, shivering in the dark, and tied into a chair so small her legs had to be drawn up under her. Though by now she was almost five years old, she could not speak a word and seemed unable either to see or hear.

The neighbors had her removed to the county home where she got food, massage and massive doses of vitamins. But the food had to be liquid because she couldn't chew and, since she had never seen herself nor been able to explore herself, she had no idea what to do with her body. She tried to talk but all that came out were vague sounds like "da." She tried to stand up, but stumbled and fell.

Worst of all, though Anna was well cared for now, she didn't smile or show affection in any way except as a dog does, by rubbing her forehead against her nurse. A smile is imitative. In the busy county home, with one nurse to dozens of children, nobody had the time to stop and smile at Anna, so she didn't seem to have faith in her ability to smile back.

Then came a surprise. At the age of six, she was transferred from the county home to a private foster home. Within a comparatively short time she was smiling, feeding herself with a spoon, munching doughnuts and bumping down the stairs by sitting down on each step one at a time as she came down.

Kingsley Davis, who wrote up Anna's story for a scientific journal, attributes her progress in the foster home to the fact "she now had the undivided attention of one woman, a woman who was using the same common-sense methods by which mothers from time immemorial have socialized their infants—unremitting attention, and countless small rewards and punishments mixed always with a sympathetic interest and a hovering physical presence." All these Anna was getting for the first time in her life.

Unfortunately, the new state of affairs was too good to last. The foster mother found she couldn't keep Anna. She was sent to a small school for defective children, not because there was any proof of brain damage, but because there seemed to be no other place for her to go. She was now seven and a half, grossly overweight since she walked with difficulty and was also making up with almost constant eating for the years she had lost.

In the school her progress slowed down again. At nine, she had just begun to babble a few words like those of a two year old, to master bowel-control, wash her own hands and brush her teeth. At this point, she caught pneumonia and died.

But did she really die of pneumonia or give up the struggle to live? Would she ever have become survivable? Would she ever have learned to answer the basic questions: "Who am I" and "What can I do?"

THE NORMAL CHILD DOES LEARN

The normal infant happily does learn to answer these questions. She does so through exploration of her body, then by putting her body through endless tests that give her confidence in what her body can do. And as she does all this she develops strong feelings about herself. Mainly the feeling of approval or love.

A normal infant approves of her body from the moment of birth; loves it just as it is. If she happens to be born with a mouth that is large and wide, then large mouths are the thing to have. If her nose is short and snub, then short snub noses are fine. And, oh, what pleasure she gets from her hands and feet and fingers and toes, whatever their shape! For what other hands and feet and fingers and toes does she know?

Later she may compare herself with friends or neighbors and suffer acutely by comparison. Her nose may seem awful, her feet impossibly big. But not now. Now her self-approval is boundless, as she touches and explores herself with ever-growing delight.

But soon she starts to develop more than a body image, she begins to develop a person image, or self-image. As her brain cells become better and better connected, she begins to look upon herself as a total person, a self, a "me." And she approves of this total self as well.

Now thinking of herself as a self or person is a long step forward from thinking of herself as merely a body. For a body can exist alone. A person exists in a world of persons, relates to them, seeks to please them and gets their approval, too.

Now a baby begins to get this sense of herself as a person when she begins to recognize that she is a continuity—a continuity that changes from day to day but remains basically the same. As she begins dimly to realize that the people around her each day call her by the same name, speak to her in a similar tone of voice, treat her with the same essential kindness and warmth. Realize that, though she is the most dependent and helpless of all newborn creatures, she has one potent weapon at her command—a cry. A cry that in some miraculous way makes the people around her bring her food, change her when she is uncomfortable, fondle her when she is lonely, pick her up and soothe her when she cannot rest.

When they do not respond to her this way she becomes puzzled and anxious, since she can do nothing for herself. But mainly they do respond, and it is this gift of a cry, and the fact the cry does make others come quickly and kindly to her aid as a rule, that develops in her what Harvard's Erik H. Erikson calls the first foundation of happiness—a sense of inner goodness or basic trust. Trust in herself because she can get the food and warmth necessary for her survival. Trust in others because they are willing to provide these with reasonable speed.

HOSPITALISM

This sense of basic trust is so indispensable that babies who do not develop it soon after birth are seriously harmed. There is a disease called "hospitalism," in which babies left for a long time in hospitals or asylums where they get the best of care and food, but from indifferent nurses, become seriously retarded or actually die. Instead of basic trust, they develop mistrust. And this mistrust destroys the vital enthusiasm they need to fight to even start becoming normal, or to stay alive.

FRUSTRATION COMES WITH TEETHING

But nothing lasts indefinitely. The best developed feelings of trust or inner goodness soon become disturbed as the time for teething arrives, and the baby makes its first brush with frustration and rage.

Frustration and rage come at teething-time because a baby now instinctively tries to bite her mother—bite the very person who has been contributing most to her sense of basic trust. She tries to bite her because teething is her first real encounter with pain, and the only action that promises relief from this particular pain is biting. So she bites her mother's breast if she is nursing, her mother's fingers if she is offered a bottle, or any part of her mother within reach.

But since no mother relishes being bitten, she shies away, or at least, utters a sharp "no!" This "no" puzzles the baby, who has probably never been disapproved of or scolded before. Still, she tries biting again, and this time her mother may get angry to the point of slapping her hard.

The slap makes her doubly puzzled. Her "good mother," her "kind mother," has suddenly become a "bad mother," a frightening mother, and her instinct is to fight back. But she can't fight back much because she simply hasn't the power to do so. Besides, she feels she must have done something to deserve the slap, so her "good mother" has not only become a "bad mother" but her "good me" has become a "bad me." She turns some of her rage back in on herself and punishes herself. In this way, conscience is born, and a crisis in development is passed.

Dr. Erik Erikson says that people the world over, of every religion and race, have a dim remembrance of some kind of "original sin" they committed, and for which atonement to a universal "earth-mother" must be made. He relates this remembrance of sinfulness to the baby's wanting literally to bite the hand that's feeding her, and turning some of her rage back in on herself. This rage against herself brings a feeling of guilt and a need for self-punishment. She punishes herself by condemning herself as a "bad me," and atones for her sin by becoming "good" again. With atonement the sin is paid for, and her sense of basic trust is restored.

THE WEANING RAGE

But soon her trust is again shattered, this time by the experience of weaning.

Weaning, in its own way, is as painful as teething. It's not easy for a baby who has been sopping up milk from a soft breast or bottle suddenly to be made to substitute a hard cup or spoon; to munch and chew strange foods with effort where before she sucked liquids that easily slid down. So again she responds with anger or rage. And again another round of feeling herself a "bad me," and atoning by self-punishment, follows. In this way more conscience is developed, and another crisis in growth is passed.

THE LOST PARADISE

The crises aren't passed without leaving some lasting scars. These scars include feelings of incurable nostalgia and dislike of change. The nostalgia comes from the leaving of Paradise as symbolized by the breast and the forced entering into a harsher world, making us forever homesick for what we have left behind. For the breast was a Paradise where, with no more effort than to reach up and grasp it, deeply satisfying nourishment from the Tree of Life was once ours.

All religions tell not only of a Lost Paradise, but also of hope. And hope is based on the sense of basic trust we keep forever once we develop it. Hope and faith in a God who will help us; faith also in the people around us who will aid us to become the good and happy person we expect ourselves basically to be.

So, in spite of homesickness, in spite of the Lost Paradise, our normal baby moves on with hope and trust—moves on to the Promised Land of infancy, and enters another growth stage.

✳✳✳ 6 She Gets Independence, But Experiences Shame

Every great life-change is a dramatic one, especially for a child. Each child is like a voyager in a strange country; everything he experiences is utterly astonishing and new.

Soon after teething and weaning comes the dramatic change from horizontal to vertical. From being totally dependent on others to standing up, acquiring his first taste of independence. From being ignorant of how small he is, to discovering he is very small indeed.

HORIZONTAL TO VERTICAL

The world looks very different from a vertical position than it does from the horizontal one. Lying in her crib, our girl-child had limited vision; she saw people mainly as heads or half-bodies as they bent over her. Now crawling, then pulling herself upright, she suddenly sees them whole. Little wonder that for a while she stands still and stares at them wide-eyed, for she's staring at them as if seeing them for the first time.

She also stares because they suddenly look so big. In the crib, with no standards of comparison, she felt as huge as they were. Now she discovers that older brothers, sisters and parents are Goliaths, while she is a pygmy. So shame and inadequacy enter her for the first time; particularly enter a girl-child, who is even tinier than a boy of the same age, as she realizes she is no longer the center of the universe with all the magic powers she was so sure she had.

HEIGHT MAKES RIGHT

"Height makes right" says the Topeka, Kansas, psychiatrist Dr. Karl Menninger. It certainly does when height is something one hasn't. The remembered shame of having to start so small is another of the memories that never quite leaves us. It's one reason a little girl so much enjoys being picked up and carried on her father's shoulders, or strutting about on stilts. Being carried high or strutting give her for a few moments the pleasurable illusion of being taller than the rest of the world. Starting small also is the reason she now boasts, "My father can lick your father" (as if even a father who doesn't pick her up somehow extends her size) or later boasts, "I have more toys, more clothes, more money, more of all kinds of things than you have. I can extend myself with these, or with a taller hat, higher heels, or a bigger car."

Shame at suddenly discovering she's so small is also the reason a toddler hides behind her mother's skirts, as if to "bury her head in shame." Or dreams the universal nightmarish dream of being caught naked in public while people point at her accusingly and she sinks to the ground.

For remember it consciously or not, our original discovery of being inadequate is so overwhelming we keep some of it to the end of our days.

SHE GETS JEALOUS

Jealousy is another result of a little girl's suddenly discovering she's so small, especially jealousy of a new baby in the house.

On the days when a toddler feels particularly tiny and helpless, she may become so jealous she slips back and tries to be a baby herself. Instead of walking, she may demand to be carried once more, or demand a bottle instead of a cup, as if to say, "See, I'm just a baby, too. Love me and protect me as much as you are loving and protecting her." So one minute she may obviously adore the new baby, the next show great jealousy of her rival. Indeed, around the age of two jealousy may be far more evident than adoration, and lead to violent scenes unless her mother manages to convey to her the fact that she has enough love for both.

But the point is, a normal infant does not stay back. Once she has become upright she does not demand a bottle again indefinitely, nor ask to be carried again for years.

WALKING AND HOLDING ON

But discovering she is so small and non-magic jolts a tiny girl's confidence in herself in other ways, too. As she starts to walk, the feet that looked so reliable in the crib turn out to be not reliable at all. She takes a few fine steps but unexpectedly her legs buckle under her and down she goes with a thump. Her howl when she falls down is therefore not only a howl of pain; it is a howl of rage at herself for being so clumsy; plus a howl at the floor for unexpectedly coming up and hitting her in the face.

Also, the fingers that looked so competent in the crib prove incompetent as well. She grasps eagerly at things, but her unreliable fingers unexpectedly drop them, and she is stunned and surprised again.

Why does an infant drop things when she is trying so hard to hold onto them tight?

Yale's Dr. Arnold Gesell says it's because her release-mechanisms develop faster than her control-mechanisms. By the age of two, she has lost some of her original grasping ability. She can release things from her hands by dropping them or throwing them, yet not control them enough to hold them tight. It's the same with her legs. When first she walks, she finds it easier to run than to walk sedately because the release-mechanisms in her legs propel her up the block but the control-mechanisms that slow her down are not yet in good shape.

Then, too, throwing things and running about are positive powers, and she can only overcome shame by accomplishment. So she gleefully practices throwing and running every moment she can, the way a swimmer practices a new stroke.

THE CONTROL OF HER BOWELS

The matter of release and control is most evident in the matter of bowel-training, over which mothers and infants can get into such tussles they become major battles indeed. Yet this is still another matter of a release-mechanism developing before a control-mechanism. Babies release bowel movements without any control over them because the special muscles of the rectum that let them be retained or released at will do not develop until around the end of the second year. So an exasperated mother may keep an infant sitting on a training-seat for half an hour without anything happening, then she may get up and let go. Or she may let go before she is put upon the seat, simply because the right controls weren't working at the right time.

INDEPENDENCE OF WILL

But getting bowel-trained is far more complicated than this.

After the sense of basic trust, the next sense an infant develops is a sense of independence of will. After the total dependence of the crib stage, developing such a sense is indispensable for healthy development. And there are no parts of her body she resents interference with more—interference that seems to threaten her new-found sense of independence —than her rectum, vagina or mouth.

For her rectal, vaginal and mouth openings are the parts of her that guard her body's integrity, and she rightly objects to having them tampered with without her permission. She objects to having her mouth tampered with as in forced feeding. She objects to having her genitals tampered with in any way. And she objects to having enemas shoved into her rectum, or having something ordered out of her rectum as "training" seems to do. She also objects to having her wastes ordered out because they were once an intimate part of herself.

Like all of us, a child is deeply interested in anything that is, or ever was, a part of herself. Hair is a part of herself, so she is deeply interested in it and looks at the locks cut off by the barber with great curiosity long after she has learned to take hair-cuts without fear. She examines a pulled tooth that was once part of herself with great curiosity, too, sometimes even asks the dentist if she may take it home to save.

So too she looks upon her wastes not only with curiosity but with a feeling of ownership. She will control their release or hold back when she is able to, but only with her consent.

In addition, she may actually enjoy her own wastes, and upset her mother greatly by playing with them, particularly when her mother has built up in her mind a picture of her little girl as an "angel child."

The Temple University psychiatrists, Drs. O. Spurgeon English and Gerald H. Pearson, explain why she may want to play with them:

It must be stressed against the opposition of one's sense of aesthetic values, that the child is naturally quite intrigued by, and enamored of, its own excretions. He or she finds their proximity to his body, when warm, quite satisfying. He finds them in no way filthy, disgusting, or unpleasant to sight and touch as we do. He would like to touch and play with them in a quite uninhibited manner, and often does so in spite of the careful vigilance of those who supervise him. Many a mother has been surprised and disconcerted to find her child occupying himself with smearing feces over himself, the bed, and over the walls of the room.

Any child is prone to do this, and no mother who experiences it should be frightened about her child's nature, or worry that he has more primitive or animal heredity in him than the next child. He is merely being an average child and following the dictates of the pleasure-principle. He need only be washed and told he can be given something more acceptable to play with than the contents of his own body. The promise should be kept by providing plasticine, modeling clay, or sand as substitutes for the instinctive tendency to play with material of such consistency. This displacement of interest to something more socially acceptable forms the beginning of sublimation.

A clear picture of the gradual substitutions the child adopts in his efforts to sublimate his original interest in feces has been well shown by Ferenczi (a pioneer researcher) when he points out that feces are brown, moist, soft, have a bad odor, and are worthless. The child turns to mud-pies which have all the characteristics of feces minus the odor. He then turns to sand and relinquishes the characteristic of moisture. From there his interest turns to bright stones and trinkets, and he relinquishes softness. Next he adopts stamps, coins and money, gaining more color than the original brown, and at the same time gaining something of social value. The adults in the environment should provide opportunities for these substitutes to take place.

All of these are important considerations to remember in reducing the struggle over the bowels.

GIRLS TRAIN EASIER

Still, girls train easier and quicker than boys do, more because they tend to be more passive than boys and so give in faster in matters where deference to the will of others is involved.

Girls train even more easily if they are not made to feel that their budding will is being "broken"; if they get a taste of general independence before they are asked to conform here. Indeed, if they are first allowed to develop some general independence, they often discover it gives them more of a feeling of self-confidence to be trained than not to be trained. As with learning to tie their own shoelaces or put on some of their own clothes, learning to control their own bowels gives them the wonderful feeling of "I did it myself."

Girls also train more quickly because, with their more sensitive skins, they are more sensitive to dirt than boys are. Though this is not always an unmixed blessing. A little girl who becomes so fastidious she never lets her clothes get one bit mussed, or who runs shrieking from every speck of dirt in sight, worries doctors far more than a reasonably messy little girl. For life contains a lot of messy experiences, particularly for women, and the time to prepare for these is in childhood.

The exciting experience of childbirth is extremely messy. So are the exciting experiences of sex-relations, breast feeding, or nursing the sick. Little girls who become so proper they can't accept these later because they are so "dirty" lose important life-experiences as a result.

Accepting dirt reminds me of the story of the city boy who took a summer job on a farm.

The first day he went into the barn, the boy said, "This barn stinks." The farmer, who loved his barn, replied, "No, it smells like a barn." Soon the boy got close to the cows, and said: "These cows stink." "No, they smell like cows," the farmer replied. Then the boy began to shovel manure, shouting, "This manure STINKS!" "No, it smells like manure," replied the farmer, who loved his manure because it fertilized his fields that raised his crops that put money in his pocket and contributed to his pride.

DIRTY WORDS

A little girl who has been too quickly and harshly bowel-trained, may also pay her mother back in another unexpected way. Outwardly surrendering but inwardly rebelling at the methods used, she may take to using dirty words instead, these dirty words being her way of getting back at her mother by taking her feces and transferring them symbolically to her tongue.

CONSTIPATION

There is the matter of constipation, too, since girls tend to be much more constipated than boys. (A long-standing joke among doctors is to speak of women as "the constipated bipeds.") Part of their constipation may be sheer "no" saying, since saying "no" also develops at this time as part of her new independence of will. Again it is as if she were saying, "You insist I throw my waste products out. All right, I'll be as independent as I can and hold them in." And since moving the bowels is extremely subject to habit formation, an early "no" habit may long persist.

And part of her constipation may be merely due to the fact a little girl is not nearly as constipated as her mother thinks. There are especially wide variations in normality here. Doctors insist that any soft, well-formed movement in an otherwise healthy person is normal for the person involved, no matter how often or seldom it occurs. Because of this fact, one healthy college student had a neat sign posted in her room which read: "I have a perfect right to move my bowels only once a week, and not to have the matter further discussed."

MUST GO FORWARD

"The ability to say a firm, friendly, guilt-free 'no' when necessary is an invaluable asset through life," says the child-guidance counselor Dorothy Barclay. The normal child starts to learn how to say this "no" as a toddler, but luckily she also says "yes," and says it in innumerable ways.

For most children play the game of life like the game of "I Pack My

Trunk," a game in which one thing is added to another while the original ones remain. So first they "pack in" a sense of basic trust; then they add a sense of independence of will, and go on adding from there.

They weather the teething rages if they get hard things to bite on instead of their mother, and if they get to understand that weaning is not a punishment, and that the relations between them are still basically good.

They weather the weaning-frustration if they are weaned gradually instead of quickly, and if they aren't asked to tackle weaning at the same time they are asked to tackle bowel-training, since two new difficult jobs at a time are too much.

They weather the setbacks they encounter when they first stand upright if they're given their heads, but with reservations. For as Dr. Erikson says, they will feel less small and unsure of themselves if they're not allowed to experience too many things that fill them with doubt and shame; if they're helped to "stand on their own two feet" to the extent they're able to, but no more.

And they weather them all because of the curious fact of "infant amnesia."

INFANT AMNESIA

Infant amnesia has puzzled people for centuries: Why is it that the most important things that ever happen to us happen while we are infants, yet we develop an amnesia about these things—no memory of them further back than around the age of three? Some researchers answer by saying it is because our brains aren't fully formed before the age of three. Others believe it is because so many of our early experiences are just too painful to remember; analysis may uncover them after much digging, but most of us would rather not face them if we can avoid it. We had so many violent ups and downs in those early years, so many experiences that caused us anxiety because we were too immature to cope with them, that we have somehow determined never if possible to face those years again. So we consciously forget them though we unconsciously remember them and their influence remains powerful. We forget them and forge ahead.

We forge ahead around the age of three from the stage when we develop some shame and independence, to the stage when we develop initiative and love.

✳✳✳ 7 She Gets Initiative and Learns to Love

Now here's a paradox: infants know rage, they know shame, but they don't know love.

Babies don't love. Adults love them, gurgle and coo at them, and they often smile and gurgle, too. But in the beginning these smiles and gurgles are mainly imitative. For love calls for giving; love isn't possible until one is a person; love takes surplus energy. And babies aren't persons yet, babies haven't got surplus energy. They need almost all they have to meet their own problems and have little to spare.

Life has been compared to a cup of water. In the beginning the cup is generously filled by the people around us, because our very existence depends on it. Later the cup becomes full and overflowing. When this happens, we have water with which to fill others in turn.

But the cup isn't filled quickly. When an infant runs to you with outstretched arms, she is pleading with you to love her, not saying "I love you." She doesn't begin to say this, move on from being a receiver toward becoming a giver, until around the age of three or four. Then she moves in a rush.

THE STATE OF INITIATIVE

Age four is the age of initiative. And initiative differs from independence of will. When she first got some independence, and developed new powers like walking and using her hands, the question a child kept asking herself was: "What can I do with these powers?" Now that these powers have been more perfected, the question becomes, "What *may* I do with them? What is acceptable?" And the answer is, "Make or create."

So with fingers that grasp more securely, she starts furiously to make things, mud-pies, drawings, castles, houses out of blocks. She also starts to make people in the sense of making friends. Her circle widens and she becomes related to more and more adults in addition to her father and mother, learns to give love as well as seek it outside her own family. Still, her central affections are reserved for her own parents. She forms an intense love-triangle consisting of her mother, her father and herself; becomes more feminine and endearing in her actions toward her father, even announcing as if to prove it, "I'm going to marry my father when I grow up."

Until now, too, she had few relations with children outside her own family. But around four, she begins to notice them more actively, to play better alongside them and even a bit with them. And she begins also to notice other children's bodies, and wants to know how they differ from hers.

At first she merely notices that some children dress differently than she does, or wear their hair in different styles. From there she goes on to notice that they urinate in different positions, and from there it's no time at all before curiosity makes her want to see if they're different in other places, such as the genitals, as well.

Many doctors believe that the ideal way to satisfy a little girl's curiosity on this point is to satisfy it very early, before the age of four, by letting her observe naked babies. Nudity is most natural in a baby, and she can look at them casually and observe their physical differences without the point being stressed.

They also believe little girls start to become modest about their own bodies around the age of four or five, and can be mildly encouraged by their parents. This modesty should be neither ignored nor anxiously pressed, they say, since the behavior of healthily modest parents who neither hide their own bodies nor exhibit them unduly, is usually the best help they can give in creating healthy modesty in a child.

With all of this, many little girls are still curious not only about the bodies of little boys but also of other little girls, to assure themselves that other little girls' bodies are like their own, and to see what their own genitals look like. So they may pull up their friends' dresses and peek at what's under them, or play doctor and explore that way. This curiosity is also legitimate, since it is based on the same drive that makes her open every drawer and closed door, or peer into every visitor's handbag, because the insides of closets and drawers and handbags are mysterious and challenging, too, and it's a dull-witted child indeed who doesn't want to find out as much as she can about the universe around her that is still so new.

Having seen the bodies of a few babies or other girls, the normal child is content for a while. Peeking and "playing doctor" may be natural steps in her development, but having served their purpose, she drops them and goes on.

WHERE DO BABIES COME FROM?

She goes on to questions like "Where do babies come from?" For she can't help but also notice during this intensely investigating time that babies come as if from nowhere. But "Where *is* that nowhere? And *how* do they come?" she wonders. It's another mystery she must explore.

Yet here a simple answer satisfies her, as long as it's an honest answer and does not go beyond the questions she has asked. She will be grateful for simplicity and honesty even though she doesn't grasp what she is told all at once, and it has to be repeated again and again.

TALK, TALK, TALK

There's probably no human gift greater than the gift of speech. For speech is the chief way by which we communicate or relate to each other. We may see each other, touch each other, but we must above all speak to each other or we are left tragically isolated and alone.

As Dr. Jane Pearce says, "Every human being seeks to communicate with every other no matter what the differences are, including language, between them. . . . If Crusoe had not found a way to communicate with Friday, Friday would have found a way to communicate with Crusoe, because all humans need to know what is occurring with other people of whom they are aware."

Given their keener senses and greater general awareness, little girls, when they do start to talk, talk earlier and better than boys do. And by four or five they are talking away like mad.

Speech will always be one of the girl's greatest assets, as well as one of her greatest weapons. For since she is smaller and less physically strong than a boy she can never lash out with her fists as successfully as he can, even if society would let her. So when she becomes frustrated or angry, the main way she can lash out is with her tongue.

FRUSTRATION AND ANGER

Now frustration comes increasingly to all of us as we become more and more aware the world is not nearly the warm and friendly place it seemed from the cradle. So, just as an infant becomes frustrated when she stands up and finds she is not as powerful as she thought; she becomes even more frustrated as the people around her stop her from doing many of the things she would like to do, stop her more often in civilized communities than in primitive ones. They stop her from eating any and every time she wants to; they stop her from crossing a busy street when she wants to; staying up as late as she wants to; grabbing other children's toys. And she expresses her frustration over many of these prohibitions in aggressive behavior. As her hands become more expert at obeying her, she sometimes uses them to try and hit her brothers and sisters, hit them in preference to her mother, but hit her mother on occasion, too. She also talks back to them, makes faces at them, uses her tongue to express her anger, gives them a literal "tongue-lashing," which for her is better than lashing with her fists.

Soon after lashing out this way, however, she feels guilty—especially if she has lashed out against her indispensable mother. Because of this, many doctors believe it is pointless for a mother to try to be too good, too lenient, too impossibly "perfect." For some hostility toward a mother who controls her child is inevitable no matter what she does, and expressing hostility toward a too-good or too-permissive mother makes a little girl feel even more guilty than she would otherwise feel. A mother, therefore, can be reasonably firm if for this reason alone.

GIRLS LESS DESTRUCTIVE

Yet there are two kinds of aggression. One is constructive aggression; the other destructive. Destructive aggression is an "acting out" of anger or frustration against other people in such a way that the other people get really hurt.

Now girls may feel as much anger as boys do, but boys around four are much more likely to act out this anger in really destructive ways. Boys kick other people hard more often, hurl things at them more often, wrestle and fight much more to the point where other people get hurt. They do this because their stronger muscles allow them to, and because they identify more with their aggressively male fathers. Studies show that in families where fathers are habitually absent, as on business trips or away at war, boys are not as aggressive as in families where fathers are regularly at home.

There may also be a hormonal reason, or "drive," for a boy's greater aggression. Testosterone is the more specifically "male" hormone, and boys as well as girls have a welling-up of sex hormones around this age. Dr. Lewis Terman quotes studies in which small boys were given extra male hormones by injection and their behavior became even more aggressive than before.

Then, too, sheer vital energy plays a part. By the age of six, boys are seven per cent ahead of girls in muscle strength and vital energy as measured by the ability to grip hard and hold on with the right hand. By the age of ten, boys are 35 per cent ahead. At no point, therefore, can girls sustain acts of destructive aggression as well as boys.

On top of all this, there is the general attitude of society; habit and training seldom permit a girl to show as much destructive aggression. Girls are more often taught to be "little ladies" and hold themselves in, while boys are excused with "Boys will be boys." Since normal means survivability for the group even more than personal survival, these restrictions are usually necessary restrictions, since uninhibited girls *can* get into more trouble—sexual trouble, at least—than uninhibited boys.

But as a result some of a girl's anger becomes expressed in tension releasing habits that turn her aggressions inward against herself instead. So there is more ear-pulling, nose-twisting, grimacing and nail-biting in girls than in boys.

TEARS AND TENSION

What a complex thing growing up is!

Love comes strongly in around the age of four or five; hostility and aggression come in. So do fears.

A baby in the cradle fears little except sudden loud noises and falling, as we saw. For fears beyond these require imagination, and a baby in the cradle has little imagination. Fears also require movement; a baby has to be able to walk around and see things that inspire fear, and a baby cannot move. Above all, fears are protective devices warning one to fight danger or run from it, and a baby can neither fight nor run.

But around four and five a child can move about freely. She can wander around and get to fear places like dark attics and dark woods. She has also developed imagination and can imagine the desolation she would feel if her parents were to leave her, or her fright if the lions and tigers she sees in picture-books were suddenly to come alive and do her harm.

Because of their keener senses, and smaller size, and less physical strength, girls suffer much more from fears. In Dr. Lewis Terman's study of over six hundred boys and girls from age five on, almost twice as many girls were described as "excessively timid" or "having a strong tendency to worry" or being more "nervous" or having "more marked fears." The only nervous habits more common in boys were stuttering or bed-wetting. Dr. Terman theorizes that boys may stutter more because more is expected of them, and they are afraid they cannot live up to these greater expectations; they therefore become caught in a conflict that disturbs their speech.

The bed-wetting, he believes, may be an acting out of hostility with destructive aggression against their parents or other adults who they feel have wronged them in some way. For there is no better way of getting back at an adult than by continual bed-wetting by a child who can control his bladder but does not want to bother to do so. It's one of the few really potent weapons he has.

Luckily, fear and anger are not the only emotions of children around the age of five. There are plenty of happy emotions, especially the happy ones provided by the same imagination that causes the fears. For now little girls can imagine themselves as happy queens, or graceful ballet dancers, fluttering butterflies, or drifting clouds.

They also invent delightful imaginary playmates, including big animals that are friendly and kind. This reminds me of a story.

Jars of strawberry jam kept mysteriously disappearing from the home of a small girl named Virginia. When scolded, Virginia kept insisting it was the work of an elephant who came in and stole the jam. But finally she was caught red-handed. Red-mouthed, too, with obvious jam smears all over her face and hands. Yet she still insisted it was the work of an elephant.

"How did the elephant get into the house?" her mother asked.

"He broke down the wall."

"But the wall isn't broken. How did it get fixed?"

"The elephant mended it."

"How did the jam get on your hands and face?"

"The elephant put it there while I took my nap."

At this point the mother decided to be very modern. She would call in a jury of Virginia's peers to give their verdict on the case.

So she carefully assembled twelve other five year olds and presented them with the evidence: the disappearing jam, the smears on Virginia's hands and face, the unbroken wall, the story of the elephant who did it all. Then she sent the jury out to deliberate.

They were back in a few minutes with a unanimous verdict. "Maybe it was an elephant," they gravely announced.

THE LOST PART

Elephant or no elephant, there's one special fear which is not based on imagination—a fear that to a little girl can seem real indeed. This is the fear that a part of her has been lost.

All children are frightened by crippled or deformed people. This is because crippled or deformed people seem to them to have something missing, and a child's image of herself and of other people is mainly a quite perfect image. Anything missing is therefore greatly upsetting.

Now, in the course of her curious peeking a little girl can't help but notice that she seems to be missing a part that boys have, a penis. It's an obvious "plus" where she seems to have a "minus," a "something" where she seems to have a "nothing." Maybe she once had this "plus," too, and lost it, like a cripple who has lost a leg. Worse, maybe she did something "bad" to make her lose it, though she can't possibly figure out what the particular "bad" was. Still, she feels she is being punished for doing this mysterious "bad" thing, feels it keenly and gets very guilty over having done it, whatever it is, but keeps this feeling to herself.

For this reason, even though she does not spontaneously bring the matter up, Drs. English and Pearson believe mothers should manage somehow to broach the subject and assure her that her vagina is not inferior to, but merely different from, the penis she never had; assure her also that someday she will have something boys won't have, breasts like her mother's, plus the privilege of bearing a child.

In fact, at this age any favorable comparison that can be made with her big and magic mother is most reassuring. The knowledge that someday she will resemble her is one of the most comforting thoughts a little girl can receive.

WISHING SOMEONE DEAD

As if the guilt over having had a penis and lost it as a punishment weren't hard enough for a tiny girl to cope with, there is also another special kind of guilt: guilt over wishing some member of her family dead.

Since five is the age of imitation, a little girl may be for the first time engaged in a competitive struggle with her sisters and brothers for a more favored position in the family—a struggle especially with her older sisters and brothers who seem to have many advantages she doesn't have merely because they arrived on the scene first. If she is angry because her parents do not seem to be treating her as well as they treat them, she may start a knock-down, drag-out struggle with them—a struggle she is bound to lose in a well-run household, but one which leaves her feeling anxious and guilty again, because during the course of that struggle she may have had fleeting thoughts of wishing them dead. So once more her conscience makes her mete out punishment to herself to atone for these wicked thoughts.

Now all of us wish someone dead at certain times. We wouldn't dream of doing anything to kill them, but we can't help wondering what would happen if Uncle Ezra would die and leave us his fortune, or Aunt Maggie would die and leave us her beautiful house. We have such thoughts but they soon go away.

But a little child still lives in her magic world. So if Uncle Ezra chokes on a chicken bone months later, or Aunt Maggie is run over by a car, she is sure her thoughts were responsible, just as superstitious people are sure when they believe the "hex" they put on someone made them die.

So a little girl suffers keenly. Indeed, as Dr. Erik Erikson says, around the age of five a little girl's conscience is at its cruelest and most demanding. There is no moralist like a child moralist. And no one who can punish herself quite as much.

The adults who surround a child can help her counter the anxiety, guilt and shame that may be welling up inside her now. They can do this by giving her sympathetic understanding, and if a near relative does suddenly die, by telling her frankly it was not her fault. That it was an illness or accident that caused the death just as an accident or illness causes some plants to die; or, if they prefer, use the explanation, "It was the will of God." Anything rather than let her bear the heavy burden of believing it was her fault, and that she is a "murderous me" who deserves to hate herself as a result.

✳✳✳ 8 The Comfort of Her Thumb

If there's one habit that drives an adult almost as crazy as bed-wetting, it is thumb-sucking. This is far more common in girls than in boys. It's so common doctors consider it completely normal up to a certain age, since it is a comforter and tension-releaser par excellence.

Yet many adults cannot bear to see it. A mouth full of thumb disgusts them, if only because thumb-sucking seems such a pointless act. Sucking on something with even the least bit of nourishment, like a lollipop, seems to make sense. On an empty thumb? None.

More, while a child is sucking she gets a sort of "lost" look, as if she were retreating into a world beyond the adult's control. It's the kind of lost look a dog gets when he's burying a bone. In burying it he is doing something instinctive that doesn't seem to make much sense either, because he may never dig the bone up. But while he is doing it, he can't be reached. Also, a frantic mother is sure thumb-sucking will spoil her daughter's good looks; push out her mouth and ruin her teeth. So at all costs, out that thumb must come.

Yet thumb-sucking is an instinctive act, and often starts even before birth. X rays show babies in the womb with their thumbs in their mouths, and right after delivery newborn babies often go to it immediately again.

Why is thumb-sucking so practically universal?

Temple's Drs. O. Spurgeon English and Gerald H. Pearson think one reason is that it provides extra sucking practice.

One of the few things a baby must be able to do right away for survival is to suck and take in nourishment. But few do it perfectly. They suck in unwanted air and have to be bubbled; they suck too fast and spit up. So they often need more practice and get it not only from sucking on their fingers but also toys, bed-clothes, blankets, "sucking blankets" so highly prized they are toted around all day.

Dr. Benjamin Spock tells of a study in which babies fed every three hours sucked their thumbs less than those on a four-hour schedule. He also tells of an experiment with newborn puppies in which milk was dropped straight into their mouths by an eye-dropper so that the normal act of sucking their mother's teats was by-passed. These dropper-fed puppies sucked their own and each other's paws until the fur was almost worn off. They were going to get that practice—or else!

RHYTHM

Then there's the matter of rhythm. Thumb-sucking often is a rhythmic act. The thumb is sucked almost as if it were accompanying a tune. Now there have always been rhythmic rocking-chairs and rhythmic lullabies to lull a tired, tense child to rest. Having learned the tranquilizing effect of rhythm furnished her by others, a child uses it herself. It's a matter of the self comforting the self.

PLEASURE AND HABIT

Next there's the matter of sheer pleasure and habit. Most learning proceeds on the pleasure principle. We find out something is pleasing, and we tend to repeat it until it becomes a habit; we find out it's unpleasant, and we tend to stop. Cigarette-smoking is a prime example of pleasure repeated until it becomes a habit. Cigarette-smoking is a combination of something to do with the hands plus the pleasure of titillating the sensitive nerve-endings of the mouth.

Yet once a habit is formed it doesn't even have to be particularly pleasurable to be continued; it merely has to be familiar. That's why many smokers go on smoking long after the original pleasure has gone, gamblers go on gambling though they lose steadily, or collectors go on collecting expensive antiques until they barely have room for one more.

Of course, if the habit does continue to be pleasurable, it becomes even stronger. The combination of pleasure plus familiarity is hard to beat.

And some of the strongest habits we have are those that have to do with the mouth, because the mouth is the earliest organ that gives pleasure. If we've been fed milk early and often, we crave milk until the end; if soup or coffee, we're miserable without them. We may rationalize and defend coffee, saying we need it for stimulation. But we will drink coffee every morning, mid-afternoon or whenever as much for the sake of putting something familiar in our mouths as for anything else.

The *British Army Instruction Manual* asks this question: "What do you do when you come upon a dying man?" The answer is: "Offer him a cigarette, then ask him if he'd like you to write to his mother." They too put the comfort of an old established mouth-habit first.

SELF-COMFORT ABOVE ALL

Because of all this, researchers like Dr. Arnold Gesell of Yale believe that while almost all children suck their thumbs at one time or another, the habit seems to reach a peak around the age of two, when the teething and walking frustrations are at their height. It tapers off around five when they acquire some initiative and control, but is normal in varying degrees until around the age of eight, when it tends to stop of its own accord, because by then the child has learned to release tensions in many other ways like skating or riding a bicycle, which involve rhythmic motions of the feet.

Dr. I. Karelitz of New Hyde Park, Long Island, even tells of seeing grown women, ill and afraid in a hospital, sucking their thumbs to release tension before falling asleep. Says Dr. Karelitz, "None of us ever grows up completely. We all tend to slip back for a few moments into childish behavior in times of stress. These women were comforting themselves in a way that was familiar, and probably less harmful, cheaper and as satisfactory as a sleeping-pill."

Will thumb-sucking deform the mouth by pushing the upper teeth out? The best-informed opinion says no. It may sometimes affect the soft baby teeth, but the soft baby teeth fall out around the age of five when the stronger, more permanent teeth come in. These permanent teeth are not affected, because the buds of the permanent teeth have been ready, locked in the jaws, long before coming down, and once they are in position up in the jaws thumb-sucking cannot budge them. Even if it could, most serious thumb-sucking has been given up by the age of five anyway.

What about causing crooked teeth? Again the answer is no. Crooked teeth are usually an inherited tendency.

Remember, too, how hard it is to straighten crooked teeth. It takes years of wearing strong metal clasps to coax them into a new position, and then they sometimes go back. The jaws and teeth are among the hardest substances in the body. It's almost impossible to push them out of place by something as comparatively mild as rubbing by a small thumb.

Of course, there can be some harm from thumb-sucking, but it's psychological harm, not physical harm. Psychological harm results when a child begins to depend on it so much for pleasure and comfort that she becomes a withdrawn child who has stopped trying to make friends.

The little girl who mistrusts life instead of trusting it, who has almost no independence of will or of initiative because both have been so thoroughly squelched, is usually the one who becomes the all-day sucker. As Erik Erikson puts it, such a child "finds his thumb and damns the world." To try and stop her at this point by using harsh measures like applying bitter substances or strait-jacketing her elbows will only succeed in making her still more unhappy and mistrustful. Worse, it will focus her attention still more on her thumb instead of on the friends or other ways of finding the comfort and pleasure she desperately needs.

I once saw an example of this. A smart-looking woman had brought her small daughter with her while she shopped in a fashionable Fifth Avenue store. The child was well behaved, but naturally wanted to get some joy from touching some of the pretty things herself. Her mother sharply reprimanded her. "Don't touch anything! Stop it this minute!" she cried. The child did stop, but a moment later her thumb flew to her mouth and from an eager, interested child she became a "lost" child wrapped back in herself. There was no place in the store for her to sit quietly; she had no toy to play with, and she could hardly stand still and contemplate while her mother deliberated and finally picked out an expensive gown. What else was she to do to while away the time except give herself the rhythmic comfort of sucking her thumb?

What would have happened if her mother had tried to yank the thumb out? Either of two things. She may have obeyed and let it be taken out, or she may have rebelled and stubbornly kept it in.

The stronger urge in a girl is usually toward giving in because a girl tends to be much more passive and pliant than a boy. Besides, a girl's essential relation is always to her mother, and while she is small and dependent, she does not dare to do anything seriously to disrupt this relation. In a showdown, therefore, she will usually surrender in order to preserve whatever she can of her mother's goodwill.

But whether she stops sucking her thumb or continues, surrenders or rebels, she may begin to distrust her mother for denying her this kind of comfort if her mother obviously indulges in much mouth-comfort herself.

Many a little girl is forcibly made to give up her thumb before she is ready for it, while at the same time she constantly sees her mother poking cigarettes, cocktails or other pacifiers into her own mouth. What conclusion can she come to, then, but that her mother is a cheat? For children are never fooled. They know when a parent is telling them lies.

ISOLATED BEHAVIOR

In June 1959, Dr. Leo Kanner, then director of the Children's Psychiatric Clinic of Johns Hopkins Hospital, read at a medical meeting a paper called "Everyday Problems of Normal Young Children." It had to do with isolated pieces of behavior, and started this way:

In 1931, I had in my office a distinguished visitor . . . one of the country's leading pediatricians. In the course of our conversation he asked me what I thought of a person who had been enuretic until the age of thirteen. Did I, as a psychiatrist, think he could be considered normal?

I replied that normalcy or a departure from it cannot possibly be defined in terms of an isolated behavior item. My visitor then disclosed smilingly that his reference to the enuretic boy was taken from a page out of his own unwritten autobiography. Yet I can assure you that he grew up to be a sane, superbly adjusted, and well-liked member of society.

As a matter of fact, is there anybody in this audience who has gone through the years of infancy, childhood, and adolescence, without ever experiencing any kind of emotional quandary and manifesting it in the form of one or another behavior problem? Only those with a very poor memory will deny that at some time in their early years they have had experiences which figure in an inventory of abnormal traits.

From there, Dr. Kanner went on to discuss nail-biting as an example. Nail-biting, he said, was described only a few years ago by a leading European authority as a "stigma of degeneration," and by another as an "exquisitely psychopathic symptom." But a recent American study showed that among a large group of unselected tenth-graders, 29 per cent were still biting their nails and 37 per cent had done so in the past, adding up to the startling total of 66 per cent. "It is hardly realistic to assume that two-thirds of our nation's youths are degenerates, or exquisitely psychopathic," Dr. Kanner continued, "especially when a survey of 2500 naval recruits showed about 25 per cent of them still biting their nails around the age of eighteen.

"Normalcy or a departure from it cannot possibly be defined in terms of such isolated behavior," Dr. Kanner insisted.

There are innumerable children who suck their thumbs at times when they are bored or frustrated. This means that there are innumerable children, as there are adults, who are at times bored and frustrated. There are many children who chew on their fingernails when they are tense. This means there are innumerable children, just as there are adults, who are tense at times. There are many children who sob when they are unhappy, who throw themselves on the floor when they are driven into a corner, who have nightmares after an exciting moving picture, or who stubbornly refuse to kiss Aunt Ellie, especially when they know Aunt Ellie has halitosis.

All these are everyday reactions of normal young children who will remain normal unless parental perfectionistic disapproval will cause them to suffer unconditionally, and become guilt-laden, literal-minded stuffed shirts.

Over and over again, Dr. Kanner stressed that he as a psychiatrist was far less concerned about fidgety children than by over-quiet, withdrawn children. For to him the over-quiet, withdrawn child often spells a goody-goody who has become frightened into practically giving up the struggle to grow.

He then gave two examples of children who had given up the struggle. One was a little girl brought to him because she still couldn't walk at the age of four. He found that her father, a determined perfectionist, had decided he would make her walk very early, just to prove it could be done. So hour by hour, he stood her on her feet and moved her legs forward before they were ready. The result was, she became so discouraged she didn't dare try to walk again long after she really could.

The second was a little girl of nine who didn't talk. It seemed her mother had decided baby-talk was nonsense, and had continually corrected her speech, trying also to make it perfect until the child also gave up. She had now been silent for six years.

NORMAL FOR ONE'S AGE

So we come to a further definition of normal. It is normal for one's age.

For not only do some parents try to push their children toward the impossible, they also have got the idea that such-and-such should start or stop exactly on a certain birthday, and are terribly upset when the particular day rolls around and they do not. Much of this misunderstanding comes from books that are not read carefully, books, for instance, like those of Dr. Arnold Gesell. In the introduction to each chapter, Dr. Gesell is careful to say "*around* a certain birthday," but many people skip introductions, and get wrong ideas.

Actually, it is as unrealistic to expect certain things to happen to a child precisely on a certain birthday as it is to expect the March winds to start blowing on the stroke of midnight of March first, and to continue blowing exactly to the stroke of midnight of March thirty-first. Nature just doesn't work that way.

In human beings, there are far more individual variations within the norm than there are in weather. In fact, says Dr. Milton E. J. Senn of the Child Study Center of Yale University, you can throw away all precise timetables of growth and development after the age of two. Before the age of two, most babies develop at a pretty uniform pace. After that, there are so many spurts and lags in individual youngsters that all you can expect is a general pattern. Definite changes on definite dates are not in the cards.

In this sense, such tension-caused habits as nail-biting, ear-pulling, thumb-sucking and fidgeting are normal traits under the age of nine in general, with one of those proverbial exceptions that prove the rule being the boy who was still wetting his bed at thirteen.

For you might call habits like nail-biting and thumb-sucking "scaffold-behavior." They are like the scaffold of a building—something needed temporarily, but discarded when a more solid structure has been built.

Normal children discard much of their scaffold-behavior since psychological scars, like physical scars, often heal spontaneously as they become over-ridden by healthy growth. So in due time the nail-biters will stop biting, the ear-pullers will stop pulling, and one bright morning the thumb-sucker will take her thumb out of her mouth and never put it back in except occasionally, like the frightened women in the hospital who were temporarily slipping back into childhood and allaying their tensions in an old familiar way.

As Dr. Lauretta Bender, former professor of psychology at New York University, says: "Growth is a stress, but a stress that does not last indefinitely. . . . One thing we should never forget is that, whenever follow-up studies are made on problem-children of any category, results in an unexpectedly large number of cases have been much better than the doctors predicted."

❊❊❊ 9 The Word You Cannot Say

This book has two purposes. One is to explain a little girl to her parents; the other is to explain a woman to herself, as she remembers herself when she too was a child. And in the course of that explanation, to help her understand and forgive herself a little for what she may think of as "wickedness" or "unforgivable sin."

The "sin" that particularly calls for understanding is the one summed up in what the writer Hannah Lees calls "the word you cannot say."

That word is masturbation.

It's a word that can't be said largely because of its history, since almost everything bad that ever happened to humanity was blamed on masturbation for five thousand years. When people suffered nervousness, impotence, sterility, insanity, even something as far-fetched as tuberculosis, masturbation was accused of being the cause. So people spoke of masturbation as "venereal pleasure," "self-abuse," or almost anything to avoid it, as if they feared the very word might call down those curses on their heads.

But, as Dr. Abram Kardiner, chief of the Department of Psychiatry of New York's Columbia Presbyterian Hospital, says, "In this instance for five thousand years humanity has been wrong. We know now it was mostly the old story of putting the cart before the horse. For centuries people observed that nervous children indulged with especial freedom in masturbation, so they leaped to the conclusion it had *made* them nervous. For centuries people observed that insane people indulged in it to excess, so they decided it had *made* them insane. And knowing nothing of the true cause of the other inflictions, they blamed masturbation once more."

UNIVERSAL AND NORMAL

Actually it was the other way around. Children who were already nervous were the ones who indulged with unusual freedom. The same with the insane who had already lost all other controls. Moreover, the most careful modern studies show that practically every child in the world masturbates to some extent at one time or another. If this led to insanity and the other miseries attributed to it then practically every person in the world would be sterile, miserable or out of his mind!

Drs. English and Pearson call masturbation "a universal and normal phenomenon in human growth and development," and they point out that the mother who says her child never indulged in it is the mother who so frightened her child the first time she caught her at it, that the child never again attempted it in her presence. And the mother who says she herself never indulged in it is one who was so thoroughly frightened by *her* mother that she buried the memory and forgot she ever did.

Masturbation, of course, is a word that disturbs people particularly when talking about girls, because they consider it a sign of undesirable sex-interest. But it is common to all children, and the normal girl indulges in it only occasionally, and then only at certain periods in her life.

Before we discuss these periods, let's decide not to use the word masturbation any more. Let's substitute a better and more accurate term, genital play.

STARTS UNDER A YEAR

The first time a child may play with her genitals is when she is about a year old. The first year of life, you will remember, is the time of the great discovery of the physical self. Just as a baby accidentally discovers and plays with her fingers and toes, so too she may accidentally discover and play with her genitals. For they're all part of the wonderful being she is discovering as herself. Besides, a baby's vagina, like her mouth, is a "part that turns in." To explore such a part with a finger that juts out is as natural as sucking her thumb. But, curiosity satisfied, she soon drops the matter as a rule and does not turn to it again until the age of three.

RESUMES BETWEEN THREE AND SIX

Around three or four, as you remember, is the age that little girls begin to notice the genital differences between themselves and little boys, and to fear that some vital part of them has been lost, since they don't have something boys obviously have. This fear of having lost something may propel them into doing what people do who fear they have lost some money—look in their pocketbooks over and over to reassure themselves it is still there.

So, too, a little girl may feel her vagina over and over to reassure herself she has something more than a mere "minus" or "nothing" in the place where a boy has that obvious "plus."

(Boys of this age may constantly touch their penis for the same reason. They may have seen a little girl who seems to have "lost" one and want to make sure this hasn't happened to them. Dr. Benjamin Spock tells of a little boy who kept repeating that his baby sister was "boo boo," his word for injured. Her lack worried him greatly until he was reassured she was all right.)

RHYTHM AND RELEASE

Then there are the matters of rhythm and release of tension. Indeed, rhythm and release of tension are such integral parts of genital play, just as they are of thumb-sucking, that some authorities consider one mainly an advanced form of the other. Advanced because anything that has to do with sex is a higher stage of development, because it leads to creativity, than anything that remains a mere activity of the self like "damning the world and sucking one's thumb."

PLEASURE

And of course there is always the element of pleasure. Sex was meant to be pleasurable, just like eating, or people might simply pass it by.

Drs. Pearson and English think the early discovery of genital pleasure is especially important in a girl-child because a girl will almost inevitably suffer some pain and discomfort through her genitals. She will need the memory of pleasure to balance this pain and discomfort; make them more bearable when they come.

Drs. English and Pearson still use the old-fashioned word masturbation and express it this way: "In order to function sexually, men and women need to have some feeling developed in the genital area. Masturbation is an aid in bringing feeling to that area and centering it in the sexual organs. Children who have been made to feel ashamed of the sexual desire that leads to masturbation, and who have been made afraid of sexual feeling by having been threatened with injury, will repress and dam back upon themselves this feeling. By punishment and threat of injury . . . the parent runs the risk that the grown woman will be frigid.

"Frigid women can, of course, have sexual relations and become pregnant, yet it is important for the race that they not be frigid. When women become frigid and do not allow themselves to have sexual feelings, there is a danger that they may be unhappy in marriage, or fail to have warm feelings towards their children, or both. They are also more prone to develop neurosis and psychosis; they have less to contribute emotionally to marriage, and their whole joy of living is reduced."

And prevention of frigidity starts very early. Indeed, ideally a little girl should accept her femininity and everything that goes with it during her pre-school years. For it is during these years that her female sex hormones first begin to well up within her in amounts enough to be measurable—well up and start to make her feel like a woman in many ways. One way of making her accept her femininity and feel good about being a woman is to reassure her over and over that her vagina is just as good as a little boy's genital organ, even though it is not as apparent to the eye, and that touching it occasionally will do her no harm.

On the other hand, threats of punishment for touching her vagina may have the very opposite effect of what is intended. Threats of any kind, as we saw, usually succeed only in fastening a person's attention on the area involved. After being threatened, a girl may feel compelled to touch her vagina even more often than she ordinarily would, the way one keeps touching an aching tooth or a loose button on a coat, just to prove it is still there, or intact.

Besides, the child who indulges in genital play to an extreme extent is already as a rule a hypersensitive, nervous and tense child. Threatening her is sure to make her still more nervous and tense. Study after study have shown that the tense, nervous child, made worse by threats, is the one who indulges more. The thing to do instead, most doctors agree, is to release her tension in other ways. Buy her a bicycle she can ride on energetically. Take her on a long, quick walk after supper or play ball with her in a long, hard play to relax her and tire her out before retiring—all, of course, without mentioning why.

Still, if the mother feels she simply *has* to mention why on occasion, explaining that too much is too much, no harm will be done as long as threats are not involved. For another part of normal is a growing ability to handle anxiety and frustration. Some anxiety and denial of pleasure are inescapable in life, as well as some resentment of the person—usually a parent—who imposes them. If the genital play has gotten so out of hand that the child indulges in it in public, or there is so much the whole family is frantic, the mother may have to court this resentment. But if she uses distraction and substitution in the positive way she did when her child was an infant and insisted on putting everything in her mouth, the situation should be kept within bounds.

FEAR OF VIOLENT FEELINGS

In any event, genital play is usually dropped around seven or eight of its own accord. It is dropped for the simple reason that a child becomes frightened of the intensity of her own feelings. A little girl, naturally more sensitive than a grown-up, is easily frightened by any intense experience, and orgasm or sexual climax is a tremendous one. Women describe it by comparing it to a sneeze: ker, ker, ker, *choo*. At the *choo*, the entire nervous system is involved. While few girls play with their genitals to the point of orgasm, still the very excitement leading up to it can be shattering. So after some good feeling has been developed in the genitals by a certain amount of exploration, they usually drop it and go into what is known as the latency, or "resting" period—a period in which they are probably freer from sexual drives than at any time in their lives except extreme old age.

A very special fear usually besets the parents of a girl-child during the stage of genital play. This is the fear that a girl may break her hymen and lose her virginity as a result.

Let's look at the hymen and see if this is a rational fear.

The hymen is a piece of membrane located at the entrance to the vagina. Strangely enough, no one has ever discovered a use for this membrane. Most structures of the body have a definite purpose. The hymen? As far as we know, none.

Most people, to be sure, visualize the hymen as a solid piece of membrane and deduce from this that it was put there deliberately to guard a girl's virginity. But it isn't solid; it has openings. Otherwise, the menstrual and other fluids couldn't come out. The hymen also comes in a bewildering variety of sizes and shapes. Some girls are born with hymens that have thick membranes and some with thin; some with hymens with one small opening and some with hymens with several small openings; some with hymens with one large opening, and some with hymens with several large openings. And some, to thoroughly confuse the picture, are born with hymens that are all open—shaped like doughnuts or hollow rings, with no membrane across the middle at all.

A surprising number of girls are born with the all-open or doughnut type, and those girls born with one or more openings often have these openings as big at birth as they ever will be. The vagina itself grows during childhood and adolescence. Oddly enough, the openings of the hymen tend to stay the same size.

So an examination that reveals one or more openings means exactly nothing as far as virginity is concerned. The girl may have just been born that way.

Also, an examination may reveal a membrane so tough it can't possibly be broken by ordinary means. A few engaged girls have heard so many stories about the "horror of the wedding night" that they actually go to a doctor and ask him to open the hymen wider in advance. But the doctor does not always find this easy to do. He may have to use a fairly sharp instrument and take several visits before the job is done.

Then, as Oregon's Dr. Goodrich C. Schauffler points out, the hymen is exquisitely sensitive to pain from about the age of three on. The other parts of the vagina have few sensitive nerve-endings, but the hymen has many. It would take a brave and callous child to inflict on herself the amount of pain necessary to break its tough membrane by stroking alone. Most genital play in childhood involves merely the clitoris where the sensations are pleasant rather than painful. The hymen is almost never involved, and no physical harm is done if it is.

To cap it all, says Dr. Bernard Glueck, director of research at Hartford, Connecticut's famous Institute of Living, there is far less genital play observed in little girls than in little boys.

❋❋❋ 10 "But She Doesn't Eat a Thing"

Every child under the age of nine is a food problem. At least she is a food problem to her mother. Her mother is sure she either doesn't eat enough, eats the wrong things, or eats at the wrong time. No matter what she does, it isn't right; mealtime can be the tussle of the day.

EATING TOO LITTLE

The most common complaint is eating too little. "But she doesn't eat a thing," her mother wails, "not a thing!"

This complaint usually starts around a child's second year. For during the first year, most babies eat like mad women. They eat for maintenance; they eat for growth. An average girl-child at birth weighs around seven pounds, and is about twenty inches tall. A year later she weighs around twenty-one pounds and is almost thirty inches tall. This means that in a single year she has become three times as heavy and one and a half times as tall—an amazing growth job that burns up a lot of food.

But during her second year this amazing growth slows to a comparative walk. During her second year her weight increases by an average of only seven pounds as against fourteen the year before, and she adds only four inches in height.

Slowing down this way, how can she possibly need as much food her second year as her first?

EMOTIONAL RESERVES

But nothing about food is simple. Infants seek nourishment not only for physical but for emotional reasons. They eat for pure pleasure; to achieve what Dr. Arnold Gesell calls "a delicious glow."

This pleasure is particularly intense for a newborn because eating is almost her sole pleasure. When she's bored or unhappy, she can hardly read a good book, look at television or chat with her friends on the phone. So when feeding-time comes around, she snatches her bottle and drains it eagerly, since life holds little more.

After her second year there are the joys of walking, talking, drawing pictures, solving puzzles, and so on and on. Her pleasure in eating fades sharply as these come along. And she begins to dawdle over her food, since eating now isn't half as exciting as the great, wide, beautiful, wonderful world she has to explore.

GIRLS NEED LESS FOOD

Besides, girls need less food than boys do in any event. They need less because their bodies are smaller and they are not as full of explosive energy, and so burn up fewer calories just as small, slower-moving cars burn less gasoline.

Even a girl who's as active and big seems to need fewer calories than a boy—as much as 25 per cent fewer. For females are simply more efficient and can more easily "make do." No matter how much a mother pleads and coaxes a little girl to "take just one more spoonful," she can't alter this fact.

DR. DAVIS BABIES

Mothers not only fuss and fume because they think their daughters are eating too little, they think they are eating the wrong things. "She won't eat anything but ham sandwiches" or "She won't touch bananas and you know they're so good for children." The complaints have no end.

Can a child be trusted to pick her own food? Will she inevitably get sick if she insists on eating this and pushing away that? Enter here a pioneer woman researcher, Dr. Clara Davis of Mt. Sinai Hospital in New York.

Dr. Davis rounded up from orphanages a group of infants about a year old who had never tasted anything but milk. Since they had tasted only milk, other habits hadn't entered the picture yet. Since they were orphans, no one had had the time to coax them to eat. They were quite unspoiled.

Dr. Davis sat the infants in high chairs and arranged for nurses to carry in trays at each meal filled with a large selection of foods, to set them down with no remarks or comments, and to feed only those an infant reached for. The trays contained cooked meat and raw meat, cooked vegetables and uncooked vegetables, cooked fruits and fresh fruits. The foods were also varied as to color and position, so that one day there were yellow carrots in the right-hand corner, another day green beans in the left, so that these considerations couldn't be of influence either. But every article of a normal diet turned up in due time, with the exception of rich sweets.

The experiment went on for a full six months in some cases, in others for years. Three times a day the laden trays were carried in, the children were silently fed their own choices, and the nurses silently went away. Then back in the kitchen every scrap of food left was weighed and measured, and compared with what had been served. Even the food spilled on the floor was salvaged and accounted for; nothing was overlooked.

Dr. Davis gives a delightful picture of a nine-month baby with rickets, confronted for the first time in his life with food other than milk.

He looked at the tray for a few seconds, then reached for the dish of raw carrots and plumped the whole of one hand into it. The nurse took up a spoonful; he opened his mouth and she put the spoonful in. He sucked the carrots off the spoon, made a few chewing motions and swallowed them. Back went his hand to the dish, and the proceeding was repeated over and over until most of the carrots had been eaten. Lettuce he tried, but he apparently thought little of it, allowing the second spoonful to run out of his mouth and not touching the dish again. Within three days, he had tried almost all of the articles, eating little of some and much of others. He had answered our first question; he could and would indicate his choice of foods without suggestion from anyone when given a chance to do so, and would eat an adequate amount.

He also showed a decided preference for such things as eggs, eating as many as five at one meal, then skipping them completely for a week. And while he still had active rickets he ate eagerly of vegetables and fruits, then cut down on them as his rickets disappeared. On top of all this, he never vomited, never was constipated, and never gave any evidence of abdominal discomfort or pain.

The other children acted similarly. As for quantity, each infant soon found out just about how much he needed and more or less stuck to it, unless a cold or other illness was coming on. From twelve to twenty-four hours before a cold set in, appetites became spontaneously poorer. From twelve to twenty-four hours before the fever went down, appetites came back.

In quality they preferred raw food to cooked. And as they began to recover from a cold or fever, interestingly they chose more vitamin-rich raw beef and carrots than usual. And at certain periods they had a marked preference for beets. All the infants devoured beets for the first six months after weaning, then seldom touched them until they were recovering from a cold or fever, when they devoured them again. The vitamins in beets? The sugar? Some other substance their small bodies craved at this time? Dr. Davis couldn't be sure. But she felt it was something they undoubtedly needed to balance out a lack.

HABIT AND MEMORY

While Dr. Davis' experiment proves a great deal about natural, unspoiled babies, it proves little about those who have already developed fixed eating patterns. For few things are as susceptible to alteration by habit and memory as food.

An Italian can crave hot peppers all his life because they happened to be in a dish that satisfied him when he was very hungry and very young; a Russian can crave herring with sour cream. Americans enjoy cake with thick icing, not only because it "tastes good" but because it is associated with memories of joyful occasions like Christmas or birthdays. Each time we eat cake we go back to a happy childhood day, and hope to recapture the pleasures we felt when the sweet morsels originally rolled on our tongues.

It is also for this reason that we dislike certain foods. If liver was repeatedly offered us on a day we felt irritable or tired, or if Aunt Emma who lived with us made a wry face every time liver was served, then liver almost surely lands on the "no" list before it gets a fair trial.

Add to this the fact that children have very keen taste-buds, and that these keener taste-buds are located mainly in the roof and sides of their mouths, and you can see why children push away foods like sharp cheeses that offend their taste-buds. Why, too, they relish huge pieces of candy like sour-balls or taffy. The large pieces titillate their mouths and they get such satisfaction from them they repeat the sensation until it wears itself thin.

KEEN IMAGINATIONS

Then, children have keen imaginations. A food that looks like what it is to an adult can look to a child like something quite offensive. A "wiggly" food such as a creamed dish may remind her of a wiggling snake. A "mushy" food like soft-cooked eggs may remind her of vomit, and children vomit far more than adults. A dark-brown food like a stew may remind her of a bowel-movement, and while at one period in her life a bowel-movement may have fascinated her, at another it can have the opposite effect. Especially to a fastidious little girl, such similarities may be very real, as real as the zebra or donkey she's sure she saw this morning in the back yard.

LITTLE HARM IN PREFERENCES

Doctors say there is little harm if food-dislikes or food-preferences based on a child's early habits persist through life. If a child hates spinach but substitutes string beans for it, or if she learns to like neither and substitutes oranges for both, parents can remember that fruits have about the same vitamin-content and nourishment as vegetables. And fish has about the same as meat, hamburger or lamb stew, so for practical purposes it makes little difference which is preferred.

It's lucky for the human race that this is so; otherwise mankind could not have survived, since the available foods differ throughout the world. Yet in the course of evolution the Chinese have learned to extract enough nourishment to keep quite healthy, living mainly on rice, the Mexicans on beans, the Indians on corn, the Yugoslavians on fermented milk. And in some parts of the world the milk comes from cows, in some from goats, and in some, except for human milk, there is no milk at all.

For this reason, Drs. Pearson and English think it's largely a waste of time and energy worrying about what a child should or should not eat. As they put it,

There are more superstitions about beneficial and harmful varieties of food among civilized human beings than about anything else in life, with the possible exception of excretory habits.

The child should eat rhubarb, he should avoid sugar, he needs green vegetables, fish will develop the brain, carrots are good for the hair, etc., etc., ad infinitum. They take no account of the scientific fact that they are prevalent only in America, and that other cultures have equally healthy people who have been raised by the application of an entirely different set of ideas. There is no single article of food the ingestion of which is necessary to life and health.

ANOREXIA NERVOSA

There is an abnormal condition having to do with food which is something else again. The Greeks had a name for it: *anorexia nervosa*, meaning a loss of appetite due to emotional reasons. This is a true loss in which a person eats practically nothing, and which lasts so long that serious malnutrition is the result.

Adolescent girls are the chief sufferers from *anorexia nervosa*. Adolescent girls, as we shall see, can become so overwhelmed by pressing life-problems, they actually stop eating and die. Children seldom do. To most children, the pressing problems of living are still a long way off. Also, the ordinary child has such a basically good appetite that it soon sends out an urgent hunger-signal after a temporary halt. Doctors agree that a child under normal conditions of love and understanding will never voluntarily abstain from food long enough to be hurt.

But there can be temporary *anorexias* in children, too. The most common of these comes from forced feeding—when a new food is forced on children too vehemently or too soon, and they become for a time uninterested in all food as a result. For there is all the difference in the world between being gently guided toward a new food and having that food forced on you. Forced feeding brings on a feeling of helplessness and rage it's almost impossible for the person doing the forcing to understand.

When the first African Negroes were captured, the American slave-dealers resorted to forced feeding to keep them alive. When the Negroes couldn't or wouldn't eat from fright and despair, the dealers used cruel devices resembling screwdrivers to push the nourishment down their throats. Mothers who shove in a mouthful of unwanted vegetable or cereal are doing something similar. Both are violating their child's integrity and creating a situation she literally "can't swallow." The ground for feeding troubles are being laid.

Other situations that can make a little girl feel so helpless or angry she can't eat are when she is constantly corrected at the table, when her parents have frightening quarrels in her presence or when she is seemingly abandoned because a new baby has arrived on the scene.

All these again usually affect a girl more than a boy. For a boy can work off some of his anger by whacking a baseball, punching a punching-bag or picking a fight with another boy who may be merely a spur-of-the-moment substitute for the parent he doesn't dare hit back. Girls can't do these things nearly as easily. Society doesn't encourage them to do them and they themselves rarely have the inclination or the energy. Until the rage-provoking situation is righted and good parental relations restored, the best a little girl often can do is to kick a can—or not eat.

❋❋❋ 11 Is It Glands?

From not eating we swing to overeating.

The biggest single reason mothers have for bringing little girls to hospital clinics is that they want them reduced. At a certain point the same mothers who begged for tonics to cultivate their child's appetite begin to worry about their thick legs and dumpy shape; they want them made graceful and attractive and slim, but quick.

But they don't want it done by diet. Heaven forbid! They want it done by injections or "shots." They can haul in a youngster so heavy she can hardly waddle, but they still insist "Obesity runs in our family" or "It's all a matter of glands."

ONE IN TWO HUNDRED

They're right about the glands. Overweight is a matter of glands— for one child in two hundred.

For when women get into a quiet corner and discuss glands as a cause of overweight, they mostly mean thyroid glands. Not more than one woman in two hundred has a thyroid deficiency. What's more, when she does, she's more apt to be skinny than fat.

The comforting thought that a lack of thyroid makes people fat was thought up by a doctor named Van Noorden back in 1894. His idea was, since thyroid helps burn up food, when you don't have enough thyroid you don't burn up what you take in. So all you have to do is keep on eating as before, take some thyroid as medicine, and, presto, the pounds will melt away. But Van Noorden himself abandoned his theory a few years after he proposed it, because it simply wasn't borne out by the facts.

Actually, a lack of thyroid usually keeps a person thin because the very lack causes a poor appetite. A child with a low thyroid output seldom has the urge to eat much, so her weight naturally tends to stay down. Also, a child with a true thyroid deficiency tends to suffer from delayed teething, cold hands and dry, pale skin. She is often mentally and physically retarded as well.

Dr. Walter Eberlein gives this rule:

If a child has continued to grow in height as well as weight, a slow thyroid is almost never a vital factor in her development.

A thyroid lack causes marked stunting of growth, and most fat children tend to be tall for their age. Also, fat girls tend to pubesce earlier than skinny girls. They seldom give evidence of any kind of mental or physical slowing down. The thyroid therefore is almost never at fault.

Meet now another remarkable woman who blazed a research trail on eating problems, Dr. Hilde Bruch.

Dr. Bruch's original contribution was in proving that obesity does run in a family—but again in a different way than most people think.

What this brilliant young doctor from Germany did was this: she decided not to take on face value the statements of mothers who brought their little girls to obesity clinics as to the amount these children ate. She would organize a team of researchers who would visit their homes day in and day out and see for themselves.

She got permission from a hundred families to do this, and started publishing her findings in the *American Journal of Diseases of Childhood* in 1939, and has checked and rechecked them ever since.

This is what she found:

WHAT THEY ATE

A normally active child of five can utilize about 1500 calories a day. This includes the amount needed for maintenance, for exercise, and for growth at that age. A normal child of ten utilizes much more—about 2500 calories a day—since around ten a much bigger growth spurt begins. But Dr. Bruch's little girls were eating between 3000 and 4000 calories a day, or about twice the amount they could possibly use up without storing a lot as ugly fat.

In addition to all the extra calories they had almost no conception of a balanced diet. They ate almost exclusively what was easiest for their mothers to fix and tastiest for them—starches and fats.

One ten year old regularly ate for her lunch three large sandwiches (meaning six pieces of starchy bread), a piece of rich cake (more starch plus fat), half a dozen bananas and apples (starch plus a lot of sugar) and several glasses of milk.

The Italian children got starchy macaroni and spaghetti at every meal. The Jewish children were downing a side dish of rich sour cream at every meal, not realizing sour cream is precisely as full of fat as sweet cream. And those who didn't drink enough milk to suit their mothers were given extra candy and cookies "to make up for it," or had chocolate syrup added to every glass.

Vegetables and salads were hardly ever eaten. Eggs in any form were dismissed as "boring." Some of them even seldom ate meat.

Many children also snacked more food between meals than at meals, but "eating between meals didn't count." And one mother whose child looked like a chubby balloon explained: "She used to drink a lot of water. I thought the water was blowing her up, so whenever she asked for a drink, I gave her milk instead."

WHY THEY ATE

Why would a mother push such enormous quantities of food into a little girl? Why would she let her eat and eat until she got worried over her appearance, then hustle her off to a clinic to beg that something be done?

Dr. Bruch discovered there were strong emotional reasons at work here, too. Not only strong, but deep. The reasons were deep because it's very hard to get the mother of an overweight child, or the child herself, to see the truth. If you ask the mother why her little girl eats as much as she does, she will usually give one of three excuses: "She needs it because she's growing," "She's always hungry" or, indignantly: "It isn't so much!"

But the hunger excuse leaves out appetite. For as Dr. Bruch explains, hunger is something physical—the actual contractions of an empty stomach. These contractions do not begin until the stomach is empty and stop when the stomach is reasonably full. Appetite, on the other hand, is psychic—related to previous sensations of pleasure, taste and smell.

Hunger is primitive and elemental. It imperiously demands relief and is quickly satisfied. Hunger comes after an actual fall in blood-sugar and goes away as soon as there is a rise. Appetite includes the emotions of wishing, longing. And wishing and longing are quite insatiable. Many a fat child eats the way a drunkard drinks. The stop-signals of satisfied hunger are ignored until the moment when she can literally take no more. The cause of insatiable longing is usually that something is wrong in her human relations. In some way she feels life has cheated her. It is well summed up in this story:

A man was walking down the street and saw a small boy crying bitterly.

"Why are you crying?" the man asked.

"I losted my penny," the boy replied.

"Oh, don't cry. Here's another penny," said the man.

At this point the boy began to cry harder than ever. "Now what's wrong?" asked the puzzled man.

"If I had the penny you just gave me, as well as the one I losted, I would now have two pennies," sobbed the small boy.

That's what ails many fat people of all ages. Somehow as a child they have "losted their penny," or, worse, they think they have. Life always owes it to them; it cannot be made up. So they try to make up for it by filling their stomachs in a way that's more socially approved than drinking. Yet since the penny is always a lost one, they are never satisfied; they eat eternally and non-stop.

More, they tend to continue to eat infantile foods like ice cream, milk or cake, rather than go on to more sophisticated tastes. They get stuck in a babyish pattern and go round and round in it, like a phonograph needle that's stuck in a groove.

MOTHER MORE THAN CHILD

In Dr. Bruch's study, it was the mothers even more than the children who had "losted their penny" and got stuck in a groove. Many of the little girls didn't yet feel that life had cheated them, but their mothers did. By the process of identification, they were trying to make up for their own feeling of lack by stuffing their children to the hilt.

That's why Dr. Bruch agrees that fatness does "run in families." It happens so often in a setting where the mother buys and cooks the food and so plays the tune to which everyone does the dance.

After many interviews and much probing, here is what the researchers found:

At least 70 per cent of the too-fat little girls were only children, or children who had been born after another child died and so had to make up to the mother "for all she had missed." Then, almost all the fat children came from poor homes rather than middle-class or well-to-do homes. The poorer mothers remembered that as youngsters their own lives had been very hard. Now their children would at least have tables groaning with food.

One woman, who at first kept insisting her child didn't eat much, later admitted: "I stuffed her like a goose because I enjoyed watching her. But since she couldn't finish it all, I didn't consider it 'much.' "

Another mother was getting a kick out of using her child as a feeding model the way farmers sometimes do their calves: "The neighbors call my daughter in to set the pace when their children aren't hungry," she boasted. "It works!"

Still another forbade her daughter all sports and activities because she had never been permitted them, kept her sitting at home watching TV or being otherwise inactive while her friends were out playing, by bribing her with extra pie and cake. "Food is almost the only interest she has now," the mother said.

While some mothers kept their children in a state of perpetual infancy mainly to flatter their own egos, several mothers of husky eight and nine years olds were still bathing them and dressing them. One of these said bluntly, "I lost another child at birth, so this one became a baby twice."

GUILT

People do a lot of things as an antidote to guilt—and the guiltier they feel, the harder they try. One woman put her guilt-feelings in a nutshell when she confided, "I nearly killed myself trying to get rid of her before she was born. But after she came, we were all crazy about her, especially me. I never could deny her a thing."

IT MAKES YOU GROW

Of course, a common reason for stuffing was the notion that extra food insured extra growth, with the parents who were small themselves particularly intrigued by this idea.

What these parents forgot is that food has little to do with growth;

it's not so much quantity as it is fresher, cleaner and better food. Children in the old days used to live, in the winter especially, mostly on canned, dried or salted food, from which practically all the vitamins had been cooked out by the intense heat needed to preserve it. In the summer there was the dread "summer complaint" from tainted milk. And all year round there were crippling fevers like typhoid and rickets that set a child way back, since a child does not grow while she is ill in bed.

Doctors feel that the chief reason children are taller today is that they are spared most of these childhood setbacks and so grow to the full potential of their individual capacities. Stuffing them beyond their natural limits will not make them grow more.

CAN A CHILD DIET?

Can a fat child diet? Rarely before adolescence. She simply hasn't the strong motivations like dating, or improving her appearance she later will have.

At the Children's Obesity Clinic of New York University I saw an example of this not long ago, as I watched a child called Ellen who was eleven years old and tipped the scale at 165, at least 45 pounds too much.

Ellen was bursting with enthusiasm. Her father had brought her, but she insisted she had come on her own accord, since she was dying to lose the whole 45 pounds, in the four months before her next birthday, and by golly she would!

The doctor in charge, Dr. Elizabeth Bergman, looked Ellen over carefully. Since she was tall for her age rather than short, since her cheeks were rosy rather than pale, and since she was obviously intelligent rather than backward, she was hardly, from her appearance, one of the rare cases of glandular lack. True thyroid-deficiency cases, as I said, have a low rate of metabolism. Ellen's was high plus eight.

Next the doctor asked Ellen what she had been eating. Her answer was refreshingly honest. She said she ate anything in sight, adding for emphasis: "I can gobble up a whole can of marshmallow paste in a couple of gulps."

She also said she had begun to eat this way three years before, after an illness involving a high fever. Many people start to eat voraciously after a severe illness, which is the reason behind the popular belief that "an operation makes you fat." They start to eat heavily because we all tend to go to extremes. Nature intends a little overeating during convalescence to make up for the time of deprivation. But nature doesn't intend it to last indefinitely. Children who have been ill, however, find convalescence a delightful state of affairs, mainly for the attention and fuss that goes with it. If they're not careful, laden trays and snacking can become a habit. Again they're addicted or hooked.

Ellen was now so addicted to food that when she said she wanted to eat anything in sight, she was stating sober truth. At many obesity clinics, instead of talking about calories they have little papier mâché dummies made up to look like a three-ounce hamburger, an average-sized baked potato or the like. These are shown as standards to the would-be reducer as easier to keep in mind.

When Dr. Bergman showed the dummies to Ellen, she got so excited merely looking at them that she actually drooled. She couldn't resist touching them, and as she left she blew kisses at them, giggling, "They look so cute."

I followed Ellen later to the lunch-counter in the building. She did order one sensible meal, under the strength of her new resolution. But could she keep it up? A child that drooled at food-dummies? I'll wager not until the years had given her far firmer motivation and strength.

Ellen's mother couldn't help her either. Almost no mother can at that age.

For pestering now by a mother tends to make the situation worse. The same mother who has been lavish in her praise for stuffing can't suddenly turn around and withdraw praise for the same reason, for to do that only mixes up a child and succeeds in convincing her that her mother is suddenly withdrawing her love.

Doctors even warn parents to go easy in withdrawing food from child diabetics for this reason. Far better, they say, to let a youngster's physical health suffer a little than have her vital belief in her mother's love suffer a lot.

✳✳✳ 12 She Goes to School and Learns to Work

There are two kinds of aggression as we saw—destructive aggression and constructive aggression. The destructive kind is a result of anger or hostility and expresses itself in breaking, destroying, moving against. The constructive kind is the result of a desire to cooperate and expresses itself in building, creating, moving toward a positive goal.

The positive goal may be becoming a member of the Peace Corps, and helping to eradicate illiteracy in a foreign land. It may be marching in a Civil Rights demonstration and helping right ancient wrongs, it may be organizing a local club to fight pornography disguised as "comic books." But however constructive aggression is expressed, it involves working lovingly and cooperatively with others toward a better world.

The normal person feels both hate and love for himself as well as others, but he feels more love than hate. He never stops trying to advance humbly toward the ideal of working cooperatively with his neighbor and loving him as himself.

A girl around five or six starts to learn how to work with and love her neighbor when she enters school. Learns to do this in a broader way than with her sisters and brothers and parents, since she now enters a wider circle of people to whom she has to relate. And she does it first by developing a sense of industry. Up to now, one of her chief jobs has been learning how to master her own body; now she must learn how to master her work-tools.

HER WORK-TOOLS

Her main work-tools are reading and writing and 'rithmetic—for the classic three R's that are the basis of all the others to come. Before she can master these, however, she must learn to do something else she has never had to do before—organize her time to meet deadlines imposed by school. Up to now she pretty much ate when she was hungry, slept until she felt like getting up, went to the bathroom without asking permission, and played until she was tired or bored with a particular toy or game. Now she has to get up in the morning so that she gets to school at the proper moment and organize her afternoons so that her homework gets done for the next day. She must also increase her attention-span beyond the boredom stage—pay attention to subjects that seem dull or difficult whether she feels like paying attention or not.

INCREASED ANXIETY

These changes inevitably generate some anxiety in her. For entering school is a great climax for her—a step up the rung of life's ladder that the word "climax" means. For above all, entering school means, too, her first real tearing away from the protection of her kind and forgiving mother, and becoming subject to a teacher who necessarily has a minimum of forgiveness for infractions of various kinds.

One way for her to minimize this anxiety is to accumulate things— the special things that are the tools of her new trade, such as pencils and pencil-boxes, rulers, tubes of bright paints, a satchel in which to carry her possessions. These give her something literally to "hold onto" and so make her feel more secure. An even better way to minimize her anxiety is for her to achieve some measure of success as quickly as possible—bring home colored pictures for her mother to admire, earn good report cards her father will be proud of, get a gold star or other token of achievement for anything from winning a relay race to becoming the best errand-runner in the class.

"Praise youth and it will prosper" is an old Irish proverb. A little girl desperately needs such praise now in order to become more sure of herself, just as she will keep on needing it all her life.

MAKING ALLIES

Still another way of minimizing her anxiety is to make some allies her own age. Before this, she had few real allies, mostly playmates who played alongside of her. Now she wants some she can play *with*. Children she can invite home after school, and get invited to their homes in return. Allies she can walk home with from school without her mother tagging along. For how can she possibly develop the self-confidence to make such allies if her mother is always on the scene and "no one wants to play with me!" becomes her greatest complaint?

DOGS OR OTHER PETS

Another way of increasing her self-confidence at this time is for her to acquire a dog or other pet. For a dog is a long step ahead of the stuffed teddy-bear or wooly animal she used to take to bed with her to comfort her in the dark. A dog is alive, a dog is grateful. And once trained, she can boss him as much as she pleases; he will remain docile and not talk back. With all the new adults who are bossing her around and telling her what to do, it's a fine balance for her to have a live creature she can order about in turn. Dogs are also like an endless succession of "good mothers"; they flatter her shaky ego with boundless love.

When dogs or other pets are out of the question, plants are a good substitute. For plants, too, are docile and grateful; plants, too, accept praise or abuse, yet show their love by growing and giving joy. So pets or plants increase their sense of mastery, and thus increase her ability to master herself and her tools.

READING JAGS

Still another way of quickly increasing her sense of mastery is through reading. Reading is in some ways an even greater achievement than talking. We can talk only with those who are near us; through reading a child can ally herself with the world of children everywhere.

Girls are famous for reading omnivorously as soon as they can. They go on such reading jags they can't wait to get home with a library book, but must devour its fascinating pages as they meander through the streets. They read much more than boys do, if only because boys are too busy playing the strenuous games they need to work off steam.

In a questionnaire given to grammar school boys and girls asking them to list what made other pupils popular with them, boys listed traits like "good at games," "likes to take chances." Girls listed "not quarrelsome," "not a show-off" or "doesn't fight." Among its other blessings, her eagerness to devour books keeps a girl so busy she doesn't have the time or energy to do much quarreling or fighting. It keeps a girl busy until the tomboy burst starts around the age of nine—a burst that brings with it an increase in all kinds of activity and aggressive behavior, as she starts in earnest the long, slow job of pulling away from her mother and becoming a person on her own.

✳✳✳ 13 Negative, Tomboy and Difficult

A girl starts the long slow job of pulling away from her mother by standing on her head. Or doing other "unladylike" things like climbing a barn roof, hurling insults at the neighbor children, or insisting on wearing the sloppiest of blue jeans. "What has come over my little darling?" her mother moans. "She used to be so sweet and feminine and obedient. Now she flounces around like a tomboy, and won't listen to a *thing!*"

MOTHER WAS MAGIC

This change is all the harder to bear because up to now a mother has been magic in her daughter's eyes.

It's hard to realize what a mother has meant until now to a girl. A father has been one thing: he has been a creature who spelled affection, shagginess and spicy male odors, but who has not had the time to get as close as a mother, the person who has been always *there*. A mother is the one who's been rushed to for band-aids, to solve puzzling problems, to be given a breathless report about what happened in school. Even if she worked out by day, she has still been mainly the judge who made most of the decisions at night. So gradually she has become as much a fixture in a small girl's life as the living room sofa, or the clock that ticks reliably upon the shelf.

But a mother has not only been omnipresent, she has also appeared all-powerful—she was the one who could do with ease almost all the things that seemed so difficult for a little girl. She could make flowers grow, cakes rise, long sums of arithmetic come out right. All these were as simple to her as to a fairy queen when she waved her wand.

Like a fairy queen, too, a mother could change her face and figure at will. A little girl has been pretty much stuck with her own looks. A mother could lounge around all day in flat-heeled shoes, pale from lack of make-up and with frowzy hair. But when she went to a party at night, lo! she became a rosy vision in shining silks, half a mile tall.

Then, Mother has had still another magical power: she could foretell the future. When she said a ballet was going to be performed in the school auditorium, it was performed; when she said the circus would come in the spring, it did come. It never occurred to the little girl that her mother learned most of this from reading the daily paper. A mother just *knew* things. It was as simple as that.

THE WILL TO BELIEVE

The American philosopher William James coined the famous phrase, "the will to believe." Children have this will to a marked degree. They "will to believe" their mothers are mainly good, kind and virtuous because it's comforting to believe it and relieves them of the responsibility of thinking difficult things through for themselves. They also will to believe their mothers are all-powerful because, as far as they are concerned, it is a fact. And girls have this will to believe even more than boys. They have it because they're basically passive or receptive. One of the main psychological differences between girls and boys is that the male is basically active and the female basically passive, a difference that continues all their lives. Women sit still while men jump around; women cheerfully stay close to home while men are impelled to climb Mt. Everest or rove into space.

This does not mean that the normal male is completely active or the normal woman completely passive, of course. But there's no question that women have a stronger drive in the direction of passivity than men have, and this drive complements the man's active drive as a hook complements an eye.

Because of this basic passivity, it's easier for a girl to say "yes" to those around her than it is for a boy. A girl may go through occasional "no" periods, but she finds it simpler as a rule to agree or give in rather than to fight. So, as a little girl she dresses in the fluffy ruffles her mother picks out for her, and puts on her rubbers and mittens with less struggle when told. And she puts this obedience into words that warm her mother's heart. "You're the best mommy on the block! I love you, Mommy!" she says over and over, with only a rare, "You're the meanest mommy I know!"

MORE IDENTIFICATION

Then a little girl says "yes" to her mother more often than not because she identifies with her mother, puts herself in her more passive, less active, mother's place. For it is far easier to identify with someone of the same sex you are. No matter how much one tries, no girl or woman can imagine just what it is like to be a man, or a man a woman. That is another reason a girl develops a closer tie to her mother than to her father. She has the extra bond of identification. So the silver cord between mother and daughter can be woven into very thick strands.

EVERYTHING SEEMS CHANGED

But around the age of nine comes a stunning change. Around nine the mainly passive little girl becomes suddenly quite active. The pliant child who mainly said "yes" starts vigorously to say "no." The demure angel throws her fine ruffled dresses into the closet, stamps her feet and sasses back to a point where she can become a veritable pest.

The time from around nine to eleven in a girl has been called the "negative age," the "latent age," the "tomboy age." Most parents would settle for the "difficult age," though it still isn't as difficult as in a boy. Dr. John Levy says that, whenever a child this age is brought to a principal's office by a teacher who says "I can't do a thing with this brat," the chances are six to one the complaint refers to Johnny rather than to Johnny's sister Mary. That is, the chances are six to one in a public school. In a private school, they're ten to one, since private school boys have often lived in homes that have permitted them to get even more out of hand.

Still, age nine to eleven is a difficult age in a girl, too, because it's such a new and bewildering age. Before, a girl grew upward like a spring plant pushing slowly through the soft earth. Now she's more like a tree breaking through a hard rock. For she is experiencing an all-over burst of power and energy such as she has never known.

A BURST OF POWER

Various human drives have been called the life-force. Curiosity is one. Libido is one. Power, or energy, is another—and possibly the strongest because it combines them all.

It is energy, or power, that pulls an ovum into the woman's tubes and makes it combine with a male sperm. It is power, or energy, that divides the one life-cell that results into two cells, four cells, eight cells, and eventually the millions of cells that make up a baby. It is power, or energy, that propels an infant to stand upright on her two wobbly legs instead of remaining in her play-pen. And it is a burst of power around nine, a strange, mysterious power that wells up inside her from her hormones, that are increasing by leaps and bounds, that pushes her to take her first real steps in the direction of joining the world of her peers, and getting herself some real friends.

NOT EASY TO WIN FRIENDS

Now, theoretically, joining the world of her peers and getting herself friends should be easy, but actually it isn't. Youngsters are suspicious of taking on a newcomer unless their admiration is won, as children who move to a new neighborhood well know. So she uses some of her energy to perform some of the feats of physical wonder children her own age can admire and understand. She climbs the highest fence in sight, turns the most daring somersaults or does her best to win a relay race. She even quits dancing school if the crowd thinks dancing school is "kid stuff" or "sissy." For while "tomboy" is a compliment, "sissy" is the worst of insults, and she will do anything to win the crowd's praise.

SHE DONS THE CURRENT UNIFORM

Equally to impress the crowd, she dons the current uniform. It may be a sloppy shirt, a dirty raincoat, disreputable sneakers, but it is visible proof of her willingness to sacrifice. The uniform is her fraternity-pin, her admission price to the club.

And in the current uniform, horrible as it may be, she wiggles all over—even more than before. She grimaces, tweaks her nose, pulls her ears, fiddles with pencils or shakes her buttocks until her parents are driven into a mad daze.

(Later these same parents will be equally dazed when she sits still for hours and daydreams, seemingly impossibly "lazy." Ah well, all in good time.)

WORKING OFF TENSION

But much of her present activity is also for the purpose of working off the tension she's bound to feel at the mere thought of joining her peers. Activity is another classic defense against anxiety. Just as the tense father-to-be paces the floor of the corridor, or the hostess whose guests are late runs back and forth to the kitchen or arranges and rearranges the table, so the nine year old works off steam by wiggling her hands, her feet and her seat.

The seat-wiggling, incidentally, strengthens her pelvis, that still-clumsy pelvis whose strength will stand her in good stead some day when she bears a child.

Her defiance and sassing back are part of the same picture: her need to use some of her energy to make the intense effort needed to break out of the cocoon of the family and join the world of her peers.

But just as she moves her body clumsily, she sasses clumsily. She swings from the most ardent idealization of her mother to the harshest criticism, from the most extreme words of worship to the most violent words of hostility. That is, she does if she's normal. Psychiatrists say this vacillating back and forth is far more healthy at nine than to continue with undiluted adoration of her mother. For continuing to do nothing but adore her is a sign of psychic infantilism. It takes courage to grow. Constant uncritical adoration may be merely evidence of a lack of that courage, an inability to go forward and learn to say "no" to the many things she will have to say "no" to in life.

So the normal girl starts now in earnest to criticize her mother, but also does it clumsily—as clumsily as she took her first steps on skates. She uses her mother as a target and, at the same time she may be praising her wildly at school, attacks her wildly at home.

But her mother isn't enough of a target for her new-found energy and hostility. She digs up boys and girls as enemies—especially boys—"pretend" enemies, if nothing better turns up, like the kids across the street she barely knows. Using her favorite weapon, her tongue, she hurls insults at them, using fine-sounding phrases like "you igorote" or "you insignificant piece of humanity." What matter if she doesn't quite understand the meaning of these insults? They are loftily designed to "slay" her enemies by laying them low.

ONE FRIEND

But underneath all this huffing and shouting, her personality is still a weak one, and no one knows this better than herself. So, even more than enemies, even more than friends in general, she needs one particular friend—one bosom pal or chum of her own age and sex whom she freely chooses, and to whom she can passionately attach herself and discover the union there is in strength.

This bosom pal she needs so that she can giggle and titter with her; walk arm in arm with her; confide some of the secrets with which life suddenly seems so full. The secret of wanting to stay out after dark, and feel guilty about it. The secret of wanting to defy her mother, and feel guilty about that. Sexual secrets like the pubic hair and tiny breasts that may be starting to develop because of the great increase in her sex-hormones, and wondering whether they are developing alike in both.

Psychiatrist Helene Deutsch of Boston says one such bosom pal is a genuine necessity at this time. "Despite her noisy self-assurance," says Dr. Deutsch, "she is aware of her inadequacy, and needs someone as insignificant as herself in order to feel stronger, doubled as it were. She wants someone who resembles her and who, like herself, is undergoing the suffering of feeling insignificant. She can endure the burden of secrecy, of feeling that the surrounding world is hostile, the torments of guilt, with greater ease because she endures them with another."

But this relationship must be monogamous if it is to have real value. The two girls must remain faithful to each other, tell each other everything, yet exclude all others, especially grown-ups, from their confidence. Because of this, it is most difficult for any older woman to get close to a girl of this age. Not only mothers but all "motherly women" are suspect. Social workers who try to deal with pre-teenagers find that, if they must get close to them for any reason, it has to be with the casual, non-authoritarian attitude of a girl friend. Pre-teens could take authority before, and will crave it again. It is anathema now.

The most vital secret a girl is sharing with her chum, or "bosom friend," is the secret of adult sex relations, what these relations really are like. She may have been told a little about adult sex relations before, when she asked about where babies come from, but she wasn't particularly paying attention to the answers. Even though she asked the same questions over and over, any simple, general, honest answer about babies satisfied her. As a small girl she was no more able to understand the complicated matter of adult sex relations in detail than she was able to get a true conception of God.

But now she has matured to the point where she is listening. With her sex-hormones so rapidly welling up in her, she is listening intently as if to a radio tuned to a new and powerful wave-length. More, in addition to listening, she may be doing some thinking and observing on her own. And the first reaction she often gets about adult sex relations is that they involve pain. She may have actually heard the sounds accompanying intercourse coming from her parents' bedroom at night when they thought she was asleep; she may have been told stories by her friends who have heard their parents; and these strange sounds are commonly interpreted by children as coming from acts of brutality. The strong male is attacking the weak female, and she is fighting him off or resisting. The woman is suffering great indignity and distress.

It is also common at this time to get the impression that childbirth is invariably very painful. In this sense women are the worst enemies of other women. There is hardly a girl alive who, during these extremely impressionable years, hasn't heard some older woman boast about how she "almost died" in childbirth and go on to give a description of the event, blow by harrowing blow. The same story-teller seldom tells of the joy that followed the experience; she takes this for granted. Besides, joy never holds an audience like suffering. Ask any newspaper editor which gets him more readers, a description of a murder or a pleasant picnic on the green.

A GIRL WORRIES MORE

Should the woman who is telling of how she suffered happen to have a mixed audience, including a boy and a girl, it is the girl who will be much more upset by the tale. For she will be identifying with the woman in agony while the boy will not. The boy may laugh the story off —after all, childbirth will never happen to him! But it probably will to the girl, so she becomes the littlest of pitchers with the biggest of ears.

Yet there's another and equally potent reason she listens so avidly. This is the basic feminine attraction to suffering, an attraction stronger than in any man.

Now attraction to suffering doesn't mean a girl or woman enjoys suffering in the sense that she consciously seeks it, though many people have misinterpreted it this way. It means she likes to hear about suffering, talk about it, relieve it when necessary and, in time, learn how to use it for a pleasurable end.

THE SPLIT IMAGE

A pre-teen hasn't yet learned how to use suffering, however. She is still at the stage of being merely attracted to it. Stories about it mightily capture her ears and her imagination, and the fancied brutality of adult sex relations drive a further wedge between herself and her mother.

For how can this brutal act be perpetrated on that magical woman? How can she allow it, when she has definitely implied conception was a romantic and beautiful act. Told all those pretty stories about the birds and the bees, even if she didn't go as far as Simone de Beauvoir's mother who told her that "babies are born by sliding gently out of the anus" and insinuated that they get in the same gentle way? With all these contradictions about the sex act, she'll never, never believe her mother again!

The same with the contradictions about childbirth. There was a song popular many years ago called "Somebody's Coming To My House." The chorus went:

> Somebody's coming to my house,
> Somebody's coming to stay,
> Father feels so happy, he's jumping for joy,
> All he keeps saying is, "I hope it's a boy."
>
> Welcome is waiting the stranger
> Who'll come to brighten our lives.
> I can hear Mother croon, "He'll be president soon,"
> When the cute little stranger arrives.

In spite of the song's cheerful words like "jumping for joy" and "brighten our lives," many girls were so preoccupied by the stories about suffering they pounced only on the word "croon" and whispered to each other it must mean "groan." Papa might be happy about the coming baby, but Mother was groaning, and they convinced each other it was so.

Dr. Abram Frantzblau of the Hebrew Union Theological Seminary says this strong impression of sexual suffering gained in childhood by both boys and girls often results in what he calls a "split mother-image." A split between the picture of a truthful mother and a lying mother; a mother who enjoys sex and its consequences and one who lets herself be brutalized.

Sometimes this split never heals. When it does not heal in a boy he may remain permanently divided, unable later to be faithful to his "pure" wife because he dares not repeatedly "attack" her, while at the same time he is potent with a "disreputable" mistress who deserves the fate she gets.

When it persists in a girl, it may result in her naturally desiring relations yet at the same time being desperately afraid of them and feeling the same about childbirth. The time to heal that split is early in life. If a mother can't bring herself to talk frankly on the subject, to tell her daughter that sex relations and childbirth are both deeply satisfying for a woman even though some pain may be mixed with them, she can at least buy her daughter a sane book. Otherwise, much lasting misery can result.

The late Dr. Irving Fischer of Mt. Sinai Hospital used to tell of getting extremely worried every time a young frightened pregnant woman came to his office for a check-up persistently accompanied by her mother. He knew she was identifying with a frightened mother who had never had the wisdom or courage to correct her daughter's fright by off-setting it with happier tales. He heaved a big sigh, and got set for a difficult birth.

A DELIGHTFUL CHILD

With all her sassiness and energy-bursts that make her often so difficult, with her intensified curiosity about sex, a girl around nine or ten is still a delightful child at that. For she has usually attained a surprising amount of psychological maturity for her age and does not use her tongue solely as a destructive weapon by any means.

A study of over three hundred boys and girls done in a Hebrew orphan asylum confirms this. They were studied as to the kinds of nicknames they commonly gave each other. As many as 39 per cent of the boys gave derogatory nicknames based on physical defects, such as "gumpty" or "fatso" or "cross-eyes," while only 7 per cent of the girls did the same. The majority of the girls gave flattering nicknames like "curly" or "blondy" or "cutie-pie."

The girls' kindly nicknames reflected their greater compassion, human understanding and warmth.

✳✳✳ 14 The Mystery of the Hormones

Women like to describe themselves as "a bundle of nerves." But "a bundle of hormones" describes them as well, if not better. For hormonal energy is at least as important to a woman as nervous energy. And what her hormones are, and how they behave, explains her mystery almost better than anything about her you can learn.

PUZZLED FOR CENTURIES

The knowledge of hormones is very new. For hormones come from tiny glands that are hidden in odd corners within us, and until recently people knew almost nothing about the working of the inside of the body, since the only knowledge they had came from autopsies, and you can't learn very much about the living from the dead.

Men were puzzled for centuries about the problem of energy—that strange spark within us which is ignited at the moment of conception, flares brightly during childhood and adolescence, burns almost steadily during the middle years, then dies down slowly until we enter our long last sleep.

Where does this energy come from? What force within us takes this original spark, adds to it something as seemingly simple as the food we eat, and converts it into a power so great it can create new life in turn, build an immortal cathedral, write an immortal poem, reach for the far-away moon?

ONE ANSWER: THE SEX GLANDS

One answer the ancients stumbled on was that some of this energy source lies in our sex glands. The male sex glands are an exception to the rule that glands are hidden inside the body, for they lie on the outside for all to see. So observers as far back as the writers of the Old Testament noticed that if a man's sex glands were injured or removed, he was affected out of all proportion to the tiny glands' size. He became not only sterile but weaker all over; his hands lost their grip, his muscles their tone. His energy was so lessened he was content to sit out his days guarding locked-up ladies in a harem rather than march off to battle again.

Butchers noticed the same thing about male animals. No one knows who first thought up the practice of taking out the sex glands from roosters to make them quieter and their flesh more tender; of altering the tomcat to stop him from roving and the bull to turn him from a ferocious, bellowing creature into a placid ox. But people seem to have known enough to do this since history began.

But what about the other tiny glands that were in time discovered? What was the influence on energy of the shield-shaped gland in the neck called the thyroid, from the Greek word for "oblong shield?" Or the adrenals, that rest on top of the kidneys and got their name from "renal," for kidney? Or the pituitary, that hangs down from the base of the brain like a cherry from a stem? Did these, too, have a general energy function? Or did they have merely a local function, or no function at all?

The thyroid, they decided, had merely a local function—to beautify the neck. In the eighteenth century, Thomas Warton gave this poetic description of the thyroid's job: "It contributes much to the rotundity and beauty of the neck, filling up the vacant spaces round the larynx, particularly in females, to whom for this reason a larger gland has been assigned, which renders their necks more even and beautiful."

Then the pituitary, men thought, merely gathered up the waste products and mucus from the brain and used them to lubricate the throat, for which reason they called it the pituitary, from the Latin word *pituita*, meaning "mucus" or "spit." The ovary merely gave forth some kind of "irrigating fluid" for the uterus, and the adrenals had no discernible job at all.

ENTER BERTHOLD

With rare exceptions, men dismissed these tiny glands this way until the year 1848, when a German professor by the name of Arnold Adolf Berthold came upon the scene.

Berthold decided that, if he couldn't peer into or do experiments on living people, he could on living animals. He also decided that, to really prove something, he had to do more than take out a part of a body and see what happened; he had to put back the part, or as near a duplicate of it as he could, and see what happened then. This is what Berthold did.

He took four young roosters as his experimental subjects and divided them into two pairs. From both pairs he skillfully removed the testes, or sex glands. The results were what had always happened—the roosters, young though they were, became listless and fat; their showy red combs became pale and shrank to almost nothing; they lost interest in the formerly alluring female barnyard world.

Now he made an incision in the abdomen of two of the roosters, and transplanted their sex glands back. Even in this odd place, inside of their stomachs instead of outside, the testes showed what they could do. They recharged the roosters with so much new energy, Berthold discovered, they soon regained practically all the bright-red, fighting power and interest in females they had lost. But the other two—the pair that did not receive the transplants—remained as lethargic as before.

Then Berthold decided to do still another experiment. He killed the two roosters in whom he had replaced the testicles and hurriedly opened their abdomens again, for he was eager to know if the energy impulses had been transmitted to the rest of their bodies through their nerves, as everyone had always believed. But to his surprise they had not. The only other way they could have acted, he reasoned, was through the bloodstream. And so he made another discovery. "The testes act upon the blood, and the blood acts correspondingly upon the entire organism," he wrote.

He had hit upon the idea of the substance that was later to be called a hormone, from the Greek word *Hormao,* meaning "I send a message" —or "I excite"—a substance that sent energizing messages from one part of the body to the other through the bloodstream, with that stream acting as a wireless system to carry the messages around.

Unfortunately for science, however, Berthold published his discoveries in an obscure medical journal under an obscure title. Or maybe it was just that he thought his colleagues would laugh at him for fooling around with this kind of thing, or that the year 1848 was a year of such huge political turmoil in Germany that people were too busy to mind. At any rate, his work received hardly any notice until many years had passed.

ENTER BROWN-SEQUARD

But another researcher's work did receive attention—attention both good and bad. This researcher was the Franco-American Charles Edouard Brown-Sequard.

Brown-Sequard was a brilliant and famous scientist. After lecturing and practicing in such varied places as the island of Mauritius, London and New York, he settled down in Paris as professor of Experimental Medicine at the Sorbonne. Here he became enthralled with the idea of rejuvenation, and at the age of seventy-two, feeling weak and tired, decided to try an experiment that was bold indeed—an experiment on himself. He removed the sex glands from some vigorous dogs, boiled them down into a concentrate, and injected this concentrate into his veins.

He did this over and over. In what seemed like no time at all, he felt so excitingly strong and well he couldn't wait for publication but hurried to announce his vitality out loud. On a June night in 1889, he proudly declared to a group of fellow scientists at a medical meeting, "Everything I have not been able to do for several years on account of advanced age, I am able, today, to perform!"

As he went on with more details that sounded like straight "Fountain of Youth" stuff, he received the usual "Fountain of Youth" skepticism. But Ponce de Léon had been a mere adventurer; Brown-Sequard was a highly respected doctor. In the end they felt he couldn't be dismissed. His declaration made such headlines it became one of those shots heard around the world.

The trouble was, the shot proved too loud. No sooner had other old men descended on Paris in droves to seek the new elixir than Brown-Sequard crumpled up and became as tired as before. The men who had come to listen now remained to scoff, and their scoffing made the whole matter seem like the disreputable joke it was never intended to be.

For Brown-Sequard had also discovered several other things. One was that a lone experiment proves nothing, and that the vital step of using animals as subjects before human beings cannot be skipped. Another is that aging tissues can be stimulated only up to a point; Berthold had used young roosters; if he had used old ones, the response he got would probably have not been at all the same.

THE QUEST GOES ON

Since Berthold and Brown-Sequard, many men have gone on with the hormone-quest, and by the 1920s so much that is fascinating had been learned that, as Dr. Edward Schumann puts it, "In the 1920s the story of the hormones burst like a meteor on the medical profession. The amazing concept of their influence on the human economy, especially on a woman's economy, astonished the medical world."

Today we know even more than we did a few decades ago, particularly about women. We know that not only the sex glands but a whole host of glands are sources of her energy, and that this energy rises and falls as her hormones rise and fall, in a way that is quite different from that in a man.

LIKE A TELEPHONE SYSTEM

Picture a great telephone system with a control center or central operator that sends messages to telephone receivers miles away. Sometimes the ringing messages are steady and quiet; sometimes they are loud and insistent. But always, as long as the telephone system is hooked up, the messages can fly back and forth. The glands are hooked up to each other as in such a telephone system. In this way they send messages to each other and to the rest of the body, with the bloodstream acting as the "wires" that carry these messages around.

There are four glands important to our story—the thyroid, adrenals, sex and pituitary. The thyroid first.

THE THYROID, OR STEADY-ENERGY GLAND

The thyroid is the steady-energy gland. Day in and day out, as far as we know, it pours forth a hormone called thyroxin which sends messages to our digestive organs to control the rate at which our food is burned and our food-wastes thrown out; to our minds to control the rate at which we think; to the whole of our bodies to control the rate at which we develop and move.

You might say that birth begins with a thyroid-burst, because it is mainly the thyroid that makes a normal baby's appetite start to quicken, its body to lengthen, its mind to brighten, its nerves to tingle, and its skin to glow. But let that same baby be born with a defective thyroid and it stays slow and lethargic, stunted in height, dry in skin, poor in appetite, severely constipated and backward in mind. But thyroid hormone given as medicine must be given as soon as possible, certainly before the age of two when an infant's brain has gotten all its nerve cells fully formed and connected, if it is to help, by starting to reverse matters and do its energizing job.

In order to do all the things it can do, the thyroid gland has the entire blood supply of the body going through it each hour, which is faster than to almost any other part of the body. The blood goes through this way almost all our lives, though its effects are a little different in women than in men.

One way in which they are different is that girls and women cannot eat as much as men, no matter how big they are. Another is that a woman's thyroid enlarges during pregnancy to help her meet the baby's extra demands. And it also enlarges during puberty to help her change over to a more mature form of sex-functioning than she had before. In Roman days, for instance, it was standard practice to measure a girl's neck as one way of discovering if she had become pregnant because, if she had, her neck-band had become too tight. And in both men and women, in old age it is the natural waning of the thyroid that makes them feel colder and move more and more slowly.

THE ADRENALS,
OR SPECIAL-OCCASION GLANDS

There are many things a good housekeeper keeps on hand—bread and butter for everyday occasions, plus reserves of meat or jars of jam for special emergencies like unexpected guests. But life is far more complex than keeping house. Life is full of crises and special-emergency occasions. Illness is such a crisis or special occasion. Childbirth is such a crisis or special occasion. A death in the family causing a great burst of sorrow is such a special occasion. And it is the adrenals that not only send out little squirts of energy-hormone in varying amounts during the day, but in crises send out extra amounts to give us a quick boost of energy to carry us through the emergency.

The adrenals give this extra boost by causing our hearts suddenly to beat faster, our blood-sugar to rise, our whole bodily processes to be so speeded up that we can fight like mad or run with the wind, as ordinarily we cannot.

To help them do these special emergency jobs, the adrenals have a blood supply that is even richer than the thyroid. Six times their own weight in blood goes through the adrenals every minute, giving them the richest blood supply of any part of the body, and letting them mobilize all our resources at once.

But such mobilization has its price. After a period of adrenal-burst, a phase of adrenal-exhaustion sets in. That's why we feel so tired after an illness, or while a wound is healing, or when a loved one has just died. We were too busy fighting or running to feel tired *during* the crisis, but once it is over we fold up like a sprinter after a hard race, and stay folded up until a fresh supply of adrenal-hormones can be built.

And the older we get, the longer it takes to build up a fresh adrenal supply. Montreal's Dr. Hans Selye says you can figure almost to the year how old a person is by noting how long it takes a certain wound to heal. Children get over wounds quickly; they hurt one minute and are practically healed the next. But with each decade the speed of healing goes down until while old people can still weather crises, they need longer rests between.

THE UP-AND-DOWN ENERGY GLANDS

Nature is remarkably inventive. She has given us daily-energy and emergency-energy glands. She has also given women something else, monthly-energy glands. These are her ovaries, or sex glands.

A woman's sex glands serve several purposes. They energize her all over, they prepare her for mating, they cause eggs, or ova, to ripen within her ovaries, they thicken the lining of her womb—and they do these jobs in distinct up-and-down monthly waves. The main hormone made by a woman's ovaries is called estrogen, from the word *estrus,* meaning "heat." Estrogen is the hormone that prepares her for mating and ripens the eggs. The second hormone made by her ovaries is called progesterone, from *pro,* meaning "in favor of," and *gest,* meaning "birth." Progesterone, or the in-favor-of-birth hormone, prepares the lining of her womb to receive the fertilized eggs. (Often, for simplicity, the two hormones are lumped together under the name "female sex hormones" though they are quite unlike, as we shall see.)

Now estrogen and progesterone are made not continuously but on certain days of the month only. On some days of the month estrogen alone is made; on other days, both are made; on still other days, practically none is made. On some days of the month, too, a lot of sex hormones are made; on some days, very little. That is one reason a woman feels so much more energetic on some days than on others; a reason, too, she's often such a puzzle to the people around her—called an angel or a devil, an Eternal Feminine or an Eternal Eve. But then, until she understands her sex hormones, and the fact they do go up and down during the month, she's a puzzle to herself, too.

NO 100 PER CENT WOMAN

Equally puzzling is the fact there's no such thing as a 100 per cent woman; or, for all his protestations, a 100 per cent man. Each of us has some of the other mixed in; in fact, a lot of the other. The most cuddly, round and feminine-looking woman is never *all* woman. She has enough female hormones to throw her over in the direction nature intended her to be, but she has a good deal of male hormones in her as well, with the two performing different functions and making her whole.

WHAT FEMALE HORMONES DO

What do her estrogens, or female hormones, do for a woman, in addition to ripening eggs and lining her womb? They surge up at puberty, developing her genital organs and breasts and causing menstruation to start. They let her become pregnant, with all the great changes pregnancy entails. They favor the deposit of calcium in her bones. They give her skin its rosy hue, so that during pregnancy, when her estrogen tides are particularly high, she literally glows. They favor the retention of water in her body, making her soft and pleasing to the touch, and, possibly most important, they help protect her against a whole batch of crippling illnesses like heart attacks and strokes.

WHAT HER MALE HORMONES DO

What do her androgens, or male hormones, do for her? They give her the big growth-spurt of puberty. Thyroid and estrogen have some effect on her growth; androgen, still more. They give her much of her sex-drive. Estrogen gives her some sex-drive; androgen more. They burn up some of her excess fat. Castrates with little androgen are often fat and flabby; young boys and girls at the height of their androgen-spurt are lean and firm. They temporarily coarsen her skin during adolescence, and sometimes bring the hated acne. Most important, they give her reserves of hidden strength.

Thus, added together, her male and female hormones complement each other. They make a woman into a blend of feminine sex-attraction, motherliness, softness and warmth, and add to it all some masculine strength.

WHERE HER ANDROGENS COME FROM

Here's another mystery: Where do her androgens come from? The bulk comes from her adrenal glands.

All the glands are complex and remarkable. The adrenals are so complex they are made up of two sections and make some twenty-five hormones we know of, including, rather surprisingly, sex hormones—both estrogens and androgens. They make so many sex hormones, indeed, they are often referred to as "the third sex gland." The adrenals are thus a combination of regular glands, reserve-energy glands and sex glands. In their reserve and sex functions, they come to a woman's rescue at many times in her life in a very special way.

THE PITUITARY OR CONTROL GLAND

The soldiers in World War I used to enjoy going around chanting, "If it's the bugler's job to wake up the camp each morning, whose job is it to wake up the bugler?"

If they'd been scientific-minded, they might have chanted, "If it's the job of the thyroid, adrenals and ovaries to supply us with energy, whose job is it to supply energy to them?" The answer is the pituitary. For in some ways the pituitary is the most remarkable gland of all.

The hormone system is like a telephone system, as I said, with the pituitary as the central operator. For in addition to its many other jobs, such as influencing the growth of the entire body, the pituitary controls and sends messages to all the other glands. Without a sound pituitary the other glands are "out of order." They cannot do their job.

There was, for instance, a young girl named Celia in Schenectady, New York, whose pituitary was severely damaged at the age of nine. Though her other glands had not been hurt, she stopped growing completely, she never menstruated and at twenty she still had the smooth face and straight body of a child. Worse, without a well-working pituitary, Celia had so few special-situation hormones to fight stresses with that a minor illness suddenly carried her off.

In normal girls this does not happen. In normal girls the pituitary-central that sits up under the brain sends out its "go" messages to the branch-stations of thyroid, ovaries and adrenals, and as these receive the messages they do their appointed jobs.

"STOP" AS WELL AS "GO"

But there's something even more unique about the gland telephone system: This is the fact that the branch glands do not always respond when the pituitary calls. At times they get overworked or tired and decide to "take the receiver off the hook." When this happens, they refuse to accept more "go" messages from the pituitary. Instead, they send back "stop" messages *to* the pituitary, asking for a rest.

Also, when the branch glands are tired, again as in a telephone system, they route messages through the pituitary to each other. When the ovaries get overworked, they send messages to the thyroid, asking it to help them out. When the thyroid gets tired, it calls for the aid of the adrenals, and so on, as the occasion demands. Thus back and forth, to and from the pituitary, and round and round to the other glands as on a busy party-line, the hormone messages fly. And this stop-and-go, back-and-forth, round-and-round hormone system is even more complex in a woman than in a man.

It is because her gland system is so complex that it is exceedingly tricky for a woman to take extra hormones as medicine. Hormones are not like aspirin. If you take two aspirin tablets and then two more, you end up with four. If you take two hormone pills and then two more, you may end up with almost none.

For the extra estrogen pills may be just enough to overwork a woman's own sex glands to the point where they send back an unusual number of messages to her pituitary to "stop," and her pituitary may become so effectively stopped it does not send out more "go" messages when otherwise it would. So she ends up with actually less of her own sex hormones than she had before—so many less that she is actually worse off than when she began.

DOESN'T WORK PERFECTLY

But even though this is the gland pattern, none of it works out with machine-like perfection, since "normal" was never meant to mean "perfect." To change the metaphor a little, a normal woman's body works rather like an old-fashioned double-tray balance scale. No matter how good a scale it is, it never stays quite in balance; it only reaches toward balance. The least touch makes it tremble and changes the up or down position of the trays. So, too, for a while the pituitary end of her scale may be up and her ovarian end down, then a slight shift will send her ovarian end up and her pituitary end down. And just when things seem to get settled to where they weigh out evenly, her scale starts trembling again.

At some times in her life her scale trembles more than others. Then there are such noticeable shifts in her balance she experiences the shock of great change. One of these great changes comes around the age of eleven.

✳✳✳ 15 She Pauses and Listens

Nothing in growth is sudden; it only seems sudden. The bud is there before the flower; the sap before the leaf. Nothing in growth is achieved without struggle. There are periods of rest, or pauses, but these are only breathers to give us time to gather strength to go on.

One of these pauses for breath in a young girl's life comes around the age of eleven. The tomboy stage has tapered off; she has not started really to become a woman. She is an in-between, a pubescent, pausing before she takes the plunge.

A DELIGHTFUL AGE

"A girl of eleven," says W. H. Auden, "can be a most remarkable creature. No longer a baby, she has learned self-control, acquired a sense of her identity and can think logically without ceasing to be imaginative. She does not know, of course, that her sense of identity has been too easily won—the gift of her parents rather than her own doing—and that she is soon going to lose it. . . .

"But one cannot meet a girl of this kind without realizing that what she is—by luck and momentarily—is what, after many years and countless follies and errors, one would like, in the end, to become."

What one would like in the end to become! Yes, and to stay! If only one could stay at the delightful age of eleven, straight and slim and virginal, standing, as another poet long ago said, "with reluctant feet where the brook and river meet."

But time never does stand still. Soon breasts begin to develop. Bellies and buttocks grow round. Hair begins to grow in the crotch and under the arms. The straight virginal body, the temporarily calm child, is no more.

THE PHYSICAL CHANGES

Preparation for the new physical changes started long ago, as early as the age of four. Girls under four are almost indistinguishable from boys. As babies in the carriage there's so little seeming difference between them that passers-by are always making proud parents angry by confusing "hes" with "shes." And even after they start to toddle, if their haircuts are alike and they are dressed in identical pants, except for a certain delicacy of feature, it is hard to tell little boys from little girls.

But around the age of four, under the prodding of her pituitary, a girl's ovaries begin to produce enough female hormones to be measurable and set her apart. These hormones influence her entire body and give her a subtle feminine look. Equally important, around four she begins to *feel* feminine. She starts this through a process called identification, or putting one's self in someone else's place.

The person a little girl starts to identify with is her mother. She starts to play with dolls and "mother" them the way her mother is mothering her. She plays house and furnishes the house with imaginary furniture, pushes a toy carriage and hugs a teddy-bear in a different and more protective way than her brother does. For her mother has become a model for her to copy. The long voyage toward becoming a mother herself has begun.

MORE CHANGES

Around the age of eight, her pituitary causes many more female hormones to accumulate within her, so she climbs another rung of the feminine ladder. Now her knees and shoulders become visibly plumper than a boy's, as her hormones change the quality of her flesh and make it softer. Her bones develop differently, too, and become jointed differently, so that while a boy throws a ball overhand, she throws a ball underhand in a way that will persist throughout life. And the features of her face become comparatively smaller and more delicate than a boy's, in a way that will also remain. It is because of this delicacy of feature that women's hats always look so ridiculous on a man.

Around ten, a girl's estrogens really start to rush in by leaps and bounds. Now her physical changes become noticeable indeed. So do her psychological changes. Since her hormones have a direct influence on her nerves, the "good" child, the "steady" child, becomes at times the touchy child, the irritable and weepy child, as all kinds of things that didn't upset her before upset her now.

One day, for instance, she cheerfully picks up her own room, or hangs around the kitchen not only to lick the icing off the bowl but to volunteer help with the ironing or with the cooking of a simple meal. But the next day, what happens? A scene like this:

Mother (to daughter): "Would you please iron these handkerchiefs?"
Daughter: "When?"
Mother: "Now."
Daughter: "You're always picking on me!"
Exit, slamming the door.

Or with her best friend:

Friend: "That skirt's pretty, but it's kind of short, isn't it?"
Girl: "Who said so?"
Friend: "Me."
Girl: "You're always criticizing! Some friend you are!"
Weeping, exit once more.

INTERNAL CHANGES

But her biggest physical changes are her internal changes. First, the changes in her uterus.

A girl's uterus at birth, remember, was comparatively large. This was due to the influence of her mother's great supply of estrogens upon her uterus while she lay curled up in the womb. But within a week after birth her mother's hormones were withdrawn, and her own hormones were still tiny in amount. So her uterus promptly shrank and stayed small throughout childhood. But around ten or eleven it has regained its original birth weight and size; then, under the influence of her own rapidly rising hormonal tide, it starts to grow fast.

Oddly too, her uterus around eleven not only grows, it changes its position. A child's uterus lies almost straight up and down. Around eleven it slides down and turns over until it lies almost flat and parallel to her vagina, or from front to back.

OVARIAN AND VAGINAL CHANGES

Her ovaries were also tiny throughout childhood. But around ten or eleven they too start to grow quickly until they become about the size and shape of pecans, and the ova, or eggs, within them start to ripen to prepare for the fertility to come.

Another rather worrisome change occurs in her vaginal secretions. There are always some secretions in the vagina, just as there are always some saliva secretions in the mouth. During childhood, though, these vaginal secretions are alkaline in reaction. Starting at puberty, the estrogens change them from alkaline to acid. Some kinds of bacilli dote on living in an acid medium, so a bacillus called Doderlein's may make itself promptly at home in a young girl's vagina as a result. Once there, Doderlein's can multiply rapidly, causing a whitish discharge. Doderlein's is more upsetting than harmful, however, since it is a normal inhabitant of the vagina during the childbearing years.

BREAST AND BELLY CHANGES

But no vaginal bacillus and no uterine changes can upset a girl as much as breast and belly changes. For a vagina and uterus remain discreetly hidden. Breasts and bellies show.

We are living in a period of body-emphasis, almost of body-worship. Some part of the female body has always been emphasized. In Imperial Rome it was the breast. Fashionable women wore their dresses so low-cut they even exposed their nipples, which were further emphasized by being painted bright gold.

In the Middle Ages, when the death rate was appallingly high and fertility correspondingly worshipped, the accent shifted to the female abdomen. If you look closely at paintings of the Middle Ages, you will notice that the women of fashion are standing with their abdomens pushed forward as if perpetually pregnant, since pregnancy was definitely "in."

But came the Victorian days, and there was another shift. Now breasts and abdomens were "out," while buttocks were "in." What were bustles but devices to call attention to the alluring buttocks beneath?

In the 1920s buttocks, breasts and abdomens flew out of favor, while legs burst forth from under the shortest of possible skirts. And as this is written, both legs and breasts are "in" again with a vengeance. Particularly breasts. Small wonder then that their development, or lack of it, obsesses the growing girl. She's concerned when they grow so fast they make her embarrassed. She's worried stiff when they don't grow fast enough to make her look immediately like Sophia Loren.

When they don't grow fast enough, she often wastes time and money rubbing them with drug-store "development creams," stuffs them into "falsies" or pesters her mother to buy her a purely status bra-size 28AA. When they grow too fast, she wears bras so tight she can't breathe or hides them under loose blouses and enormous sloppy shirts. For in breasts and feelings about them, there seems to be no middle road.

GROWING LOPSIDED

It is equally upsetting when her breasts seem to be growing lopsided, or when one grows faster than the other.

The reason for this is that when the pituitary sets the cycle going that results in sexual maturity, it does not do so evenly at first. Just as menstruation usually starts irregularly, so does growth of the breasts. One breast may for a while be more sensitive to the hormonal-stimulation it gets. But the slow breast will usually catch up in time. It may not catch up perfectly, to be sure, but then, who ends up with two eyes with exactly the same vision, two ears that hear exactly the same sounds, two feet of exactly the same size or a profile exactly the same from both sides?

The wise saying of the Emperor Marcus Aurelius, "There is no excellent beauty without some strangeness about its proportion," certainly holds true.

BREAST PAIN AND TENDERNESS

Growth is a stress, and stress includes pain. Since a girl's breast grows at a tremendously speeded-up rate during puberty, a few shooting pains almost always accompany this growth. So do tenderness, a feeling of fullness, even a small amount of milky discharge from the nipples. But all are normal, including the milky substance, which should be ignored unless tinged with blood.

The painful tenderness can be reduced by drinking fewer fluids and eating less salt. But puberty is the start of the age of food-fads, with fluids like soda-pop and foods containing much salt, like salami and hot dogs, heading the list. So this isn't always easy advice to follow. Yet, if a girl remembers that eating salt causes fluids to be retained in her body, and many fluids cause much breast-tenderness, it will help her to understand.

And if she can't bring herself to give up salt and soda-pop, doctors recommend that her mother get her a firm, preferably padded, uplift brassiere, to be worn even at night. The brassiere helps, says Dr. Goodrich Schauffler, if only because it proves her mother is sympathetic with her secret concerns. So he advises she get one until, as he puts it in a delightful phrase, "she grows into her normality."

BRUISES AND SHUDDERS

Dr. Schauffler also advises she be reassured that bruising or hitting her breasts will seldom cause harm. There has been so much talk of cancer lately that every bruise or encounter with a basketball causes shudders. The only bruises to watch are those that do not heal over a period of many months. But young people in the main override all kinds of blows with healing growth.

And both mother and daughter should be reassured about small breast-masses or lumps that are unusually tender to the touch. Dr. Frank Adair, chief of the Breast-Cancer Service at New York's Memorial Hospital, says people get so upset over these, fearing they certainly mean cancer, that not a week goes by but a dozen girls are rushed to him for examination as a result. He usually ends up advising them to calm down and come back in six months if the lumps have not disappeared. They seldom do come because the lumps were caused by the same uneven hormone-spurt that caused one breast to grow faster than the other, and they almost always correct themselves in time.

Besides, the breasts, like other organs such as the uterus that are subject to much growing and shrinking, are particularly prone to lumps and masses during puberty when they are developing fast, or the menopause when they are shrinking. Dr. Adair calls this "faulty growth control" and says much of it turns out to be within the normal range.

Not only do a girl's breasts and genital organs get a big growth-spurt during puberty, her entire body does the same. After a short period in which she has hardly grown much at all, she starts around ten or eleven to shoot up like the proverbial weed. This is because her pituitary, or chief gland, is not only sending out a slew of messages to her sex organs in preparation for the mighty menstrual process that is soon to get going, it is also sending out a stream of messages to her long bones—the bones of her legs, thighs and arms—to grow longer and make her increase in all-over height.

These growth-messages from her pituitary reach a peak around the age of ten or eleven, or just before menstruation may be expected to make its bow. The average starting-age for menstruation in the United States used to be thirteen. With better nutrition, it is now twelve or even eleven, though the normal range is between nine and fifteen. (A start earlier than nine is called "precocious puberty," and a Dr. Van Haller in 1751 recorded the odd case of a girl who started as early as two and continued more or less merrily until the age of fifty-two, though that was odd indeed. Precocious puberty is for some reason more common in girls than in boys; the girls to whom it happens also tend to be very bright.)

When a girl does start to menstruate, whatever her age, her big growth-spurt usually starts to slow down and to stop entirely within a year or two. This is because after that time the ends of her long bones close, and, once these ends are finally closed, growth in height is not possible any more. Dr. Maria New of Cornell Medical School says that once a girl starts to menstruate, she may expect to grow only about two inches more.

The general rule, therefore, is: The earlier the start of menstruation, the shorter a girl is apt to end up; the later the start, the taller she is apt to be. Though heredity also plays a part; tall parents are obviously more likely to have tall daughters, and short parents short.

Most girls don't worry nearly as much about being short as they do about being too tall, for the simple reason that very tall girls find it harder to get beaux who are taller than they. One way to slow down a girl who seems headed toward becoming a six-footer, and who hasn't started to menstruate, is to bring menstruation on by taking sex hormones. Not all doctors like to give them for this purpose, however, and will do so only after X raying her wrist to see whether the ends of her long bones are closed or soon to close, as well as taking tests to determine what her own sex hormone count is. For another general rule is: If a girl, or anyone else for that matter, has enough hormones of her own, of any kind, taking more will do her no good and may do harm.

UNEVEN GROWTH

Whether a girl ends up tall or short, her growth during puberty will not be even all over her body. Her feet, for instance, will grow faster than her hands, so that for a while she looks and feels "all feet." Her nose will grow faster than the rest of her face, so that for a while she looks and feels "all nose." And her belly will seem to grow faster than any of them.

Her belly grows because her internal organs are suddenly getting so big her still narrow pelvis and hips cannot make room for them, so there is no place for them to go but out. Also, the angle of her pelvis changes at puberty. During childhood, the angle of her pelvis to her backbone was straight up and down. Now her upper backbone continues straight but at her pelvis the angle becomes curved in a marked "S" curve. So not only does she get the much-hated potbelly of puberty, but sometimes she gets "lordosis," or a jutting-out rear end, as well.

GAIN IN WEIGHT AND APPETITE

Weight-gain during puberty goes hand in hand with height-gain. In fact, if a girl grows rapidly in both weight and height, it is usually a pretty sure sign menstruation is not far away. In a California study, girls almost ready to menstruate were found to be gaining twice as much and growing 30 per cent faster than girls who were not.

Part of this weight-gain is due to the fact that her muscles are getting heavier. Part is due to an increase in the output of her thyroid gland.

For when her pituitary prods her sex glands into action, it prods her thyroid as well, with a peak prod around twelve. This thyroid-burst is one reason for a girl's touchiness at this age, as well as for her marked boost in appetite, as formerly "picky" eaters often become almost insatiable now. "Food is mostly all I think about, especially after meals," is the way Martha, a bright twelve year old, put it. Add the gain in weight, as a result of all this eating, to the egg-shape caused by the potbelly and the sudden sticking out of her rear end, and you get the famous "awkward age" when no clothes seem to look right.

But around fourteen, the thyroid-burst tapers off, and the mad eating-jag usually stops. The potbelly also goes away as her hips get wider, she stands up straighter, her waist gets smaller, and her insides fall better into place. So around fifteen she becomes a Junior Miss with a brand new "figger"—a more womanly figure now.

A NEW SELF-IMAGE

But does this change to a new figure make her immediately happy? It does not. Each great change in her body calls for a new way of handling herself. The protruding breasts, the wider hips, the longer legs, the new spine-angle, and the feet so big she hardly recognizes them, alter her entire sense of balance. This, plus the crazy high heels she insists on trying to wear, make her stumble all over herself so that she almost has to learn how to walk again, as she did originally at the age of one.

TWO KINDS OF AWARENESS

Everyone has two kinds of awareness, an inner awareness and an outer awareness. Inner awareness is the attention we give to our bodies; outer awareness is the attention we give to the world. This awareness shifts constantly back and forth. It shifts at different times of the day; it shifts at different times in our lives.

A baby is almost all inner awareness. The demands of its stomach are so insistent it makes almost everything else unimportant. But during the toddling stage the outer world begins to fascinate a baby, as it discovers with eyes of wonder the cocoon of its home. Soon its horizons become even broader. A child of five or six is so full of outer awareness she can stare out of a train window entranced for hours, or get so involved with a new toy she forgets to go to the bathroom, while during the tomboy-stage the urge to move and explore propels her to look outward still more.

But now comes puberty and lo! the coin is flipped over again. Now a girl can become so full of inner awareness again she can almost seem to her distraught parents like a hypochondriac. Every new hair on her legs is horrible, every breast-pain ready to take her to death's door. "I just can't stand it, Mother. DO something!" she wails.

Part of this obsession with her body is due to the fact that girls are necessarily concerned with their bodies. Part is a mask to conceal her worries over the future and what it will hold. For a girl at puberty is like a traveller at a crossroad. She has a long way to go, and fears that havoc awaits her if she takes a wrong turn.

Where will she end? Will she become really pretty and popular, able to love and be loved? Will she get married and become a mature woman like her mother? And if she does become a woman, does she *want* to become one, or would she rather stay as she is?

Dr. I. Newton Kugelmass says that before puberty, a girl often thinks very little about the problem of becoming a woman or of accepting femininity and all it brings, even though ideally she should. She goes through the various cute or tomboy stages, hardly giving the subject a thought. But during puberty she becomes so sensitive to the great changes going on within her she can ignore it no more, and her anxieties about it reach a height.

Also, accepting femininity as a child was largely determined by her mother's attitude. If she had a mother who constantly lamented the fact she was born a woman, a loud-crying *mater dolorosa* who bemoaned her sad lot, insinuating that "all men are vile," and warning her daughter about "wicked strangers who might offer her candy and do dirty things," a little girl can have easily concluded the dangers far outweigh the advantages. If she could help it, she wouldn't become a woman at all! She would remain forever a carefree child!

But at puberty her rapidly rising tide of sex hormones—a tide that gives her a vague tingling in her vagina and develops other parts of her body—pulls her inexorably in the direction of adolescence and womanhood. As a result, she can become so torn with conflict she feels caught in a net. It is because of this conflict that Dr. Kugelmass believes nervous habits like nail-biting and hair-tweaking may now reach a peak.

Dr. Irene Josselyn of Phoenix, Arizona, believes it is because of this same conflict that a pubescent girl often talks so much about her bodily pains. A pubescent girl, Dr. Josselyn says, is like a pregnant woman, worried about the future and what it may bring; so it relieves her to talk about her body, too. Besides, it is much easier for a girl to point to a growing breast and say, "It hurts," than it is to point to a vague fear, and much easier to make other people understand when you do.

AWAY FROM BOYS

The same fear of the future and what it may bring makes the normal girl stay away from boys now. Indeed, her dread of boys is so great she shuns them as much as she can.

The following story told by a father in Charlotte, North Carolina, was quoted in *Life* magazine.

The little girl waited in the living room of her home in Charlotte, N.C., perched uncomfortably on a piano bench. Across the room her father put down the paper, and started for the kitchen. 'Before I was two steps away,' the father recalls, 'I felt her tug at my sleeve. I'll never forget the scared sound in her voice: "Daddy, don't leave me!" she yelled. Then it struck me. My daughter is eleven. Here she was waiting for a little squirt to knock at the door, pin a corsage on her long evening dress, and take her off to their first dance. In that moment I understood her fear. She was facing a situation no eleven year old is prepared to handle. She was so pathetic that I was really upset.'

The father was referring to the current practice of eleven and twelve year olds dating with boys, a practice that many towns, like the town of Charlotte, have decided to stop. For people in these towns realize that such a practice is no more natural than forced hot-house tomatoes are natural. It is a result either of a mechanical imitation of grown-ups or stampeding by the crowd. The proof lies in the fact that when little girls do fall for it, they mainly sit and glare at the boys—and the boys glare right back.

THE RETREAT AGE

The anxieties of a pubescent girl rise to a climax around thirteen. It is this climax that makes age thirteen not only the "awkward age" but the "age of retreat."

During the retreat age, she may retire for hours on end to her room, answering the call of no one, or, if she lives in the country, retreat to the woods and fields. In her room she may sit silently, looking at her developing form in the mirror. In the fields, she may merely lie on her back and think. But this looking and thinking is a special kind of looking and thinking. It is an absorbing and a listening; a listening to her inner signs, an absorbing of the shock of change.

Walt Whitman, who had a good deal of the feminine in him, beautifully expressed this mood of listening in his "Out of the Cradle Endlessly Rocking." Here he tells of his solitary trips to the edge of the shore:

"For more than once dimly down to the beach gliding,
　Silent, avoiding the moonbeams,
　　blending myself with the shadows,
Recalling now the obscure shapes, the echoes,
　　the sounds and sights after their sorts,
I, with bare feet, a child, the wind wafting my hair,
Listen'd long and long."

So, too, the pubescent girl pauses and recalls the obscure shapes and sounds of her lost childhood, just as before she recalled the lost paradise of her babyhood. So, too, before plunging into the sea of menstruation, she listens long and long.

✳✳✳ 16 Menstruation:
A Tide Rises and Falls

Of all the new things that are about to happen to a pubescent girl, menstruation is the biggest. For nothing is as shattering as first menstruation. Nothing, unless it is first childbirth, hits with such impact. The beginning of the monthly periods is an experience she remembers for life.

She remembers it for two reasons: It is surrounded with mystery. It has to do with blood.

To most of us, the sight of blood means trouble. We know that if we are cut or hit, blood usually flows. If we are wounded, more blood flows. And blood, we have been told, is the precious life-substance. To lose even a small quantity can be dangerous. To lose a lot can bring hemorrhage and death.

Now, suddenly, a girl loses what seems like a lot of blood and loses it for baffling reasons. She hasn't been cut or hit; she hasn't been wounded. Why then does it flow out?

More, she loses this baffling blood from a place that up to now has been strange and forbidden; loses it in a way over which she has no control. If she has not been prepared for the experience, she may panic. Has the genital play she may have indulged in for a while anything to do with it? Is the uncontrolled flow something for which she will be punished, as she may have been punished as a child for wetting her pants? Or worse, is it evidence of some mysterious disease?

A SUICIDE ATTEMPT

Havelock Ellis tells of a suicide attempt after a first menstruation. In his classic *Studies in the Psychology of Sex,* he tells this story:

"A few years ago a case was reported in the French newspapers of a young girl of 15, who threw herself into the Seine at Saint-Ouen. She was rescued and on being brought before the police commissioner said that she had been attacked by an 'unknown disease.' Discreet inquiry revealed that the mysterious malady was one common to all women and the girl was restored to her insufficiently punished parents."

Of course, few girls react in a way as extreme as attempted suicide. But far more girls reach puberty without knowledge of the subject than most people realize. Statistics show that only five per cent of girls know anything in advance, even in these modern days.

NOT LISTENING

This lack of knowledge, however, is not always as much the parents' fault as Havelock Ellis implies. Some mothers honestly do try to tell their daughters about menstruation before it happens. But Dr. Helene Deutsch makes the point that many girls deny they have been told anything for the simple reason they were not listening. Memory is always selective, so no matter how many questions girls may have asked on this or other subjects relating to sex, they usually have not been listening to the answers if these answers were unpleasant, especially if they came from someone as close as a mother, and even more especially during the shy and sensitive pre-teen years. They therefore often forget what they have learned, and have to learn it all over again later, when the matter has become more urgent, from a doctor or a book like this.

HIDDEN HOSTILITY

Other girls deny advance knowledge because of hidden hostility to their mothers, since some mothers, instead of telling them nothing, give actually wrong or sadistic information.

There was, for instance, Eleanor, whose mother used menstruation as a subject for teasing. Eleanor as a child was very thin. When other women were present, her mother would often remark on this thinness, then giggle and titter with her friends and hint that "someday something would happen to fill her out." But she refused to tell Eleanor what this something was, just saying, "You'll see!" as if the matter were some great private grown-up joke.

First menstruation came by chance to Eleanor in school the day after she had taken a ride on a roller-coaster. She became petrified at the sight of the unexpected blood, and figured maybe the ride had something to do with it. Maybe it had injured her somehow; maybe now she would need an operation, and the "filling out" would come as a result. Nor did it help when she got home and her mother dismissed the matter by saying curtly: "This is what I was expecting. Now forget about it, except to remember it will come back next month."

But it didn't come back the next month, or the next, or the next. Menstruation is so intimately connected with the nervous system that fear can easily suppress it. In Eleanor's case, she was so bewildered and frightened she didn't have a period again for a year.

Now, as Dr. A. E. Rakoff of the Jefferson Medical School points out, it is quite common to menstruate irregularly for several months or even a year after the start of the flow—to be irregular in frequency, amount and length of days—since the pituitary and ovaries are not yet working together in a well-regulated partnership. But in this case the natural tendency was certainly heightened by fear.

In another instance, a mother used menstruation as a deliberate punishment. Josephine had just gone through the normal tomboy stage and, when her first period arrived, her mother announced: "That's what you get for being so unladylike as to climb trees. Now you're splitting up the middle as a result." I don't have to say what a fearful thought "splitting up the middle" is. It was enough to stop Josephine, too, from menstruating again for a year.

Still another mother, on the day of her daughter Jennie's first period, simply gave her daughter a hard slap across her face. Jennie also thought the slap was a punishment, if not for climbing trees, then for doing the "dirty thing" of uncontrollably menstruating. Actually, the slap was done in accordance with a notion you had to slap a newly menstruating girl to keep the color in her face, since otherwise she would lose her color because "all her blood was running out the other end."

Of course, few mothers behave in these extreme ways. Some merely avoid the matter as much as their daughters because it seems such a touchy subject they just can't bring themselves to discuss it. So they either postpone it until the last minute or, if they do bring it up, they run through it like a steam-roller, as something to be gotten over with fast.

MENSTRUAL BLOOD AS POISONOUS

One reason mothers are so embarrassed is that they find it hard to get over old beliefs imbibed from *their* mothers—beliefs like those that preach menstruating women are "poisonous" or "unclean."

The belief that they are poisonous is very old. Some cultures believed they were so poisonous they segregated them in special menstrual huts where they were served special foods from special pots, after which the pots were destroyed for fear they might be used again and contaminate the entire tribe. Other cultures slung up newly menstruating girls in dark huts in hammocks, stung them with nettles, or made them wear special bonnets that hung down over their faces to protect men from their "evil eyes." And the Roman writer Pliny was quoted for centuries after he declared that if a menstruating woman entered the door of a winery, the wine would turn sour; if she stirred milk, it would curdle; if she sewed, the thread would knot; if she touched flowers, the flowers would immediately die.

England's Mary Chadwick thinks things like the segregation in dark huts and the stinging with nettles were forms of initiation-rites, testing a girl's fitness to enter womanhood as many societies test boys, while the slinging up in the dark in hammocks was symbolic of being halfway between heaven and earth or between death and rebirth, death being the earth and the heaven rebirth, to symbolize the fact a girl was now dying as a child and being reborn into a new life.

MENSTRUAL BLOOD AS GOOD

Yet some cultures thought the blood of menstruating women was powerful and good. A medieval tale held that if a warrior's sword were whetted with it, his sword would become doubly keen. An Italian belief had it that if an unfertile woman borrowed a sanitary napkin from a fertile woman, she would become blessed with children. Still other people gave women during their periods the awesome power of foretelling the future, or raising up storms against an enemy at sea.

BIBLICAL BELIEFS

The danger-myths, though, far outweighed the power-myths, since they were unhappily reinforced by the Bible. The Bible uses the word "unclean" to describe menstruating women, and many Biblical scholars think this a most unfortunate translation from the original Hebrew since the same word was used to describe lepers.

The Old Testament declared a woman was ritually unclean whenever an "issue of blood" was coming forth from her body. By virtually unclean, it meant that she could not enter the temple or other sacred place, or touch any hallowed thing; she had to remain separate and apart until she had gone through a purification ceremony every month like the Jewish ceremony of *mikvah,* or after-menstrual ritual bath, which made her acceptable again.

The reason for this, says Dr. Frank M. Gross, Jr., Hancock professor of Hebrew at Harvard, was the ancient fear of any "issue" from the body, including the issue of male semen or sperm. Blood was feared because it might be "bad blood" which might spread disease; semen was feared because semen was powerful in both good and bad ways. Semen could bring about conception. Semen could also spread disease. But since it was *men* as far as we know who wrote the Bible, the burden of badness and the need for purification was still put upon the women, who were also chastised as "unclean" after the act of giving birth. And to rub it in, they were doubly unclean after giving birth to a girl, possibly because a newborn girl often seems to menstruate in a small way.

Leviticus XII states: "If a woman has conceived seed and borne a male child, then she shall be unclean for seven days; according to the days of her separation for her infirmity she shall be unclean and she shall continue in the days of her purifying for three and thirty days. . . . But if she bear a maid child, then she shall be unclean for two weeks, and she shall continue in the time of her purifying for sixty and six days."

The editors of the Modern Interpreters' Bible suggest it would have been far kinder to say the same thing in essence this way: "When a woman has borne a son, proper feeling requires that she remain in seclusion for a week; then the child (if a male) is to be circumcised. Even then, she is to stay at home for a month, and her first journey abroad shall be to a temple or a church."

Put this way, there would be less suggestion of punishment for a normal and necessary process like birth or menstruation, and women might have found far better ways to describe menstruation than "falling off the roof" or "the curse."

STOP AND GO; RISE AND FALL

I said that the interplay between the pituitary and ovarian glands works like a telephone system—the pituitary gland is the central operator that sends out "go" messages to the ovaries to produce female sex-hormones to raise the tide, and when the ovaries have produced enough they send back "top" messages to the pituitary and the tide falls.

It is the fact that the pituitary-ovarian exchange does work both ways that makes the system so complex and astonishing, since it only works this way during the reproductive years. Before that, while a girl is still a child, it works in only one direction, with messages flashing from pituitary to ovaries only, and the tide constantly rising. But after puberty the two-way system starts, and the child becomes changed indeed. She changes into a woman who is very different from a little girl and also very different from a man, for a man has no tides like hers. A man's androgenic hormones are produced quite evenly throughout the month.

If you wanted to sum up the essential difference between a girl and a woman, or between a man and a woman, it might be this: A woman has female hormone-tides that each month rise and fall, and she has emotional tides that rise and fall at the same time.

The rising and falling of these tides take place roughly over a twenty-eight day period. I say roughly because the human body is not a machine, so the period seldom comprises exactly twenty-eight days. But twenty-eight days is the standard so it is used here as a base.

THE TIDE STARTS TO RISE

The first day of this twenty-eight day period is the first, not the last day, of the menstrual flow, since it is easier to tell when the flow starts than when it ends. This first day is called Day One.

On Day One a woman's pituitary sends a "go" message to her ovaries using them to make estrogens. The ovaries respond slowly at first, but by Day Five when the flow as a rule is over, they get up speed and start making them in earnest. As this happens, the tide begins to rise— rises until it reaches a peak around Day Fourteen. As it rises, three things happen: The estrogens stimulate a woman's whole body and make her "feel good." They thicken the lining of her womb. They ripen an ovum or egg.

Thousands of eggs, you will remember, have been lying patiently in her ovaries since birth, waiting to ripen and be released. Now, during the first half of the menstrual month, one of these eggs does start to ripen. On or about Day Fourteen it becomes fully ripe and bursts forth from her ovary with the quiet drama of a ripe flower bursting from a bud. This bursting forth of the egg is called ovulation; the day of its bursting is called Ovulation Day, and the event is the high point of the first tidal wave.

The wave can be expressed in figures: As computed by Dr. Herbert Kupperman of New York University, during the low days of the actual flow, a woman's body only makes about 20 units of estrogen a day. At the high point of Ovulation Day it makes 80 units, or a full four times as much.

A SECOND WAVE RISES

An egg having burst forth and a high point reached, the ovaries now signal the pituitary to "stop" as both take a brief rest. But the rest is short. Soon the pituitary is urging the ovaries to get busy again. As a result, more sex-hormones are poured forth and a second wave starts to rise from about Day Fourteen on.

But this second wave is different from the first because it is a double wave. In a moment we'll see why this is so. Before we do, let's see what happens when an egg bursts forth.

AN EGG BURSTS FORTH

When an egg bursts forth from the ovary, a little spot is left on the ovary at the place from which it has burst. This spot is yellow and is called the "corpus luteum" or "yellow body." Urged on by the pituitary, this yellow body also starts to make sex-hormones of its own. At the same time, the egg starts on its journey down one of the Fallopian tubes toward the womb.

The egg does not go directly into a tube. Instead, each tube has at its top a cluster of tiny "fingers" that flutter about, catch the egg, and suck it into the liquid the tube contains. When the egg has been sucked in, the tube starts a series of rhythmic movements that wave it on its way.

About halfway down the tube, however, the egg may be stopped in its tracks because the goal of the whole process has been achieved—it has met up with a male sperm which was recently deposited in the vagina and has found its way up into the tube. If such a meeting has taken place, the sperm has probably entered the egg and started a new life. If this has happened, the egg is now a fertilized egg and as such it continues on through the tube and into the womb.

But the womb must be ready to receive and nourish the fertilized egg so that it may start immediately to grow. And that's where the hormone made by the yellow body comes in. For the special hormone made by the yellow body is called progesterone, from *gest* meaning birth or gestation, and *pro* meaning in favor of. Progesterone is thus the "in favor of birth" hormone.

During the second half of the month, therefore, or from about Day Fourteen on, both estrogen and progesterone are made. Estrogen is made by the ovaries as before; progesterone made by the yellow body is added, making a double wave. The estrogen continues to stimulate a woman's body all over; the progesterone stimulates her womb in particular; stimulates it to develop a lining that is far richer and thicker than the lining it had during the first half of the month—a lining rich enough and thick enough to let the fertilized egg burrow into it and start its nine-month adventure of growth.

THE WAVE MOUNTS HIGHER

During the second half of the month the double wave mounts to a peak just as the first one did. Urged on as usual by the pituitary, the double wave mounts to a peak around Day Twenty, when the ovaries once more signal the pituitary to "stop." The pituitary rests from about Days Twenty to Twenty-eight, during which time both hormones are withdrawn, the wave falls, and menstruation begins. That is, menstruation begins if the egg has not been fertilized, in which event it simply shrivels up in the tube and slips out unnoticed with flow.

Menstruation is thus a regression, a throwing off by the uterus of the rich, thick lining that was specially prepared to receive and nourish a baby had one been started by a fertilized egg. The lining is thrown off for the simple reason it is not needed. It is discarded much as a cake that is not needed may be discarded by a fastidious hostess because an expected guest did not arrive. And as it is thrown off, the wave falls to the lowest point of all.

The wave stays low for a few days, then since nature is a persistent girl who constantly tries to get a new egg fertilized, the whole monthly process starts again with another Day One.

Menstruation has been poetically described as a cry of disappointment. Disappointment by a woman's body that all its work and preparation for a baby have gone for nothing that month. So the sad womb weeps, and tries once more.

NOT BAD BLOOD

The true story of menstruation has only been known for about fifty years. It explains why menstrual blood is not "bad blood," or "unclean blood" or a throwing-off of accumulated poisons, as the ancients in their ignorance believed. On the contrary, the discarded lining is just about the freshest and cleanest kind of blood, with no odor attached, since it is made brand new every few weeks and thrown away merely because a still newer lining is about to be made.

The story also explains why menstruation is not a "curse," and has nothing to do with being "sick" or "unwell." For how can a girl be "cursed" when she is preparing for the greatest of all creative acts—the creation of life? And how can she be "unwell" when she is going through a natural process—a process in which she loses only about three or four tablespoons of blood during the entire flow—three or four tablespoons that are so mixed with water and other fluids they merely happen to look like more?

Perhaps most important, the story explains a woman's feeling-changes as the month rolls by. The fact that on certain days she may feel so irritable and jumpy she thinks she's jumping out of her skin—on other days, fine and at peace with the world. On certain days heavy to the point of bursting, with abdomen and breasts all swollen, on others, light and gay and ready to waltz.

THE HORMONES STIMULATE

Remembering that both estrogen and progesterone are stimulating hormones, let us review the month again and see why these feeling-changes take place:

Days about One to Four, or the days of the actual flow, are the days of very low hormones, so these days a woman is apt to feel droopy and low as well. But comes Day Five and the tide starts to mount rapidly toward Day Fourteen. During Days Five to Fourteen, therefore, her body is flooded with estrogens reaching a peak on Ovulation Day, making her feel best of all so far.

After Ovulation Day progesterone is added to estrogen, making her feel still better. Her good spirits rise to Day Twenty which is the height of the double wave.

But after Day Twenty, the double wave starts to dip, and as it does, both hormones are rapidly withdrawn. During the week of withdrawal, particularly during the last half of it or Days Twenty-four to Twenty-eight, she may feel tired and depressed, all the more so since the dip is such a contrast to the previous week when the double wave was mounting. And during the menstrual Days One to Four, she may feel bluest and most tired of all.

But comes Day Five, when the flow is over and a new wave starts to rise. She feels fine and fit again, and once more ready to conquer the world.

This still does not explain everything about the menstrual month. There is still the paradox of Days Twenty to Twenty-eight.

Theoretically, since these days contain the peak of the double wave, a woman should feel best of all, but some women feel just the opposite. This is because estrogen and progesterone are not only stimulating hormones, they are water-retaining hormones. Progesterone in particular causes water to be retained by the body, so much water indeed that it can make a woman water-logged and tense. "Pre-menstrual tension" is the name for this water-logged state of affairs.

A woman suffering from pre-menstrual tension may find her head aching from excess water that presses on the delicate nerves leading to her brain. She may find her breasts heavy and swollen with excess water, her abdomen distended with excess water, and her whole body feeling generally miserable from top to toe.

While many doctors believe this water is put there for the purpose of strengthening the tissues around blood-vessels of the womb that will nourish a new baby if one has been conceived, the woman who gets a real excess of it may be extremely upset for a while. So upset that one woman I know had a perfectly good nose fixed during this time just to "cheer herself up." Another left a perfectly good husband. A third quit a perfectly good job. Other women become dismayed when they discover an unexpected weight-gain of several pounds from water—dismayed especially if they happened to start on a diet just then and do not know what is involved.

Yet the water starts to go away like magic as soon as the flow starts with Day One. If it doesn't, Seattle's Dr. Robert N. Rutherford suggests that since salt causes even more water to be retained, salt be restricted during the pre-menstrual week. And if that doesn't work, he suggests taking diuretics or water-eliminating pills during the pre-menstrual week.

Even without salt-restriction or water-eliminating pills, by Day Five the woman who a week ago was sure she hated her job, hated her husband, and couldn't bear her appearance, gets a new burst of well-being as a new hormone tide starts to mount. For every woman's pendulum swings back and forth, back and forth, with the rising and falling of her monthly tides.

The pendulum swings so surely that doctors can do tests that tell with remarkable accuracy what day of the month a woman is in. Gynecologists can take a little vaginal fluid, or a few cells from the tissues of her uterus, put these under a microscope, and know from what they see how much estrogen and progesterone are circulating within her. The uterine cells, for instance, at one time will show a beautiful fern-like pattern; at other times they will not. The vaginal fluids at one time will be thick and opalescent, at another thin and clear.

Psychiatrists like Chicago's Dr. Therese Benedek also believe they can tell what time of the month a woman is in by her dreams and emotional state. Some years ago Dr. Benedek did an experiment in which she carefully recorded the dreams and emotions of her women patients day by day. She then compared her findings with those of a gynecologist. Their records tallied to a remarkable degree.

Since a woman's tidal waves rise and fall this way, from puberty to menopause, when people say, "You never can tell with a woman," they just haven't bothered to find out if she's at high or low tide.

MORE MENSTRUAL MYSTERIES

Understanding the tides does not explain all the menstrual questions and mysteries. There is the question of cramps. There is the question of "middle pain." There is the mystery of the girl who hasn't started to menstruate by the age of 16, and many more. Let's take them one at a time.

What is the right age to start menstruation? There is no one "right age." Around eleven or twelve is average in the United States today, but the normal range goes as low as 9 and as high as 15. If a girl hasn't started by 16, however, she probably has a faulty pituitary that has not been successful in stimulating her ovaries enough to start the process.

Girls of this kind suffer a good deal, since in addition to not menstruating they usually have undeveloped breasts. And while they can cover up their lack of development by athletic achievements, as a rule they are miserable underneath, shy and introverted and feeling they don't "belong." It's a toss-up who is more inwardly anxious—the girl who is ready to menstruate and vaguely fears it, or the girl who hasn't started at the expected time.

Dr. Benedek tells of a patient of hers who had not started at the age of twenty-two. She was nearly six feet tall and still growing, with no breasts, no pubic hair, no evidence of ovarian activity of any kind. She suffered greatly, she said, because she "felt like a woman though actually she was just a tall little girl." After hormone-medication plus psychotherapy, she began to spot a little, though her menstrual periods were only token periods. But she was grateful for even this small sign of femininity, especially since her breasts began to develop too.

Now theoretically, since it is a girl's pituitary that is at fault in such cases, the medication given should be pituitary hormone. But at the present time a reliable pituitary hormone has not been developed for this purpose. The little available is for research mainly, and extremely expensive. So what is given instead is estrogen and progesterone, given as nearly as possible in imitation of their natural production in the body— that is, estrogen throughout the month, progesterone added during the second half, then both hormones withheld until the uterine lining that has been built up is shed.

But this is not true menstruation in the sense it includes ovulation, so the girl cannot become fertile or conceive. And since the hormones used are replacements for those she lacks, they must be taken indefinitely if even token periods are to result.

The earlier the treatment is started after age 16 too, the more chance there is of good results. Dr. Robert N. Rutherford points out that treatment is often delayed by mothers because they fear the necessary vaginal examination "may destroy their daughter's virginity" or be a "potentially traumatic experience." But he believes the trauma of staying infantile and not achieving periods, even token periods, is far greater than the trauma of an examination sympathetically explained and carefully performed. Besides, a good doctor can often do such an examination through the rectum instead of the vagina, and learn almost as much.

INDUCING OVULATION

As I said, the ideal treatments include ovulation, and until recently that had never been achieved. But as this is being written two doctors, one a Norwegian and one an Italian, have succeeded in inducing ovulation in formerly infertile women with huge injections of the special pituitary hormone that is not generally available. These injections are prohibitive in price, often have to be repeated several times, and so far have caused the birth of an unusually large number of twins, triplets and quads. But they may become perfected—who knows?

Even when a girl does start to menstruate of her own accord around eleven or twelve, she probably does not ovulate for several years anyway, since the development of fertility is a slow process and takes a longer time than does the establishment of menstruation itself.

Dr. Ashley Montague of Princeton tells of studies done on thousands of women all over the world who were married in their early teens and did not use contraceptives of any kind. Comparatively few of them ovulated or conceived until their twenties.

There are of course exceptions. Everyone knows of some teenage mothers, but they are not the rule. And when teenagers do become mothers, they are usually neither physically nor emotionally ready for the task. Physically they are not ready because too-early motherhood may stop them from completing their own growth and development. Emotionally, they are not ready because too-early motherhood can be overwhelming. And the younger the girl, the more overwhelming it can be.

This is particularly true if she is not married and has to go it alone. In a Salvation Army home for unmarried mothers in Richmond, Va., I saw older teenagers going about the business of caring for their babies with a certain amount of competence. The younger ones were mechanically going through the motions, and looked positively dazed.

As if to prove that girls in their teens are not intended to become mothers, nature makes the age of maximum fertility between 20 and 30.

Women who have been married for some time and have been using contraceptives, often stop using them in their thirties and are surprised when they find it difficult to conceive. They immediately blame the contraceptives, thinking they have hurt them in some way. In all likelihood, no. It is simply that in their thirties their natural fertility has fallen off. It may therefore take them several months or years to get pregnant, and in their forties even longer, though it is not impossible until after the menopause, as women with so-called "change of life" babies can testify.

MENSTRUAL PAIN

"Woman-pain has seized my body. Let the gods tear this pain out." This inscription, scratched by some nameless Assyrian woman on a clay tablet some 3000 years ago, probably refers to menstrual pain. For what girl or woman has not at some time or other suffered such pain? Who has had all her periods free from discomfort or cramps?

Cramps are irregular, shooting, doubling-up pains in the lower abdomen that come with the first day of the flow, last a short while and then go away. What causes them? Rather unexpectedly, ovulation. Few girls suffer cramps until they ovulate. And since a girl doesn't ovulate until several years after menstruation has started as a rule, she doesn't suffer them until she does.

Here's the reason ovulation is the cause. During the first half of the month, as you know, estrogen alone is made by the ovaries. During the second half, or after ovulation, estrogen plus progesterone is made. And estrogen alone builds up the uterine lining a little.

Estrogen plus progesterone builds up the lining a lot. You might say a one-layer cake lining is made by estrogen; a two-layer by estrogen plus. Now the uterus has to expel this lining by squeezing motions. Each time the uterus squeezes, a little lining is thrown off. So cramps are rhythmic rather than continuous. They accompany the squeezes—a cramp for each squeeze.

Then the uterus of a beginner is quite inefficient at squeezing. It has not yet had time to build up good strong muscles to do the job well. Take a month in which ovulation has occurred, so that a two-layer cake has been made. Add to this a uterus inefficient at squeezing. The result may be jerky squeezes that give pain, especially on the first day of the flow when there is a comparative lot of lining to be thrown out.

THREE IMPORTANT "BUT'S"

There are several important "but's" that soften this statement.

First, it is not normal to have a lot of cramps—an amount that really incapacitates. A study of 4500 girls found that those who do have a lot add up to less than 3%.

Second, it is not normal to have cramps continue after the end of the teens. By the age of twenty or so, the uterus has usually built up strong enough muscles to do a better job.

Third, it is not normal to have cramps continue after the first pregnancy. Labor and delivery really do give the uterus a workout, and this workout increases its efficiency at a tremendous rate.

Fourth, it is better in some ways to have cramps than not to, because cramps are usually an indication that ovulation *has* taken place. And since ovulation is necessary for a woman's highest kind of functioning, cramps may be taken as one bit of proof that nature is readying her for the job.

Yet normal or not, and helpful or not, bad cramps can be relieved. Doctors stress simple remedies like short bed rests, drugs like aspirin, or soothing baths.

By stressing aspirin, they mean that most of the other advertised remedies are merely aspirin in another form. Indeed, so many kinds and sorts of things have been recommended for cramps, few better than aspirin, that the late Dr. E. C. Hamblen of Duke University humorously expressed it: "The long list of remedies which have been hailed as successful in menstrual pain merely bears witness to the willingness of women to report relief when they are convinced their physicians need encouragement."

By stressing soothing baths, doctors mean warm baths not too hot or cold.

The New York psychiatrist Dr. Emy Metzger tells of her experience on the staff of a mental hospital in Vienna in the days when there were no tranquilizers or other soothing drugs for disturbed patients, so they had to be kept in tubs of warm water to soothe them instead. When their menstrual periods arrived, it was expected that these patients would become even more disturbed and they were taken out of the tubs. "Bathing has been considered unfit for menstruating women since time immemorial, and it is the first rule of medicine to do no deliberate harm," argued the doctors who took them out. But Dr. Metzger suggested leaving them in the tubs, at least for a trial. To everyone's astonishment, the warm water helped them instead of hurting them; they felt better in every way.

The old idea that baths were to be forbidden during menstrual periods was based on the fact that in ancient times most bathing was done in public pools or streams, and it wasn't so much that the water would harm the women as upset the men who dreaded this particular kind of blood. But now that baths are taken in private, now that we have tampons, and especially now that we know this blood is not dangerous, the taboo no longer makes sense.

And if a soothing bath is not available, an electric pad or warm-water bottle is also helpful, though it should be placed at the feet, not on the abdomen as is commonly done. Heat placed directly on the abdomen can make the uterine squeezes come even faster, and the whole idea is to slow them down.

Things doctors say never to do for cramps are to use opiates, or to stay in bed for several days.

Opiates like phenobarbital or codeine can be extremely habit-forming, as well as lowering the pain threshold. The more they are used, the less tolerance there is to any pain when they are stopped.

As for long bed rests, a Philadelphia study divided a large number of girls suffering from cramps into two groups. One group stayed in bed for several days, the other took exercise including vigorous sports like basketball. In the second group, the pain disappeared in half the time.

All doctors agree that the old idea that menstrual pain is caused by a "tipped womb," that is, a womb that happens to lie slightly at an angle instead of flat, has gone with the wind. A tipped womb has no more to do with cramps than a tipped nose. So the insertion of a pessary to try and change its position also makes little sense.

SUPPRESSION OF OVULATION

If the cramps are bad to the point of being unbearable, what doctors usually do these days is to suppress ovulation. They use hormones to do this, taken practically always by mouth.

The hormones used are estrogen, progesterone, or a combination of both, and they are given *outside* the normal rhythm. That is, more hormones are given during the first half of the month than would naturally be made by the body, enough more to "stop" the pituitary before it can cause the release of an egg. And without the release of an egg, a two-layer lining that is difficult for an inefficient uterus to expel, is not made.

Doctors suppress ovulation for only a short time, though, because sex-hormones soon cause an increase in the size and power of the uterus that is often just enough to tide an adolescent over her period of inefficiency, so she soon gets to the point where she can expel any amount of lining with ease.

They also suppress it only for a short time because the menstrual process is very strongly affected by the emotions. Once a girl has had a few periods without cramps, she's apt to change her memory of the experience. She feels better because she expects to feel better; she also gets over some of her fears like the fear of staining her dress. And if she has an intelligent mother who cooperates by expecting her to feel better, half the battle is won.

FEMININE MASOCHISM

Then a girl feels better about menstruation as time goes by for still another reason. This is something called "feminine masochism." It rates a discussion since the term "masochism" is greatly misunderstood.

The literal meaning of the word masochism, says Dr. Leon H. Saul of the University of Pennsylvania, is the "enjoyment of pain," derived from the eighteenth-century nobleman named Masoch who is reputed to have enjoyed it. But to enjoy pain one must deliberately seek it, then having found it, one must deliberately prolong it and keep on prolonging it to the hilt. People who deliberately get themselves whipped for enjoyment, or who insist on being beaten before they can enjoy sex, are true masochists. But such people are abnormal and rare, especially women. Few women enjoy being whipped, or can bear to see others whipped. The ones who moan, "My man doesn't love me any more; he hasn't beaten me lately!" are a tiny, degraded minority no matter what the wiseacres say.

Normal female masochists are different: they are merely women who accept pain when it's unavoidable with as good grace as possible, and incidentally get some pleasure from it. This difference is so important let me repeat it: An abnormal female masochist is one who deliberately seeks pain and suffering. A normal masochist is one who accepts pain or suffering when unavoidable, possibly gets some eventual pleasure from it. In other words, she is a women who finds victory in defeat.

Many psychiatrists believe that without this kind of normal masochism women as a race could not have survived. For there is much more inevitable suffering in a woman's life than in a man's. Almost no woman entirely escapes menstrual discomfort, she has to have the ability to accept it when unavoidable, and find it may lead to the pleasure of pregnancy. Almost no woman entirely escapes pain in childbirth; she has to have the ability to accept this too, and to discover it leads to the pleasure of having the child. In sex, almost no woman escapes a sense of shock when her body is first invaded, she has to have the ability to accept this invasion, and discover it leads to pleasure as well.

MIDDLE PAIN

Now to "middle pain."

The Germans call middle pain *mittelschmerz*, and that's what it is— a short, sharp pain that comes during the middle of the month rather than during the flow. Middle pain is worrisome because it doesn't seem related to anything. But it is related; it is related to ovulation. Middle pain is a pain in one of the ovaries as an egg bursts forth.

The vast majority of women have no idea that ovulation is taking place unless they take their temperature and notice that it drops about half a degree. A few women know about it through this quick pain. Still, women get worried about it because they think the pain may also mean something like appendicitis or other abdominal trouble. If they keep a diary, and note that the pain comes at almost the same time each month, the worry is gone.

Once it is gone, however, doctors suggest that the diary be discontinued. It is not wise to keep looking for any kind of pain since, people being what they are, looking for pain can help bring it on. It's like feeling the dentist's drill in your mouth before he has started, or getting seasick before the boat has left the dock.

TOO LITTLE FLOW OR TOO MUCH

Women also worry if they think they flow too seldom, too frequently or too irregularly. They even worry if they flow every twenty-eight days, but not every twenty-eight days "on the dot."

This should be said in headlines: *No woman flows every twenty-eight days on the dot.* She can flow from twenty-one to forty days apart and still be within the normal range. What is more, she can on occasion skip all over the place.

In 1939 Dr. L. B. Arey did a study of 1500 women all over the world. There were British, American, German, Hungarian women, and more. Each kept careful records for many months, and Dr. Arey didn't find a single one who was regular for any significant length of time. While the most common interval was twenty-seven days apart, the same women sometimes had periods that were as much as 69 days apart. And many women had flows 125 days apart, or menstruated only three times a year. The flow itself lasted anywhere from one to seven days, with four and a half days being the most common length.

In general, Dr. Arey concluded, the average adult woman can expect a third of her periods to vary two or more days from her own expected times, and occasionally very much more.

He summed up his findings this way: "The woman whose periods occur with precise regularity is a creature out of a fairy story. She simply doesn't exist."

NERVOUS CONTROL

One reason that menstrual periods can vary so much is that the glands that control the hormonal waves are affected by the nerves. Because of these nervous influences, any kind of stress can upset the timing —even something so comparatively mild as the stress of an ocean voyage or a change of climate. And strong stresses like fear or anger can upset the periods far more. Fear of pregnancy, for instance, can delay a period just when a woman desires it most; but let her take a test that proves she is not pregnant, and the fear disappears and the period arrives.

Similarly, fear can bring on an unwanted period. Nervous brides often fix a wedding date on which they are sure they will not be menstruating. The day arrives and lo! they are flowing anyway.

Dr. Helene Deutsch tells an interesting story about the power of fear or anger to bring on a period out of its usual time. In her book *The Psychology of Women* she tells this tale:

Many years ago, as a young medical student, I followed with great interest a court case concerning a marriage problem. A husband had asked for a divorce and as his only reason told the court the following story. By profession he was a travelling salesman who returned home only at irregular intervals. In the preceding two years, he said, every time he returned home he found his wife menstruating. In his eyes this was sufficient proof that she no longer wished to have marital relations with him even though she assured him in all sincerity that it was only a coincidence, a kind of bad luck for which she was not responsible. The psychiatrists rejected the husband's theory, even though it was already well known that menstruation can exert a tremendous influence upon psychological life. They were ready to admit that mood-changes could accelerate or retard menstruation for a short period, but the enormous and recurrent influence described to them by the husband seemed to these experts impossible. The only person ready to accept the husband's interpretation was the old judge, who had a keen intuition and a broad knowledge of human nature. He granted the divorce, and subsequent events proved the husband's theory to be correct.

As to cramps, there is the story of the girl who never had them until she became a nurse and had her first brush with the shattering experience of death and of the girl who had cramps only when falling in and out of love.

ABILITY TO FUNCTION

Because of the endless things that nerves can do to the menstrual periods, and because there are women who have their periods only three or four times a year, Dr. E. C. Hamblen of Duke University bases his definition of normality here on the ability to function. He puts it this way: "Any woman who can bear a child is basically normal no matter how much pain she occasionally has, or how often or seldom her periods appear."

Dr. Milton E. J. Senn of Yale expresses this thought in a different way: "The number of variations within the normal is tremendous. This makes our work, when we are dealing with human beings, very difficult and complex. In deciding whether something is pathological or not, we must make sure we are not falling into the error of disregarding human differences. In dealing with the human being, we must be aware of his similarities in comparing him with others, but also be aware of the pitfall of considering someone deviant merely because he is different. His difference may not be unusual for *him*."

Dr. Senn is a pediatrician, and he was writing mainly about children. But his words have such a direct bearing on women that the last sentence is also worth repeating. "His difference may not be unusual for him."

ABSENCE OF MENSTRUATION

Obviously, a woman cannot bear a child if she never menstruates at all, because with no menstruation there is no ovulation, and without ovulation that vital egg is not available to be fertilized. Yet there are girls and women who flow for years, then suddenly stop.

This sudden stopping may be due to several reasons. One is plain malnutrition. When a girl is seriously undernourished, either as a result of eating next to nothing in an effort to keep her weight abnormally low, or as a result of eating mainly a crazy diet like pickles, hot dogs, and fudge sundaes, she can stop menstruating simply because she is not getting enough vitamins to keep herself in good health, or because her energy is so low she has barely enough to keep herself alive, much less enough left over to perform a vital function like menstruation. Women in concentration camps often stopped for this reason. In her book, *The Walls Came Tumbling Down*, Henriette Roosenburg told of her near starvation in a concentration camp, and how both she and almost all the other women there stopped menstruating, losing their sex-desire as well.

Malnutrition can also delay the start of the periods. Right after the First World War in Vienna, when conditions were very bad, 73 per cent of the girls between fourteen and fifteen years had not started. A few years later, when conditions were much better, only 24 per cent of the same age group were in the same spot.

Other studies show that girls from upper, better-fed groups start as a rule two years younger than those from lower, undernourished groups.

And in the sixteenth and seventeenth centuries, when health conditions in general were terrible, a survey of medical records shows that girls started way behind the early Greeks and Romans who lived better in many ways.

In America today, with probably the best nutrition standards in the history of the world, girls are starting earlier and earlier all the time— much earlier than in Asia and South America. It used to be believed that girls in hot countries started earlier than girls in temperate or cold climates. Not so. Food and health seem to play a more important role.

PSYCHIC REASONS

Other reasons for an absence of flow are emotional, such as a rebellion against femininity.

Some adolescent girls continue to rebel against becoming females. They may rebel consciously or unconsciously, but they rebel just the same. They see growing-up and becoming brides or mothers as something vaguely "dreamy" and "romantic," but suppress what they consider the "disgusting" part. A few repress it so strongly they actually stop developing and retreat to the stage of infancy, where they eat almost constantly the way a baby does, and become very fat. The fat further hampers their development, since it keeps them from a normal amount of dating while it stops their periods, too.

When such girls begin to eat more sensibly and reduce, and especially when they can be led to face both the pleasant and unpleasant parts of growing-up, they often do begin to date. And the very dating, plus the weight-reduction, often brings on the menstruation that had been suppressed.

NAPKINS VERSUS TAMPONS

What about the small internal pads known as tampons? These are not a modern invention, as many people think. They go back to the time of the early Greeks and probably before.

The "father of medicine," Hippocrates, described a soft internal roll made of lint worn by the women of his time. Egyptian, Assyrian and Babylonian records tell of similar devices, and tell, too, how the aristocratic Byzantine women insisted on those made only from the finest wool. In fact, throughout history the women who worked hard wore internal protection almost exclusively, while the more sedate and leisurely, who could afford elaborate and concealing clothes, wore the larger and more cumbersome kind. This difference extends into modern times: the poor nomad women of Mongolia still use tampons much more than the richer Turkish women who lead sedentary lives.

But the questions are: *Should* a woman wear them when she has a choice? Are they immoral, as some Catholic women have been led to believe? And can they do harm, especially to virgins? No more than twenty-five years ago, a large group gathered in London to debate these very questions, some of them protesting strongly against "such things being foisted by shops on young girls."

One of the most comprehensive studies on the subject ever made was done in 1945 by the pioneering Dr. Robert Latou Dickinson, for several years president of the American Gynecological Society and official adviser to the U. S. Government on questions of maternal health.

(Dr. Dickinson was so concerned with all problems relating to women, he hung beautiful paintings on the ceiling of his office, instead of on the walls, so that his patients could look at them during examinations and so distract their minds. He also never considered a patient just a "case." If he was scrubbing up for an operation in a hospital and a nurse announced, "Doctor, your hysterectomy is ready," he would rebuke her with, "That is not a hysterectomy. That is charming Mrs. Jones." A tiny, eager, bouncy man who was still practicing at 85, he is also said never to have forgotten a name.)

In an article printed in the *Journal of the American Medical Association,* Dr. Dickinson attacked the problem of tampons with characteristic zeal. First he figured out that the average woman menstruates for some 35 years, roughly from age fifteen to age fifty. If she does this every month, these 35 years add up to some 425 periods. Leaving out four pregnancies and recoveries, this leaves about 375 periods. Counting ten napkins per period, she uses the staggering total of 3750 napkins in the course of her life.

Dr. Dickinson was honest about these menstrual napkins. He called them 3750 "nuisances," then proceeded to inquire whether or not some of the nuisance could be eliminated. He decided it could.

A group of 6500 women was the basis of his study. Each woman was carefully measured, then asked a series of questions, and this is what he found: The average opening in the hymen of a virgin is about one inch in diameter. The average opening in the hymen of a married woman after intercourse is 1¾ inches. The average opening after child-birth is 2¼ inches. But the smallest tampons are less than a half-inch in diameter—7/16 to be exact. This means they are slightly less than half the size of the average virginal opening. Their chances of doing harm are therefore exceedingly remote. "The tampon has a caliber that does not impair standard anatomic virginity," is the way Dr. Dickinson sums this up.

Some girls, to be sure, are sensitive when first they begin to use them—they find difficulty in inserting them, or experience a small amount of pain. For these Dr. Dickinson suggested a gentle stretching by the gradual insertion of a tampon with its tip well lubricated with cold cream, this to be practiced between periods, preferably in the relax-ing atmosphere of a warm bath. Or as an alternative he suggested gentle stretching by the repeated use of warm vaginal douches. "The douche is a good educator," he said.

Dr. Dickinson found several positive advantages to tampons. First, they do not chafe as ordinary napkins do. Second, they produce no odor since menstrual blood is practically odorless; it is only after it has been exposed to the air in a place with no ventilation that odor develops. Then, they do not produce erotic feelings, since there are no nerve endings in the actual canal in which the tampon rests.

Dr. Dickinson did find, though, that most women would be more comfortable with an outer napkin during the first day of the flow, since that is when fully half of the lining of the uterus is expelled.

A CATHOLIC VIEWPOINT

In his standard text, *Fundamental Marriage Counseling*, Dr. John R. Cavanagh, psychiatrist, Knight of St. Gregory and special lecturer in the School of Sacred Theology, Catholic University of America, also goes very carefully into the subject of tampons. He discusses the accusa-tion often made that tampons are a direct stimulus to masturbation, and denies this in the following words:

There is no doubt that a vaginal tampon could be used for the purpose of masturbation, just as any other similarly shaped material could also be used. This has little to do with the practical question as to whether or not its routine use to restrain the menstrual flow would induce or lead to such prac-tices. The internal tampon, when inserted in the vagina, does not ordinarily lead to erotic excitation. The vagina is a relatively insensitive area. Goodell [another researcher] calls it 'the great silent area of the pelvis.' The vaginal sexual response belongs if anywhere to the vaginal orifice or opening. The erotic stimulus of the stationary internal protection is therefore negligible compared to the moving pressure of any external protection.

The selection of the type of menstrual protection is a matter of choice as to what is more convenient to the woman, and has no moral implications.

Dr. Cavanagh then goes again into the question: Is there any physical harm; can tampons impair later ability to have children by causing infection? Again he answers no.

There is the practical fact that more than two billion menstrual tampons have been sold and used without any proof of harm or impairment to the health of women. It is also true that in most medical centers, the internal vaginal tampons are commonly used either as a menstrual protection or as a useful and beneficial appliance between menses. An absorbent menstrual tampon cannot block the flow and be a cause of inflammation of the pelvis.

Dr. Cavanagh further quotes a study made by Dr. K. J. Karnaky and published in the *Western Journal of Surgery and Gynecology* for April 1943. Dr. Karnaky tested 2000 women, among them 110 nurses, and concluded in favor of internal menstrual protection, going so far as to tightly pack them into several women whose extremely profuse bleeding called for abdominal surgery. He ends with the statement, "All the findings and conclusions of the above were confirmed at Loyola University, Mercy Hospital Clinic."

PSYCHOLOGICAL VALUE

Dr. Irving Fischer adds a final note on tampons. He finds they have a psychological value. He believes they have a definite role in preparing a woman for the casual handling of her genitals when the need arises. Many women decide to plan their families after they are married, but find themselves unable to use a diaphragm as a contraceptive. This is because they have been so harshly punished as children for touching their genitals, they now find themselves blocked. He feels that the use of tampons in adolescence helps break this block. And Dr. William Bickers of the University Hospital of Beirut, Lebanon, puts it simply: "Girls who have used tampons make better brides."

ACCEPTANCE

As the years go by, the normal woman comes to accept menstruation philosophically. She is not unduly worried when an occasional period is delayed. She is not unduly worried if she has her periods as often as every twenty-one days or as seldom as forty days, since these are within the normal range.

Above all, she comes to accept her periods as a bother, but seldom more. A bother, but not lastingly painful. A bother, but not "unclean." A bother, but not poisonous to anyone. A bother, but indicating mainly one is at low tide.

Yes, a bother—and a bit of a mess. But accepting that mess is one of the signs of maturity. For what isn't a bit of a mess at times, including many experiences that lead through suffering to pleasure? Isn't cooking a meal messy, but doesn't it lead to the pleasure of eating? Isn't washing one's hair or putting on make-up messy, but don't they lead to the pleasure of looking well?

In her novel *The Rosemary Tree*, Elizabeth Goudge told of a precocious five year old who was asked by her mother how she always managed to get so dirty.

"I just live," the little girl replied. "Living is dirty work, but I like it."

Menstruation, too, is "dirty work." But women learn if not actually to like it at least to accept it for what it is—the badge of femininity. The badge can be worn in misery or in pride. It is normal to stress the misery at first, then have it give way to pride—pride in the fact it lets a woman do what no man can do, bring forth new life.

✳✳✳ 17 Intense Awakening

Life means constant change. Nothing ever stands still. At the very moment the night is darkest and coldest, day is about to break. At the very moment winter is at its wildest, spring is on the way. The universe has been defined as "something that is always changing but remains essentially the same."

Girls, too, are always changing but remaining essentially the same. They change in small rhythms from energy to fatigue, then back to energy again; from hunger to satisfaction, then back to hunger. They also change in large rhythms. They change in monthly cycles as their hormones rise and fall. And they change dramatically during adolescence or the intense awakening years.

SCHOOL

As a child, she learned something about the outside world in school. She duly memorized and recited the facts that in Holland they produce large quantities of cheese and that South America is bounded on the north by the Isthmus of Panama. But she didn't learn what it is like to wrest a living from Dutch soil or to steer a boat around South America. The Dutch and South Americans remained for her mostly quaint, picturesque people whose problems in no way touched hers.

STORIES AND FAIRY TALES

She got a little more sense of reality in childhood, oddly enough, from fairy tales. For fairy tales contained not only picturesque, quaint and presumably "good" people, but also witches, ogres and wolves that wanted to eat up Little Red Riding Hood. But the trouble here was, she knew these were fairy tales. She was sure that at the end of each story somewhere, somehow a Good Fairy, a Prince or a Knight in Shining Armor would appear and set everything straight. So she did her shuddering and shivering over the wicked characters, cuddled comfortably in a big armchair, confident that soon all would come out right. This indeed is the central belief and credo of the normal child: that the world is a safe place in which virtue always wins. For no child's story ends with the death or destruction of the heroine; no child would be able to stand it if it did.

So a kind of canopy hangs over the little girl, a warm, sheltering canopy that keeps her feeling safe and snug, with reality far away. And since the first goal of living is personal survival, and a child has so much plain surviving to do, so many problems of her own to meet and solve, she is not ready yet to take on the problems of the world. Almost every known civilization has erected such a canopy, has entered into a conspiracy to keep children as much as possible from knowledge of the harshness of things. People seem always to have known that to do otherwise would only make children terrified and prematurely old.

During the teens, slowly, gradually, a girl's canopy starts to lift. The adults around her start to lift it. Urged on by new psychological forces within her—as new as the physical forces that bring on menstruation—she herself begins to lift it. In addition to growing, she begins to "grow up." A much more intense awakening is begun.

Insanity has been called a "flight from reality" because the insane run away and retreat from a knowledge of things as they are. Adolescence can be called a "flight into reality," because during these years a girl comes to grips with it. She gets a heightened inner awareness that makes her own pains and aches more biting; she gets a heightened outer awareness that makes her more conscious of the painful truths of the world.

PERSONALITY STRENGTH

The main task of adolescence is developing the personality strength to accept these painful truths. Accept the fact that Good Fairies do not always appear in the nick of time, and even when they do they are not all good; a little bad is inevitably mixed in. Accept the fact that the Fair Knight's armor is not all spotless, yet it is armor just the same.

AMBIVALENCE

This realization that good and bad exist simultaneously everywhere is called ambivalence. It is the feeling that we can want to be both cruel and kind to someone else, as well as cruel and kind to ourselves, at one and the same time. And this is something extremely hard to accept at first. Hard enough as it applies to others; even harder as it applies to ourselves. For accepting it means accepting the dark forces that lie in the part of ourselves that psychiatry calls the unconscious; the part hidden from everyday knowledge, but flowing like an underground stream that occasionally bubbles to the surface and makes its presence known.

It is the unconscious that lets us love and hate someone else or love and hate ourselves at one and the same moment, love consciously and hate unconsciously or the other way around. And this is hard to accept because we all yearn for simplicity, yearn to keep our childhood faith that black is pitch black and white snowy white. Life is so much simpler believing in a George Washington who never told a lie than a George Washington full of contradictions! In a saint eternally saintly who never, never is revealed as falling from grace!

But living has never been simple. Growing up means coming to grips with this normal mixture of good and bad, with the good predominating but the bad unmistakably there. Coming to terms with imperfect parents who are a mixture of kindness and cruelty, but hopefully more kindness than cruelty. Accepting ourselves, too, as a mixture of kindness and cruelty, independence and dependence, but hopefully more kindness and independence than not.

It takes a long time to acquire the personality strength to accept these contradictions, which is one reason adolescence takes so long.

A BURST OF ENERGY

Nature helps a young girl start by giving her a great burst of energy —a burst almost as great as the burst which let her get born. This energy is a combination of physical energy and psychic energy. The pause at around thirteen is over, and she bursts forth with a tremendous break.

Marilyn Monroe, telling of her break into adolescence, told an interviewer:

The whole world which was always closed to me—I felt just like I was on the outside of the world—then suddenly, everything opened up. Even the girls paid a little attention to me just because they thought, 'Hmmm, she's to be dealt with!' And I had this long walk to school—2½ miles to school, 2½ miles back—it was sheer pleasure. Every fellow honked his horn—you know, workers driving to work, waving, you know, and I'd wave back. The world became friendly.

All the newspaper boys when they delivered the paper would come around to where I lived, and I used to hang from a limb of a tree. They'd come with their bicycles, you know, and I'd get these free papers and the family liked that, then they'd all pull their bicycles up around the tree and then I'd be hanging, looking kind of like a monkey, I guess. I was a little shy to come down. I did get down to the curb, kinda kicking the curb and kicking the leaves and talking but mostly listening.

And sometimes the families used to worry because I used to laugh so loud and so gay; I guess they felt it was hysterical. It was just this sudden freedom because I would ask the boys, 'Can I ride your bike now?' and they'd say, 'Sure.' Then I'd go zooming, laughing in the wind, riding down the block, laughing, and they'd stand around the block and wait until I came back. But I loved the wind. It caressed me.

As in Marilyn's case, this energy is unchanneled at first. Just as Marilyn rode with the wind to nowhere and back, so too all adolescents flit about, savoring first this, then that. Just as the bewildering varieties of food at a smörgåsbord are first tasted and rolled on the tongue before we settle down and concentrate on two or three, so a teenage girl tastes conservatism and radicalism, the life of Bohemia and the life of a "proper lady," crazy love and sedate love, coyness and boldness, before she can channel her energy and make a choice.

DEVALUATION OF THE MOTHER

But her hardest job is not so much her channeling energy as it is pulling away from her mother. She pulled away a little before puberty, to be sure, but the pull was nothing compared to this one. For this time she is "playing for keeps."

The teenager starts this pull by a strong devaluation of her mother. The very woman who most of the time during childhood seemed "the most wonderful person in the world" now suddenly becomes a "dope." She becomes such a "dope" that one girl tells how surprised she was when a neighbor stopped by one day to ask her mother for some financial advice. Maybe *before* her mother might have been able to give such advice. But now?

This devaluation is merely a way of lessening a girl's own sense of guilt. It is a basic psychological premise that whenever we want to pull away from someone or something, we first lessen our guilt by devaluing it. If we want a divorce, we devalue the husband we once adored. "He's no good," we cry. "We were grossly deceived!" If we decide to leave a job, we devalue the office or the boss. "The boss is a tyrant!" we shout. "Nobody could get ahead with all those climbers around!" Anything to lessen our own guilt by shifting the blame.

So the adolescent blames her mother for everything. If a job isn't done, her mother used the wrong tone of voice in suggesting she do it. If her room isn't picked up, her mother didn't remind her in time. Her mother was firm when she should have been gentle, or gentle when she should have been firm. Her mother is impossible on all counts.

But then there is another shift. She rethinks the matter and decides her mother isn't nearly as bad as she made her out to be. So she now feels guilty for ever believing she was so bad, and hurries to make up.

HER OWN DECISIONS

She also makes up for another reason. She still needs her mother very much. After all, her mother has been helping her make all kinds of decisions, such as when to do her homework, how late to stay out at night, how much of her precious allowance to spend. Theoretically, she thinks, she should be making such decisions for herself. But making one's own decisions is difficult, especially when one is new at it and one's personality is wobbly in the extreme. So one minute a girl tries desperately to control her own actions; the next she gives up the effort, rushes back into her mother's arms, praises her and asks her to take over again.

Indeed, Dr. Irene Josselyn points out that the chief complaint she gets from teenagers in trouble is that modern parents do not take over enough; do not set limits for their children or make rules to guide them, to give them an excuse for not doing what they really don't want to do but haven't the courage to say no to against the crowd.

They may prefer to have limits set by people other than the parents they are pulling away from, but they can't carry by themselves the burden of all the decisions to be made. Their resentment of authority often masks great relief that someone is carrying part of the burden for them. When parents back out and refuse to carry it, the girls feel abandoned. They want their parents to stay firmly in the picture no matter how often and how loud they seem to protest.

DOUBLY GUILTY

Also, when parents back out of the picture altogether a girl feels extremely guilty. Some resentment or hostility against parents by adolescents is as normal as in childhood and a "perfect" parent gives a child no legitimate excuse for this hostility, so she feels even worse than she does toward obviously bad parents. Overpermissiveness, therefore, makes for havoc on all counts.

Still, firm parents don't solve everything either. Permitting a parent to take over too completely only makes a girl feel childish again, and fighting the desire to remain childish is a prime step in growing up. So after a while she devalues her mother again and tries to make her own decisions, just to prove she is not a child.

In this way she teeters back and forth like a circus performer on a tightrope, balancing herself desperately to avoid a bad fall.

She balances so precariously she can become a wreck. What with learning to control her own actions, feeling guilty over criticizing a mother she still needs very much and in acute conflict between her aspirations of purity and her growing sexual needs, a young girl can fall into a state of spiritual and physical exhaustion.

Much adolescent fatigue, overeating and oversleeping, says Dr. Carl Binger of Harvard, is due to this exhaustion, especially in girls away at camp or school for the first time. Overeating and oversleeping can then become a way not of restoring strength but of avoiding problems. It's as if one could dive under the covers or sit at a table forever and never emerge.

Yet teetering back and forth is the normal adolescent pattern. It is far more abnormal to remain passively dependent, and never to teeter or to criticize one's parents at all.

Indeed, teetering and criticizing are so important that the psychologist Dr. Erich Fromm sees them as the main way of avoiding adult neurosis. For the main problem in adult neurosis, in his view, is not sex-repression but the problem of the perpetually "good child" who never has learned to grow up and make decisions on his own; who was so frightened at the merest thought of parental criticism that he promptly buried it—buried it so deep it later became almost impossible to dredge up and put into words.

MARY ASTOR'S STORY

The story of the actress Mary Astor is a case in point. She tells in her autobiography how for most of her adult years she was a seemingly hopeless alcoholic.

Now alcoholism is a complex matter; it can stem from many causes. But there's no doubt that one of them is that the alcoholic is trying to escape from almost unbearable anxiety and tension—anxiety that stems from many reasons, among them a failure to grow up. The alcoholic has remained fixed in immaturity, and tries to solve practically all his problems by oblivion. And this oblivion he secures the way an infant secures it—by a bottle, through the mouth. Like an infant, too, he falls down and expects to be picked up and comforted, gets filthy and expects to be cleaned, lives in a world in which everything, he hopes, will come out all right as in Fairyland, if only he postpones facing his problems indefinitely by retreating into an alcoholic haze.

Mary Astor was such an alcoholic until the age of fifty, when she found religious and psychiatric help that let her unburden herself, write her book, and be healed.

Mary's main problem was her inability to criticize her father, not her mother. Her real name was Lucille Langhanke, and her father was an overbearing German, so overbearing, indeed, that neither she nor her timid, childish mother were ever able to stand up to him. In any dispute he simply shouted them down.

At the age of twelve, Mary, who was an only child, happened to win a small-town beauty contest. This decided Papa; she would leave school, become an actress and support them all. From then on, he devoted himself to planning Mary's every move. If between jobs she tried to find a few friends, he called her "lazy" and "good-for-nothing," shouting "Isn't your own family good enough for you?" and personally chaperoning her everywhere to make sure she found no friends. He even forbade her to close the door to her own room at night so he could keep an eye on her in bed.

By the time she was sixteen, Mary was earning a good salary. Any other girl would have spoken up. She did not have the courage. She had one wild, dreamlike love affair with John Barrymore, which she somehow managed while rehearsing with him for a picture, then became completely passive again. At nineteen, though by now she was earning $2,000 a week in Hollywood and they were living in a fine house, she was still accepting five dollars a week from her father as pocket-money.

She also was chaperoned everywhere. Her mother, father, or chauffeur accompanied her at all times. Mealtimes were especially oppressive, with her father constantly shouting at her and telling her what and how much to eat. "I had no appetite," she writes. "The food tasted like cotton and sand, but to quiet that strident voice I choked it down. . . . Yet I did not protest. Largely from the habit that had been ingrained in me, I sat there passively. . . . I think I had become too lazy mentally to rebel, too afraid of the consequences, too weak morally to face the changes this rebellion would bring. It was easier to continue my submissive existence . . . easier to escape to the solitude of my room (I was permitted to close the door now) or just to sit on the balcony and dream at the moon. . . ."

HARDER AGAINST MOTHER

The normal teenager also dreams at the moon. But unlike Mary she gradually finds the strength to throw off choking domination and strike out on her own, especially against the too-strong bond with her mother. For the central bond in both boys and girls, again unlike Mary, is almost always with the mother, so that criticizing her is far harder than criticizing a father even of the sternest kind. This is because motherhood has been so exalted, so emotionalized, that questioning a mother always seemed more of a sin, a sin like questioning THE MOTHER in the sense of the Universal Mother or the Mother of God.

And this is true even if the mother has long since been dead. For her influence has been so strong that her teachings have been taken in by her children and made into their own. The result is, she continues to live inside of them long after she has gone. Her portrait, in death as well as life, in effect still hangs over the mantel, pointing an accusing finger at them if they do anything of which she would not approve.

This internalizing of the mother's teachings is not all bad, to be sure. In childhood it had great positive values. It developed conscience; it taught a youngster how to obey many of life's rules. But adolescence is not childhood, and adolescents are not children. If a teenage girl or boy continues to be as passively dependent on his mother's teachings as he was before puberty, neurosis or great unhappiness can come about.

Here is another story in point.

THE THREE PRIESTS

In the town near where I live there are three brothers who are all priests. This is unusual; in many Catholic families one son becomes a priest, but seldom three. I happened to remark on this one day, and this is the story I was told: When the mother was first married, she had an unfortunate series of miscarriages; time and again she conceived but could not carry the pregnancy through. Since she ardently desired a child, she made a vow to God that if He would give her a living son, she would give the boy to the Church. Soon after this, to her great delight, three sons were born to her, all strong and well, and she decided to give all three. When the first son came of age, she told him of her vow, and he consented to do as she wished. When the second son came of age, he did the same. But the third son rebelled. He literally got down on his knees and begged her to release him. She was adamant. She played on his guilt-feelings with exhortations like: "You wouldn't want your own mother to suffer eternal hellfire because of a broken promise, would you?" Though the promise was entirely of her making, not his, he could not stand up against such pleas, and gave in. Even though his mother died before his final vows were taken, he could not break away. The two older brothers are content enough in their vocation. He is a most miserable man.

MERELY DIFFERENT

Children can remain emotionally bound to their parents without going to such extremes. They can feel guilty merely because they did something different than their parents expected, even when this difference brought them happiness and success.

Men can feel eternally guilty because they became good psychologists instead of passable furniture manufacturers or good musicians instead of indifferent ministers. Women can feel nagging doubts because they chose a secretarial instead of a teaching career, or did not become as good cooks as their mothers. And this can happen even when their parents didn't command them to become teachers or manufacturers; when they merely became victims of their parents' highly charged expectations which worked on them as strongly as explicit commands.

I know one grown woman who gets an anxiety attack while doing something as seemingly innocuous as buying herself a new blouse. Her mother had always preached: "Clothes are rags! Clothes are rags! It's all right to spend money on things like books or travel because those things are cultural. But clothes are beneath an intellectual woman's contempt." The result is, though she is a well-known painter, she still gets so excited while buying a garment she cannot sleep for guilt, and usually winds up punishing herself the next day by rushing it back. She doesn't know *why* she takes it back; she only knows she has to. For she has long "forgotten" her mother's teachings; they persist only as this vague feeling of doing wrong.

UNMARRIED DAUGHTERS

Daughters are far more likely than sons to react this way. After the short tomboy-burst, their tendency toward passivity tends to take over and retard girls from developing the personality-strength to strike out on their own. Everyone knows one family in which a daughter has remained unmarried, not because she didn't have an opportunity to marry but because she simply could not resist her mother's pleas not to leave her, or get over the notion her mother would in some way punish her if she did.

These are the daughters who develop into the traditionally "bitter old maids." They may be outwardly good and virtuous but inwardly they are usually seething with rage. This bitterness and rage has nothing to do with "sex starvation." There is no such thing as sex starvation in the popular sense of the word. It is rage against themselves for lack of courage to grow up, bitterness against their mothers for not helping them to. That is why daughters usually vacillate in conduct from weak obedience to vengeful spite.

Girls' tendency toward passivity also helps explain why there are still twice as many cloistered nuns as monks. It is simply not so much of a struggle for a girl to give up the world and let someone else take over for her as it is for a boy.

NOT EASY

Growing up is one of the hardest jobs in the world. For a girl especially it means fighting the desire to remain a cute, dependent child and moving on toward the rewards that courage brings. But the normal girl does move on. She moves out from under the canopy of childhood and works through to a more realistic appraisal of herself and other people. She learns to see her mother in particular as a human being much like herself with faults as well as virtues, and worthy of respect for her virtues alone. When she achieves this, she becomes reconciled to her mother and loves her again.

This reconciliation doesn't come quickly; it takes many years. And while it is coming, a teenage girl is left in a dilemma: with both her mother and father temporarily out of bounds, what will she do with her brimming burden of love instead, a burden she feels she must expend on someone else or she'll burst—and soon?

✳✳✳ 18 Full and Brimming Over

The adolescent girl starts to solve the dilemma of her over brimming love by giving more love to herself.

This matter of love for oneself is much misunderstood. There is a good and a bad way of looking at everything, so people like to downgrade self-love one moment by calling it sinful, preaching, "If you want to be good, don't love yourself at all; lose yourself and love others instead." Then the next moment they turn around and shout, "How are you going to get ahead if you are always thinking of others? Hold on to what you have! Make your pile!"

These contributions come from the idea that love is a limited thing; that we have only just so much, like a single piece of cake. If we give a tiny bite away, we'll have that much less for ourselves.

But love is limitless. The Bible was clear on this point when it commanded, "Love thy neighbor as thyself." The ancient scholars who wrote the Bible knew that you have to love yourself before you can love your neighbor; that love is a learned thing, and loving yourself is one of the ways to develop that learning.

Dr. Erich Fromm interprets the Biblical commandment this way: "If it is a virtue to love my neighbor as a human being, it must be a virtue and not a vice to love myself since I am a human being too. There is no concept of man in which I myself am not included. . . . An attitude of love toward themselves will be found in all those who are capable of loving others. . . . If an individual is able to love productively, he loves himself too; if he can love only others, he cannot love at all!"

STARTS AS A CHILD

A little girl starts to love herself as a child, but it's a weak love because she is weak as a person. In adolescence her love grows stronger because she grows stronger.

WITHDRAWN AND SOLITARY

While she is developing in this strength, a teenager may again retreat to her room and stay there for hours. Asked what she is doing all this time, she probably replies, "Nothing." That isn't true. She is trying to develop self-love by looking hard at herself in the mirror—examining her fingers, her toes, her nose, as she did as a baby long ago. But while she knew no other fingers, toes or nose, then, now she does, and she's trying to see if hers "measure up" against those of the rest of the world. As a rule she decides they don't measure up very well, for an adolescent has far less confidence in herself than she had as a child. So she retreats, and looks, and reflects and looks some more, trying to find some part of herself of which to be proud.

"Praise youth and it will prosper," is an old Irish proverb. Earnestly seeking praise from those around her, she is at least seeking some basis for praising herself.

PULL TOWARD HER FATHER

With all this, she doesn't stay in her room indefinitely at this stage. She emerges and, rather to her family's surprise, switches intensely to a new love object—her father. During the very time she pulls hard away from her mother, she is pulling strongly toward him, giving him an amount of affection she has not given him in years. And she demonstrates this affection in the time-honored feminine ways of ruffling his hair, running to fetch his favorite lounging jacket, smiling up at him with a special smile whenever he comes home.

This pull toward her father comes about for two reasons. The first is her rising tide of sex hormones. This rising tide makes her greatly interested in all males, and her father is obviously a big, friendly male close to home. The second is that, close as he is, her father has seldom been as "magic" as her mother, if only because her mother has usually been the mouthpiece for both. So it is easier now to keep her father in perspective. She does not have to rebel against him quite so much in order to free herself from suffocating family ties.

But the pull toward her father doesn't last either, though it has great value for her development, if it happens at the right time and season. So while she is giving him intense affection, he is giving her a lot of affection in return, and this affection teaches her the valuable lesson that she can someday be fully lovable to a man.

She is not yet ready for such a love; no girl in her early teens is ready for full male love. But it is important for her to learn that she will one day be ready. For a girl's psychosexual development is much more complicated than a boy's. His first strong attachment is to his mother, a female, and he remains attached to the female gender. A girl's first strong attachment is also to her mother, a female, but to attain full maturity she has to change genders to the male. Her father's companionship during adolescence greatly helps her to make this change.

MUSIC AND POETRY

"O World, I cannot hold thee close enough!
Thy winds, thy wide grey skies!
Thy mists that roll and rise!
Thy woods, this autumn day, that ache and sag
And all but cry with colors! That gaunt crag
To crush! To lift the lean of that black bluff!
World, World, I cannot get thee close enough!"

When Edna St. Vincent Millay wrote these lines, she was expressing the over-brimming love a teenage girl next gives to nature. And with her usual intensity, she gives it exclamation points and all. Sunsets, which before she may hardly have noticed, are now "simply divine." So are flowers, and the crescent moon and the deep stillness of the winter woods at night.

Then she loves music, especially popular music. How she dotes on it when it echoes some of her own jagged rhythms. She listens to it endlessly with rapture, particularly when the lyrics are sad. Because of her natural attraction to suffering, she sits and agonizes by the hour over the woes of the homesick sailor, the lovelorn soldier or the cowboy far off on "the lone prair-ee."

Cheerful music does not give her half as much pleasure as sad music, especially when she feels like the teenager Marie Bashkirtseff, who wrote in her famous diary:

"I love to weep, I love to give myself up to despair, I love to be troubled and sorrowful. I regard these feelings as so many diversions, and while I ask for happiness, I find myself happy in being miserable."

This "happiness in being miserable" will, in certain ways, be with every girl all her life.

GIRL FRIENDS AND WOMEN FRIENDS

But while music and poetry are fine enough in their way, a teenager's real need is for people. Girl friends, both old and new. Her girl friends now become the objects of such passionate devotion that the well-known "crushes" of adolescence are the result.

She may even have crushes on two completely different sets of girl friends—girls bright and girls dumb, girls on her own side of the tracks and girls on the other. This is another way of exploring and testing reality. To find out more about the good and bad in people, she needs them both.

It is important to note here that these intense crushes are seldom evidences of homosexuality. True homosexuality among women is quite rare.

Crushes do have an erotic tinge if you look hard enough for it; there is much hand-holding, kissing and putting of arms around waists. But to label this kind of thing homosexuality is a misnomer. It is usually nothing of the kind.

To the normal girl, crushes are mainly adventures in human warmth, and as such just another step along the long road to maturity. It is a step that cannot be by-passed, any more than adolescence itself can be by-passed; it would leave her much poorer if it were.

But girl friends are still not enough outlet for her warmth. She also spills over with love for women like teachers, club leaders and camp counselors. Her crushes on these mother-substitutes are legendary, too. They are often even more intense than those of her chums, since they serve a double purpose; they are outlets for confidence as well as her affection.

All adolescent girls tend to be secretive. Much of what is happening to them is so new and disturbing they find it almost impossible to talk about with someone as close as a mother or even a friend. But they may be able to talk about it with an older, dispassionate woman. So older women outside the family often perform a function much like that of Catholic priests—they become sympathetic ears to which a girl can unburden herself without fear of betrayal.

HEROINES OF HISTORY

But older living women are still not enough. Next, she pours some of her over-brimming love onto the heroic women of history and, again, the more tragic the better. Our teenager goes on a reading spree and devours the lives of a Joan of Arc, a Florence Nightingale, a Mary, Queen of Scots, and is inspired to emulate them all. She decides she will don a suit of white armor and ride forth to liberate her country like Joan, or put on a white cap and relieve suffering like Florence or die gloriously on the scaffold like Mary. And if neither a suit of armor nor a scaffold are handy, she will at least grab a bedpan and become a nurse's aide. Anything to be as heroic or as tragic as they!

She often doesn't wait for the future to live out her dreams. She does this here and now.

During the summer of 1962, *Time* magazine reported that ten thousand teenage youngsters were enrolled in a project called Operation Kindliness, sponsored by the United Community Services. In cities like Boston, Philadelphia and San Francisco, they were enthusiastically doing everything from skinning rabbits for the medical researchers at Peter Bent Brigham Hospital to giving permanent waves to psychotic women at state hospitals, all, of course, without pay.

One delighted mother said of her daughter: "She goes charging out of here every morning like Florence Nightingale riding on Paul Revere's horse." A teenager enrolled in Operation Kindliness described her own feelings: "I just love the beach in the summer. Really I do. But —well, I like this better."

It added up to a fine example of love expressed in a practical way.

OF COURSE, MEN

But girl friends, older women and humanity in general still do not use up all of her love-energy. She has plenty left to be used in the way it was always meant to be used—in getting ready for mature sexual love. Yet aside from the problem of changing genders, this is far from simple again.

It sounds so easy in the story books for a girl to get ready for personal sexual love. All she has to do is to wait for Mr. Right to come along and woo her, then happily leap into his arms and mate. But it never works out quite that way.

One of her biggest difficulties is to straighten out what her parents have told her about men. For the very same parents who have idealized marriage and urged her to hurry toward it may have also told her "men can take advantage of you" or "never kiss a man" or just used the generally blasphemous statement "all men are bad."

The psychiatrist Dr. O. Spurgeon English tells of a Philadelphia girl who landed in his office as a patient after being constantly warned by her mother against "men who cruised around in cars ready to pull you into white slavery." The mother explained, "Of course I wanted her to get married. But I figured that if only I could frighten her enough to get her through high school safely, I'd be greatly relieved."

How, under such circumstances, could the girl know Mr. Right from Mr. Wrong? It's like being told for years that all food is poisonous, then suddenly being urged to eat.

FEAR OF MALE GENITALS

But even without confusing parental cautions, a girl has her own built-in fears, among them the fear of male genitals.

There is almost no girl who has not seen male genitals in one form or another by the time she has reached her teens. If she hasn't seen those of human beings, she has seen those of animals like horses, dogs, bulls. And these male genitals can appear very large and threatening, particularly when erect.

For there is a basic difference between male and female sexual anatomy: male genitals invade; female genitals are invaded. And invasion of any kind is a threat since it goes against our feelings of bodily integrity.

We don't like needles stuck into our arms, even for worthy purposes like polio shots. We don't like enema-tips shoved up our rectums even for worthy purposes like pre-operative cleansing. We don't like dentists poking into our mouths even when they are "just looking" and cause no pain. We just don't like to be invaded, and that is that.

The fact that some day a shy, fearful girl may welcome the particular kind of invasion that is sexual is beside the point. In youth she does not, and it will take her a long time before she does.

So this shy, fearful girl is faced with a dilemma: She is naturally afraid of males. She may have been warned against males. She is irresistibly pulled toward males.

She solves the dilemma by approaching them the way one approaches a haunted house one is afraid of but irresistibly pulled toward —she draws near them a step at a time, taking the longest possible way around.

IDEALIZATION OF DISTANT MALES

Her first long-way-around step is idolizing distant males. Some of her female heroines may be women like teachers who are close to home. But not her male idols. These in the beginning are either great men of history who are conveniently dead, or great men of the entertainment world who are far away.

So adolescence becomes the great age of gazing ardently at pictures of a Beatle in a movie magazine, stretching out on a sofa and mooning over Bing Crosby's voice on records, or joining a fan club and getting a TV star's autograph by any ruse.

These distant idols are worshipped because they present no problems. No questions can come up like, "What shall I talk about if he does ask me for a date?" —"What shall I wear?" —"How shall I act?"— because she knows none of them will ask her. So she can dream away endlessly about them and never worry about what would happen if, horrors! she should meet one of them face to face.

If she lives where there are no movie or TV magazines (girls in the heart of Africa or Greenland go through the same stages), she pins her dreams onto a Prince or Tribal Chief. When the present Duke of Windsor was the young, dashing Prince of Wales, girls all over the world swooned over him as regularly as later they swooned over Frank Sinatra. The one was as glamorous and distantly safe as the other. The principle was the same.

DEAR DIARY

Then a girl takes the long-way-around step toward men through her diary.

What would she do without her "Dear Diary," a place in which to confide passions so sacred they cannot bear to be lit by the light of common day? Girls have surely kept diaries in one form or another ever since the first teenager learned how to write.

One of the most famous of these adolescent diaries is that of Marie Bashkirtseff. Marie fell madly in love with a Duke who qualified as a properly distant male because she had merely passed him without speaking half a dozen times in the street. She nevertheless records her desire to become a world-famous singer with hundreds of men courting her, and the moment of triumph when she spurns all except him:

"To see thousands of persons, when you appear on the stage, await with beating heart the moment when you begin to sing; to know, as you look at them, that a single note of your voice will bring them all to your feet; to look at them with a haughty glance—that is my desire. And then in the midst of this the Duke of H—— will come with the others and throw himself at my feet. But he shall not meet with the same reception as the others. Dear, you will be dazzled by my splendor and you will love me."

Life magazine recently published excerpts from a modern American girl's diary: "I was thinking about it, but now I know it; I love Randy. . . . Went to church and thought about Randy; prayed for him. . . . Randy and Marianne are going steady; it makes me sick, I hate Randy. . . ."

The words are more prosaic than Marie's. But the principle is the same.

Diaries are therefore not to be laughed at. Psychiatrists like Dr. Deutsch say that, like the worship of distant males, diaries are useful ways of preparing a girl for a more realistic approach to men, so most valuable in working off steam.

LONELY HEARTS AND PEN PALS

Lonely Hearts and Pen Pal Clubs work off steam in much the same way.

Since a girl almost never meets, or expects to meet, a Lonely Heart or Pen Pal, she can appear in her letters to them as grand or as sophisticated as she would like, and not be found out.

Sometimes, however, complications do arise. There are rare instances in which a girl gets so worked up she not only writes Pen Pal letters but answers them herself, signing a man's name to boot. Since she answers them herself to bolster her stock by showing the answers around, and for this purpose usually makes them highly passionate, the letters may get back to her parents who will be led to believe she is having a wild affair when she is having nothing of the kind. And because a girl who does answer her own letters would rather die than admit it, it may take a good deal of patient sifting to get at the truth.

Occasionally, there is even a girl who goes further than to write herself letters—she insinuates or boldly states she has been the victim of rape when nothing of the kind has taken place. There is little question but that some of the tales of assault told by southern girls would prove to be products of fantasy if they were dispassionately investigated before a lynching mob arrived on the scene. This is doubly tragic because fantasied seductions or other sex experiences are more likely to be reported by girls during adolescence than at any other time.

DAYDREAMS

Then there are the outlets of just plain daydreams. Daydreams of marvelous marriages, daydreams of splendid careers, daydreams of how she will decorate her home down to the last magnificent detail.

Daydreams are as valuable as diaries, since they make life bearable during a time of stress and conflict. The teenage girl, neither a child nor an adult, caught and vacillating between the two, often feels rejected and misunderstood, a Cinderella imprisoned by wicked forces pushing her this way and that. Like all people who feel imprisoned, she takes refuge in dreams. She escapes from the difficult present into thoughts of tomorrow and better days.

"If I cannot dream, I might as well die." Surely all people who have felt themselves prisoners, for whatever reason, have said the same.

FOOD FADS

Even in her everyday eating, an adolescent daydreams and tries to escape from herself into a strange and shinier place.

Peep into a lunchroom near a high school and what do you find? Are the girls munching away on plain cheese sandwiches and milk? Seldom. They are attacking hot dogs made even hotter by mustard, spicy salami made spicier with ketchup, sundaes heaped with whipped cream and fudge. Then a week later they are going to the other extreme and picking away ascetically at so-called "health foods" like raw carrots, lettuce and nuts.

Some of this strange eating, like the longings of a pregnant woman, is due to her changed chemistry. Since all life-patterns tend to repeat themselves, some are due to her defiance of her mother, who may have forbidden things like hot dogs and salami. The rest is due to her intense quest for adventure.

It is a rare teenager who can travel to foreign countries. But juggling the chop suey with chopsticks in a mysterious-looking "Chinese den," gobbling up spaghetti in an "Italian joint" or savoring curry served by a turbaned Hindu in an "Indian palace" are substitutes. All are ways of stepping out into a widening world.

CLOTHES FADS

Clothes fads are another way. There is no one more eager for the latest cry from Paris, Hollywood, Honolulu or wherever than a teenager. As a child she had to be docile about clothes. With little or no pocket-money, she had little or no say. But now that she commands a fair allowance or earns her own money, she goes to every extreme. The American garment industry reports that while adolescents make up only 17 per cent of the population, they buy a big 35 per cent of the clothes.

But it isn't only how much a girl buys, it's what she buys that flabbergasts adults around her. If heels are high, hers are so high she can barely totter in them; if skirts are skimpy, hers are so skimpy she can barely navigate down the block.

Even more puzzling, she may languidly descend to supper one evening dressed head to toe like a Theda Bara vamp, complete to green eye-shadow, black mascara and slinky, trailing gown. The next evening she may do a switch and glide in as a demure maiden in pink ruffles. This is more dream-stuff. Not at all sure yet of who she is or what she is going to be, by trying on various kinds of clothes she is literally trying on various dreams.

She also dresses to increase her sense of belonging. A teenager needs desperately to feel she's part of a group. She demonstrates she is "in" by wearing the group-costume of the moment, whether it's a sack, a shift, or a feminized version of a zoot suit, since not to wear it would mean she's out.

She also dresses to bolster her ego. Her figure is so new and exciting, coming as it does after the shapelessness of the potbelly stage, she decorates it to show it off to the hilt. She wears bouffant skirts that trap air beneath them and give her a graceful swing, wide belts that accent her tiny waist, stretch-pants that accent her tiny hips and sweaters that reveal more than they conceal.

BECOMING AN ACTRESS

> "I want to go upon the stage,
> And wear a wig, and feathers,
> I envy each tragedian,
> The laurels that he gathers."

The anonymous person who wrote this must have been a teenager. Because of all the ways of trying on dreams, becoming an actress is the most popular. It is an almost universal glamour-dream among teenage girls, along with newspaperwoman, private detective and policewoman.

Actress is the most popular because acting seems to combine everything. First, acting is exciting, and the teenager is dying for excitement. Travelling, staying up late, meeting new and glamorous people—acting promises the excitement of all.

Second, acting is the quickest way of exchanging unsureness for sureness. A girl can try on different clothes of different kinds of people, she can try on their whole personalities as well and hide behind a mask, assuming a new character with each role. If she's a lowly sweeper of the hearth, lo! she can become a Cinderella in a coach of gold; if she's a poor goose-girl, she can become a Queen.

Then acting is a showing off of the body. And for the first time in her life, as we just saw, a teenager has a body she wants to show off. What profession could be more alluring than one in which she can show it shining in silks and satins under flattering lights?

Above everything, acting sounds like a cinch. A director tells her how to recite the grand speeches someone else wrote, how to move to show off her beautiful body best. This is infinitely more appealing than studying hard herself to get an A in English or mastering shorthand. Yet for this "easy work" she will get all that wild applause of a grateful audience! Not to mention the pay!

And she wouldn't be feminine if she didn't prefer to be a "suffering" or tragic actress. For, as Marie Bashkirtseff said, there's a certain happiness that comes from being miserable, and women are masters in extracting some pleasure from pain.

The adolescent girl in particular is a master at it. The adolescent world is so full of jangling outbursts followed by quiet solitudes, anger followed by ecstasy, violent adorations coming on the heels of violent hates, it is no wonder the adults around her often see only the pain and ask themselves in desperation, will the scale ever settle down? Will they ever be able to forget this stormy time and feel like the old lady who said, "Thank goodness, there were no adolescents when I was raising my girls!"

ALWAYS BACK TOWARD NORMAL

They will be able to feel like the old lady someday. They will forget most of the storm in time. For the pull of life is always back toward the normal. Adolescence is a rocky road that can neither be skipped nor detoured, but most young people come out at the end of the road in far better shape than seemed possible when they were bumping along.

Adolescent girls, for all their intensity, come out quicker and better than boys. Delinquency is the most serious acting out of hostility, and the United States Childrens' Bureau, analyzing returns from 76 juvenile courts, reports the delinquency ratio of boys to girls as a huge six to one.

Adolescent girls also express less anger in general, and more positive compassion. In a study of anger in 550 boys and girls of high school through college age reported by Dr. Lewis Terman, the only field in which girls reported more anger than boys was over social injustice like "hearing friends unjustly abused" or "seeing boys make fun of older people" or "seeing a person treated unfairly because of his race." Anger of this kind is aggression expressed in a constructive way.

So settle down in time a girl's scale usually does, no matter how wildly it had seemed to tremble. And when it does settle down, the diaries are carefully locked and stored away in the attic, the Pen Pal letters are bundled up and dropped into a dresser-drawer and the worship of distant heroes becomes far less. She gives up the million-to-one-shot dream of living the abnormal life of a glittering star, and turns her dreams instead to jobs like teaching, social work or something that can no longer be postponed—her relations with the real boys around her.

Gradually she discovers these boys aren't nearly as frightening as she used to think, and she gets up the courage to go out on single dates instead of group dates since she now can dispense with the support of a group. Soon she will get mad crushes on these boys just as she got mad crushes on her girl friends. Soon she will be declaring she "loves" many boys in turn, though she may not love any of them. She may merely be "in love," which is something else again.

While she is getting ready for mature love, other problems about her body demand her attention. Let's take a look at some of these.

❊❊❊ 19 Obsessed with Her Body

Since it is healthy and good to learn to love oneself, a young girl does this, among other ways, by learning to love her body. If she loved it as a child, she loves it infinitely more now. Curiously, too, she derives strength from that love, as it becomes for her what Dr. Helene Deutsch calls a "narcissistic guard"—a defense against destroying blows.

The French writer Albert Camus tells of young girls: "Every year the young girls come into flower on the beaches. They have only one season. The following year they are replaced by other flower-like faces, which the previous season still belonged to little girls. For the men who look at them, they are yearly waves whose sight and splendor break into foam over the yellow beach."

Waves are a particularly good metaphor for girls, since they have those giant waves inside them, too. The girl who disregards this wave-like effect on the people around her, and goes around constantly ungroomed and sloppy, is a sick girl who probably doesn't love her body enough to preserve it by eating or washing or rest.

Doctors notice this kind of body-indifference most keenly in mental hospitals. They notice that when girls—or women of any age—are emotionally ill, they go around constantly dishevelled and dirty. It's a happy sign when they start to put on lipstick again, scrub their faces or comb their hair.

The normal teenager goes to her usual extremes, and is concerned with her body almost to the point of obsession. She is obsessed with her skin, with her nose, her toes. Even if they are good, she wants them to be better. And if they aren't good—quick, Watson, bring help!

HER SKIN

Of all that obsesses a girl about herself, her skin obsesses her the most. This is natural. Skin is changing and ever mysterious; it changes not only according to our health and our emotions, but according to the weather and the time of day. We can be pallid in the morning, rosy at noon, gray with fatigue at night. We redden more on a hot day than a cool. We become red with rage or pale with fright. Small wonder, then, that skin is a source of never-ending interest, and that we are eternally aware of what is happening to it, particularly to the skin on our faces.

THE AGONY OF ACNE

Yet nature has chosen the teens, of all times, to subject a girl's face to horrid disfigurement. Just at the very moment when everyone is starting to tell her that "her face is her fortune," the smooth, fair skin of her childhood is apt to give way to pimples, blackheads or boils.

This kind of disfigurement is as old as history. The Greeks had a word for it, as they had for so many things. They called it acne, meaning "point" or "bloom." The "bloom" probably referred to the extreme redness of some of the pimples, and the "point" to the blackheads. But whatever acne refers to, adolescents hate it, and with reason. For doctors estimate that at least twenty per cent of girls and a whopping sixty per cent of boys get acne at one time or another. You might call it Teenage Public Enemy No. 1.

People have always wondered why acne appears at adolescence and not before. All kinds of answers, including sex-practices, have been given, most of them wrong. The real cause seems to be the new wave of hormones that floods the body and changes it in so many ways.

When puberty arrives, it brings with it a rush of estrogens, or female hormones, as we saw. These estrogens keep a girl's skin soft and clear. But along with the estrogens, she also gets a comparatively large rush of androgens, or male hormones—an amount far greater than she ever had before. And these androgens have an adverse effect on her skin. They make it tougher and harder, and alter the working of her sebaceous glands.

These sebaceous glands in the main do a beneficial job. They throw onto the surface of the skin a waxy substance called "sebum," which mixes with the perspiration to form an invisible coating that helps protect the skin from invasion from bacteria. But under the influence of her large new rush of androgens, the openings of the sebaceous glands become thickened and clogged. The sebum, instead of being freely thrown off, then clots at the ends of the glands, especially the glands of the forehead, face, chest and back. Stuck there, it turns black on exposure to the air. Blackheads are not "dirt"; they are merely plugs of waxy substance turned black. Or, instead of turning black, the plugged-up places may become infected and develop into pimples or boils.

Why do girls tend to get more acne at certain times of the month, notably just before menstruation? Why do their faces remain clear for days, then suddenly a few pimples appear? These questions, too, have always puzzled people, especially since it does not work the same way in boys.

The answer is hormones again. Girls do not produce sex hormones at a steady rate. Estrogen rises high during the first half of the month and falls low during the second half, dipping down most sharply just before menstruation occurs. So before a menstrual period there is less estrogen to do its protecting and nourishing job. But while estrogen dips down before menstruation, androgen remains up. Androgen is now relatively higher than before. Since there is little or no estrogen to balance it, androgen becomes the villain in the case. Androgen coarsens the skin and makes the detested acne appear.

ESTROGENS AS MEDICINE

Since it is too much androgen that causes acne, and estrogen balances androgen, doctors are now giving acne-plagued girls extra estrogen to supplement their own supply. A formula like that in the birth-control pills is being used in cases that warrant it, often with great success.

ANTI-BIOTICS

Anti-biotics are also used, since anti-biotics check infection anywhere within the body, and acne as we just saw is an infection too.

But anti-biotics have their problems. Acne is a condition that can go on for months or years, and anti-biotics taken over so long a period tend to destroy not only the unwanted bacteria that are causing the trouble, but also the wanted bacteria that normally inhabit the intestines and help in the digestion of food. So taking anti-biotics for months or years may prove a case of throwing out the baby with the bath-water. The destruction of the helpful bacteria may cause stomach upsets, or a most annoying itch, around the rectum in particular. For this reason, anti-biotics are usually reserved for severe flare-ups, and then given only in small doses over short periods of time.

X-RAY

X-ray, surprisingly enough, is less harmful than too many anti-biotics, if it is given by a competent specialist. Dr. Marian Sulzberger, former Chairman of the Department of Dermatology of the New York University Post Graduate School, believes the fear of X-rays has been greatly exaggerated. "Many adolescents with severe acne," he says, "are being deprived of this effective and safe treatment simply because the patients or their parents have been given to believe that X-ray is always dangerous no matter how small the dose. Severe acne is often helped by X-ray which is within the safe-dosage range."

LOCAL TREATMENT

Luckily, for ordinary acne, the kind most girls get, the best treatment is still home treatment. The use of salves, lotions, plain hot water and soap.

The salves and lotions have to be special salves and lotions, however, and like X-ray, they have to be prescribed by a doctor or a skin-clinic, not bought at random from the corner drugstore. For no two skins are alike. A lotion or salve that will work for a brunette may burn the hide off a blonde or redhead, and it takes an expert to determine which kind is needed for whom. Indeed, doctors say one of their biggest jobs in acne is undoing the harm caused by girls who rush out and buy themselves any old stuff after reading some alluring ad.

Moreover, since the emphasis should be on drying creams and lotions that will help dissolve the fatty plugs that are causing the trouble, buying ordinary creams which are oozing with fat and grease, are also to be avoided. But girls fall for ads here too. They read fancy descriptions of so-called "nourishing creams" or "vitamin creams" and forget that the skin is mainly a one-way street, with nourishment going from inside to outside, not the other way round. Nourishment for the skin comes from within, from eating proper food, as does every other kind of nourishment. It cannot be obtained from the rubbing on of all the creams in the world!

Above all, say doctors, a girl with acne has to learn to leave her face alone. Keep her hands away from those pimples and blackheads; resist the temptation to squeeze or tamper with them in any way.

This is very hard to do because there is something about a pimple that makes us yearn to touch it. We are as tempted to pick at it as we are to scratch an itch. Yet almost all the permanent scars left by acne are caused not by the condition itself, but by over-zealous picking and squeezing. So doctors cannot advise a girl strongly enough: leave her poor face alone. Let the pimples come to a head by themselves. Scrub the blackheads several times a day with plain soap, hot water and a rough cloth. But aside from this, hands off.

IT GOES AWAY

The best news about acne is that it almost always goes away of its own accord. A good doctor can make it go away faster but it goes away in time even without him.

It goes away around the early twenties as a rule. It does so because by that time a girl's body is secreting a full complement of estrogens, enough to balance any androgens that may be causing trouble. Also by this time the emotional turmoil of adolescence is over, and anger and excitement throw still more than usual androgens into the blood. Around 20 therefore a better state of both physical and emotional health has been achieved.

All this is important to remember because many youngsters have been made to suffer unnecessarily over acne, since they have been taught that in some way it is connected with sex-practices when it is not. It can be stated positively: acne has nothing to do with the presence or absence of sex-intercourse. Acne has nothing to do with the presence or absence of genital play.

People used to think there was a relation between acne and sex because the early twenties was the age when most young people got married, as well as the age when acne usually disappeared. But young men or women can marry and establish regular sex-relations and still have acne; complete ascetics can have it disappear.

About the only relation between acne and sex is that even the most persistent cases of acne almost always get better during pregnancy. This is because during pregnancy a woman's natural supply of estrogens not only goes way up; it stays way up. This huge supply of pregnancy-estrogens balances the androgens that have been causing the trouble. It is as simple as that.

Meanwhile, acne should be regarded with sympathy while it does last. Dr. Marynia Farnham tells of young people becoming actual "acne-hermits" because their families pooh-poohed the matter and merely laughed at them when they could have helped them instead. She has known acne-plagued girls who were perpetually too "sick" to go to parties; girls who refused to attend even their own graduation exercises because somehow they had gotten the idea that acne was connected with shameful sex-practices that now "showed."

Another reason why acne usually goes away in the early twenties is that the emotional stresses of adolescence are mostly a thing of the past. Androgens are not only "strength" hormones, they are "fight" hormones. Emotions like anger or excitement bring out the fight re-action and throw extra androgens into the blood, with the result that the acne gets worse. But calm down again, and the acne fades.

This is another reason why boys get more acne than girls. Ado-lescence brings boys a greater rush of androgens than girls under any circumstances; but boys heighten the androgen effect by getting angrier and more excited than girls.

THE MEN WITH THE TATTOOS

They tell the story of an Englishman working in Africa who fell in love with a native girl. She would have none of him unless he covered his face with tattoos, as was the custom in her tribe. He retreated deep into the forest with an old woman skilled in tattooing, and underwent the ordeal. He was gone so long that the girl got tired of waiting and took up with another lover. Furious, he decided to have his tattoos re-moved and return home. The removal was successful—to a point. His face appeared clear and unblemished as long as he was calm. But when he remembered how he had been jilted and his furious feelings returned, the angry blood would rush to his face and the hated marks, faint but distinctly perceptible, would appear.

NOSE WORRY

Next to being obsessed with her skin, an adolescent is obsessed with her nose. It is amazing how many hours she can spend looking in the mirror and deciding her nose is "all wrong."

Partly she is right. An adolescent's nose does grow faster than the rest of her face. And since it's a "part that sticks out," and so unusually fascinating, for a time she *can* look almost all nose. If she inherits a tendency toward a really big nose, or a hooked one, the situation is ob-viously worse. Girls with big noses are so self-conscious they think up all kinds of ways to avoid being seen in profile. They will never be caught in a snapshot that way, and will keep turning their heads forward with a quick movement even on ordinary occasions. One girl covered her nose with her handkerchief, as if she had a perpetual cold, every time she got up in class to recite.

This preoccupation with her nose isn't all vanity, however. The plastic surgeon Dr. Gustave Aufricht points out it may be just the opposite. "Vanity," he says, "is a desire to excel over, or be different from, our fellow men. The girls who hide their noses are seeking to be like other people. They are trying to be inconspicuous, to melt into the group."

Since adolescence is the time when the need to melt into the group is strongest, a nose that may seem not particularly big to others may loom enormous to its owner. A vicious circle can then be set up. Because she feels like an outcast, she can become more shy and timid than the usual teenager. The more shy and timid she becomes, the more the other boys and girls will ignore her, so even more shy and timid she will become.

A study done at Johns Hopkins by Drs. Milton Edgerton, Wayne Jacobson and Eugene Meyer confirms this. Extreme shyness and timidity were the outstanding characteristics of a group of girls and women seeking nose operations, and this shyness and timidity had become most pronounced during the ages of twelve to fifteen.

Not that all the patients were twelve to fifteen. At least a third were between twenty and forty, had good jobs or were married. Still, they felt unhappy to the point of being constantly anxious and jittery, and they took out their jitteriness by snapping at the world. One married woman with a good job said, "I hope my nose operation will make me want to be less nasty with people." Another said, "All that's wrong with my friends is my temper." It's as if they had to snap at people before people snapped at them.

Still another girl in her twenties, dateless since high school days and severely depressed since her second term at college, left school and came back home, explaining, "I was living like in a vacuum. I just did homework all the time. I would sit in my room alone on Saturday nights and cry for hours." And the married women in the study admitted their marriages were full of tension, again blaming their noses. (It is well known that to many people the nose is equated with the genitals. An ugly nose may spell ugly and unattractive genitals to the woman involved.) Or it may just be equated with anxiety they can't put their hands on. As Dr. Edgerton says, "All their no's became equated with their nose."

It is of great interest, too, that most of the older women in the Johns Hopkins study, though married, were still having difficult relations with their mothers. They still felt acutely their mother's attitude toward them, especially if their mothers did not wholly approve of their looks. Some were sure they weren't "pretty enough to suit their mothers," or weren't as pretty *as* their mothers. This hurt even more than if they thought they weren't pretty enough for their husbands. Indeed, they hadn't dared be operated on until they had got their mother's consent.

But, with her consent, it was noticeable that after the operation their relations with her were greatly improved; they were also more sure of themselves in every way. One put it, "It was as if a veil had been lifted between me and other people, and for the first time I saw them as the good people they really were. So I could be more relaxed with them, too."

These reactions didn't happen immediately, though. For the first few days after the operation their anxiety and general sense of unworthiness was as strong as before. This was because the operation had drastically changed their self-images. And a self-image is something that has taken a long time to build up; it is not changed overnight. So, much as a girl may have longed to have her appearance altered for the better, the very alteration may upset her at first.

Suppose, she may think, her friends don't recognize her? Suppose, not recognizing her, she becomes even more isolated than before? There is no fear as great as the fear of loss of identity, of becoming a stranger in a strange world. This is the terrible fear of amnesia, or of having to cry out to someone you once knew and loved, "Look, look, this is me!"

Then some girls were afraid their new faces, even if recognizable, might bring about a loss of control. A sixteen year old said this before her operation: "I don't know whether it would get the better of me. If a girl has her nose done and she's radically changed and she's beautiful and gets rushed by boys and just because of the change in the nose everybody is paying much more attention to her, that naturally will all go to her head. She couldn't remain shy if she was. She would actually be forced to come out and have a personality change. If I had any control over it, I definitely wouldn't want to change inwardly but I don't know whether I'll have control or not."

After the operation she was worried sick for fear she might change inwardly and get ready for the boys to rush her—and they wouldn't. How awful she'd feel then!!

NEVER SATISFIED

There is also the matter of plain dissatisfaction. There are always some girls and women who spend all the money and time an operation costs—and then are never satisfied. One day I was in the office of a plastic surgeon waiting to interview him for this book. A really beautiful girl was impatiently waiting for him, too. "What," I wondered, "is she doing here?" When I had a chance, I asked the nurse. "Oh, she's here trying to convince the doctor to do her nose over," she replied. "First, it was too long, now it's too short. Then it will be too wide, then too narrow. But it's almost impossible to improve on an operation involving bone structure once it's done. Besides, what can you do to please a neurotic girl like that?"

Such girls have projected all their emotional and social problems onto their faces, and are trying to solve them from the outside in, instead of from the inside out. For this reason, plastic surgery is not for everybody. Certainly it is no magic wand to make a nasty temper un-nasty, a neurotic person un-neurotic or a shy, withdrawn person suddenly blossom out. A nose can be fixed in a matter of hours; habits of behavior take much longer to fix.

For this reason, too, many surgeons refuse to do nose-plastics on some people until they have first had one or more sessions with a psychiatrist. The surgeons realize they may be expecting them to do the impossible, and have the sense, born of long experience, to refuse.

HEALTHIEST YEARS

The teens are the healthiest years of our lives. Childhood diseases are practically a thing of the past; new illnesses are at a minimum; teenagers just don't get sick to any extent.

Yet how girls, at the height of their anxious period, worry about themselves just the same! They worry not only about acne and noses, but about odors, big or small breasts, too much hair on legs or chin, and hair the wrong color or the wrong kind on their heads.

If this weren't enough, their mothers worry for them about things like high heels and the harm they may do to their feet, wire bras and the harm they may do to their breasts, permanents and teasing and dyes and the harm they may do to their hair.

The fact is, this is such a worrisome time one can get ill just from worrying.

BAD SMELLS

Americans are obsessed with odors. "Bad breath" and "B.O." ads form a common part of our advertising.

Little girls don't smell; their sweat glands and sex glands are comparatively inactive. But after puberty they become very active and adolescents do smell.

In fact, all adults smell. They have skin-smells, breath-smells, hair-smells, armpit-smells, genital-smells, feet-smells. Odors in all these places are normal. Yet Americans fuss about them to the point where they are constantly dabbing on creams, lotions, liquids and sprays. The French think they're crazy. The French know that under the right circumstances, people can find each other's odors downright attractive. But, since we live in a culture that does fuss about them, we must conform.

Body odors are caused mainly by the decomposition of natural waste-materials, including perspiration and skin particles. These don't have an odor when fresh; only when they've been exposed to the air for some time.

Girls perspire much less than boys do, except under the arms. Men perspire, for instance, much more in the feet because of their tight, heavy shoes which lock the perspiration in.

But some girls perspire more than others or have worse breath than others because they eat highly spiced foods like raw onions or salami. Onion or salami sandwiches are among teenagers' "passions." After gorging on these, mouthwashes don't do much good, for as long as the spices remain in the stomach their odors will keep coming out through the mouth.

Spicy foods eaten at night can still show up on the breath in the morning because during sleep the production of saliva, which helps to neutralize odors, slows up greatly. The moral here is "Help by brushing the teeth before going to bed." And if the odor persists all day, use dental floss to get out the offending food particles hiding between the teeth, not a mouthwash that merely covers one odor with another for a short time.

Both girls and boys perspire more all over as a result of strong emotions, just as acne gets worse as a result of these. Exam time, for instance, is a bad time.

Just before menstruation is another bad time for girls. This is because all the glands, including the sweat glands, are temporarily more active at that time. But pre-menstrual or even menstrual odors are not nearly as noticeable as self-conscious girls think. A daily bath and regular changes of napkins will almost always keep them under fine control.

Is it true that a girl's hair smells during adolescence more than when she was a child? Yes, it is. The same sebaceous glands that act up on the face during acne, are also on the scalp. The greasy material they secrete clings to the hair, and the dust particles and microbes that are always in the air in turn cling to them. A weekly shampoo will wash them away. Meantime, few boys will get close enough to sniff these odors and make faces—again in spite of those fearsome ads.

UNWANTED HAIR

Unwanted hair on the face or chin is in the same category as smells —not nearly as obvious as girls think. Women like the "bearded ladies" of the circus are so rare as to be freaks, and then such hair is usually of hormonal origin. The "ladies" in question have many more male hormones than their due share.

Small amounts of unwanted hair can be removed in several ways. First, there is plucking by tweezers. This is fine for odd hairs or as a hurry-up solution on the face. But the trouble with plucking is the roots haven't been affected, any more than grassroots are affected when you pull out a few blades from the lawn.

Then there is rubbing off with wax depilatories, or shaving. These also are like mowing the lawn; the hair invariably grows back. Shaving, of course, is the cheapest and, no matter what anyone tells you, does not coarsen hair or make it grow back faster. Coarsening is a natural process that happens with age. A baby's hair is as soft as down. Few grown-ups can say the same.

Wax depilatories cost more than shaving. Besides, many people discover they are allergic to the chemicals involved. They should never be used on the face as there is great danger of their getting into the eyes.

Third, there is electrolysis, practically permanent and almost 100 per cent safe, if done by a really experienced and competent operator.

Here's how it works. A fine electric needle is introduced into the hair-canal, as far down as the root of the hair-follicle. This needle is the negative terminal of a low electric current which passes through the patient, who completes the circuit by holding the positive pole in her hand.

The current destroys the tissue of the hair-follicle. When the tissue has been destroyed, a bubble of hydrogen appears on the surface of the skin. This bubble is a sign to the operator to turn off the current and pluck out the hair, which is now literally "off because it's out."

Electrolysis demands patience on the part of both the operator and the girl, and patience is something adolescents are notoriously short of. But it takes quite a while to get rid of hairs one at a time. There may also be a slight irritation or swelling after each session, but this irritation is relieved by cold compresses, or it just goes away by itself.

Selecting a competent electrolysist is also a problem. But most skin specialists know at least one good one, and will recommend one if asked.

PERMS AND DEVILS

Girls and women being the creatures they are, they have always worried, among other things, because they thought they had too little hair, or too much.

In medieval days they thought they had too much. During the Dark Ages the idea got around that devils resided in the hair, particularly sexual devils, so women with a lot had to hide it under caps or kerchiefs, or cut it off when they retreated to nunneries, while orthodox Jewish women had to cut it off when they got married and put on ugly black wigs instead, so as not to attract other men.

During other ages, women worried about having too little hair and dreamed of hair long and lovely enough to excite the senses of men. From the Grimm Brothers' "Rapunzel, Rapunzel, let down your hair," to the poet Robert Browning who lamented the vanished hair of ladies of long ago:

> "Dear dead women
>   With such hair too,
>   What became of all the gold
>   Used to hang and brush their bosoms,

hair has been a great love of men. So whatever the current fashion, women spend a lot of time and energy on their hair. They tint it, curl it, uncurl it, tease it, pompadour it, singe it, tonic it or fluff it up with wire-rolls that make them look, as they walk down the street, like Medusas in shorts.

Also, they permanent it, or as the English fondly say "give it a perm." One even sees mothers dragging little girls as young as seven into beauty parlors for perms. Mainly, they drag them out again in anger, complaining the perm didn't take. Of course it didn't take. Until the sex hormones that nourish the hair come in strongly at puberty, the hair is much too fine to stand being chemically waved.

The New Yorker magazine once ran a cartoon showing a group of women coming out of a beauty parlor, with the caption, "Most of them look as if they hadn't been waited on." Before menstruation is established, that caption certainly applies.

DYED AND DEAD

Dyed hair used to be dead hair. One heard horror stories like that of the woman who woke up the morning after a dye job to find all her hair fallen out on the pillow. Seldom any more. Dyes today are pretty safe. Still, the hair can look dead, especially if a girl goes in for shoe-blacking black or tow-headed straw, and then doesn't bother to use oil-shampoos to put back some of the oils these harsh dyes take out. There are also occasional girls and women who are allergic to dyes. While their hair doesn't *fall* out, they do get severe headaches or skin eruptions, in unexpectedly remote places of their bodies such as around the genitals. To play safe, a "patch test" should be done each time before a new dye is used, though even if the patch test seems to work, sensitivity may develop during the actual dyeing. If that happens, the dye should be immediately shampooed out, then any that's left neutralized by a rinsing with peroxide, and the peroxide in turn shampooed out.

Dyes can also be very obvious. It isn't true that "nobody but her hairdresser knows for sure."

I was eating lunch one day at Altman's crowded tea room in New York. I found myself sharing a table with three teenagers who were chatting away like old friends. But something was definitely wrong with their appearance. "I have it," I said to myself. "It's their hair. They're all redheads, and none of them was meant to be. They simply don't have the skin for red hair."

Being a curious creature, I spoke up. "Do you mind if I ask you a personal question? Have all of you dyed your hair?" "Of course we have," they giggled. "Why, does it show?" "It shows," I answered. "What's more, I'll guess you all go to the same beauty parlor and use the same dye-pot." "Of course we do," they giggled again.

I changed the subject at that point. But I thought, "Why didn't someone tell them before? Why didn't someone say frankly that red hair on them was obviously wrong?"

For someone has to tell us; we can seldom see it for ourselves because we seldom see ourselves as we are. We do mayhem to our appearance by deciding on impulse to become blondes when our skin is swarthy, or go in for coal black when we are basically fair, just because we are at the moment too passive or too defiant of our mothers to resist those lovely pictures of someone else.

BECOMING A PERSON

Besides, dyeing one's hair no more solves any real problems than bobbing one's nose. That is, it doesn't for a girl who has the guts to become a *person*.

A person is someone who knows what she wants in life, but knows that getting it won't be easy.

A person is someone interested in ideas, as well as things. Things are well enough in their way, but humanity has not advanced by things, but by ideas. Ideas on how to do a better job and, better still, how to improve sanitation, cure infections, fight plagues, keep food more wholesome, build more comfortable houses, communicate with each other better and express more love.

As always, a story is in order.

There was a girl from Atlanta, Georgia, named Geraldine who was eternally dissatisfied. She expressed it in dyeing her hair first blonde, then red, then black. She became, in fact, a "beauty parlor addict" which in its own way is as insidious as a drug addict. Whenever she didn't know what to do "for kicks," off to the beauty parlor she went.

Now Geraldine happened to be an excellent swimmer and had recently saved a friend from drowning. But she didn't think about that; she tried to get a lift in other ways instead. Not a week went by but she was back taking a "beauty shot" of some kind. If it wasn't a dye-job, it was a haircut, a facial or a massage. Anything to let somebody do something *to* her, instead of doing or remembering what she had done herself.

OBSESSED WITH HER BODY

Eventually Geraldine landed in a psychiatrist's office. She wasn't sick enough to need it, but she sought psychiatry as another kind of kick. The psychiatrist was a very sane woman. She learned about the life Geraldine had saved, and got her talking about that, boasting about it even. Boasting about it and using it to raise her self-esteem. After a few sessions Geraldine was able to cut down on her beauty drugs and use some of her energy in volunteering as a guard at a children's pool instead.

It wasn't easy. No change is easy. But what it did for Geraldine's morale when, for the first time, she could answer the question "Who am I?" with, "I am a life-guard," instead of "I am just another girl with pink, green or yellow make-up and hair."

CONTACTS AND CONTESTS

"Men never make passes at girls who wear glasses."

Dorothy Parker said this but she was wrong. Men not only make passes at them; they admire them, make ardent love to them and marry them. There even was a recent Miss America contestant who paraded in glasses—and won. And 33 per cent of all Americans wear them today.

Still, some girls get upset over wearing them. The modern answer is contact lenses if one can stand the trouble and expense.

Contact lenses cost anywhere from a hundred to five hundred dollars. A Seattle doctor whose daughter insisted on getting them told her he guessed the lenses themselves were worth three dollars. The rest went toward the time involved in teaching her how to put them in and take them out.

Contact lenses often take weeks to get used to, with big tears running down one's face while one does. And since they are so tiny, they fall out of the eyes without warning in a dark movie-house or while crossing a busy street, and get lost. Besides, it is the rare girl who can wear them all day long, since they are foreign bodies in the eyes no matter how well they fit. They sometimes begin to irritate after a few hours; then they have to be taken out and the eyes rested before they can be put back in again.

With all this, a few girls swear by them since they are invisible and reflect no lights. And those who are really near-sighted find they can often get better correction with them than with anything else. They certainly do away with the very thick lenses that extremely near-sighted girls used to have to wear.

OUCH, MY FEET!

I once knew a delightful old doctor, a foot-specialist, who had an office that looked out on New York's Fifty-seventh Street, where all day long women of fashion paraded by. Between patients, he used to amuse himself by looking out the window at the women, rubbing his hands and chuckling, "They'll all come to me yet!"

Not all of them came, of course. But it's surprising how many did, a large proportion still in their teens. The statistics tell the tale.

Ninety per cent of us are born with perfect feet—the kind of feet you see in children, straight and square. But by the time we are twenty, at least 75 per cent have foot-troubles, and the miseries get worse as the years go by. One American company that manufactures so-called foot-remedies admits to doing a business of $35 million a year. And almost every candid snapshot of a girl shows her with her shoes kicked off under the table, or the pained expression on her face that says, "Ouch, my feet!"

BUNIONS

One of the chief foot-miseries is a bunion. Doctors call it a "hallux valgus." and define it as "any big-toe joint that juts away from a line parallel to the center of the body."

Some of us make our own bunions; others are practically born with them. Dr. Paul W. Lapidus, of New York's Hospital for Joint Diseases, stresses the born ones. Some of us, he says, are born with feet shaped more like a hand with the big toe flaring out and away like a thumb. Then we stuff that out-flaring toe into a hard, tight, in-flaring shoe and keep it there for years. A bunion is almost sure to result.

But this isn't all that happens. When we stuff our feet into tight shoes this way, nature tries to keep the two hard surfaces of shoe and sticking-out big-toe bone from rubbing against each other by forming a little cushion over the big-toe joint. This cushion becomes full of a soft fluid, and is called a "bursa." But alas! this bursa doesn't stay soft and cushiony. If the rubbing continues, it too gets hard and inflamed.

So now we have three hard surfaces rubbing against each other—big-toe joint, shoe and bursa. If the rubbing goes on, wretchedness is our lot. The wretchedness of pain, and eventually the wretchedness of arthritis. Both are a cry for help.

Almost as common as trouble from a bad bunion is trouble from a bad arch.

The human foot is wonderfully intricate. It was designed some twenty or thirty millions of years ago to do all kinds of good things, such as carrying us barefoot over uneven ground. For carrying us over uneven ground it was designed as a tripod, with the weight distributed mainly over three places—the heel in the back and the two big and little toes. We were meant to shift back and forth constantly among the three. The middle toes were mainly designed for swinging in trees. They were made curly and flexible, so they could curl around the branches and hang on. But few of us live in trees any longer, or use our middle toes for swinging from trapezes the way circus-performers do, so our middle toes have little to do. And almost none of us bounce around any more barefoot on bumpy ground except maybe girls on farms or in summer camps. Instead, we bang all day long against rigid pavements or rigid roads. So, with our middle toes practically useless, the rest of the tripod gets our full weight all at once instead of letting the weight shift back and forth. Either our long arch or our cross arch drops under the strain.

When our long arch drops, the result is called "flat feet." When our cross arch, or metatarsal, drops, it is called by the mouth-filling word "metatarsalagia."

Curiously, flat feet, which have had by far the worse publicity, usually give less trouble. For many flat-footers were born that way and their feet get adapted to their flatness and learn to function pretty well. The proof of this pudding is that many ballet dancers have flat feet and dance away without giving it a thought.

A Queen of Spain once took a publicity-trip through her kingdom. Thinking to please her, the women of one town offered her a gift of a pair of hand-embroidered stockings. The gift was curtly refused by the courtier whose duty it was to pass on such things. "The Queen of Spain officially has no legs!" he snapped.

Modern girls do have legs, and these legs do give pain in other odd places besides arches or bunions. Pain across the ball of the foot is one of them. This is different from the occasional pain of flat feet because it comes from that dropped metatarsal, or cross arch.

When the cross arch drops, the idea is to shift the weight away from the arching place by placing a built-up leather bar on the outside of the shoe. This bar is placed not over the arch itself, but just behind it, so that the weight of the body hits the bar instead. Or metatarsal pads can be placed inside the shoe, also just behind the cross arch.

Many women develop a corn on the little toe. Corns, like bunions, are the result of two hard surfaces rubbing against each other—hard leather and hard toe.

Extremely pointed, narrow shoes make the situation, of course, far worse. In fact, pointed shoes, as I write this, are giving doctors a field day. They say they are amazed at the staggering number of girls and women who come to them begging to have their little toes cut off, as Cinderella's sisters did, so they can squeeze their feet into even smaller and more pointed shoes! They don't seem to realize that it's the old story of nature abhorring a vacuum; as soon as you remove one toe, the others start to move over to fill in the empty place. If that isn't looking for trouble, nothing is.

But then young women have always looked for trouble as far as their feet were concerned—or let men talk them into it. Everyone knows about the old Chinese custom of deliberately crippling the feet from birth. Richard Carter, writing in *Life* magazine, describes this pretty custom: "To achieve the lily foot, as it was called, the feet of a Chinese girl-child were literally squashed in half. First the four small toes were tightly bound beneath the sole. A year or so later, when the toes were successfully deformed, the child's heels were doubled under too, until they approached the tip of the toes. The result was a foot that could fit into a silken boot no larger than a teacup, and a girl who could never walk again, but at most merely totter, quivering all over."

Then there was the crazy fashion called the "chopine." This was a high wooden clog like a stilt that originated in oriental harems but was enthusiastically taken up by European women. The chopine ran as much as two feet high so its wearers couldn't walk at all unless held up by servants on either side. Yet the chopine lasted in fashion for over a hundred years, with respectable women making up stories to defend it by saying it protected their feet from the dirt and damp, and courtesans not bothering to defend it at all.

Maybe some of this crazy foot-business came about because, as Havelock Ellis said, the female foot has always been a male fetish, and the last part of the body to be publicly uncovered. Many centuries after the breasts were bared, for instance, the foot was still hidden. Maybe people wanted the foot hidden and shown only to selected males as a sign of great intimacy, he believed. And since high heels enhance the daintiness of the foot and make it seem more removed from the everyday world, they gave the chosen men who were allowed to see it a greater thrill.

But whatever the reason, there is no question but that young men like high heels, and that young women impose this imprisonment on themselves to please them as well as to cater to their own vanities—because high heels make the foot look smaller and the legs look longer. So they totter about on them no matter how much they hurt.

Granted, many girls insist they cannot wear anything but high heels. They swear that when they switch to low, their calves hurt. They are right. Calves do hurt when one switches all at once. This is because the constant wearing of high heels shortens and tightens the tendons that run up the back of the leg. When these tendons are suddenly pulled down into normal position, they cry out.

But tight tendons can gradually be loosened. One way to do this is to plant both feet, without shoes, firmly on the ground quite far away from a wall, then to place both hands against the wall with palms turned out and to push against the palms, swaying the body back and forth and keeping the knees as straight as possible. This will exert a strong pull on the tendons and stretch them again. If this is done about a dozen times a day for a few weeks, flat shoes can be worn in comfort again.

Here's a piece of good news for young women. They get far less "athlete's foot" than men.

Athlete's foot has little to do with athletics. It is caused by a fungus like a tiny ringworm that likes to make itself at home between perspiring toes. It probably got its name because men perspire more than women, and athletes perspire more than most. But the fungus isn't choosy; any perspiring feet will do. Give it enough warmth and moisture and it grows and starts to itch.

That's why athlete's foot is far more common in the spring and summer than in the winter. People's feet are simply warmer in the spring and summer. That's why hikers tend to get it more than stay-at-homes, especially if they hike in heavy, closed shoes.

The American soldiers on the Island of Guam had a lot of trouble with athlete's foot. Then they noticed the natives didn't. They threw away their heavy, closed shoes and walked around barefoot until they were supplied with light shoes or sandals. It worked. That's another reason women get less of it. Their shoes are lighter and more open. And if they do get drying powders and lotions, they will usually get rid of the fungus in a short time.

PIANO LEGS AND BOW LEGS

You don't see nearly as many bow legs as you used to, because mothers now have the good sense to give their children vitamin supplements, or, if their children happen to be born with bow legs, to have them corrected at once.

"Piano Legs," or thick legs, are something else. There's little that can be done about these except to reduce all over. And even that doesn't help too much, since thick legs are more a matter of weight-distribution than of all-over fat.

TOO FAT

American women think they weigh too much, and start thinking so during the reawakening years.

In fact, adolescent girls think so much about overweight that, next to menstruation, it is their chief worry. Dr. Arthur Roth, director of the teenage clinic at the Kaiser Foundation Medical Center in Oakland, California, says that at least 15 per cent of the girl-patients come to the clinic because they want to get thinner. The doctor thinks most of them have fine, healthy figures and don't need to get thinner at all. There are only a few adolescent girls who are genuinely heavy. The others go to extremes, as in everything else, and compare themselves to abnormally skinny models.

Some girls, to be sure, are reasonably slim as children, but blossom out at puberty and stay blossomed out.

In their case, bad mathematics is the cause. The relentless mathematics of calories.

A calorie is a unit of power, or energy. It takes a certain number of calories a day to power us just as it takes a certain number of gallons of gas to power a car. But there's this difference; cars use fuel only when they are moving; we use fuel even when we seem to be lying still.

For even when we seem to be lying still, our hearts are beating and our lungs are breathing in and out. This takes a certain number of calories, and is termed the amount needed for "resting energy." Then there are the calories needed for "moving energy," and finally those needed for "growth energy."

Now doctors estimate that at the beginning of the growth-spurt of puberty, a girl uses about 2200 calories a day for the combined jobs of resting and moving. At the peak of the spurt, or during the time that she is both shooting up fast and getting menstruation established, the amount goes up to 2400. But once menstruation *has* been established and the growth-spurt ended, it drops back to what it was at the end of childhood, or 2000. This drop usually takes place around the age of fifteen in a girl. If she continues to eat as much now as she did before, she is almost bound to store the extra amount as unwanted fat.

Why does she continue to eat so much when she doesn't need it? Why isn't the amount of food she takes in more or less automatic, as it is with, say, a healthy cat, who usually gobbles from his dish just about what he can use, then stops?

But our development is far more complex than that of animals. We start out in life with a pretty good food-regulating mechanism, as the experiments with babies showed. But we lose this mechanism early. Soon all kinds of factors enter in, the chief of which is memory, especially the memory attached to the pleasant experiences of childhood—the days when we were very avid because we were very young.

Before we know it, we find ourselves trying to recapture those happy experiences by eating the foods that are associated with them. We do this all our lives; we do it in particular during adolescence when we feel tense and unhappy and restless and, sure no one loves us, decide we will love ourselves. And we will express this love by doing what our mothers once did for us—stuff something into our mouths.

But eating is more than a solitary pastime; it is a social event.

Is the crowd going down to the drug-store for cokes? A teenager simply must go along and have a coke, too, even though ordinary cokes are crammed with calories that may be the last thing in the world she needs. Is the crowd having a late snack of fat hamburgers or fattier bacon sandwiches? She downs a couple, too, though her dinner was more than enough.

Give up late-snack bacon sandwiches and cokes? That's like being asked to give up her friends!

Nothing in life is simple. The awakening years are particularly complicated. For then we are torn between wanting love from our parents and wanting to defy them. If our parents dare to tell us we are getting too heavy, we will eat all the more just to prove who's boss.

This is what happened to Judy Garland during her teens, only the "parent" Judy was defying was the studio for whom she was working. The columnist Joe Hyams tells how Judy sang in vaudeville from the time she was a kindergartner. Soon she was being spotlighted as the best of three sisters because she had such a big voice. But this meant professional school instead of regular school, and few childish pleasures like swimming because she might catch a cold and miss a day's work.

By the time she was thirteen, she was a movie star. In Hyams' words, "Judy grew up with M-G-M as her father and the whole world as her audience. Her mother often used the studio as a disciplinary threat and used to tell Judy to behave or she'd tell the studio on her. . . .

"The only thing Judy could do that she liked to do was eat. She stuffed herself with food at every meal. She sneaked in double malts between scenes, nibbled on chocolate bars at school, and grew unphotogenically fat. An M-G-M executive sent for her.

" 'You look like a hunchback,' he told her. 'We love you, but you look like a monster.'

"After this incident, a humiliating directive was sent down from the front office. No matter what Judy ordered for lunch, she was to be given only a small bowl of chicken soup.

"Judy's comment today is brief. 'The soup was well salted with my tears.' "

Then there's the matter of exercise. Teenagers take less exercise than they did before.

Everyone knows that exercise burns up calories. But as Professor Arthur Jersild of Columbia University points out, "One mark of childhood is a strong desire to be active. One sign of growing maturity is a strong inclination to sit down." And this desire to sit down comes much earlier and stronger to girls.

Even the girls who were tomboys at age eleven now make up all kinds of excuses to get out of gym. From junior to senior high school, says Dr. Jersild, the gym-excuses increase 400 per cent. This is due neither to illness nor menstruation, but to sheer lack of interest. They say they simply do not want to muss their fancy hairdo's or to get big muscles, or they just can't be bothered changing their clothes.

WIDE VARIATIONS IN WEIGHT

But since there are wide variations in normal weight as well as in everything else, Dr. Roth insists again that the typical girl is still not too fat, and that overweight is really a problem of the much later years.

To prove it, here are some tables of normal weight-ranges for ages thirteen to fifteen, according to bone structure:

Height in Inches	Weight in Pounds		
	13 Yr.	14 Yr.	15 Yr.
53	62-82		
54	66-85		
55	69-90	70-91	
56	73-95	74-96	
57	77-99	78-102	82-106
58	80-103	83-108	86-111
59	84-109	86-112	90-117
60	87-113	90-117	95-123
61	91-118	94-122	98-128
62	95-124	97-126	102-132
63	100-130	101-131	105-137
64	104-135	105-137	108-140
65	108-140	110-143	111-144
66	112-145	113-147	114-149
67	116-151	117-152	118-153

With all this, some girls with large frames never succeed in getting down to any extent no matter what they do.

For there is still a difference we don't understand in the way different people seem to be able to burn up food. Dr. William Wilkins of Johns Hopkins tells of a pair of 12 year old twins, one of whom weighed 87 pounds and had not pubesced yet, while the other weighed 143 pounds, was 3 inches taller, and had full breasts and pubic hair. Yet both ate about the same amounts. Why then were they so different? The speculation is that one twin inherited most of her genes from one parent, the other twin from the other. But, as I said, we don't really know.

ANOREXIA NERVOSA

A far more serious problem than over-weight during the intensely awakening years is anorexia nervosa, or the nervous inability to eat. This is confined almost exclusively to girls and may be the basis for the stories of girls who "simply faded away," since girls with their strong tendency to express emotions through the mouth have been known to die from it. They have been literally unable to swallow the complexities of adolescence, and slow death has been the result.

Dr. I. Newton Kugelmass says the great complexities they can't swallow are usually sexual, since the disease occurs mainly in sexually over-developed girls. By this he does not necessarily mean that such girls are indulging in any kind of sex, but are obsessed by sexual conflicts and thoughts. They have been known to blurt out to sympathetic ears questions like:

"Do all women almost die when they have babies?" "Can you get the sex-disease from someone breathing in your face like a cold?" "Can you get cured if you've had it, or do your children become idiots?" "Can you go crazy just from bad thoughts?"

Caught between these fears and conflicts and their natural romanticism and idealism, they have been left in a state of such suspended animation they could not extricate themselves, and starved to death.

The psychologist Dorothy Baruch describes their dilemma this way: speaking of both boys and girls: "Implicit in the teen-agers' questions and wonderings lie complaints that the sex education he's had, has attempted to stop him from believing that pleasure is permissible. It has failed to give him release from the fear that punishment must come as the result of enjoyment; that hurt or injury will result. It has failed to relieve him from self-condemnation. It has failed to answer his desperate need to like himself should he enjoy his body's feelings, and to know deeply and well that he is still a good person with human dignity, and that enjoyment does not turn him from a man into a beast."

Dr. Baruch believes that girls in particular need to have the horror stories counteracted by being firmly told, "Sex is basically good." Because knowing it is good, they will be more able to wait for full consummation.

As one girl said after hearing of the good side: "That helps a lot. I've been wondering if I could hold out until marriage. Lots of girls don't. I think they're mainly curious. Now that I know what it's really like, I won't have to do actual research myself." Nor will she have to stop eating as a form of resistance against her too-anxious thoughts.

TOO TALL, TOO FAST, TOO SLOW

"Too tall, too fast, too slow." These worries tag right along after too fat or too thin.

"Too fast" means a girl is developing ahead of her friends her own age. This worries her because she feels "different," something teenagers hate to feel.

"Too slow" means she is slow at developing, so again she feels different. If an underdeveloped girl of twelve tries to play with older girls, she may be rebuffed; playing with younger girls, she may be teased. In either event, the situation makes for much unhappiness. Dr. Roth says that one of his most rewarding moments came when a girl shouted happily to him across a busy waiting-room, "I've had it!" meaning that her long-awaited first menstrual period had arrived, and she had joined the crowd.

Yet late-maturing girls have an easier time in general than early-maturing because adults don't expect as much of them, and boys feel they are no threat. And too tall girls have the hardest time. Boys feel that very tall girls are a great threat and dislike going out with them, while tall girls feel self-conscious with short boys. This, plus the fact that adults usually expect more of tall girls than they are ready for, makes some tall girls crawl into a shell and take a long time to come out.

HYPOCHONDRIA AND ANXIETY

But most of these difficulties are usually ironed out in time. The early-maturing girl's friends catch up with her. The late-maturing girl starts to mature. The small girl grows. The tall girl stops.

Meanwhile, there's anxiety. When Professor Paul Landis of Washington State College distributed a questionnaire among 5000 students, asking "What disturbs you most?" he got answers like, "Being self-conscious of my new body," "Being afraid others won't like me," and "Being afraid I won't measure up."

The reassurance a teenager desperately needs is that she *will* measure up; she will be able to face the future as countless girls have done; above all, that normality has wide limits and ten chances to one she is within them.

As Dr. Roth so nicely puts it, "If the ultimate goal is to reach the time when everyone can take just the right amount of a 'Drink Me' potion like the one that made Alice in Wonderland shorter, or the proper size 'Eat Me' cake which opened Alice out 'like the largest telescope that ever was' . . . then let us hope that such a goal is never reached. Do you want to live in a world where everybody is the same size, has the same complexion, does things the same way, thinks as everyone else does about everything? I don't."

❋❋❋ 20 Time for Decision

From childhood, boys and girls step along quite different paths. They both struggle to acquire a sense of basic trust instead of mistrust, of self-reliance instead of shame and doubt, of initiative instead of guilt; they try earnestly to get themselves friends and learn how to work.

But there the sameness ends. When things get too tough for small boys, they have the privilege of exploding into violent or negative behavior. They can rough-house, play hooky, put smelly cheese behind the radiator or tacks on the teacher's seat. Most of this will be tossed off with a "boys will be boys." Not so with girls. A little girl is supposed to remain a "nice child" or a "little lady who doesn't muss her pretty clothes." And she more or less succeeds. You remember that at age ten far fewer girls than boys were brought to child guidance clinics because of behavior problems their parents couldn't cope with. And this wasn't because they didn't have negative feelings like their brothers had; it's just that a combination of habit and custom made them manage somehow to hold themselves in.

A REVERSAL AT SIXTEEN

But by sixteen or seventeen, things change. A girl isn't so successful at holding herself in any more. Around sixteen or seventeen Mary becomes almost as openly restless as her brother.

What is happening to her that she can no longer hold herself in?

Two things: First, for probably the first time in her life, she feels strong enough and free enough to express what she thinks. Second, she is smack up against what psychiatrists call an "identity crisis." Even as short a time as a year or so ago, she could play at living, endlessly try on new clothes and colored hairdo's, imagining herself someone else. Now she must choose, select one dominating identity. Work at becoming not merely *a* person, but a specific *kind* of person. Playtime is no more.

Yet making a choice is harder today than it ever was, because never before in history has a girl had so much to choose from. In older, less progressive societies, there was usually one main role cut out for her, and she followed it—or else.

In Biblical or agricultural times, she had to be a hard-working, productive wife and household manager. A thousand years before Christ, Proverbs 31 wrote the instructions plain: "She seeketh wool, and flax, and worketh willingly with her hands. She is like the merchants' ships; she bringeth her food from afar. She riseth also while it is yet night, and giveth meat to her household, and a portion to her maidens. She considereth a field, and buyeth it; with the fruit of her hands she ploweth a vineyard. She layeth her hands to the spindle, and her hands hold the distaff. She maketh herself coverings of tapestry; her clothing is silk and purple. . . . She maketh fine linen and selleth it; and delivereth girdles unto the merchant. . . . Favour is deceitful, and beauty is vain; but a woman that feareth the Lord, she shall be praised." And while the passage doesn't mention it, she was to do all this while almost constantly pregnant, or busy nursing and raising the results of her pregnancies. Small wonder then that beauty was vain and the command to dress in silk or purple seldom achieved.

As for deciding on schooling, there was little time for that for a girl, beyond learning to count on her God-given fingers. Nor was there even much time for love. A man like Jacob might toil seven years for the wife of his desire, then after getting the wrong girl toil seven more. But once he got her, the Bible is quite silent on the subject of married love. The stress was always on duty—a woman's duty in particular to follow her husband wherever he might lead, bear him as many children as possible and work from before dawn to sunset.

MEDIEVAL TIMES

In medieval times, however, the rules changed, at least for a woman of the upper class. Her role was to be that of a Romantic Lady who inspired chivalrous knights. She was to spend her time perfecting the arts of beauty, talking vague "love talk" and managing her trailing sleeves and intricate headdress with grace. There is hardly a word in the romantic literature about her rising while it was yet night, planting vineyards or laying her hands to the spindle. Instead, she was as much as possible to be an inspiring angel in human form.

MORE CHANGES

In the eighteenth century, the rules changed again. Now divinity in bodily form was out, while her ideal role was to perfect her intellect, as well as to have affairs with innumerable lovers, affairs replete with trappings like secret messages, trusted go-betweens, men hiding in closets —all the paraphernalia of what the French call *amour*.

Came the nineteenth century and intellect and *amour* were out. Sober Victoria ruled the waves, so the stress was once more on a woman prudish and passive, living almost completely through her husband and worshipping him as the essence of the lordly male. Tennyson expressed this when he wrote of the ideal Victorian wife:

> "Her faith is fixt and cannot move,
>   She darkly feels him great and wise,
>   She dwells on him with faithful eyes
>   I cannot understand: I love."

SUFFRAGETTES AND FLAPPERS

But worship of the male didn't last either. Soon suffragettes were starving and chaining themselves to fences, to wrest the vote from the lordly male. Lucy Stoners were refusing to take their lordships' names; frivolous flappers took their names but gave them no children, while other women were demanding half-a-dozen children plus an education plus a full-time job.

Is there any wonder that the modern girl at the climactic age of seventeen, with all of these roles to choose from—dutiful homemaker, romantic lady, submissive female, intellectual job-holder—is restless and confused? Whichever she chooses, she knows the course will not be easy or straight?

What makes it even harder is that the choice often hits a girl full-blown. Little boys have usually been asked all their lives by doting relatives: "What are you going to do when you grow up?" Many little girls have been dismissed with, "Look at her beautiful eyes and pretty curls!"

SHE DECIDES ON COLLEGE

Then our girl around seventeen decides she wants more than pretty curls, wants to go to college and preferably a college away from home. Her biggest job is sometimes not to make grades good enough to get into college, but to convince her family to let her go.

And some families do not convince easily. Some still argue that if there is a choice between brother and sister, it is brother, hands down.

The families who act like this are probably still influenced by ancient ideas like that of Aristotle, who thought the female had a "sort of natural deficiency," or by ideas like that of Governor John Winthrop of Colonial Massachusetts, who argued that the wife of a fellow-governor in Connecticut had gone insane because she had worked too hard at trying to learn how to read and write. "If she had attended to her household affairs and such things as belong to women," wrote Governor Winthrop in 1645, "and not gone out of her way to meddle in such things as are proper to men whose minds are stronger, she had kept her wits."

Are girls' minds inferior? Is a girl mainly a foolish "dimwit" or "bird brain" who can't balance a checkbook, much less do something more complicated like run a business, as TV comedies and cartoons like to quip for cheap laughs?

Not if you look at the results of modern I.Q. tests, which show girls are quite as intelligent as boys, though in different ways.

Quoting the writer Morton Hunt,

"From the age of four on, boys do better than girls at abstract words, arithmetical reasoning, induction and telling what is wrong with an absurd picture, while girls do better at language items, social questions and esthetic problems such as matching shapes. (Similarly, on college entrance exams, senior high school girls do as well as boys in an overall sense, but not subject by subject; they are markedly inferior to the boys in physics and in mathematical aptitude, but notably superior in English composition.) But none of this supports the traditional position of women. For the differences between the average score for boys and the average score for girls on the several types of I.Q. test items are not large, and do not show them to be two unlike species of human beings. Boys average better in arithmetical reasoning—but that does not mean most boys do better than most girls. The larger part of each group lies in exactly the same range of excellence. Most girls are better than most boys in verbal ability, and a minority of each sex is exceptionally excellent or poor, creating minor differences in the 'overall averages.' "

The notion that there are large differences, Mr. Hunt goes on, comes from the fact that we tend to think in terms of opposites—positive versus negative, good versus bad, active versus passive. So we are tempted to go on to think of male versus female, when they are not versus each other at all.

"To classify girls in terms of opposition to boys, calling them illogical and boys logical, for instance, is in itself a piece of elementary illogic. To state the truth accurately requires at least three propositions:

(1) Some men are highly logical, and so are some (but not quite so many) women.

(2) Some women are exceedingly illogical, and so are some (but not quite so many) men.

(3) Most men and women are in the same range of innate capacity for logical thought, which is far too little for the good of the human race."

Even within these small differences, a great deal depends on previous experience. A Yale University psychologist, Dr. G. Alexander Milton, was puzzled by the fact that a group of high school boys did seem to do a great deal better on certain logical problems. But then he remembered that one of the problems had had to do with a tramp rolling cigarettes from old butts. How many cigarettes, he had asked, was the tramp able to roll from 72 butts if it took six butts for each new cigarette? The correct answer was fourteen new cigarettes, but the girls had said only twelve. The blind spot lay in the fact that the twelve cigarettes yielded twelve new butts which the tramp again rolled to make two more, and the girls hadn't got this right because few girls roll their own. But Dr. Milton changed the problem to making extra cookies from leftover scraps of dough, which is something many girls do, and now most of them answered right!

Summing up, Mr. Hunt quotes another psychologist, Dr. Paul C. Berry, who concludes that most of the intellectual differences between boys and girls in our culture are due to the fact that many children grow up with the ideas constantly hammered into them that boys are reasonable creatures and girls intuitive creatures, and this results in a certain number of women without the ability to use their native abilities because they are just plain rusty. As Dr. Berry puts it, there are some women who can't think because they think they can't think—and so don't try.

So much for a girl's mental abilities. What about her body? What is the truth of another old-fashioned notion—that she "cannot stand the rigors of college life?" That since a man has a bigger head, a heavier frame and more powerful muscles, he is stronger than she?

The question is: Stronger for what? For hunting lions, for killing his fellow men with clubs, cutting down trees with a huge axe, tilling the soil with a heavy plow? Maybe. But hunting lions, cutting down trees by hand or tilling with a plow are hardly as important as they used to be. And when it comes to the real test—the test of true biological superiority—women are the stronger sex by far, not only in childhood but right along the line.

Consider some more vital statistics. Adult males are now more prone to heart disease, bronchitis, pneumonia, ulcers, anemia, tuberculosis, accidents and infections. Blindness is one-third more common, gout is almost completely a male monopoly, and even in cancer the statistics favor female cures against male. But the final test is the survival of which I spoke in an earlier chapter, and in nearly every civilized country in the world for which the United Nations has collected data, the life-expectancy for a newborn girl is five to seven years longer than for a boy.

But strength is not only a matter of longevity; it is a matter of being able to meet crises. Here are a few more things to ponder:

During World War II in London, nearly 70 per cent more men than women were found to be suffering from emotional shock as a result of the constant bombings. In the concentration camps on the Continent, far fewer women broke down. Women taking necessary injections to prepare them for army service fainted far less often than men. And studies by the U.S. National Aeronautics and Space Administration show that women will probably even prove in the long run better able to stand the hazards of space flight—better both psychologically and in the actual handling of controls.

Granted that women tend to have highs and lows of energy rather than a steady supply because of the up-and-down rhythm of their sex hormones, all this still hardly adds up to their being the "weaker sex" or the "lost sex" or the "second sex" or the "dim-witted sex," as the silly jokes like to say.

On the other hand, it doesn't add up to women being just like men either. For men and women are not alike, but complementary. There are small but profound differences between them, so that together they form a unity, but of subtly different parts.

The Danish writer Isak Dinesen expressed it:

> In order to form and make up a Unity, in particular a creative Unity, the individual components must needs be of different nature; they should even in a sense be contrasts. Two homogeneous units will never be capable of forming a whole, or their whole at best will remain barren. Men and women become one, a physical and spiritually creative Unity, by virtue of their dissimilarity. A hook and an eye are a Unity, a fastening; but with two hooks you can do nothing. A right-hand glove with its contrast the left-hand glove makes up a whole, a pair of gloves, but two right-handed gloves you throw away. . . . An orchestra is a unity, and may be perfect as such, but twenty double-basses striking up the same tune are Chaos.

> A community of but one sex would be a blind world.

Yet, knowing all this, a seventeen-year-old girl still has to ask herself, "If I do get to college, shall I let the brains I have show? Shall I study as hard as I am able, make as good grades as I can, or more or less hide my mental abilities for fear that showing them will keep me a hook without an eye?"

Alas! These questions are not easy for her to answer, since getting the reputation for being a "brain" *will* often hinder a girl from getting a man.

It will hinder her because men, and young men in particular, are desperately afraid of "pushy" women. They are afraid for a basic reason that has to do with sex.

A man's part in the sexual embrace can be summed up as the three P's of Pride, Pleasure and Procreation. Pride is in many ways the most important because a normal man's part in sex is active. He cannot even begin to engage in intercourse without doing something active like having an erection. Then he cannot complete it without maintaining that erection for a fair length of time, and carry everything through to discharge or orgasm. All this is extremely visible and positive; whatever he does, or fails to do, is there to be seen. And if the accent is the least bit on failure of this visible activity, his pride is deeply touched. He is not virile or "manly." He is a mouse.

A woman, on the other hand, has the receptive or responsive part to play in sex. Her vagina is not an active organ in the same sense his is; the most she does as a rule, once intercourse has started, is to meet her partner halfway. Indeed, she can meet him even less than halfway. She can do practically nothing, merely simulate pleasantly, and the act can be completed. Her pride will not be touched.

Now men are deeply afraid that abnormally pushy women will put them on their mettle sexually; will make demands on them they cannot visibly meet. And they carry over this sexual fear into many other spheres of life. They run from too obviously successful or aggressive women whom they call "man-eaters" or "devils" or "teasers," with the result that many girls still have to play dumber than they really are, in order not to frighten off beaux.

Similar reasons persuade girls to let boys do almost all the courting, the telephoning and asking for dates, the paying of bills like restaurant checks, all the other active things that affect a young man's public pride.

An old-fashioned girl, of course, has let men do things like these for centuries. Custom and teaching made her automatically let men pick up handkerchiefs for her she was well able to pick up for herself, open doors she was well able to open, carry packages she had more than enough strength to carry herself.

A modern girl who has sat all day next to a boy in college, or has a job as good as his, often has to deliberately remember to let men do such things for her. She often has to remember to seem to know much less about politics than she really does know; or, when playing games like ping-pong, to stop herself short and let her fiancé win when she can easily beat him.

"Acting dumb" this way is even harder to follow, of course, when the advice she gets from home is contradictory.

When Uncle Henry telephones her at school on Sunday and asks: "Did you have a date last night?" while on Monday mother writes, "Don't go so deep into philosophy no man will be good enough for you." When on Tuesday Aunt Mary sends a note advising her, "Prepare for a profession. You have plenty of time to get married," and on Wednesday Grandma says, "Aren't you engaged yet?" a girl can be confused for fair.

Yet this kind of confusion is perhaps unavoidable in changing times like ours. It may be unavoidable altogether, since a girl's role has never been clear-cut and never will be.

Yet getting as much education as possible is still vital, if only because education develops a girl's personality as nothing else can. Education in its best sense adds to the moral strength she originally got from her parents, the new and different kind of strength she gets from the wider college world. And this double strength prepares her for greater happiness at the end of her days. Modern women who usually start childbearing and child-raising in their twenties have another twenty or more years to live after their children are fully grown. And it is a pitiable sight to see such older women spending these twenty years running frantically from one game of bingo to another, taking one cruise after another, or just sitting on a park bench in places like Miami or Los Angeles staring into space. Their own biological gifts, plus the miracle of today's medicine, have added years to their life, but not life to their years.

The only thing that can add life to one's years is to continue to create and to grow, and an interest in creating and growing comes from habits of work and of curiosity learned when young. The girls who start college and drop out before they get a degree—and they add up to almost 50 per cent of those who enter—seldom acquire these habits. The girls who do not even finish high school certainly do not.

The skimpily educated "baby doll" may be appealing enough to get by and have a wonderful time at eighteen, nineteen or twenty. She hardly will be at forty, fifty, or sixty. The aging doll who still dresses like an adolescent is either boring or pathetic. Men run from her like the plague. In fact, as men get older they often do a turnabout and find intelligent women a source of genuine comfort since older men are more sure of themselves, and do not feel as sexually threatened.

Speaking as an older man, Ben Hecht says, "There are many exciting personalities to be found who can stimulate you, but I have come on few who can make you feel content, as if some human sunlight were warming you." It is this quality of contentment men ultimately seek in a woman, and they do not find it in an eternal child bride or baby doll.

A COMPANION TO HERSELF

Education, to be sure, does not solve all a woman's problems. There have always been women with little or no education who had this quality of human sunlight; who continued to function well in old age as warm grandmothers. But the proof that education does solve many problems is shown by the fact that sociologists find divorce far less frequent among college-bred couples than among those who are not, and report that attendance at night school or college refresher courses by both men and women has gone up in the United States alone from two hundred thousand to two million in the past forty years.

And if nothing else, education makes a woman continue to be a good companion to herself. Every second woman in the United States is a widow by the time she is seventy, and so technically alone again. A single woman is never completely alone as long as she can continue to hobnob with the great minds of the ages through books.

❈❈❈ 21 True Love

All of us suffer the same basic fears—the fear of loneliness, the fear of rejection and inferiority, the fears of pain, illness and death.

When we are young, illness, pain and death seem far away. Loneliness and rejection do not. The adolescent girl feels herself one of the loneliest people in the world. Her greatest dread is the dread of emotional isolation—of being "left." No adolescent has sufficient emotional resources within herself to carry on for very long alone.

So whether a girl in her late teens wants a college education or not, she certainly wants and needs to fall in love. Full and brimming over more than ever, she wants a real relationship with a real boy—a boy as lonely as she.

Love has been described in so many ways one can't begin to count them. Two of the best modern definitions are those of psychoanalyst

Erich Fromm and writer Ben Hecht. Fromm calls love "the union of two lonelinesses." Ben Hecht describes it as "the only gateway out of solitude . . . the sudden hilltop of companionship that adds a sense of genius to living." Speaking of his own early love-days, Hecht goes on: "All that was sweet in living lay in those warm hours, in those hours he bloomed like a field of poppies; his heart opened to rain, wind and light; he looked on himself with new eyes; he visited humanity and felt the nearness of God."

WOMEN DIFFERENT

This sudden hilltop of companionship comes with the same blinding radiance to both boys and girls. Still, there are differences between male and female lovers.

One difference is that fantasy-life continues much longer in girls. Once a boy gets into a relationship with a real girl, he is apt to give up his fantasies about "dream women," such as movie heroines or pin-ups. A girl does not. She often continues her dream-life much longer—even after an actual male is on the scene.

Sometimes this "dream lover" is a national hero like a Beatle, with girls getting together in fan-clubs to adore him. Sometimes, more curiously, it is a person in the girl's own past, a person who continues to haunt her as did Nina's dead fiancé in O'Neill's *Strange Interlude*. Sometimes it is a religious figure whose bride she yearns to be.

The dreams in these instances may have an almost obsessive character, as seen in the mass feminine hysteria over the death of Rudolf Valentino, a hysteria far out of proportion to his fame. Thousands of girls and women stood in line night and day in order to get a view of his body, and came away in a trance—girls and women with perfectly good friends and husbands of their own. Valentino could have been nothing else to them but a full-blown dream lover. If he couldn't be seen and touched in life, he had to be seen and touched in death.

FROM ABOVE

It is interesting, too, that a great many male dream lovers are imagined as coming down from above.

The myths and stories of all ages tell of women dreaming of a beloved who will come down to them this way—a god from Olympus who will catch them up in his strong arms, an eagle who will enfold them with his mighty plumage, a knight who will swoop down, lift them onto his high horse and carry them away. Men dream otherwise. They dream mainly of mermaids who will rise up from the sea below.

This difference in dreams is probably a symbolizing of the actual sexual scene—the man enfolding from above, the woman enticing from below. It has been carried over by modern women in the worship of the airplane pilot or astronaut—the tall, strong Lindbergh or Shepard who triumphantly glides down from the skies and receives an almost hysterical kind of female love.

The English psychiatrist Dr. Esther Harding says that a common feminine dream is that of an airman swooping down from overhead in his plane, with the dreamer catching hold of part of the plane and being carried up and away with it into the heavens as if by some kind of magic kite.

NORMAL IN ADOLESCENCE ONLY

Dr. Harding makes the point that while this obsession with dream lovers is common and normal during adolescence, it is not in later years. If clung to persistently, it will make it impossible for any real man to satisfy the woman. One real man may be dismissed as "too short," another disdained as "too dumb," another shunted off as "too poor," while still another is "so awkward he falls all over his feet."

These criticisms, of course, are sometimes valid and genuine, but when they persist and all available men have something wrong with them, they suggest that all the men around are being compared to a Dream Prince who does not and cannot exist.

SOUL-MATES

Another common characteristic of late adolescence is the looking for "soul-mates," and this again is more common in girls.

"Soul-mates" also have a somewhat dreamlike character. A girl falls in love instantly without even getting a good look at a fellow "across a crowded room," or she falls in love after drinking a magic love-potion as in the opera *Tristan and Isolde*. But unlike *Tristan and Isolde* or *South Pacific*, where the instant passion lasted forever and a day, in real life this kind of love usually disappears as quickly as it came. The spell is broken and the glamor is gone, until she falls "madly" for someone else. "He's divine," she sighs today, and "He's impossible," she shouts tomorrow, until she finds a new divinity next week.

Dr. Harding thinks dream lovers and soul-mates, passing as they should be, are not occasions for laughter. They are necessary steps in a girl's development toward a more mature kind of love. They postpone actual sex-relations and give a girl time to have an emotional experience she needs first.

They also release a great store of creative energy—a store so great it doubles and triples the energy-burst of puberty. There's an old saying that "the engaged girl blooms." The girl who is merely advancing toward engagement—advancing by way of slow emotional experience—becomes too as a sleeper who awakes.

Under the impetus of a similar awakening, sculptors have burst forth with the creative energy that formed great works like Pygmalion's Galatea. Musicians have created great music as did Beethoven while under the spell of his Immortal Beloved. And painters have painted as did Renoir his glorious series of Golden Girls, and Mary Cassatt her glorious series of Golden Children.

This burst of creative energy may be the true meaning of the ancient proverb, "It is better to have loved and lost, than never to have loved at all."

WOMEN AND PAIN

But perhaps the most important difference between male and female love lies in a girl's greater attraction to pain.

There's little question that girls and women seem more attracted to pain and suffering than boys. Girls are enormously attracted to professions like becoming medical missionaries, nurses or Sisters of Charity, where they get great satisfaction from relieving suffering, while it is common knowledge that a sick or retarded child will often receive far more of a mother's devotion than a healthy child, and be mourned more if it goes.

But above all, Dr. Helene Deutsch believes women are attracted to suffering in love. "Every girl and woman," she says, "longs in her heart for at least one great romance that includes suffering and pain."

Maybe this suffering gives their love a sense of high drama it otherwise would lack. Maybe much of the pleasure comes as a result of the suffering, just as the pleasure of resting comes after hard work, or of eating after hunger. But the stories of the great romances of history that women sigh over always seem to mix pain with pleasure. Eloise suffers tortures over her beloved Abelard, Juliet agonizes over her Romeo, and Joan of Arc's story would shrink to nothing without her painful love affair with France and her tragic death.

I repeat, however, this is quite different from seeking suffering for its own sake, or deliberately prolonging it when it can be cut short. The well-worn tale about the woman who boasts, "My husband doesn't love me any more; he hasn't beaten me lately," is describing a most abnormal type. And when the German writer Nietzsche said, "Visiting a woman? Get out your whip!" he was promptly countered by an Englishman who replied, "Nine out of ten women would have torn the whip out of his hands. That's why he was careful never to go near any of them."

Even the large number of women who are attracted to alcoholics, to the point of yearning to marry them, want to do so with the idea of reforming them, or of getting eventual pleasure out of what they have achieved. But it is not normal for women to enjoy staying with an alcoholic, or any other severe neurotic, if tragedy is going to be the result.

Finally, the normal woman not only does not seek pain, she does not brag about unavoidable pain when it does come. Nor does she continue to wallow in it all her life. It's all very well for an adolescent to go crazy over songs about economic cripples, and wail:

> He doesn't hang diamonds around my neck
> And all he has is an unemployment check.

Later this kind of song should not be nearly as appealing. And certainly, says the psychiatrist Dr. Leon H. Saul, the girl or woman who always has "terrible" menstrual pain, "terrible" childbirth pain, "terrible" pregnancies, is emotionally sick.

TO MARRY OR NOT

St. Paul said, "It is better to marry than to burn," and women do burn to be married. What's more, they burn earlier today than they have for a hundred years.

A woman burns and yearns for marriage because marriage not only means sex, it means social status, entry into the adult world and founding a family. And mating, getting married and founding a family are deep

biological instincts in a woman. Besides, she was in all probability
brought up in a married family, so marrying becomes the natural thing
to do. Dr. John Levy says,

> First impressions are strong impressions. Adults cannot help reliving in
> fashion the kind of life they knew in childhood. The warmth and the intimacy
> of the family group becomes synonymous with life itself. Even if the warmth
> seems suffocating at times and the intimacy contentious, we are so bred up to
> them that we cannot exist in any other atmosphere any more than the pro-
> verbial fish out of water. . . .
>
> Idealists, troubled by the obvious deficiencies of the marriages they see
> around them, are forever devising new systems guaranteed to run with an
> oiled precision. Free love, companionate marriage, easy divorce, state care of
> children. . . . Logically almost any one of these schemes is superior to the
> curious institution we call holy matrimony. Unfortunately, logic is not very
> effective in ordering people's lives. Psychologically, these Utopian systems
> made a fundamental blunder. They ignored the point we have just been
> making: that marriage begins in infancy. . . . The most perfect system
> fails if it does not meet the expectations formed in childhood. We make
> ourselves wretched very frequently by adhering to foolish outworn ideas
> about marriage, but I fear we should be even more miserable without them.

So normal girls yearn to be married, and they yearn today earlier
than they have in a hundred years.

The greatest fear women have always had, as I said, is the fear of
being left. Not so much the fear of being left financially stranded or dependent on the bounty of relatives, as the fear of being left emotionally
stranded—everything implicit in the terrible thought, left behind by life
itself.

Today, with the memory of two devastating wars behind them and
the anxiety over total annihilation in the next war, the fear of being
left is even stronger. So women reason that if they are married and their
men go away and do not come back, they will at least have had some
shared time together, some memories built up that they can keep and
savor all their lives.

Then many girls today grasp at early marriage as a quick solution
of their identity crises. The University of California psychologist Nevitt
Sanford tells of studies showing college seniors to be far less sure of themselves than college freshmen.

They arrive as freshmen quite confident of the kind of person they
are or want to be. By their sophomore year they are less sure and start

asking: "Why have I come? What am I here to get ready for?" By their junior year they are overeating and oversleeping to postpone answering these questions. And by their senior year they are so near to having to answer them, so close to the moment when they will have to move out from the protection of school into a strange big world, they find themselves quite at sea.

Instead of facing the matter out, many girls grab at what seems the easy solution of becoming "Mrs. So-and-so."

One girl put this neatly when she said, "I can't decide whether to go home and try to solve my problems or to stay here and get married."

Needless to say, marriage would plunge her into a dozen new and more complicated problems. But that isn't how it looks during the exciting days before. As a result, today one in every eight girls is a "Mrs. So-and-so" even before she graduates.

A third reason for the rush into early marriage is financial. Young couples at the present time actually have the money to get married on. In America, young wives work at well-paying jobs, while husbands study or until they earn enough, making it much easier to walk up the white-carpeted aisle.

In Ireland, one of the poorest countries in the world, marriage is not common until around the age of 30. In 1929, when things were very bad, the average marriage age for Irishmen was as high as 35, and for women as high as 29. It has recently dropped to just over 30 for men, and just over 27 for women. Sixty-six per cent of all Irish males between the ages of 20 and 29 still remain bachelors, and vast numbers of both men and women die single.

Compare this with America, where only 7 per cent of women in their early thirties were reported single in the prosperous 1960s, against 15 per cent in 1940, a 50 per cent drop in spinsterhood in twenty years. The average age of first-time marriages in the U.S. today is 23 for men and 20 for women, with more girls marrying at 18 than at any other age.

Another reason for early marriage is that teenagers often feel themselves a group apart. They think of themselves as "we" and the rest of humanity as "they." And the we's, like all apart-groups, tend to cling together, plunging into marriage so they can cling more closely and become a twosome against the world.

Probably the biggest reason is the general speeding up of everything. Girls rush into early marriage, says Dr. Jane Pearce, with the wistful hope that all the necessary preliminary living they may have skipped will suddenly be made up now. They try to make this one tight relation make up for the chumship they may have missed, the sense of initiative they didn't develop or the independence of will. They get a "now or never" attitude that becomes exaggerated to the point of panic. They themselves whip into a lather of haste and urge a boy on. And since the boy, too, is panicky, he also needs less urging than before.

Yet with all this, tight intimacy cannot be rushed. Research bureaus tell us that engagements of three months or less are five times as likely to lead to quick divorce as engagements of six months or more.

LOVERS' QUARRELS

But whether the engagement is long or short, lovers still often quarrel bitterly while it lasts. Why do they quarrel? Why, when things are going so smooth, do they suddenly go so rough?

To understand this, we must remember that we all constantly are pulled back toward our childhood. We are children so long that we never quite get over it—no, none of us, not even the most mature.

Now a girl almost always chooses a boy, Dr. Jane Pearce believes, because he reminds her of her parents, and the relationship she had with her parents from her earliest days. Particularly the relationship with her mother and the ambivalence it contained. There was the cozy relationship with the good mother who was all-giving and a source of endless satisfaction. There was the terrifying relationship with the angry mother who was frightening when angry, or who imposed strict rules. So we get the violence and terror of lovers' quarrels when the lover acts, or seems to act, like the bad mother, and the delights of making up when the lover becomes the all-giving good mother again.

But the chosen one proves himself in time much more like the good mother than the bad, just as the real mother was probably more often good than bad, so the quarrels cease and he becomes the True Love. When this happens, for a time he is greatly overidealized, just as the original mother was, though the relationship still may fluctuate from certainty to doubt and back to certainty again. When certainty finally prevails, the girl hurls herself into his arms with a sigh of relief, and the marriage takes place.

That is why Cupid is always portrayed as an infant. He symbolizes the infant's desire for all-acceptance and all-forgiveness. And since the boy has been going through the same experiences as the girl, since he, too, is looking for all-acceptance and all-forgiveness, Cupid does his best. But he has a big job on his hands.

✳✳✳ 22 The Giant Step

So our girl in her late teens or early twenties is ready to be married. Ready to take the giant step out of her parents' home into a strange new home of her own.

THE BOY NEXT DOOR

Whom does a normal girl marry? If she is wise, she marries a man who needs her, in women the "need to be needed" is terribly strong. Then she marries a man with her general background, tastes and ideas. She may be madly attracted to the stranger, the man who is excitingly different, but it takes a brave and unusual girl to make a success of such a marriage after the excitement has worn off. And if she goes so far as to cross the color line, she has to be strong indeed. It is far better to make a go of it with the equivalent of the boy next door.

A girl usually finds things easier, too, if she marries a man a few years older than herself. An older man is more of a replacement of her idealized father than a man her own age since he embodies some of her father's strength. And while a man expects his wife to be a mother to him as well as a mistress no matter what her age, if he is much younger than she is she may again be headed for trouble. With a much younger man, her motherly drives may be so strong they get in the way and inhibit normal sexual relations. An opera-singer eloping with her young chauffeur—such marriages almost never work out.

But whomever a girl marries and no matter how propitious the situation, things as a rule are far from easy for her at the start. This is because for a girl the giant step means not only wrestling with new chores like housekeeping, budgeting, sharing all kinds of intimacies she has not shared before, but also jumping into practically the whole new world of sex.

Most grooms have had a certain amount of recent sex-experience, with genital play at least. What is more, it has been genital play to the point of orgasm or discharge. Indeed, according to Dr. Milton Sapirstein, genital play including orgasm is not only practically universal during male adolescence, it is also a necessity as preparation for marriage and mature sex relations. Orgasm to a man is such a tremendous and demanding experience, he can seldom achieve it with a partner with any degree of self-confidence unless he has first had practice in achieving it alone.

By rediscovering the capacities of his genitals during his teens; doing this moreover without the complexities that interaction with another person brings, a man builds up confidence in his ability to give and receive sexual satisfaction. Genital play in this sense is a helpful bridge in a boy's development from an immature child to a potent man able to "consummate a marriage" in the literal sense of the words.

NOT THE SAME IN GIRLS

It is not at all the same in girls.

Most girls, true, do engage in a period of genital play in childhood. But girls seldom resume it after that, since it is not a bridge or preparation for anything. But kissing, petting, necking, courting, or whatever you happen to call it at the moment, is a preparation. That's why almost every culture has permitted some form of them.

Some modern girls, to be sure, go beyond kissing and courting, and have sex-relations before marriage. But this is not the same as having them after marriage. Sex before marriage almost always involves great secrecy, as well as flouting of conventions. And while some girls can ignore conventions and achieve a good relationship with a man nevertheless, most girls cannot. Most girls need the blessings of society before they can relax and fully enjoy sex.

To a girl, moreover, the first sex-experience is seldom pleasurable. This is another reason she is fortunate if she can have it within marriage. For then it will take place with a man who has genuine tenderness to offer her, who is willing to stay around and give her the emotional support she craves after the act is over, rather than with a man who may be extremely ardent before, but hurries off after and leaves her emotionally high and dry.

And since enjoyment of sex usually includes the enjoyment of orgasm, let's look more closely at orgasm and see what it entails.

THE THREE P'S

Sex, as I said, can be summed up in three P's: procreation, pleasure, and pride. From the long-range point of view, which we must always consider, procreation is by far the most important, since without procreation there could be no continuation of the race.

Now a man cannot possibly continue the race without orgasm, because without an orgasm he cannot release the necessary sperm. But a woman can. A woman can get pregnant even though she has never had an orgasm in her entire life. This is because the release of an egg that joins up with a sperm is not dependent on orgasm. An egg is released automatically once a month by ovulation. So female orgasm is simply a nervous climax to sex-relations—a climax that women describe all the way from "the most exquisite sensation" to "a mild general glow"—and as such it is a comparative luxury from nature's point of view. It may be thought of as a sort of pleasure-prize like the prize that comes with a box of cereal. It is all to the good if the prize is there, but the cereal is valuable and nourishing if it is not.

So, since genital play or other experiences involving orgasm are necessary preparations for procreation or the full consummation of marriage in a man but not in a girl, a girl can walk up the carpeted aisle quite unprepared for what is to take place.

TALKING AND DREAMING

Then a girl is usually unprepared for sex and marriage in other ways. A man has done a great deal of advance talking and dreaming about sex. The so-called "wet dreams" that include spontaneous emissions, are practically universal. But girls seldom have comparable dreams. Nor do they talk to each other about sex as frankly as boys do. If they talk at all, it is mainly fantasy-talk on romantic subjects like love or the longing for love.

Girls also tend to delay actual sex-relations because they know a man's desire is far greater if he is granted true intimacy only after a long period of wooing; after he has fought for his woman as men have fought since prehistoric times.

All this—a girl's greater reluctance to talk about sex, her greater preoccupation with fantasy, her instinctive knowledge that she needs to delay matters in order to be fought for—postpones actual experience for her until after marriage as a rule, and brings her to the altar in a quite different state than that of her groom.

THE KINSEY REPORT

The Kinsey Report confirms much of this. One of the most significant of Kinsey's findings—a finding buried for the most part among his charts and statistics—is that boys reach their peak of sex-interest at a very early age. A boy of around eighteen is probably as sexually eager as he ever will be. He reaches a peak of sex-interest in his late teens, and from then on his interest goes straight down decade by decade until he reaches the indifference of old age. A girl's curve is entirely different. A girl's sex-interest is just beginning to be awakened in her late teens. It does not reach a peak until her early thirties. Then, instead of going down, it stays at practically peak-level for some ten or fifteen years before it starts to decline.

This accounts for one of life's little ironies: A man and woman rarely meet in sex interest until they are both in their thirties. Before the thirties, her interest has been comparatively little, his very great. In the forties his may be less than hers. Only during the thirties when his intense eagerness has subsided and hers has risen, do they meet on more or less common ground.

SHE'S "COLD"; HE'S "INSATIABLE"

This explains why, if a man and woman marry early, as most modern couples do, he may accuse her at first of being "cold" while she may accuse him of being "insatiable." But both accusations are seldom just.

The bride may not be so much "cold" or "frigid" as inexperienced. She may be attempting to do the difficult job of making an about-face and thinking of something she has avoided for years as "forbidden" as suddenly something permissible and "good."

The husband may be in a different plight. Great sex-interest does not necessarily mean great sex-power. The typical groom of twenty-two or three may have great sex-eagerness but that hardly means he is a sheik. Even more to the point, the experience he has had before marriage was hardly all happy experience. On the contrary, those very wet dreams with their uncontrollable emissions, those very experiments with genital play, may have made him almost as anxious as self-confident. The average groom is not nearly as wild as he has been painted. He is neither a Clark Gable nor a James Bond who, thanks to the courtesy of cunning script-writers, makes all women faint at sight.

He is rather a man who still has in him much of the small boy who was as terrified of sex as pleased by it. And since none of us ever forget our childhood, much of this terror remains in him no matter how grown-up and dashing he tries to appear.

But the good Lord forbid that he admit this terror out loud! Especially since it affects his pride! So instead he often does what we all do where our pride is concerned—project our failings onto someone else. Utter the ancient buck-passing cry, "It's all her fault, Lord, not mine!" And much of his insatiability may be due merely to the fact that he is trying to overcome his terror by learning to do better. And learning takes time.

That is what the honeymoon has always been for—to give both bride and groom some uninterrupted practice time, though the conventional two weeks cannot even begin to scratch the surface of all they have to learn.

THE WOMAN ADJUSTS

How does a normal woman meet this introduction-to-marriage situation—a situation that is admittedly never easy? She meets it by doing the larger share of adjusting and compromising. By not swinging from the extreme of Victorian passivity in sex to the modern extreme of expecting full pleasure on the dot.

Adjusting and compromising are dull words, to be sure, like patience. They do not have the glamour of words like "secret meetings," "dating," or "being engaged." But adjusting and compromising are what normal women have always done just the same.

Normally wise women have always done the larger share of adjusting to sex because they knew they had to. They have also done it because it's easier for them than for their mates. Here's why.

EASIER FOR A WOMAN TO ADJUST

A man has to do something active in order to engage in sex-relations. He has to first get going, then stay going, in an obvious positive way.

Now it is not simple for a man to either get going or stay going, because sex is not just a local activity, it is an extremely complicated activity involving his whole body and nervous system. All kinds of messages have to be sent from his brain and nerves to his sex-organs before he can get up the necessary steam. And if anything interferes with these messages, he can be sunk.

Animals are different, though people are always citing the example of animals. "Aren't male animals almost uncontrollable when a female comes along?" they argue. "Aren't stallions and male dogs always ready and raring to go?" Yes, they are. But only in season. In season, stallions and dogs are subject to strong hormonal pressures. When these hormonal pressures are present, they are single-minded. When they are absent, they couldn't care less.

But the human male is neither a stud-dog nor a stallion—a creature of hormones, dependent on seasons. The human male is ready for sex at all times, but he pays for this readiness by his greater nervous complications. A whole host of nervous factors like anxiety, fear or fatigue can make the human male's desire and ability to perform lessen to the vanishing point. Under the whip of stress, he can become so inhibited he cannot maintain the most attractive of relations. Worse, he cannot even start.

But a woman can. Since a woman's role in sex is mainly responsive or receptive; since she does not have the job of initiating and maintaining an erection, she is always anatomically ready. And while she cannot respond as well under stress as she can otherwise, she can for all practical purposes respond well enough.

The result is that, if she does not do the larger share of adjusting, if she becomes aggressive and "modern" to the point of demanding the kind of sex-relations some marriage manuals exhort her to demand, her marriage can land on the rocks almost before it has gotten off the ground.

THE PARADOX OF THE
MARRIAGE MANUAL

Why is this so? Why are so many of the marriage-manuals quite misleading? Why, well-intentioned though they are, do authorities like Dr. Milton Sapirstein believe they can actually wreck more marriages than they help? Because the manuals are in the main unrealistic. Because they are full of wrong assumptions, and set standards almost impossible to attain. Because they leave out emotion and urge the inexperienced man and woman on to heroic efforts to attain a merely physical "perfection" by the use of special tricks and techniques, a perfection that includes mutual, simultaneous, satisfying orgasm every time.

HAVELOCK ELLIS

To understand how the manuals went wrong, we have to go back to the great pioneer sexologist Havelock Ellis.

Ellis was one of the gentlest and kindest of men. Born in England during the late Victorian era, he rebelled against the harsh creed of his day that preached that all pleasure in sex was a male prerogative; that women had to be completely passive and have no pleasure at all. Ellis advocated pleasure for women as their natural right, and went on to describe techniques for stimulating them to that end.

The trouble with Ellis, however, is that he was writing from fantasy rather than from the biological facts. When Ellis wrote, "As (sex) desire is usually more irregular and more capricious in the woman than in the man, it is the wife who may properly be regarded as the law-giver in this matter, and the husband may find his advantage in according her this principle," he was writing out of a wish rather than out of experience— a wish based on the letters of the thousands of women who wrote him telling of their unhappy lot. And most of the writers of manuals who followed Ellis have written out of similar wishes, merely elaborating on his techniques.

THE BIOLOGICAL FACTS

The plain biological facts are these.

Mutual simultaneous orgasm is almost impossible every time. Since the average orgasm in a man takes only about two minutes to achieve from the time of entry, and in a woman eight to ten minutes, few women can have an orgasm every time unless a man is extremely experienced and controlled. If they have it about half the time, they are doing well.

To complicate the matter still further, if the man is not the "law-giver"; if he cannot set the pace but has to stop constantly and think about his technique or of the effort he is making, he may not be able to function to the best of his ability and try to give a woman any orgasm. Those ancient childish devils of fear and anxiety may step in and stop him from keeping going at all.

This is all the more true in a long-term relationship like marriage. A man may function extremely well during a short affair where excitement and novelty keep his tension high, or where he saves face by begging off and not even keeping a date that might include sex when he doesn't feel up to it. A "wolf" who sticks to a series of one-night stands may function even better if he is careful to keep switching women before his tension runs out.

But in a marriage a husband and wife are together day in and day out. And since the active burden of maintaining a day-in-and-day-out relationship is on him he has to think of himself first, not wear himself ragged trying to do what is beyond his emotional or physical means.

Yet this is what makes the situation into a paradox. When a husband is allowed to think of himself first but not ignore his wife's wishes completely, he usually does succeed in giving her a surprising amount of pleasure too. And occasionally orgasm as well.

There is also much pleasure a woman can get apart from orgasm. She can get pleasure from being desired and enfolded as the great wings of the swan enfolded Leda in the ancient myth—the myth that tells how the god Zeus fell in love with Leda, a mortal, and came to earth in the form of a swan and enveloped her with his mighty plumage as they made love.

In speculating on the meaning of this myth, Dr. Helene Deutsch says that the sex-act was probably in the beginning a mere act of violence which the weaker woman could not resist and did not particularly enjoy. But gradually it became transformed for her into an act of pleasure too.

"The violent penetration and mighty embrace . . . the powerful embrace of the prehensile arms, combined with the defensive counter-pressure, induced strong pleasure-sensations in the woman's entire body. The particular disposition in the feminine skin-surface to be pleasurably excited perhaps originates in these primitive situations . . . The story of the god who assumes the shape of a swan and envelops the woman with his plumage seems to express the feminine wish to feel the seducer's might with the whole surface of her body . . .

"Thus the need for kisses, wooing, and general tenderness before a woman today can engage pleasurably in union."

TWO KINDS OF FRIGIDITY

Dr. Deutsch also distinguishes between two kinds of frigid women —the women who are benevolently frigid and those who are maliciously frigid.

(There are very few women who are completely frigid—that is, who get no pleasure in sex at all. And there undoubtedly will be fewer and fewer all the time as girls are less subject to the kind of teaching that induces feelings of deep-seated guilt and shame. Still, about 15% of all women do suffer some degree of frigidity, so the distinctions are important.)

The maliciously frigid woman is one who uses sex as a means of punishing her husband. She says in effect, "If I can't enjoy it, then you can't either," and refuses relations altogether or grants them so grudgingly the punishment is equally harsh.

The benevolently frigid woman does not do this. She says in effect, "Even though I don't enjoy sex very much, I am gracious enough to let you do so. In this way I can at least get the pleasure of giving pleasure to someone else."

DR. JOHN LEVY'S EXPERIENCE

The psychiatrist Dr. John Levy tells of having as his patients many women who used sex as punishment. They not only punished their husbands, they punished themselves by over-riding the good memories with bitter memories—so bitter that the good moments were all but blotted out.

He tells how almost invariably, when a disturbed woman came to him and talked about her marriage, she started with endless complaints about her sex-life. She spoke of nothing but frustration; everything about it was wrong. Yet as he talked to her further, he usually found that sex-frustration was actually only part of the picture. It wasn't her main trouble at all.

On the other hand, when a happier woman came to him, she also talked about her sex-life. She too, when questioned, remembered vexations. But that wasn't all she remembered; there were good things as well. She told of the many close, tender, amusing moments that were deeply satisfying. In fact, the happier woman usually told him about the satisfying moments *first*.

This difference he found to be crucial: A woman whose marriage is basically happy dwells on the close, tender, amusing moments of sex as much as possible. The disturbed woman forgets them, dwells only on her misery and lack of "fulfillment" and ignores the rest. True, the close, tender, amusing moments may be Little Moments compared to the Big Moments the poets and ad-writers speak about so glowingly. But Big Moments are rare in everyone's life. An unbroken succession of them exists only in never-never land.

Meanwhile, the Little Moments are worth cherishing to our bosoms. Especially the amusing moments. A sense of humor is invaluable in enjoying sex. When Elizabeth Taylor said that on the night she married Richard Burton they "giggled the whole night through," she was making a very mature remark.

HOW MUCH SEX IS HEALTHY?

Another question that is always coming up is, "How much sex is healthy? Am I or my husband getting too little or too much?"

There is no direct connection between sex-activity and health, Dr. Levy answers. He says:

I would not go so far as to say that there are not a few people with strong impulses who suffer from long periods of abstinence. But I do know the dangers to health of complete celibacy, to say nothing of partial satisfaction, have been greatly exaggerated. As much harm has been done by prescribing 'sex' indiscriminately to persons married and unmarried as by the most hidebound puritanism. Similarly, there is little chance of 'sapping your strength' by excessive indulgence in intercourse. I know of only one rule to govern the amount of intercourse in marriage for the best maintenance of health: as much as you or your partner enjoy. . . .

Ninety-nine times out of a hundred the physical symptoms associated with a disordered sex-life are due to worry about sex, not to any direct influence of sexual habits. Worry and guilt do lead to neurasthenia, insomnia, pallor, dark circles under the eyes. . . . Sexual acts, whether they are peculiar in form, excessive in quantity, or rigidly repressed, do not.

WHAT IS PECULIAR?

Which acts are peculiar? Which are normal instead?
Dr. Levy answers for us again:

The sex-drive is complex, exceedingly complex, so complex that it permits
of the widest differences between one individual and the next, both in the
experiences that cause sexual tension and its mode of expression. The anatomy charts we present to children and to the earnest bridegroom or bride
are over-simplified to the point of idiocy . . . They are like a four-year-
old's drawing of a man—a circle for a head and two straight lines to take
care of the body, arms and legs. Everything that really matters is left out.
. . . The physiological basis of sexuality is simplicity itself compared to its
so-called psychological aspects.

For this reason, Dr. Levy goes on to say, no two people in the world
have the same pattern of sexual drives, which is why there is no such
thing as an ideal marriage or ideal sex-life in which two people completely mesh. For the drive for sex is like the drive for food. We are all
born with the need to eat but our choice of food is laboriously earned.
We learn over a period of many years to prefer in the main wholesome
bread to candy or cake or to the paint on toys. We also learn according
to the country we're born in to eat mainly spaghetti or potatoes or rice;
to eat a big breakfast or a small, five times a day hurriedly or three times
with great ceremony attached. And in addition we learn to crave occasional variations—spicy beans as well as potatoes, hot dogs with mustard
as well as broiled steak.

So too with sex. While our chief drive may be toward the more
standard forms of intercourse, we still may crave something different
once in a while. He says:

"Sometimes a married pair will be close and affectionate. Tenderness
will pass into a rather solemn passion. . . . At other times their mood will be
wholly frivolous. Intercourse will be just a rattling good time. . . . At times
the husband will vulgarize the act with smutty words or take a fine pleasure
in hurting his wife or forcing her to his will. Or the couple may play at an
illicit relationship, acting out a little seductive farce for their own benefit. . . .
Our uninhibited happily married couple will take all these variations and find
them good."

Wise wives will help their husbands in these various kinds of love-
play. They will do so by being basically warm and giving. And they will

not feel "used" or "put-upon" as they do so, for they will be giving out of their inner wealth.

To be sure, the ability to experience sex this way will not come quickly; it will hardly spring alive full-blown on the wedding night. Yet a woman who advances from the immature state of "being in love" to the mature state of "loving" will acquire it in time. And when she does, she will find that it leads to a true and lasting union the way a study of fancy tricks never can.

Dorothy Thompson was learning how to skate. "Gently, gently, no effort. Let yourself go," her instructor told her. "I laughed out loud, and he wondered why," she later wrote in her diary. "I thought—that's the recipe for success in love, and it's taken me twenty years to learn it! To be soft and receptive. All of grace and femininity is in it."

Gently, gently, let yourself go. Be soft and receptive. What advice could be more the opposite of that of the marriage manuals, with their deadly serious insistence on techniques?

THE FAILURE OF THE
BEAUTIFUL WOMAN

This brings us to another paradox: the sexual failure of the beautiful woman.

Here we go back to Dr. Milton Sapirstein and to what he calls the strangest of all paradoxes—the fact that the beautiful woman is far less apt to achieve a good marriage than her plainer sister. Why is this so? Why do women yearn for great beauty, yet if they happen to be born with it, or achieve it after working like beavers, often find it not a blessing but a curse? A curse that robs them of the very happiness they most desire—happiness with men?

The answer, he says, is because happiness for beautiful women is not in the cards. Outstanding beauty arouses irrational expectations in men, and these collide head-on with the expectations the beauty herself has. The result of this collision is usually disaster. Each party feels cheated because he thinks he's been taken in.

Dr. Sapirstein starts by retelling the story of the most famous beauty of them all, Helen of Troy. It is hardly a happy story. It is the tale of a woman brought up with great expectations, carried off again and again as a prize, implored by men to do something as irrational as make them immortal, then as quickly accused of making them impotent, of "sucking forth their souls" as in Marlowe's famous lines:

> Was this the face that launched a thousand ships?
> And burnt the topless towers of Ilium?
> Sweet Helen, make me immortal with a kiss (*kisses her*).
> Her lips suck forth my soul. See where it flies!

Almost all history and literature sound similar sad notes when they recount the stories of beautiful women, Dr. Sapirstein says. He writes:

They wind before us in sorrowful procession, enchanting and enchanted, lovely lost women with doom on their lips and in their eyes. They did not know they were doomed; they expected something quite different—the rare and shining destiny nature reserves for her darlings. The trouble is that their assumptions were false; they are not nature's darlings. Outstanding beauty, like outstanding gifts of any kind, tends to get in the way of normal emotional development, and thus of that particular success in life we call happiness.

The classic heroines who do wind up happy ever after are cut to a different pattern. Their expectations are modest—the love of one good man is about all they dare to hope for—and their beauty, if they have it, is not intimidating but as shy and unemphatic as they are. Women of this kind pose no threat to men. It is otherwise with the Helens, the Iseults and the Guineveres. They are, quite literally, 'stunning.' Their beauty strikes like lightning and may be equally dangerous. The man is rash who believes he can possess them and still live as other men live.

He goes on to point this up with a modern story—the story of a strikingly lovely woman who came to him for psychiatric help, opening the interview with the sharp question: "Doctor, aren't there any potent men left in the world?"

Her experience was a common one—many marriages and innumerable affairs between, all starting in high anticipation and quickly ending in disillusion. Her current marriage of only three years' standing was also about to go under. Yet while she admitted that all her lovers with monotonous regularity developed such failings as loss of erection or premature ejaculation, she insisted it was not her fault. Dr. Sapirstein writes,

It was obvious that this woman 'did something' to men, afflicting them with a radical sense of insecurity. Her attitude was a very arrogant one. Implicit was a challenge, 'Let's see what you can do. Everybody else has failed me.' Any man who came in contact with her sexually was placed in a kind of test-situation which promptly precipitated anxiety on his part and a consequent loss of healthy sexual reflexes.

And as all became decreasingly potent through anxiety, every relationship came to grief. Each man had started wooing her to distraction, but ended up with recriminations as bitter as those against Helen of Troy.

WHOSE FAULT WAS IT?

Whose fault was this? Some of course was the fault of the men.

It was the men's fault because of their exaggerated expectations. All of us have exaggerated expectations of those with whom we fall in love, but in the case of the beautiful woman these expectations become irrational; they are too big to be achieved. For the beauty appears to her lovers almost as a goddess, and when one dares to aspire to having sexual relations with a goddess, guilt and punishment almost inevitably result. Self-punishment if nothing more. Punishment to fit the crime. Such lovers, says Dr. Sapirstein, end up by psychologically castrating themselves.

But some of the fault is the beauty's too, for she too has had irrational expectations. And these irrational expectations started in childhood, so that her failure was quite foredoomed.

Let's look at the childhood of a typical beauty, and see how it differs from that of the ordinary girl.

THE CHILDHOOD OF A BEAUTY

The ordinary girl starts life as a cute baby and gets the ordinary amount of attention cute babies get. The beauty starts life as an exceedingly pretty baby and gets an exceeding amount of attention as a result. More, she gets this attention without doing a thing to win it; she just gets it and accepts it as her due.

As she grows, the ordinary little girl has to battle for her place in the sun; the beauty can remain passive and not battle at all. She becomes, as Dr. Sapirstein says, "a kind of little princess, exacting favors and services from everybody. . . . Even small boys, those demons of selfish energy, become like miniature knights in her presence, conceding her favors they would never think of granting to her less comely sisters."

Worse, the adult males in her circle begin to behave like the small boys. They too become enchanted with her and tempted to caress her too frequently or too eagerly, arousing her in a way she is too inexperienced to cope with or understand. It adds up to having the odds stacked against her healthy emotional development far greater than those against the ordinary girl.

THE ADOLESCENCE OF A BEAUTY

As she grows into adolescence, the beauty gets still more odds stacked against her. Now, when other girls start to value their looks to a reasonable extent, she starts to over-value hers tremendously; to see her body as a tool with an almost mystic power to give her what she craves. Other girls have to work to develop their resources; she can passively drift along and let her face and figure do the work for her. The result is, the world of the teen-age beauty becomes "the unreal and effortless world of the dreamer. . . . Dependent, submissive and narcissistic traits, which our society fosters in all girls to a certain degree, become exaggerated in her to the point of caricature."

Yet here the drama heightens. Badly equipped to face life as she really is, the beauty enters the field of adolescent dating competition with the highest hopes. And for a while these hopes do seem to be achieved. Boys literally fight over her while they leave her plainer sisters up against a wall. But once the boys succeed in dating her, her relationship with them is never as casual or as easy as theirs. They constantly over-stimulate her and she finds herself on every date having to fend them off. Yet they get very angry with her when she does; no matter how she behaves they accuse her of "leading them on," if she doesn't consent to kisses or more.

This puts her into a terrible dilemma: either she cracks under the strain and becomes promiscuous or she wages a furious battle within herself, represses her own aroused feelings, rebuffs the boys vigorously, and becomes the well-known "cold, unfeeling beauty." Either way the struggle exhausts her; she becomes much more tired than the usual adolescent girl.

But if she decides on marriage as a quick way out she faces another dilemma; her choice is not nearly as wide as she thought. While dozens of boys want a quick fling with her, when it comes to marriage the nice timid boys are afraid of the competition and don't even ask. The ambitious, hard-working boys also hold off because they are afraid she will prove too expensive for them and choose a girl with more moderate tastes.

There's nobody left but the very aggressive boys. Yet these are the kind who are apt to be more than usually impatient; if she frustrates them in any way, they also leave her flat. So she finds herself quite bewildered. A few months or years ago she seemed to have an overwhelming number of suitors; now her plainer sisters are busy marching off to the altar with the very ones she thought she held securely in the palm of her little hand.

When the great beauty does marry, therefore, she usually ends up marrying one of three special types: a roué who wants to use her to show the world how skilled he is in breaking down difficult defenses, a man so infantile he mistakes her beauty for strength, or a much older, extremely wealthy man who acquires her to show off his good tastes as he would acquire an expensive picture to hang on the wall.

With none of these, of course, is happiness in the cards. The roué soon tires of her and turns to greener pastures; the infantile man finds she is hardly a bulwark to lean upon; and between her and the wealthy older man there has seldom been an emotional rapport from the start. Besides, with none of these is she ready to make concessions. She expects to go on being the adored Little Princess, and when she comes up against reality she feels as if her lovely face had been smacked. She walks out before she has given the marriage half a chance, only to repeat the sad process by marrying again and walking out again.

BEAUTY AND THE BEAST

But, says Dr. Sapirstein, there's sometimes an even sadder fate in store for the beauty than multiple marriages. When all her other relationships have broken up, we sometimes find her accepting a man so ruthless that nothing can stop him or reduce his potency—the totally callous gangster or hoodlum type. This man is so far beneath her we now see the shocking spectacle of beauty in love with the beast. A Lana Turner pathetically in love with a hoodlum who degrades her to the point where her daughter feels she has to kill him to save her mother from her fate.

A more ordinary woman does not let a man degrade her that much. The self-love of the ordinary woman steps in and rescues her—the normal self-love that says, "Thus far you can go and no further. Enough is enough." But the great beauty does not have a normal amount of self-love. Starting with too much, she often swings to the extreme of too little. When a Lana Turner accepts as her lover a true beast, it is because she has reached the end of her emotional rope.

THE HOMELY WOMAN

On the other side of the picture is the middle-aged homely woman who is still going strong. Dr. Sapirstein tells of another patient of his, a homely woman who at fifty reported a highly satisfactory love-life. Her current marriage was extremely happy; she had been married and widowed twice before. And each of her lovers vowed she was the best sexual partner they had ever known, probably because she had expected little, been grateful for what came her way, and showed it in her warmth.

Dr. Sapirstein sums up the paradox this way:

(Men feel) that homely women are safe; they make no demands or arouse threatening fantasies. But men have always been terrified of the sexually aggressive woman, and as far as they are concerned any woman who stimulates them too much is automatically regarded as aggressive. The beautiful woman . . . is this, she is that. . . . The truth is, she makes them uncomfortable and they hate her for it (as they hated) Helen who dreamed too much and begot impossible dreams in men.

MOST OF US ORDINARY

Most of us, thank goodness, are not great beauties. We are comfortably ordinary women who do not expect the impossible. We may run the gamut at first in our feelings about sex all the way from the women who exclaimed, "If God made anything better, He kept it from us," to the one who declared it "a much overrated pastime." But as the years go by we get to a middle ground. We are neither cold, nor do we expect the undying ecstasy sex cannot possibly give.

"Gently, gently, no effort. Let yourself go," we keep trying to remind ourselves. "Be soft and receptive. All of grace and femininity is in it. . . ."

✳✳✳ 23 Period of Disillusion

Marriages start with an idyll. After a while the idyll evaporates and there comes a period of sharp disillusion. A shakedown in the relation of bride to groom that has nothing to do with sex. For it is a general disillusion. A state of mind that makes the bride wonder: "Why did I ever get married? And why especially did I marry *him*?"

To add to her misery, she is sure no other bride has ever asked herself such questions. No other bride ever had a dreamboat who mysteriously developed into a dullard, a saint who became most unsaintly, a fashion-plate with meticulously creased trousers who was metamorphosed into a slob who slept in his underwear or heaved his dirty socks under the bed.

She is wrong, of course, in thinking she's alone. All brides have similar shakedowns. All brides start with the earnest desire to make their marriages "perfect," then are driven to tears when they turn out to be far, far less.

A UNIVERSAL EXPERIENCE

To understand why this happens, and happens to everyone, let's go back again to the courtship days.

In the rose-tinted hours of courtship, our Hannah loved her John madly, and John loved our Hannah the same. Madly is the key word here. For the state of being in love is a fantasy-filled state of incredible, uncritical madness. A state cunningly devised by nature to lift two ordinary, shy youngsters out of themselves, make them more alive, more intense, more wonderful, and propel them together with a bang.

But nothing in life is static. Nothing can possibly stay put. After the high, mad peak of the wedding and the fling of the honeymoon, Hannah and John tend to simmer down and become once more their ordinary selves. Indeed, they have to do this. Neither they nor anyone else has the sheer emotional energy to stay up long at a peak stage. If they remained in the state of courtship intensity, they would soon find themselves as emotionally exhausted as Roger Bannister was after breaking the four-minute mile.

This, then, is what the disillusioned period amounts to: a necessary coming back to earth, a resumption of normal walking speed after the spurt of the race. And in this coming back, two things happen: our bride sees her husband more clearly; she also sees herself more clearly.

For during the courting days, if he appeared larger than life in her eyes, she also appeared larger than life in her own. She thirstily drank up his overestimation of her and really believed she was the super person he made her out to be. Now, alas, she can no longer do that; she has recognized herself as not quite as worthy of adoration either. And this is, if possible, an even worse shock than her discovery of the truth about him.

"Our disillusionment does not proceed wholly, or even primarily, from the unromantic facts we learn about our partner in the course of daily observation," writes Dr. John Levy. "It comes largely from our bored recognition of the same old self within our own breast. Our new-found charm and prowess and glamour evaporate when we can no longer read them in a worshipping gaze."

NO CHOICE

Yet there is no choice but to accept this evaporation when it comes. No choice, that is, if we want to found an enduring and stable relationship with one man that will last and grow through the years.

For the only alternative to a stable marriage is an endless series of new and seemingly "exciting" suitors, each of whom we idolize and who in turn idolize us, but with whom we must also come to a shakedown when our everyday personalities emerge from the haze. And these shakedowns tend to get sadder and more frustrating as we get older and realize that time is running out. Not as sad, maybe, as for the great Beauty, who expected so very, very much and is tumbled to earth all the harder, but sad enough. How many sad shakedowns must Barbara Hutton have had?

THE PENDULUM SWINGS

Besides, if we don't throw a tantrum and walk out of a marriage at the first slight, if we stick with our husband and determine to work things through, after a while we find the pendulum swinging again. We see him once more as the man we freely chose, and who as freely chose us. And because we chose each other freely and eagerly, much of the original attraction is still there. When we are sick, we find that he nurses us; when we are blue, he cheers us; when we are lonely, he offers us a uniquely friendly hand.

We find that glamour doesn't have to disappear from our marriage. It is there to be found, though in modified form. "Life is much more fun when you can take your wife out dancing and feel that she really is the most charming creature you ever saw, and you're a pretty interesting fellow yourself and love is wonderful . . ." Dr. Levy writes from the man's point of view. "The fact that she looks a little blowsy when she gets you a Bromo-Seltzer next morning is irrelevant, unless you still have the childish longing to live above yourself twenty-four hours a day every day. Glamour in marriage cannot be continuous, but it needn't be absent. The morning after does not destroy the reality and value of the night before.

"(But) the first step toward permanent and satisfying marriage is disillusionment, the willingness to accept oneself and one's partner on the level of everyday living, to take the worse along with the better."

REMEMBERING

It also helps during the blue moments if one deliberately tries to remember the better moments.

Edna St. Vincent Millay vividly expresses this kind of double remembering in her poem, "Souvenir."

> "Just a rainy day or two,
> In a windy tower,
> That was all I had of you—
> Saving half an hour
>
> "Marred by greeting passing groups
> In a cinder walk,
> Near some naked blackberry hoops
> Dim with purple chalk.
> I remember three or four
> Things you said in spite,
> And an ugly coat you wore
> Plaided black and white.
>
> "Just a rainy day or two
> And a bitter word.
> Why do I remember you
> As a singing bird?"

And when one does this double remembering, love returns and partly displaces disillusion—the kind of love that makes a relationship between a man and woman so intense, so inexhaustible, so basically satisfying it can last for twenty, thirty, forty or more years, with the twain becoming more and more "of one flesh" as the years go by.

✳✳✳ 24 Birth Control:
The Greatest Freedom

From the day she gets married, the most vital concern a woman has is the concern about pregnancy. This is because she knows that every act of love brings with it the possible conception of a child.

Women have always both longed for and dreaded the advent of pregnancy. Even those who longed for it the most, hoped to be able to choose their time. For of all the freedoms a woman can have, the freedom to decide when and if she will conceive is the greatest—far greater than the freedom to vote, to work, to keep her own earnings, all the things for which through the centuries she has fought. For this is a freedom that strikes to the very heart of her being. It is also a freedom on which the very essence of normality depends—a race as well as an individual able to survive, work, and love without exploding itself to death.

Yet the use of contraceptives, or birth control as it is familiarly called, has long been a matter of boiling controversy. Some religions have banned it, but to many others it has seemed reasonable and right. So we find an Egyptian papyrus dating as far back as 1550 B.C. advocating the use of such familiar things as plugs of lint soaked in honey. We find Roman women using gauze soaked in olive oil; ancient Chinese women hopefully trying wet tea-leaves; English women of the Middle Ages making magic passes over their beds, or desperately eating the parings of the hoofs of mules, hoping this might make them "as sterile as a mule." But nothing really worked until Fallopius invented a male sheath of fine linen in 1564—the same Fallopius who discovered the Fallopian tubes.

Fallopius developed his linen sheath mainly as a protection against the venereal disease which had suddenly become rife in Europe. But it was soon taken up with great enthusiasm as a contraceptive as well, though it didn't become well known until a Dr. Charles Condom introduced it to the court of King Charles II, when, like any other fashion set by a king, it suddenly caught on, and got its "condom" name.

While fine linen was better than nothing, it proved porous and highly variable in texture. A really successful sheath could not be developed until around 1843, when Goodyear in America and Hancock in England almost simultaneously succeeded in vulcanizing rubber. The far better rubber sheath for men, sold to this day in England under the name of "the poor man's friend," and the rubber diaphragm for women, were on their way.

The diaphragm is a piece of curved rubber with a thin, flexible rim that fits over the neck of the womb and prevents the sperm from entering. It is used alone, or for double safety a teaspoon of special antispermicidal jelly is put inside before it is inserted.

VITAL TO WOMEN

The diaphragm, plus similar means of barring the entrance to the womb such as a metal or plastic cap, is of particular importance because most people believe it vital that birth control be in the hands of women, not men. For to a man, having a child is a distant affair. In the heat of sexual tension, he seldom gives it a thought. Not so a woman. You might sum it up by saying that the complete act of love takes about ten minutes for a man; for a woman, nine months. The control of its consequences thus definitely belongs to her.

Yet getting this control has been extremely difficult. Just when news of the blessings of the diaphragm was beginning to spread around the world, came the Victorian hush-hush era in England and the Comstock regime in America.

Comstock was a fanatic who saw everything that had to do with sex as deviltry, and he succeeded in having contraceptives outlawed in a rider slipped into a bill outlawing obscene books and pictures. Public inertia plus other taboos let matters stand this way for half a century until Margaret Sanger came along.

Margaret Sanger was a visiting nurse who was called in one day in 1912 to attend a woman in a dilapidated New York tenement who was hemorrhaging from a self-inflicted abortion after she had become pregnant again, with many small children already to hand. Mrs. Sanger did what she could to stop the hemorrhage, then had to summon a doctor and stand by while he callously snickered at the sick woman: "Oho, so you want to have your cake and eat it too? Next time tell your husband Jake to go sleep on the roof!" But Jake did not choose to sleep on the roof. A few months later, Mrs. Sanger was called in by excited neighbors to attend the same woman: she had tried to abort herself again. But this time such virulent blood-poisoning had set in that Mrs. Sanger could do nothing except watch her die in agony. The lifelong crusade for birth control by the shy, red-haired nurse was born that day.

THREE GREAT MEN

Every once in a while, humanity produces a great man—someone who does truly original thinking and lifts people further along. In our century there have been several such men, but probably few will be remembered with more gratitude by women than the trio of Drs. Abraham Stone, Gregory Pincus and John Rock. For these men have helped women to solve the age-long problem of birth control in a new and dramatic way.

Abraham Stone was a small, gentle, soft-spoken man who, like Margaret Sanger, devoted the greater part of his life to the birth control movement. With his wife, Dr. Hannah Stone, he worked tirelessly in two directions, opening fertility clinics to help sterile couples achieve greatly wanted pregnancies, and teaching thousands of others how to avoid the pregnancies their health or pocketbooks could not afford.

But though he later became the prestigious editor of the *Journal of Human Fertility*, medical director of the Planned Parenthood Federation and professor of Preventive Medicine at New York University, Abraham Stone was not satisfied with the birth control methods then current. They were good, but not good enough. "The ideal contraceptive," he wrote in his journal, "remains to be developed. It should be harmless . . . entirely reliable . . . simple, practical, universally acceptable, and esthetically satisfactory to both husband and wife." None in use answered these specifications. Rhythm was highly unreliable. The diaphragm was both unaesthetic and unromantic to the many women who didn't like to put it in and take it out at obvious moments. And other popular methods such as douching were either harmful or of almost no value. (Many of the widely-advertised chemicals for douching sold under the euphemistic name of "feminine hygiene" were so strong they could do real damage to the delicate vaginal lining, or wash away the secretions put into the vagina for protective purposes against bacteria just as protective secretions are put into the mouth and nose. Or they were so useless as contraceptive methods they did almost no good at all.)

So one night in the winter of 1950, Dr. Stone sat with Margaret Sanger and another old friend, the biologist Gregory ("Goody") Pincus, earnestly discussing the matter until almost dawn. Dr. Pincus was a famous biologist, Doctor of Science and researcher in reproduction at the Worcester, Massachusetts, Foundation for Experimental Biology. The friends of the Planned Parenthood Federation had raised a little money for further study. Could Goody maybe start on a whole new research tack? If they put in the money, would Pincus put in his brains and time?

Dr. Pincus agreed before he realized what he had let himself in for. The amount of money raised by the federation turned out to be only $2100, a pittance barely enough to pay for the experimental rabbits needed for a few months of work. Even a year's work would take from twenty to thirty thousand dollars, and how could he know it wouldn't take as long as ten years, as similar projects had done?

GIVE IT A TRY

Still, the job was so fascinating and so important he decided to give it a try, at least.

Since a whole new tack was called for, he started thinking along completely new lines. The methods of diaphragm, condom, douches and spermicidal jellies all relied on a mechanical or clinical barrier to prevent the sperm from entering the womb and travelling up into a Fallopian tube to meet the egg. The main trouble with all of them, including the rhythm method that depended on limiting sex-relations to the infertile time of the month, was that they had to rely on human beings distracted by the high excitement of intercourse to use them at exactly the right moment and in the right way.

What about preventing the egg from being in a tube waiting for a sperm in the first place? Prevented by something done *before* the exciting sex moments? This would be revolutionary indeed!

As Albert Q. Maisel tells the story in his book *The Hormone Quest*, on further reflection Goody Pincus decided it was not so revolutionary at that. Nature was already doing this by the simple method of stepping up a woman's supply of sex hormones. Working in accordance with her basic stop-and-go arrangement, these extra hormones, notably the progesterones, were stopping her pituitary from sending messages to her ovaries to ovulate again during the two weeks of the second half of the menstrual month, as well as during the nine months of pregnancy. In fact, they were inhibiting the pituitary so well during a normal pregnancy that it was the extra sex hormones that made the pregnancy hang on, and doctors were taking advantage of this fact by injecting women threatened with abortion with still more hormones, which often worked.

But injections by a doctor, while all very well in an emergency, are expensive and time-consuming. Could a pill perhaps be developed that a woman could take herself—a pill that would do a similar pituitary-inhibiting job?

Dr. Pincus was so tremendously excited he got to work the very next morning with an assistant. They started with the classic laboratory experiments with animals. They fed progesterone by mouth to female rabbits and rats, put them into cages with males where they would mate with abandon, and watched the results. Sure enough, progesterone given at the right time prevented the rabbits and rats from releasing eggs and becoming pregnant, try hard though they obviously did.

ENTER DR. ROCK

At this point enter the surgeon Dr. John Rock on the scene.

Only forty miles from Worcester, in the Boston suburb of Brookline, Dr. Rock, clinical professor of Gynecology at Harvard, had been running a fertility clinic in connection with the Free Hospital for Women. He had helped hundreds of women to conceive who had heretofore been barren, and he, too, had been proceeding along a new tack. Noticing that many sterile women were victims of an underdevelopment of their genital organs, he had also noticed that these organs were matured in other women by pregnancy; the high tide of pregnancy hormones built them up. Why not cause a seeming pregnancy in his barren patients by the administration of such hormones, and see what came of it? Maybe their genital organs, too, would be built up so a real pregnancy could result?

And this is precisely what happened—not in all the cases that he tried, but enough to convince Dr. Rock he had something. Thirteen out of eighty women to whom he fed increasingly large doses of progesterones by mouth for three months did conceive afterward, though they had been hopelessly barren before. They conceived by what came to be known as the "Rock Rebound"—that is, they released no eggs, had no menstrual periods and conceived no children while taking the hormones—they did by a rebound reaction after they stopped.

Goody Pincus had helped Dr. Rock in his study of human eggs recovered from ovaries that had had to be removed from surgical patients suffering from some female disorder. Dr. Pincus taught Rock and his co-worker, the biologist Miriam Menkin, how to keep these eggs alive in the laboratory.

Now Rock and Pincus compared notes on the role of the female sex hormones as related to ovulation and went on with enthusiasm from there.

Dr. Pincus started on the trail of a synthetic progesterone which would be far less expensive than the natural kind he and Dr. Rock had been using. Dr. Rock started to treat his sterile patients along still another new tack—instead of giving them the hormones daily during their pseudo-pregnancies, he gave them in a twenty-days-on, eight-days-off rhythm, so that they had their regular menstrual periods while taking them instead of no periods at all. And here periods were psychologically very gratifying, for periodic flow is very important to a woman. When she is not really pregnant, she expects to menstruate, and menstruate for her peace of mind she therefore should do.

It was now not a far step for Dr. Rock, from thinking of his pills as fertility pills which would cause a temporary false pregnancy after which his barren patients might rebound and become really pregnant, to thinking of them as birth control pills which would do the same. And while Dr. Rock was an eminent Catholic, the father of five and the grandfather of fourteen, he saw a crying need in this direction, too, and started to work with Dr. Pincus along that line.

It wasn't a quick job. It took not $2100 but $300,000 in research money, as well as eight years of testing both on animals and thousands of women, before the pills were judged effective and safe.

They were tested independently by such men as Dr. Edward T.

Tyler of the University of California School of Medicine and declared effective an astonishing 99 per cent of the time.

They were also tested in Puerto Rico by Dr. Edris Rice-Wray, and declared so safe a majority of women taking them reported they felt better than ever before.

They were tested so thoroughly in England that the National Health Boards there are issuing them as a government service at cost, making them truly "the poor woman's friend."

They were tested, above all, with possible relation to cancer, and the findings were that, in addition to not causing cancer, some forms of cancer seemed actually to be helped by their use. A fear that they might cause phlebitis turned out to be quite unfounded.

In order to bend backward, however, the U.S. Federal Drug Administration at first authorized them only up to the age of 35, when the chance of conception decreases greatly anyway. To bend backward still further, it recommended they be taken for no more than four years at a time, depending on the strength of the pill prescribed. As further research was done, these limitations were removed. There is now no limit on their use.

The main drawback of the pills is that they sometimes cause a feeling of nausea or fullness when a woman starts to take them. This feeling of fullness is due to the same reasons that cause it at the beginning of a real pregnancy, but it is not nearly as bad since the amount of hormones necessary to inhibit ovulation is far smaller than that necessary to hold a real pregnancy in place. If there are any discomforts, doctors suggest the woman try a smaller dose or a different brand. Half a dose often works as well as a full, and there are already at least six reliable brands on the market, at a total cost in the United States of only about $2.25 a month.

Summed up by Dr. Edris Rice-Wray: "It is extremely rare to find a woman willing to accept any other means of contraception once she knows the pills exist."

A STILL NEWER CONTRACEPTIVE

A still newer contraceptive is being tested at Yale at the time of writing. This is a pill to stop the egg from being implanted in the lining of the womb after it has been fertilized. This pill is taken for three days after an act of intercourse that may have resulted in a conception, and has been successful so far only in monkeys. If it proves successful in women as well, it will be still another weapon in the long fight against pregnancies that are not wanted or planned.

✳✳✳ 25 It's Not Always Easy to Conceive

But contraceptives or no contraceptives, most women still do decide to become pregnant a few times after marriage. They decide this because they know that bearing a child is the only way most of us have of creating something beyond ourselves, of making life triumph over death and so becoming a creature akin to a god.

The first problem in becoming pregnant, of course, is to get started. And while some women swear they conceive "if a man so much as looks at them," others find it surprisingly hard to do.

One-tenth of all couples can't do it easily. This figure holds true all over the world, and oddly enough in animals as well. While the female always has been blamed for this—wives traditionally have been branded as "barren" while husbands have gotten off scot free—actually only about half the time does the fault lie with the female; the other half it is definitely with the male. When a famous stallion who had won dozens of races was recently sold for breeding purposes, he proved to be as sterile as a castrated ox.

Often the fault lies with both male and female. That is why a second marriage sometimes is fertile when a first is not. Napoleon and Josephine couldn't produce an heir, but she had already had two children by her first husband and he promptly had the little king of Rome by Maria Luisa. Together, they each may have had just enough wrong with them so that the combination didn't work. And no matter where the fault lies, there is no more stigma attached to it than to the inability to walk a tightrope.

Two popular misconceptions must immediately be ruled out: Infertility is seldom due to venereal disease. It is almost never due to the previous use of contraceptives. If a woman stops using contraceptives and finds she can't get pregnant right away, it is usually due to the fact that she was infertile all along and didn't know it, or her time of maximum fertility has passed.

The time of maximum fertility in a woman is from about age twenty-two to twenty-eight. After thirty, it slows down. After thirty-five, it slows down some more. After forty-five, it slows down to where it is almost non-existent. Fertility does not depart completely after forty-five, to be sure, as women with so-called "change of life" babies discover. But even after thirty it slows down to the point where conception is seldom immediate.

Also, the frequency of marital relations drops by the thirties. According to Dr. Kinsey's findings, it drops from a frequency of two to three times a week to once a week or less, and by the forties it has dropped even more. So there is that much less chance of conception than there was during the twenties when frequency was high.

Conception is a most complex affair—so complex that it has been called a "combination of clumsiness and grace." There is infinitely more to it than a jolly sperm cell from a male rushing in and joining up with a happy egg cell from a female. All kinds of conditions must be met and all kinds of hazards overcome, including the condition that the act be exquisitely timed to take place during a crucial forty-eight hours of each month.

I told a little about this in the chapter on menstruation. I shall tell more now.

HAZARDS OF THE SPERM

Sperm cells are incredibly tiny, with heads about 1/6000th of an inch across, and even thinner tails that lash about and propel them to swim. They are so tiny that they can be diverted by the slightest obstruction. And there can be many obstructions, alas!

Sperm cells start their lives in the testicles where they are constantly freshly made. The testicles in turn are suspended in a sac called the scrotum, which extends downward on the outside of the body just behind the penis.

The testicles and scrotum are outside because sperm cells are extremely sensitive to heat, and the interior of the body is too warm for them. If the testicles are subjected to high temperatures, they first diminish and later cease the production of sperm. The scrotum is also constructed of a special thin skin that makes for rapid cooling off. Thus, hazard number one: If a man gets any kind of illness that carries with it a high fever, the outside location and cooling-off device may not be enough to save the sperm. He may be left temporarily sterile as a result.

When normal fresh sperm quietly leave their birthplaces in the testicles and start travelling up toward the end of the penis from which they must be ejaculated into the woman's vagina, they do not travel in a straight line. Instead, they must pass through a maze of passages and ducts, and some of these ducts may have become temporarily blocked as the result of infection (I repeat, *not* necessarily venereal infection— there are at least fifteen other kinds).

The third male hazard is the number of sperm and the obstacles they must meet once inside the woman's genital tract.

The sperm cells, as I said, are incredibly tiny—so tiny that an average ejaculation of a teaspoonful of fluid contains the astonishing number of close to four hundred million of them. Yet, equally astonishing, almost all these four hundred million are needed to complete the job.

Many millions are needed because the crucial meeting of sperm and egg does not take place in the vagina as one might expect, but in the outer third of one of the Fallopian tubes, seven or eight inches away. And that seven or eight inches turns out to be a veritable obstacle course since the womb lies between the vagina and the tubes, and the tiny sperm cells must swim through it, upstream against more tortuous odds, with swimmers falling by the wayside right and left. It has been calculated that out of four hundred million sperm cells that start the course, only the small fraction of around two thousand are left to finish. Yet all those two thousand will be needed to assist the one which will penetrate the egg!

The fourth male hazard is that, instead of starting immediately to race straight toward the egg, the sperm first swim aimlessly for a while. Some, as they swim, get themselves caught in the folds and crannies of the vagina, where they are trapped, curl up and die. The rest may suffer a different fate: the vagina is normally acid in reaction and sperm cannot live in an acid medium, so even without being trapped they can be destroyed.

They must hurry on to the womb, which is normally alkaline in reaction and so more favorable to sperm. If they can get inside it, they will be safe.

But here another hazard awaits them; they sometimes find a thick fluid barring the entrance to the cervix, or neck of the womb. In Dr. Alan Guttmacher's words, "They get trapped in this cervical fluid like flies in flypaper." Others get past the fluid and into the cervix, only to find it not as alkaline as it should be, so they too are halted. (Doctors who treat infertility sometimes speak of a "hostile cervix." The woman who overhears them feels guilty because she thinks it implies that *she* is hostile. It implies nothing of the kind. A hostile cervix simply means chemically hostile. There just happens to be too much fluid blocking the way into it, or fluid of the wrong kind.)

But luckily, the cervix does as a rule receive most of them, and the womb in turn receives them and lets them pass through.

FEMALE HAZARDS

Let's leave the sperm for a few minutes and turn to the female side of the story.

Amazing as it seems, centuries ago it was thought the female contributed nothing to conception. The man had all the life-force, a woman was merely the inert box that carried the unborn baby around. Thanks to the microscope and the patience of thousands of investigators, today we know better. We know that the female contributes one egg, but it is an egg so vital it counterbalances all those four hundred million sperm cells.

This egg, which is far larger than the sperm cells but still no larger than the period at the end of this sentence, is released once in the intermenstrual weeks, on about the fourteenth day before the succeeding flow begins, if conception fails. As soon as it bursts forth from the ovary, it is sucked into one of the Fallopian tubes. There, gentle currents within the tube wave it down toward the middle where it waits for the sperm.

But here is female hazard number one: Some women just don't have an Ovulation Day. They enjoy sex, menstruate after a fashion and are otherwise normally female, but for some reason they don't release eggs. And obviously, without eggs they cannot conceive.

Other women do release eggs, but not every four weeks. Indeed, few women release them regularly. In the skipped months, too, conception cannot take place.

Even more important, if an egg is waiting around in the tube, it does not wait indefinitely. The waiting-time of an egg is only a few short hours, rarely more than twelve. After that, if not fertilized, it degenerates and disappears, usually by absorption. And there will be no more eggs that menstrual month.

Suppose there is a waiting egg inside a tube. Let's go back to our sperm swimmers and see what more hazards they must overcome before they can join up with that.

As they continue their race, they may find the thin tube closed against them when it should be open. Or they may race up the wrong tube—the left tube, for instance, when an egg is waiting in the right.

But finally, almost two thousand do make their goal. Two thousand sperm swim up the proper tube and start roving around, hoping by chance to encounter that one waiting egg. If it has not yet arrived, they can swim around looking for it for a short time. If it doesn't come fairly soon, they have to give up and die.

For here's where the crucial number of forty-eight hours comes in. Sperm can stay alive swimming around in the tube for only about thirty-six hours hunting for an egg. An egg can stay alive in the tube for only about twelve hours waiting for a sperm. It adds up to just about forty-eight hours out of each month that egg and sperm can stay alive and meet.

And if egg and sperm do meet, many of the two thousand sperm that finally got into the outer third of the tube that doctors poetically call the "conception chamber" may help the one winner by releasing a chemical that seems to aid it in breaking through the wall that surrounds the egg.

With the help of the two thousand, then, the sperm enters, and a pregnancy has hopefully begun.

Is it the fittest sperm that gets in, or the fastest? According to Dr. Alan Guttmacher, it is merely the luckiest. Says he, "The baby it has started off has a far greater chance of becoming president than that sperm had of becoming part of a baby, for it has won against odds of several million to one."

At this point you would think we could catch our breath and say the hazards of conception are over. But no, there are more.

Nobody knows exactly why conception takes place in the tube instead of lower down in the uterus—why the sperm has to travel upstream against all those obstacles, then join with the egg and travel back down. One theory is that the sperm can move up faster than the egg can be moved down. At any rate, travel back down is precisely what the fertilized egg now has to do, taking about four days to do it. It must retrace the pathway of the sperm and travel down to its future home in the uterus, starting to divide and grow into two, four, five, eight and more cells as it does.

But sometimes it can't retrace its steps. Sometimes it remains stuck in the narrow tube which is not built to expand like the uterus. When it gets stuck, it is called a "tubal pregnancy" and the whole thing has to be removed, tube and all, lest the tube rupture, tear a sizable blood vessel and cause serious bleeding.

Sometime, too, the fertilized egg succeeds in travelling down, but meets its final hazard when it has to burrow into the lining of the uterus, since conception is not considered complete until the fertilized egg has become incapsulated in the uterine lining that has been made thick and ready to receive it. If for some reason the egg can't burrow in, it is thrown off after all that work, and another sperm and egg have to start trying all over again.

HELP AT HAND

Of course, there is help for many of these things if they do go wrong—help that lessens the chance of their going wrong once more. Dr. John Rock estimates that, at the very least, 25 per cent of the seriously handicapped couples who seek help can get it, which means about one in four, or much better than a gambler's chance.

Some couples are easy to help, some are hard and take a long time. One doctor had about given up, until while on vacation in Europe he got a one-word cable from a couple he had been helping. "Bingo!" was all it said.

A woman can be helped by surgery, by hormone treatment to build up internal organs that have remained immature, or by the simple Rubin Test to determine whether her tubes are open or closed.

There are also things to be done for a man—if his wife can get him to go. Men are so touchy on the subject of fertility that many doctors suggest a woman try to lead her husband to a general practitioner's office rather than to a specialist's, so that no one will know what he's there for. Or if he does go to a specialist, then to try to make an appointment outside of regular hours—anything to save his pride.

Once there, a man may be helped by antibiotics to clear up old infections, by remedies like a change in diet, psychotherapy or even a suggestion for less frequent intercourse, since too-frequent efforts only make him tense and interfere with the production of sperm.

But Dr. Rock suggests that some wives not tell their husbands when it is ovulation time. Men hate to have intercourse "according to the temperature chart," even though that greatly increases the chances of conceiving. Such planned intercourse makes them nervous, and nervousness may be extremely bad for fertility, as we shall see.

THERAPEUTIC INSEMINATION

As a last resort, there is artificial insemination. Many people consider this a bad name, however, and the better name of "therapeutic insemination" is now used by specialists in the technique like Dr. Sophia Kleegman. Dr. Kleegman distinguishes between "therapeutic donor-insemination" and "therapeutic husband-insemination," depending on whose semen is used.

"Husband-insemination" is usually used when, for one reason or another, not enough sperm can enter the cervix. The husband's sperm is injected just inside the place in the cervix that opens into the uterus, giving more sperm a better chance to make the grade. "Donor-insemination," or insemination by an anonymous male donor, is used when the husband's sperm-count is much too low for doctors to expect success in any event.

Some doctors combine the two and mix in a little of the husband's semen with the donor's. This makes it possible for the couple to think that possibly the husband furnished the one lucky sperm cell after all. For the main trouble with using a donor exclusively is that he *is* anonymous. A donor is a healthy young man like a medical student who has had a strict physical and psychological examination, and who provides sperm in a test-tube for a small fee. Neither partner ever sees him any more than the inseminated cow sees the bull, so no one but the doctor knows who he is.

But the objection here is that women aren't cows. A woman generally wants to know. She wants to be part of a known triangle of father, mother and child.

Dr. Helene Deutsch tells of a patient of hers who, thinking she was pregnant by her husband, indulged in a brief summertime affair with another man, excusing herself with, "It doesn't count." She returned home to find she was pregnant all right, but not as many weeks as she had figured. Now the thought began to torture her, "Who actually is the father? Which of the two?"

When the child was born, she continued to be tortured by the thought. As a result, she found she couldn't love it. "I can't love the child of an unknown father," she kept crying to herself. It took psychiatric help to get her to accept her husband as the father, and only then was she able to give it love.

Dr. Deutsch believes this is one of the main reasons for a woman's deeper need for monogamy. Since every act of intercourse contains for her the possibility of conception, she has to stay faithful to one man at a time.

EMOTIONAL STERILITY

A woman's life is interminably caught between the poles of sterility and fertility, between too much and too little, between being panicked because she seems to be always pregnant, and frustrated because she desperately wants to be, and cannot.

Other reasons for "cannot" are nervous or emotional. These are much more difficult to treat than the physical causes for, while we know that the nerves influence the hormones and the hormones the nerves, it is hard to put our finger on precisely how.

FEAR AND GUILT

Certainly the chief cause of emotional sterility is fear—usually the crippling fear that is the result of guilt. Some doctors, not all, believe that the occasional woman is infertile because she feels deeply guilty about some specific past "sin" she has committed, or she feels just generally "unworthy." She transfers these fears to her mysterious insides, which then punish her by not letting her conceive.

The doctors who theorize in this way go on to say that she then becomes obsessed by the anxious thought, "I will never have a child," and this anxiety makes her truly spastic. This is proven to them by the reports of doctors who have done Rubin Tests on women and found their tubes wide open during all the unimportant times of the month, but closed by a nervous spasm during the crucial ovulation time. Other doctors have inserted balloons into the uterus, and recorded its contractions

much as an electrocardiogram records the contractions of the heart.
While most women, they find, have regular rhythmic uterine contractions, nervous women record wild contractions that, speculation has it,
either do not let the sperm pass through, or stop a fertilized egg from
implanting as it should. (Dr. William Bickers observed the uterine contractions of a sterile patient of his over a long period of time. When he
frightened her in any way, such as showing her a hypodermic needle,
her contractions immediately became jerky. But she was an artist, and
when he took away the hypo and put a familiar pencil and sketch-pad in
her hands and asked her to sketch while he recorded, she became relaxed
and the contractions calmed down.)

THE INFANTILE WOMAN

Then there is the sterile infantile woman. She is usually small,
dainty and perpetually in need of a prop to lean on. Her original prop
was her mother; now it's her husband. She demands constant attention
and tenderness from her husband. ("Tell me you love me! Tell me you
love me!") But the tenderness she gives him in return is not that of a
wife but of a cuddly child. She fears pregnancy because she has no
motherly feelings; pregnancy may demand these from her and make her
grow up, which she does not want to do.

Curiously, says Dr. Helene Deutsch, this type of infantile woman
often during puberty had many symptoms typically connected with
pregnancy. She vomited, had painful feelings or swellings in various
parts of her body and developed marked eating disturbances. Yet when
faced with the possibility of actually realizing pregnancy, she can't. She
may fool everybody, including herself, by spending a tremendous amount
of time and money running from doctor to doctor saying she *wants* a
child, before she is up to it. If she does eventually conceive, it is more
because life has matured her than because of anything the doctors have
done.

THE TOO-MOTHERLY WOMAN

Another type of sterile woman starts her married life as the exact
opposite of the infantile woman. Instead of having no motherly feeling,
she has a great deal. But she spends it all on her husband, and intuitively
knows that he does not want a child.

When women do conceive under such circumstances, their husbands often become so frightened of the pregnancy that they run away, become impotent or start to become alcoholics. The wives seem to sense these dangers, and ward them off by unconsciously influencing their ability to conceive.

THE HIGHLY EROTIC WOMAN

A fourth type of sterile woman is the highly erotic. She too has great warmth, even great motherliness, but she is afraid a child will interfere with her rich erotic life.

This fear is especially strong in actresses and beautiful women who pride themselves on remaining "sex symbols." It is also strong among more ordinary women during their early married years. For during early marriage sex can be so new and overwhelming that all one's available emotion is poured into it. The overwhelming experience of childbirth would make the competition become too keen, so childbirth is postponed.

Childbirth is also postponed by the kind of woman who pours all her available emotion into a great cause like civil rights, or into becoming a biologist or a doctor. Such a woman, like the motherly woman, is also rich and warm, but keeping herself sterile keeps her free for her other dreams.

THE MASCULINE-AGGRESSIVE WOMAN

Psychiatrists like to lump the words "masculine" and "aggressive" together, and for good measure add "cold."

So we get still another type of sterile woman—the cold-masculine-aggressive who marries for social and financial status and shuns feminine tasks like the proverbial plague.

Yet since no one is ever entirely predictable, the cold-masculine-aggressive woman sometimes fools us at that. She goes to the other extreme and has a lot of children, just to prove she has the masculine guts to outdo everybody else, and can!

THE WOMAN WHO LIVES WITH MOTHER

A rather surprising type of sterile woman is one who lives with her mother, or with her husband's mother.

Dr. John Rock says that not infrequently during the depression years he saw couples who came to him begging for help for sterility, and were astonished to discover they had simply never had adequate intercourse. Living with mama had kept them too shy and inhibited; they were simply afraid she was peeping or listening while they were making love.

THE EMOTIONALLY DISTURBED WOMAN

Finally, there is the deeply disturbed woman. This kind of woman was never much of a person in the first place, and after marriage her problems overwhelm her to the point where she is and has nothing—no housekeeping skills, no strength, no warmth, no anything to give to anyone.

Yet, often as not, this type also goes to the other extreme and compulsively has lots of children, as if she were trying to make up for her own poverty of spirit. When she does this, she becomes the despair of everyone, with her dirty house, dirty clothes and dirtier children. But when kindly social workers are taken in by her complaints over her large brood and hand her some contraceptives, she promptly "forgets" to use them and maddens everybody by having more.

TWO BAFFLERS

Outright sterility may be puzzling. Compulsive fertility may be maddening. Other problems are plain baffling.

The first baffler is what doctors call "one-child sterility." A woman is perfectly healthy; she has one child easily, then for years she tries but can't have any more. What's gone wrong? Her psychology has gone wrong, think men like the late Dr. Irving Fischer. She wanted her first child badly, but while she says she wants another, she was so overwhelmed by the first after she got it, she really doesn't. Only if, at long last, she learns to relax will she be able to conceive again.

A second baffler is when a woman conceives after a single act of intercourse—an act moreover that is not during her normal ovulation time. Here Dr. Therese Benedek does the thinking. Dr. Benedek thinks a woman's emotions so strongly influence her hormones that on occasion they can set off ovulation at a totally unexpected date. For an isolated act of intercourse is usually very exciting. It occurs between lovers after a long absence, or between lovers for the one and only time. The excitement causes all kinds of inner changes, and a pregnancy is set off.

Luckily all these problems are rare. Pregnancy from a single act is rare. Sterility for any reason is rare, and the emotionally sterile can get help from psychosomatic clinics which are held at many large hospitals, from private psychiatrists or from plain old-fashioned doctors who will let them talk.

There is also the most old-fashioned remedy of all—religion. Religion for centuries has helped the barren woman because of its doctrine of forgiveness of sin. God forgives us, and we in turn humbly forgive ourselves, even for the masturbation we think may have caused our sterility.

Religion is so helpful Dr. Deutsch believes it often helps where everything else fails. She tells of at least two instances of which she has known, where the Black Madonna of Czestochowa in Poland relieved women of their barrenness. It was as if the Madonna had pitted her healing power against the traditional "witch" that keeps women sterile, and won.

Dr. Deutsch believes, too, that most extreme physical manipulations that succeed in relieving sterility, such as surgery, are mainly psychological in effect. They are interpreted by the woman as a form of punishment, and having done sufficient penance, she becomes free to conceive.

MAJORITY NEED NO HELP

The majority of women do not have to seek help. Fertility is the norm for 90 per cent of humanity. Over-fertility, indeed. Since nature considers the race before she considers the individual, in all functions vital to survival she gives us more energy than we need. She gives us so much energy to seek food, we can end up by stuffing ourselves silly. She gives us so much energy to seek and consummate sex, we can replenish the earth and to spare.

So in the normal course of events, nature gives the husband plenty of sperm and the desire for intercourse so often that his sperm remains very potent. She gives the wife a cervix with the right kind of fluid to encourage the sperm, tubes that are always open, ovulation with enough frequency so that if a willing egg isn't on hand one month it is the next.

Above all, she gives fears but also the ability to overcome them. So sooner or later as a rule a woman makes a positive decision toward pregnancy; she makes this decision as her way of saying "yes" to life.

"Yes," she says, "my insides *can* function, and pregnancy will prove it."

"Yes, pregnancy is a little frightening, but I have the courage to undertake it."

"Yes, I should like my first-born to be a son, especially if he comes after the period of marriage-disillusion. For then I can recreate the fantasy of a 'perfect' relationship. I can dream he will be all the things my husband for the moment is not."

"But yes, yes, yes!"

And as she makes this series of yeses, she finds herself asking the most frequently asked question in the world.

❋❋❋ 26 "Doctor, Am I Pregnant?"

The most frequently asked question is, "Doctor, am I pregnant?" A married woman who is having intercourse asks it over and over again for thirty odd years, and if a doctor isn't on hand to give an answer, she grabs a friend, a neighbor, a mid-wife—anyone who might know.

But before she asks, she has made a guess herself. She bases this guess on several well-known signs, though some of the signs may be very misleading.

A DELAYED PERIOD

The first sign a woman usually looks for is a delayed menstrual period. Whether she fears pregnancy or desires it, comes a few days' delay and she immediately cries, "This is it!"

But we've just seen how powerfully the emotions can influence the hormones, so that the very fact that a woman desperately fears pregnancy, or ardently desires it, can cause a period to be delayed for days, weeks or more.

FALSE PREGNANCY

There is a rare condition called "hysterical pregnancy" or "false pregnancy" that dramatically points this up. Here a woman with an ardent desire for children can go through a whole nine months of missed periods plus all the other classic symptoms, and not be pregnant at all.

The last Czarina of Russia went through such a hysterical pregnancy. After four daughters she wanted a son and heir badly, and her periods stopped, her breasts became full, her abdomen swelled; she even had false labor pains. But when it came to delivery, there was nothing there. Later, of course, she did bear a son, the sick little boy whom Rasputin claimed he could cure. But first she went through those whole nine illusory months when, as they say, it was "all in her mind."

Recently a 27-year-old woman who had borne one child came to the University of Oklahoma Hospital clinic with all the symptoms of a four-month pregnancy, except that the doctors knew she had had a hysterectomy several years previously and so nothing could possibly be there. Yet she insisted she *was* pregnant, repeating: "This is just like my other one," and even awoke a few weeks later, still in the hospital, with what she was sure were "labor pains." It took much psychotherapy to convince her she was wrong, to give away her new layette and to go home.

If such extremes can happen—hysterical pregnancy was known to Hippocrates thousands of years ago—is it surprising that fear or hope can delay a period a mere few days or weeks?

OTHER CAUSES OF DELAY

Then there is plain malnutrition. Women who go on crazy reducing periods often so deplete their vital forces that their periods are skipped or delayed just as they are in adolescent girls.

There are also all kinds of stress. The stress of a new job, of a death in the family, of a drastic change in air, can wreak havoc with the menstrual cycle for a time. So one missed or delayed period may mean nothing at all; it needs at least two periods to count.

Dr. John Rock says a woman's conclusion she is pregnant on the basis of one delayed or missed period has lined the pockets of abortionists, as well as the sellers of fake "abortion-pills." A survey done in one hospital clinic showed that as many as 40 per cent of the women who thought they were pregnant were not. Yet abortionists are hardly eager to do pregnancy-tests on a prospective client with a pocket full of money to spend. So they merely do a routine curettage, charging as much as the traffic will bear, figuring she'll never be able to prove later she wasn't pregnant in the first place, or even bother to try.

BETTER SIGNS

The next sign women look for is "morning sickness." Morning sickness is the popular term for nausea, or a "funny feeling" in the stomach, that plagues some pregnant women. If a woman has had intercourse the night before and feels "funny" the next morning, again she may leap to the conclusion, "This is it!"

But one can "feel funny" in the stomach for a dozen reasons. And certainly no one starts being nauseated a few hours after conception. It just doesn't work that fast.

Another pregnancy-sign is a change in the breasts. The breasts become full, tender and start to tingle. But this sign can also be misleading, since full, tender breasts are also a sign of pre-menstrual tension.

Better signs are sleepiness and frequency of urination. At the beginning of pregnancy, some women get so sleepy they can fall asleep standing bolt upright in a jolting train. Others develop an urgent desire to urinate.

If all of these come at the same time—at least two missed periods, plus full breasts, plus great sleepiness, plus much urination, plus a little nausea—they do point to pregnancy. But they're still not proof positive. A doctor looks for more.

WHAT A DOCTOR LOOKS FOR

A doctor starts looking, logically, at the top, or the breasts, then goes down to the abdomen and vagina, using his skilled fingers as well as his eyes as he goes.

At the initial visit, he looks at the breasts and palpates them for evidence of changes in the glands. Then he tries to strip the nipples of a little colostrum—the yellow fluid that comes in before the milk.

Next he asks his patient to undress to her slip and hop up onto a special examining-table, on which she lies on her back with a sheet covering her and her knees raised high. This position has been embarrassing to women through the years. An old woodcut shows a nineteenth-century doctor examining a pregnant woman standing up fully clothed, and one end of a large cloth tied around his neck while the other is tied around hers. He is probing under the cloth, unable to see more than her face.

A modern doctor, after examining the breasts, next looks carefully at the abdomen for evidence of a change. Then he looks at the vagina for three telltale signs: a change in color from pink to dusky as evidence of an increased vaginal blood-supply, an increase in elasticity of the vaginal tissues as preparation for the delivery to come, and an increase in vaginal discharge due to increased activity of the mucus-secreting glands.

Finally, at this first visit, he gently examines the uterus for signs of enlargement and growing softness, with one or two fingers in the vagina and a hand on the abdomen. While this uterine examination is most important, a few doctors omit it for self-protection. Some patients who later miscarry swear the uterine examination "shook the baby out." Nonsense! Nothing as simple as a gentle examination can shake out a baby. Once it has securely burrowed in, a baby is a persistent little object with all kinds of shock-absorbers. Dr. Guttmacher tells of an unwed and desperate pregnant woman who jumped out of a second-story window, hoping the fall would "shake it out." She broke both legs, but the tenacious baby stayed in.

THE PREGNANCY TESTS

When all the signs are positive, a doctor still cannot say for certain from an examination alone that a woman is pregnant until about the twelfth week. If she has to know sooner, she must resort to the pregnancy-tests.

Most of the pregnancy-tests are reliable as early as the third or fourth week after conception. As I write this, other and faster ones keep coming along, but so far few have held up.

The ones that have held up are the mouse test, the rabbit test and the frog test. Women lump them together as a rule under the familiar name of the "A.Z. test," named after the two doctors who originally discovered them, bald stubby Herman Ascheim and brilliant Bernard Zondek of Berlin.

Here's how the test works: A woman who thinks she may be three or four weeks pregnant—that is, she has missed one period and waited at least a week after the time she expected it to arrive—drinks no more than one cup of fluid from 4 o'clock in the afternoon until the next morning, then before breakfast that morning takes a specimen of her urine and puts it into a clean bottle and hurries with that bottle to a laboratory or a drugstore displaying the A.Z. sign. (If she can't hurry, she refrigerates the bottle of urine until she can.)

In the laboratory, technicians inject the urine immediately into five young, virgin female mice. Twenty-four hours later, they kill the mice and examine their ovaries for signs of ovulation. If at least three out of the five mice have ovulated, they send back a positive pregnancy-report. If there's any doubt about the ovulation, they do the test again.

The test has proven more than 95 per cent accurate, and the rabbit and frog tests have proven the same, since they are merely variations of the mouse test. And it is the presence of a special quantity of pregnancy hormones in the woman that makes the tests work out.

HOW THE PREGNANCY HORMONES DIFFER

For a woman's hormones become very different in quantity after she becomes pregnant. When she is not pregnant, as you will remember, her hormones go up and down in tides each month. During the first half of the month, estrogen is made by her ovaries under the urgent messages sent them by her pituitary or chief gland. Up, up, goes the estrogen tide as her ovaries receive the "go" messages. Then "stop" messages are sent back by her ovaries to her pituitary, and there is a short rest.

During the second half of the month, the rest being over, more "go" messages are sent by her pituitary to her ovaries, this time urging them to make both estrogen and progesterone—the progesterone being the "in favor of birth" hormone that doubly thickens the uterine lining to prepare a home in case a baby is conceived. Up, up, goes the hormone tide now again until, if no baby has been conceived, more "stop" messages are sent, both estrogen and progesterone are suddenly withdrawn, the unused uterine lining is thrown off, the unfertilized egg crumbles and dies and menstruation comes with its hormone lull.

WHEN PREGNANCY OCCURS

But when a baby *has* been conceived, or pregnancy occurs, there is what amounts to a hormone revolution. Now there is no lull at the end of the month. On the contrary, estrogen and progesterone continue to rise; rise so much in order to nourish and energize the growing fetus that a woman makes many, many times the amount of sex hormones that she did before. It is these extra hormones, plus some hormones made by the fertilized egg itself, that show up in her urine and make the tests work. They do not show up in sufficient quantity until at least three or four weeks after conception, however, because before that time there are not enough to be counted.

But after that time there usually *are* enough. Enough to make a tiny immature mouse or rabbit suddenly "grow up" and ovulate, and show the changes in its ovaries that ovulation brings.

What a boon to women that these tests were discovered! That as early as a few weeks after conception she can know with about 95 per cent accuracy whether she is pregnant or not.

OTHER MYSTERIES EXPLAINED

The hormone revolution explains other mysteries, too.

It explains the extraordinary sleepiness at the beginning of pregnancy. No hormone is a simple chemical; progesterone, in addition to its other properties, is a most soothing hormone. At first a woman's great progesterone tide is so soothing it lulls her to sleep. But after a while her body gets used to the new state of affairs and the sleepiness wears off.

Next the hormone revolution explains the frequency of urination. Pituitary and estrogenic hormones are also far from simple. Pituitary hormones affect the adrenal glands which in turn affect the water-balance. With her pituitary now going full blast and sending almost constant messages to her adrenals and ovaries to keep on producing hormones, a woman's body makes a lot of extra water that must either be retained or thrown off. Her body prefers to throw it off whenever possible. One way of doing this is to throw it up. Another is to throw it out by much more urination than usual.

Then the hormone revolution explains the breast-changes. Still another job of the pituitary is to stimulate the breasts to make milk. And while the need for milk for the baby is still a long way off, the pituitary still starts at this early time to develop the milk glands. These swell the breasts, and as the pregnancy progresses other hormones made by the placenta join in and keep them swelled.

AN EMOTIONAL DRAMA

But pregnancy is far more to a woman than a hormone revolution. It is an emotional drama. A drama that, like most dramas, can be divided into three acts, each act having its special emotions that range from excitement to passivity to fear and back to excitement again, and all adding up to an experience that makes most of the other events in her life pale before it.

Let's begin to sit in on that drama now.

❋❋❋ 27 The Pregnancy Drama: Act I

Since it is a drama, pregnancy has its heroes and its villains, and is concerned with life and death. For life and death are so close to each other, a woman cannot create one without approaching the shadows of the other. So pregnancy is both a blissful time, full of promise and hope, and a myth-haunted time full of ancient fears.

The curtain goes up on Act I.

A TREMENDOUS UPHEAVAL

A woman, as I said, doesn't immediately know she is pregnant. But know it or not, conception from the very first moment causes a tremendous upheaval inside her. Every remote cell in her body is involved; you might call it a biological storm. So Act I starts off either with a storm's pleasurable excitement, or with the rumblings of threatening thunder, depending on whether the woman has longed for pregnancy or dreaded it as a "trap."

MORNING SICKNESS

The most famous evidence of thunder is nausea, or morning sickness. It is famous because it's largely expected. "Aren't you glad I haven't got morning sickness?" women ask their husbands when they don't have it. "I'm glad," they naturally reply.

Morning sickness, when it does come, has several causes, and doctors aren't sure which is the most important. One cause may be the new high level of estrogen at the beginning of pregnancy that shoots up to give the embryo extra food to grow on and extra water to drink. But this water doesn't only nourish the baby; it floods all the mother's cells. At times, some of it accumulates in her stomach and intestines, particularly while she sleeps. When it does, it causes irritation in the morning when she wakes. But as the morning wears on, some of this water is passed off in the urine or absorbed in other ways. By noon, she feels better and, as the day goes by, better yet. The storm lulls.

It takes about the same four weeks for the estrogen-level to become high enough for the woman to feel it and become nauseated as it does for her to know she is pregnant in the first place, so morning sickness doesn't usually enter the scene for about a month. But only about a third of all women get it at all these days, and only about a tenth get sick enough to remember it. Yet it's the old story of the creaking wheel; this tenth make a lot of noise.

They've made so much noise that until lately morning sickness was much more common among American and European women than among primitive Eskimo, African or Mexican women. This, according to Doctors William Kroger and Herbert Freed, is because primitive women have been traditionally more stoical and resigned to whatever fate may bring. They have talked less about nausea, and expected it less. But now that many of them have become "modern," they have started to vomit, too, mainly because it is the thing to do.

Also, until lately American and European women have found it hard to accept the so-called "animal functions" of the body—the secretions and excretions, the plain necessary dirt. The functions of conception have awakened all kinds of hidden ideas of disgust, and it's well known that disgust causes nausea. Anyone who has observed a child throw up at the mere sight of food that looks unattractive will testify to that. So American and European women, with their centuries of teaching that sex and childbirth were "dirty," or "beastly," have thrown up as a result.

ENLARGING UTERUS

Another cause of morning sickness, says Dr. Robert N. Rutherford, is the enlarging uterus of early pregnancy. A woman's enlarging uterus presses on the trigger mechanism of her bladder, making her not only want to throw up at times but also constantly to "go."

INCREASED AWARENESS

Still another cause is the great increase in her inner awareness.

We all have three kinds of awareness: an outer awareness, sensitivity to what's going on in the world; a surface awareness, or sensitivity to our skin, faces and bodies; an inner awareness, or sensitivity to our mysterious "insides." Women have much more surface and inner sensitivity than men, particularly inner, developing it first during the teens. No girl can start to menstruate and adolesce and not have her thoughts turned sharply inward at least every four weeks.

But during pregnancy this inner awareness is tremendously increased. Increased to a point that would be abnormal in a non-pregnant state. What's more, it stays; it does not go and come like the awareness of menstruation. A pregnant woman senses this when she finds she just can't stay interested in things like politics or reading serious newspapers like *The New York Times*. "What's wrong with me? Am I losing my grip?" she worriedly asks.

Nothing is wrong. During pregnancy, nature deliberately switches most of her awareness from out to in so a woman can concentrate on signals from her baby; let her watch and listen intensely to make sure nothing goes wrong. Unfortunately, this makes her more alive to her own discomforts as well. The heartburn or constipation or leg-cramps that would have gone more or less unnoticed now loom tremendous. Particularly the morning sickness, which has been so widely heralded Greek women were speaking about it thousands of years ago.

SELF-PUNISHMENT

In addition, some psychiatrists see morning sickness as self-punishment. A way of trying to throw up a desired pregnancy as a punishment for past sins.

Recently Dr. Eleanor Hamilton of New York did a special research on the worries of pregnancy. She found one of her patients, whom she calls Kit, feeling extremely guilty for stealing her husband from her sister, who was incurably ill. Kit thought that after her marriage "she had all the good things in life while her sister had none."

The baby would be the crowning good thing. But she was unconsciously trying to punish herself by throwing it up.

Norma, another patient, had once wished her brother dead. He hadn't died, but she knew she had wished it. Now, wishing relatives dead is extremely common; we all do it at one time or another. But Norma never forgave herself for the wish, and was also punishing herself by trying to throw up her desired child.

PUNISHING HUSBANDS

Still other women throw up to punish their husbands. Absent husbands more than on-the-scene husbands; particularly husbands who have volunteered for war or seem to have deliberately deserted them in other ways.

For during pregnancy, there is also a great increase in dependency. An amount of dependency that would also be abnormal at other times. The expected baby is so dependent on its mother, a woman seems to need to become extra-dependent and protected herself to balance things out.

Perhaps this is how human marriage started. Women sought marriage because they needed husbands who would stay near them, support them and protect them while they were pregnant, and men were willing to become husbands and stay around their women in exchange for regular sex and getting the child.

So when men leave their wives during pregnancy, they are more bereft than at any other time, and more apt to want to punish them. "Look at the terrible thing he has done to me!" they cry. Dr. Helene Deutsch had a patient who was a fine, intelligent woman and a skilled musician. She had had two uneventful pregnancies while her husband was home. He volunteered for long-term army service and broke the basic triangle of father, mother and child. Her third pregnancy was awful. She punished him by throwing up all over the place.

EATING TO MAKE UP FOR IT

But you can never reckon without the fact of human ambivalence. We don't want something one minute and want it the next. So many of the very women who throw up promptly feel guilty because they *have* thrown up and want the baby more than ever. As a result, they try to protect the pregnancy by eating like mad. When they eat too much and their stomachs get over-full, the extra food, plus the extra water, makes them more nauseated than ever. Then they are in a state.

IT GOES AWAY

Luckily, there's a cheerful end to the nausea story. This is that for the comparatively few who do get it these days, it usually goes away by the end of the third month. It goes away because she gets used to the high estrogen-level of pregnancy, and because after the third month her uterus no longer is down in her pelvis pressing on her bladder but has risen up into her abdomen where it can no longer press.

It also goes away for a new reason: this is the development of the placenta—a remarkable pregnancy arrangement that is like no other arrangement a woman ever has.

Placenta is Latin for "cake," and that's about what the placenta is—a large, flat, spongelike cake that forms at the spot where the fertilized egg has burrowed in. It is a cake of concentrated richness that provides nourishment and protection for the baby, and help for the mother, too.

THE PLACENTA HELPS THE MOTHER

Here's how it helps the mother: When pregnancy starts, the first hormones to leap up, as we saw, are the estrogens. The next are the progesterones. Now both hormones have been made all along by the ovaries, but the ovaries are tiny bodies and not up to the enormous pregnancy job. Especially the job of making enough progesterone to keep the uterus quiet and hold the growing baby in. That job is now taken over by the placenta.

So as soon as embedment of the egg is complete, the placenta starts to form. But since it is a special, new and comparatively large organ, it takes about three months to become fully developed. By the end of Act I, however, it is complete. By the end of the third month, it is producing enough progesterones to make the baby stay put, as well as producing enough to balance some of the extra estrogens and reduce their irritating qualities. And so the estrogen-caused nausea happily disappears.

Finally, the emotional causes disappear. There is a huge emotional change as a woman proceeds from Act I to Act II. During Act II most women positively enjoy pregnancy and decide they'd like to become pregnant again.

THE BABY AND THE PLACENTA

Now, what the remarkable placenta does for the baby.

One of the chief jobs of the placenta, as we saw, is to keep the uterus quiet. Another is to make it soft and large and provide an expanding home. This growing softness and largeness is why pregnancy at a certain point often can be diagnosed simply by feeling the uterus. If a woman is not pregnant, doctors say the uterus feels "as hard as the tip of her nose." If she is, it feels "as soft as her lips."

THE PLACENTA STRAINS

Possibly most important for the baby, the spongelike placenta acts as a fine-mesh strainer, straining out most of the diseases the mother may catch and harm the baby with, or the harmful drugs she may take. It doesn't filter out all the diseases and drugs, to be sure, only most. The drug Thalidomide that deforms unborn babies proved to be one of the exceptions. Another is German measles.

German measles is a strange disease. Its official name is rubella, meaning "red spots," and it was dubbed "German" because at first it was thought to be more common in Germany than elsewhere, which isn't true.

Rubella is strange because it seems fairly innocuous as far as the mother is concerned. It seldom makes a woman very sick, or lasts more than a few days. But if these few days happen to fall during Act I, the rubella germs can go through the still-developing placental strainer and seriously hurt the child; make it blind or deaf or damage its brain. It can do this because the baby's brain, and nerves to the eyes or ears, are also being formed during Act I. After that, they are complete and can no longer be hurt.

Queen Juliana of The Netherlands had German measles during Act I of her last pregnancy. The court doctors wanted to abort her as a preventative measure, but she was thirty-seven and hoped for a son after three daughters. She refused, and gave birth to her youngest daughter who is nearly blind.

THE AUSTRALIAN DOCTOR

The harm done by German measles was cleverly deduced by an Australian eye doctor, Sir Norman McAlister of Sydney. In 1941, Dr. McAlister was very much upset by what seemed to be a local epidemic of cataracts in the newborn. He wondered whether something that happened during their mothers' pregnancies could have caused it, and set out to track down their histories. Sure enough, 68 out of 78 mothers had had the same disease, rubella, during those vital first few months. By good detective work, he rechecked his findings around the world. Everywhere he found the same results; this common infection, almost always mild in children, too, was sometimes so severe in its effects on pregnant women it crippled their unborn.

Actually, other doctors found, rubella seems to damage whatever tissues are growing fastest when the infection strikes. At a 1960 international conference on the subject, Dr. Andrew J. Rhodes of Toronto reported that rubella can cause cataracts during the sixth week, deafness during the ninth, heart defects during the fifth to tenth and dental deformities during the sixth to ninth.

Some doctors even go so far now as to suggest that all girls be deliberately infected with German measles while young, in order to develop antibodies as a protection for later pregnancies, though not all doctors agree.

However, German measles early in pregnancy is still one of the few reasons for legal abortion in most countries, both in America and abroad.

OTHER CRIPPLERS

Other cripplers of an unborn baby that go through the placental barrier are mumps, and drugs like marijuana and heroin. Babies of addicted mothers may be, rather strangely, born addicted themselves, and have to be given gradually smaller and smaller doses of drugs until they are withdrawn.

NOTHING ELSE

But again there's a cheerful note to the story. Few other diseases or drugs we know of do go through the placenta. The dreaded T.B. or polio, which a mother may catch during pregnancy, does not. Neither do simple drugs like aspirin or mild sedatives. Also, the placenta is a two-way-passage. Some of the baby's own products happily go through it and help the mother. If she has diabetes, some doctors believe the baby manufactures extra insulin and passes some on to her, making her diabetes temporarily better. If she has arthritis the baby makes extra adrenal hormones that help that. This was how the well-known adrenal hormones ACTH and cortisone were discovered. Researchers stumbled upon them after noticing that many women's arthritis seemed spontaneously to improve while they were pregnant. So they started deliberately giving cortisone and ACTH to women who were not pregnant, with the same good results.

THE SINS OF THE FATHERS

But German measles, arthritis, diabetes and morphine-addiction are worries of only a minority of women. A far more common worry is giving birth to a child who has inherited the family illnesses. "Will my child inherit my father's diseases or those of his father before him?" is a nagging question. "Will the sins of my ancestors be visited upon my child?"

The answer is an almost positive no. A child may inherit a tendency toward a family disease, but not the disease itself. It will not be born with cancer because "cancer runs in the family," or born to be a drunk because "grandfather couldn't leave liquor alone."

There are several important reasons for this. The first is that the germ-cells of ova and sperm live a life separate and apart from the rest of our bodies. We get our germ-cells at birth direct from our ancestors, who got them from their ancestors, who got them from theirs. After we get them, we merely carry them around as we received them with little change. We may later develop gout or gallstones, but we do not pass them on in a complete form.

Second, the germ-cells contain small particles called chromosomes. And while every other cell in our bodies has 46 chromosomes, the germ-cells are splits and have only 23. This is in order that when the splits of ova and sperm unite, a new complete cell with 46 chromosomes can be formed again. And since the germ-cells *are* splits, we inherit only half our chromosomes from our mother and half from our father, and our mother and father inherited only half of theirs from each side of their families, and so on back in an endless chain to the beginning of time.

Third, each of the 46 chromosomes contains at least fifteen thousand genes which are the actual bearers of the family traits. And when the original cells split up, taking along half of their chromosomes and leaving out the other half, it seems to be pure chance which chromosomes go along, taking their thousands of genes with them, and which chromosomes with other genes stay behind. It works out to over seventeen million possible combinations of genes that have gone to make us, and another seventeen million that will make our baby—seventeen million all mixed up like red and blue and green confetti, almost every color and shape and size under the sun.

Add to all this the fact that every male ejaculation contains several hundred million sperm cells, and again it is pure chance which sperm cell, carrying which possible seventeen million genes, will penetrate which waiting ovum. The mathematics of the mixing thus becomes breathtaking. Who then can possibly predict the family traits we will pass along, or which leave behind?

We may pass along grandfather's quick wit, and leave out his drinking propensities. Pass on great-grandmother's courage, and leave out her weak kidneys. Get great-great-grandfather's red hair, but not his rugged strength.

ABILITY TO SURVIVE

This is why nature has made two sexes in the first place, and evolved this cunning plan of confetti-mixing. She has done it to insure a normal race with the ability to survive. Survive with big brains or medium-sized ones; when things are going rough or going smooth, in drought-ages or ice-ages, in times of plenty or famine, in the heat of the tropics or the chill of the poles. Survive in sufficient numbers for a majority to endure and pass on their genes in turn.

Writing in *Human Embryology*, the biologist Bradley A. Patten expresses the plan this way:

Thus there is produced sufficient stability to insure continuity and at the same time sufficient variety to insure progress. For the offspring will in the main resemble progenitors which have successfully lived in the prevailing conditions of the past, but will exhibit sufficient variability among themselves to insure that some of them shall successfully live in any conditions likely to arise in the future.

ALL MIXED UP

It should be of great comfort to the pregnant woman to remember, then, that her husband may be sent on an assignment to Alaska, and she has a fine chance of having children with the brains and stamina to follow him there. Or he may be sent to steaming Libya, and they should be able to endure there, too.

On the other hand, it is unreasonable to expect any of our children to look or behave like any particular ancestor. One may have grandmother's hooked nose, another great-grandmother's straight one; another grandfather's blue eyes; another grandma's brown. Certainly there will be *some* family resemblance, but it may be all mixed up. For each child is a unique individual, because he is the only person in the whole world with his exact blend of genes, even as you and I.

There's also no reason to expect a child to look or act like a woman's *former* husband. A strange belief persists that the child of a second marriage may, through some mysterious influence, resemble the husband of the first.

This belief was probably started by an unfaithful wife. "Oh, little Willie's temper?" she must have said airily. "That came from my ex, Joe." Nonsense. If little Willie looks or acts like a Joe, it is some current Joe. He's the only "mysterious influence" who is at work.

95 PER CENT NORMAL

Here are some recent statistics compiled by the U.S. Department of Health. Of all the millions of babies born in the U.S. each year, only 4 per cent are born with disease of any kind, plus only 1 per cent with a physical malformation. The terrific publicity on "blue" babies, cerebral-palsy babies, retarded babies, etc., can scare the daylights out of any woman who forgets that these are a tiny minority.

Put positively: a whopping 95 per cent of us are born normal— a figure worth memorizing, and repeating over and over again.

It is partly because of this normal 95 per cent that all plans for the sterilization of criminals or the otherwise unfit have usually fallen through. Not only is it a natural right to bear children, but scientists realize how small a percentage sterilization would affect. Besides, women with low mentalities have been known to give birth to geniuses, and geniuses to fools.

Genius is inexplicable and unpredictable. Who knows from what ancestor Beethoven got the genes that gave him his musical ability, Rembrandt his eye for color and form, Lincoln his compassion, Mahatma Gandhi his courage to become a living saint?

"Before I was born out of my mother, generations guided me," said Walt Whitman. To deliberately improve the human race, we'd have to go back hundreds of generations, not one. Meanwhile, nature does pretty well by herself.

PREGNANCY A DOUBLE FEATURE

Pregnancy is like a double feature, played simultaneously. There is the baby's story and the mother's story. So during each act of pregnancy we will flash from mother to baby, then from baby to mother again.

What is happening to the baby while mother is or is not having morning sickness, threat of miscarriage, unfounded worry over punishment for her own or her father's sins?

Baby is blissfully comfortable, getting started on its stupendous growth from its original cells to the approximately two billion it will eventually become.

Flash to baby.

LIFE BEGINS

We left the baby, after the cataclysmic event of union of ova and sperm, with the fertilized egg starting to journey down the tube toward the womb.

Scientists refer to an unborn child first as an embryo or fetus, and later as a baby. Most mothers simply call him "it" all along. I'll do a little of each.

As it starts its two-inch downward journey, the egg that is to become a baby is no bigger than the point of a very fine needle, or the dot over an *i*. Waved on by contractions within the tube, it is wafted down toward the womb and in a few days reaches its future home. It floats around for a day or two in the warm, dark, fluid-filled womb cavity, then burrows energetically into its thick, spongy lining.

As it burrows in, its mother may have a slight flow of blood. This is the flow that has given rise to the story that some women continue to menstruate during pregnancy. But as a rule there is only this single, slight, burrowing-in flow, then no more.

STARTS TO EAT

By burrowing-in time the original needle-fine cell has become a whole cluster of cells. As the cluster burrows in, it starts to absorb nourishment from the soft, thick lining much as a hungry plants starts to absorb nourishment from the rich, soft soil.

SOMETHING SPECTACULAR

On the ninth day, something spectacular occurs. The round cluster no longer remains a round cluster: it starts to break up into layers. One layer is the yolk sac, which fed the cluster until it burrowed in; the second layer will become the amnion and the third layer starts to take human shape. Acting on instructions from the genes which have worked out the pattern over millions of years, this third layer breaks up into body-cells, nerve-cells, blood-cells—everything that will eventually make up a living child.

As early as the nineteenth or twentieth day, for instance, a crease forms down one of its surfaces, and lo! there is the beginning of the spinal cord. On the twenty-sixth day, there form two tiny buds that will develop into arms and on the twenty-eighth day other buds that will develop into legs.

A BEATING HEART

By the end of the third week, some of the cells of the third layer have even formed a heart, and this heart has begun to beat. It is only a primitive heart, to be sure, but compared with the size of the embryo, it is nine times as large as the adult heart. And after a few days of practice, this primitive heart will be pumping away at the rate of 65 times a minute in order to circulate the embryo's newly formed bloodstream.

The beating of this embryonic heart cannot yet be heard through the mother's abdominal wall. Later, it will be heard, and it will give out a double beat like the tick of a watch. It will also beat much faster than the mother's heart, enabling the doctor to tell the difference between them.

With the formation of its heart during the third week, the embryo's development proceeds by leaps and bounds. Indeed, it proceeds so fast that by the end of the first month, though its mother often is not sure yet she is pregnant, it will have done the largest relative amount of growing it will ever do in its entire life, having become among other things, almost a whole inch long.

Geraldine Lux Flanagan tells all about this in fascinating detail in her book *The First Months of Life*. And she insists that, as the baby develops, it never goes through the actual stages of being a fish or a monkey or anything else. It always remains a human baby. The reason for the fish myth is that nature has only a limited number of basic patterns from which to build all her creatures, so for a short time these patterns may look alike, just as a blouse pattern may look like that of a house-jacket until it gets its finishing touches. So the tail of a monkey grows out of the same stub that later becomes the human coccyx at the base of the spine, and the ears grow out of the same slits that in a fish become the gills. But that doesn't mean we ever had, or were intended to have, a monkey's tail or the gills of a smelt.

THE AMNIOTIC FLUID

After the miraculous formation of the beating heart comes the miraculous development of the amnion.

Amnion is Greek for "little lamb," and the amnion is another special pregnancy arrangement that in its own way is as remarkable as the placenta.

The amnion is a thin, tough, flexible membrane that encloses the embryo completely, and is filled with a fluid called the amniotic fluid that make it the "bag of waters" in which the baby serenely floats. It was named amnion because lambs are often born still enclosed in their membranes, and this fact was probably first observed by a curious shepherd who told it to another shepherd who told it to several more, until in time one duly wrote it down.

The amniotic fluid has the special job of protecting the baby from jars and jolts. You know that you can't hurt a person by slapping him when he's underwater. Well, you can't hurt or jolt an unborn baby by slapping it, or its mother's belly. No matter what you do within reason to its mother, the bag of waters acts as a powerful shock-absorber to keep it from harm.

Can our almost universal attraction to the sea come from this original floating in a sac of protecting waters? Is that why a dip in the warm, buoyant ocean is always so soothing? Speculate as we may, we know that the baby does float in a bit of warm private ocean from the end of its first month on.

THE SECOND MONTH

The second month sees more changes. Now the one-inch-long baby is a complete miniature creature with a human face, human eyes, human ears and nose, and even the germs of human teeth deep in its human gums. Its arms, as Geraldine Flanagan tells us, have also developed from their original stubs, and added miniature fingers and thumbs. Its legs have added miniature knees, ankles and toes and, most miraculous of all, there has been added a miniature human brain.

It is during this crucial period when the brain, eyes and ears are being added that, as we saw, the baby can be hurt by those few substances that pass through the placental barrier. But, luckily, during this same period it can also be most easily influenced for good. For during this same Act I period, baby is not only becoming human, but human along its own family lines. Thus, some embryos develop larger ears or keener hearing than others, much as their families have larger ears or keener hearing. Their brain develops for better or worse much as their families have better or less good brains. Their eyes grow dimmer or sharper, their very longevity is mainly determined. Yet with all this, each baby becomes an individual, too. During Act I it develops its own footprints and palm-prints—the footprints and palm-prints that will characterize it and make it unique to the end of its days.

And all this develops day by day, month by month, according to the universal plan. The embryologist Davenport Hooker, working with several associates at the University of Pittsburgh, patiently put together during thirty years a remarkable series of pre-natal pictures. They found the plan so masterly they could tell almost to an hour how old an embryo was.

And by the end of the second month, the pictures show such a remarkable state of comparative completion that even researchers no longer refer to it as an "embryo." They, too, use the word "baby," since it is now truly a little person in his or her own right.

THE THIRD MONTH

During the third month this little person begins to move all over. Though it still weighs only one ounce, it kicks with its tiny legs, makes a tiny fist, and turns its tiny head. In preparation for life outside the womb, it also starts to practice breathing and swallowing. It does not actually breathe yet because it gets its oxygen from its mother's blood through its umbilical cord, and it does not do much swallowing because it gets its food in the same way. But it gets ready to do these things as early in its little life as this.

Davenport Hooker's films even show the three-month-old, pre-natal baby swinging his whole body back and forth for a few moments at a time, the way its mother may swing it in a cradle or carriage after it is born.

A MILESTONE

At the end of the third month, the baby passes a milestone.

Its movements before were mechanical; now they become graceful. Refinements like nailbuds have formed at the ends of its fingers, and its face has become almost pretty. The face has a delicate mouth complete with tiny taste-buds and saliva-glands, and this tiny mouth has started to practice the sucking and swallowing movements it will need in order to stay alive in the outside world. Even its genitals have formed, and if it's to be a girl, the ovaries within the pelvis already contain some of the egg cells that perhaps in turn, with the help of some unknown male baby, will develop into future babies and carry on the great chain of life.

But these developments, wondrous as they are, are not the milestone. The milestone is that, by the end of Act I, the baby passes the test of its own survival. The third month is when nature as a rule decides whether it will be aborted, or carry on and get properly born.

A "MISS"

When a baby escapes or is forced out of the womb prematurely for any reason, doctors call this premature termination of pregnancy an abortion. Lay people often call an induced escape an abortion, but a natural one a miscarriage—or, more familiarly, a "miss."

Researchers disagree on statistics here; some say ten per cent of all babies are "misses," some say twenty per cent. But they do agree that at least three-quarters of them miscarry during their second or third month of womb life.

Why do they do it so soon? Nature has the good sense to quickly discard something defective and start again. And an aborted baby is almost always defective. Either it didn't happen to form a proper germ cell during union, or it didn't burrow into the womb properly or something else went wrong.

Dr. Alan Guttmacher tells how a wonderful former teacher of his forcefully demonstrated the chances of miscarriage before the learned members of the New York Obstetrical Society. Dr. George Streeter of the Carnegie Institute of Embryology stood upon the platform in an impeccable tuxedo and took a handful of ordinary garden pea-pods out of his pocket. "Gentlemen," he said, as he casually shelled the peas, "I cannot be sure, but I'll hazard the guess that these pods will contain one or two bad, runted peas—defective germ-plasma conceptions." They did.

So, too, some human conceptions are defective or runted. And when they are, they are discarded early in the game. The uterus automatically forces them out as something unwanted, the way we automatically blink an unwanted cinder out of our eyes.

Most miscarriages, therefore, are not the result of something seriously wrong with either parent, nor are they the result of inheritance of "bad genes." They are rather the result of simple bad luck.

Dr. Edith L. Potter, a professor of Pathology at the University of Chicago, carefully examined more than 1500 miscarried embryos, and states without hesitation that they were rarely due to bad genes. In fact, she insists that even a long series of miscarriages does not significantly increase the chance that a woman's next baby will be born with a defect.

It merely means that the particular pregnancy that missed probably wasn't a good one, and it would be quite proper to begin again.

WELL PACKAGED

In spite of this, women continue to blame themselves and think that something they did "shook the baby out."

Such shaking is next to impossible, if the pregnancy *is* a good one. The baby is too well packaged and protected by its mother's tough abdominal muscles and uterine walls, not to mention its own amniotic sac. Says Dr. Guttmacher, "You cannot shake a good human egg loose any more than you can shake a good unripe apple from the apple tree." And Dr. Potter tells of another study done on four hundred wives stationed with their husbands at an air force base in Georgia. "During their pregnancies," Dr. Potter relates, "these women had traveled an average of 2000 miles each, by car, plane, train and bus. Some had crossed the continent in jouncing trucks; some had driven to Alaska and back. Five had been in serious smash-ups; one was catapulted out of a car. Twenty had been extricated from houses demolished by a tornado. Yet the miscarriage rate among these women was no higher than would be expected among women who spent their entire pregnancies placidly sewing little garments in their own homes."

MISCARRIAGE HABIT

When women miscarry three times in a row they are said to be "habitual aborters" or have the "miscarriage habit." Some doctors believe this habit has an emotional base. Dr. Helene Deutsch says she has often been called in by puzzled gynecologists to give psychiatric assistance to habitual aborters, and in some cases she found the woman wanted a child so badly and its loss was such a terrible trauma that there developed a compulsion to repeat the traumatic experience. "After every miscarriage, the wish for a new pregnancy was increased—like the desire for a drug in an addiction—and with it the tendency to miscarry," she says. "In one case the woman gave up all hope of success, adopted a child, and when she later became pregnant did not take any of the precautions against miscarriage that she had taken previously. Only then did she give birth to a normal child."

Other women break the miscarriage habit by taking specially prescribed hormones or vitamins. Even then, some doctors feel the most important factor is that treatment gives the woman renewed confidence in herself because the doctor expresses confidence in her. For success is contagious, too.

SIGNS OF MISCARRIAGE

Women expect pain to accompany miscarriage; it often does not. Bleeding is the most common sign.

This bleeding is like an exaggerated menstrual period, and is accompanied by cramps like exaggerated menstrual cramps. In addition, the blood contains shaggy clots anywhere in size from an egg to a peach. Doctors usually refer to these clots as "tissue" or "products of conception" and ask that all be saved for them to inspect. Women who don't like to handle this tissue will find a tea-strainer handy for rescuing it, after which it should be put into a clean bottle. This is no time for over-squeamishness or modesty. The doctor needs to examine the tissues to make sure that what looked like tissue was not merely a blood clot and also that he will remove what's left. He will do it by a simple operation called a "D and C," or dilation and curettage. Also, the tissue may give him valuable clues in preventing further misses.

THREATENED ABORTION

A threatened abortion may not develop into a real one, however. About half the women who start to abort, don't. That is why any suggestion of one should be reported promptly. Many doctors think a prompt taking to bed and staying there stops an abortion, but others are not so sure, which is one reason why the practice of medicine will always remain an art as well as a science. In still another study of almost two thousand women, Dr. Potter found that the quarter of them who were allowed to get up and go about their business after the worst part of the bleeding was over did about as well as the three-quarters who were confined strictly to bed.

In that one quarter, the babies must have fought to pass the survival-test, to live on to quicken and make their mothers "feel life."

So we drop the curtain on Act I and ring it up again on Act II. Enter the mother again to the center of the stage.

Act II, Scene One, of pregnancy starts with the fourth month, and brings with it a dramatic emotional change. Even a woman who has been panicked during Act I usually switches now to acceptance and joy.

One reason for this joyful feeling is that, with the "feeling of life" which comes soon after the fourth month, the baby is no longer a fantasy but a reality. As it starts to exercise and develop its muscular strength, its kicks become immensely reassuring. Even though it may not exercise for long periods at a time—it may wake, move around, get tired and go back to sleep—its kicks make a woman know it is *there*.

HER DOCTOR KNOWS, TOO

And even if the baby doesn't kick, a doctor can diagnose pregnancy after the fourth month without a test of any kind. He can do it, first, by measuring the height of her uterus.

Normally, the uterus lies way down in the pelvis. But during Act II it moves forward and starts to grow upward as well. During the fourth month, it reaches up about a third of the way between the pelvic bone and the navel. And each month thereafter it continues to increase in size and grow upward until eventually it is almost under the breasts near the border of the ribs. Since no other condition except pregnancy causes a uterus to enlarge in just this way, it is practically "proof positive" that a baby is inside.

Then, during Act II of pregnancy, there is also a noticeable increase of clear vaginal secretion, plus an increase of pigmentation around the nipples, plus the actual outline of a baby. A doctor looks for two, but measuring the height of the uterus is still the surest proof.

A DREAMLIKE STATE

Between the arrival of kicking, or feeling life, and the assurance by her doctor that her baby is a reality, the normal woman now becomes not only more joyful, she turns inward more and becomes much more passive —passive to a point that would be abnormal if she were not pregnant. She enters indeed into almost a dreamlike state.

One woman described this dreamlike state as "like riding on a boat

—you seem to sit still and do nothing, while the boat just sails you along." Another woman described it as "feeling like on a lazy spring morning when everything is in tune."

A college student put it: "So many things used to upset me. I'd lose my research paper, or people would chew toothpicks in class, or matches, and I'd get crazy. None of this bothers me any more. Maybe a pregnant woman makes a big psychological as well as a physical adjustment— maybe that explains it. I just know I feel fine and content."

While still another woman said of a friend: "She walks around looking so radiant you'd think she had a ribbon tied on the end of her belly button." The word "radiant" is the one most often used about a woman during Act II, since her face softens and shows an inner glow. Her body glows, too, since the sleepy time of Act I is over and hormones that make her more placid also paradoxically charge her with energy. Thus she only *seems* to vegetate; she is charged with energy, too.

COMPULSIVE PREGNANCY

The contented feeling and the radiance of Act II also explain something else that puzzles many people—compulsive pregnancy.

There are women who puzzle us by getting pregnant over and over though they are poor, know about birth-control methods and have no scruples about using them. They may even care little about the child after it comes, but pregnancy itself is a temptation they cannot resist. So they manage to achieve it again and again, justifying themselves by talking about "duty" or saying they "feel empty" without a baby inside of them, when actually it is the pleasure of the turned-in, dreamy state of Act II they are seeking again and again.

PHYSICAL DISCOMFORTS

Yet dreaminess or not, Act II has its physical discomfort. Almost no woman gets all of them and some women may get none of them, but here they are:

1. *Heartburn.* Heartburn is one of the most common, although the name is a misnomer, since it has nothing to do with the heart. Heartburn is essentially a harmless, though unpleasant, condition resulting from the pressure of the up-travelling uterus against the stomach. It can be helped

by eating small meals—slowly—and remembering it *is* harmless and will go away.

2. *Backache.* This again is the result of pressure—this time because the enlarging uterus puts a strain on the back muscles, and also because the pelvic joints are relaxing toward the birth event and this makes the mother walk in an unnatural way. High heels make backache infinitely worse since during pregnancy nature throws the spine backward to counteract the stomach that is sticking forward. High heels throw the stomach still farther forward so nature has to throw the spine still further backward, making the ache that much worse.

3. *Varicose veins.* These are caused by the pressure of the enlarging uterus on veins leading from the legs. Varicose veins also go away as a rule when the baby is born and the pressure is relieved.

4. *Silvery streaks on the abdomen.* These come from the great stretching of the skin and may not go away since stretched skin does not always shrink back. Pubescent girls sometimes get similar but hardly noticeable streaks during puberty when their skin is being rapidly stretched, and just plain fat women often get them, too.

5. *A darkish line down the middle of the abdomen, or irregular dark patches on the face and neck.* These darkish lines come from the pregnancy hormone changes, thought to be especially the great increase in adrenal hormones. They disappear when the hormone swing is reversed.

6. *A fine growth of hair on the face.* This hair, too, is a result of the increase in adrenal hormones, and should go away when the swing is reversed. A woman who had to have electrolysis done on her face during pregnancy met her electrolysist in a department store one day and called out, "I'm not coming to see you any more because I'm not planning any more babies!" She kept her word.

A "FEMALE COMPLAINT"

There's a special pregnancy discomfort that deserves a corner all to itself. Its official name is leucorrhea, but women usually call it simply "the whites" or "the female complaint."

Leucorrhea refers to an increased discharge of secretions from the vagina. Now there are always some secretions from the vagina, and a moderate increase in them during pregnancy is normal. These increased secretions, however, are non-irritating and clear.

But there are other kinds that are not clear or non-irritating. They are white, foamy and itchy. They also cause inflammation, and sometimes an unpleasant odor.

The white, itchy, irritating secretions come from an infection—an infection due mainly to chemical changes. The chemical reaction of the vagina is usually mildly acid. But during pregnancy, it may change to quite strongly alkaline, and there are certain organisms that thrive in an alkaline medium. When the alkalinity becomes high enough, they move in and make themselves at home.

What is worse, some of these are of a yeasty variety. They grow and multiply fast, like the yeasts used in making bread. Like another non-yeasty organism called trichomonas, they multiply especially fast in a warm, moist, sheltered place like the folds of the vagina and, as they multiply, they throw off waste products that cause the inflammation and distressing itch.

Unfortunately, "the whites" until now has been a condition easy to acquire but hard to cure. This is because some women's vaginal regions during pregnancy tend to be even more alkaline than others, and when this happens the infestation can be driven out but it tends to come right back.

Until now a standard remedy has been an acid douche of plain white vinegar dissolved in warm water, four or five tablespoons to the quart. But the United States Drug Authority is investigating something much better for trichomonas trouble—a new drug that can be taken by mouth instead of locally, and so get into the bloodstream and onto the deep parts of the vagina where the trichomonas like to hide. The cure rates are reported to be amazingly high.

EMOTIONAL PROBLEMS

There are also emotional problems that disturb the basic peace and harmony of Act II. Chief among them is the old, ever-recurring problem of the relation to one's mother.

Some women, especially young ones, identify so completely with their passive babies during pregnancy that they find themselves slipping back into dependency on their mothers again for everything, just as their babies are depending on them. When this happens, trouble brews.

The late Dr. Irving Fischer of Mt. Sinai Hospital was most eloquent on this subject: "When I see Mama coming along with daughter at every pre-natal visit; when a pregnant woman still dresses in silly clothes and acts like a little girl playing with dolls, with no seriousness in her demeanor, I say, watch out! I am not seeing true youthfulness, I am looking at psychic infantilism. Everyone concerned is in for a rough time when she discovers that her mother can't do the job for her; that she has to deliver the baby herself."

This kind of complete dependence is abnormal, though luckily not too common. As the fear of Act I gives way to the hope and expectation of Act II, most girls develop a surprising amount of maturity. This maturity makes them better adjusted to their mothers than they have been in a long time; but adjusted or reconciled on a different level—the level of equality. For now at last a girl is practically equal to her mother. So a new and happier era for them both begins.

COMPULSIVE EATING

Another problem of Act II is compulsive eating.

Many women now crave food as endlessly as an alcoholic craves drink. They crave not just certain foods, but anything and everything in sight, wanting literally to eat all day long. As one pregnant woman put it, "My chief passion in life is food. I read recipes, think about recipes, make recipes and eat the rest of the time."

There is some physical justification for this increase in appetite, since a woman's metabolism is somewhat stepped up during this time. But the stepping up is offset by her greater tendency to sit still and avoid any kind of exercise because of her awkwardness and increased weight.

Besides, no woman actually needs to "eat for two," as people used to think. Let's look at some figures that prove this point.

The total weight-gain in a normal pregnancy is between fifteen and twenty pounds; this breaks down into about seven pounds of baby, one and a half pounds of placenta, three pounds of amniotic fluid and five to eight pounds of extra water stored in the tissues as a provision against unexpected loss.

Now let's say a woman weighs 150 pounds before she gets pregnant. Even twenty extra pounds is only one-seventh more. The most she can do therefore is to eat one and a seventh times as much, not twice as much, or trouble brews.

Why then do women sometimes go on these compulsive food-binges? Drs. Kroger and Freed think they are a defense against anxiety, or a way of rewarding themselves for becoming Proud Mothers. They are a way of slipping back to childhood days when almost all anxiety was dispelled, or good deeds rewarded, by a lollipop stuck in the mouth.

Women whose husbands are far away, or not attentive enough, are especially prone to act this way, just as they are more prone to nausea. It is again as if they were saying, "If there's no one around to love me, or love me enough, I'll love myself more instead. And I'll show my self-love by indulging myself in anything I want to eat."

A SERIOUS COMPLICATION

Now extra eating wouldn't be so bad if by gaining, say, thirty pounds instead of fifteen, they merely ruined their figures. But alas! that is far from the only harm pregnancy eating-binges can do.

Formerly one of the most common and still one of the most dreaded complications of pregnancy is toxemia, a condition that can lead to convulsions and possible death. For centuries, doctors thought toxemia came from some kind of poisoning, hence the name, from "toxic" or "toxin," meaning poison. But they have found out this isn't true. Toxemia comes, as far as we know, from too much food and drink. Since a pregnant woman's body has the extra job of carrying away the baby's wastes as well as her own, grossly overloading her stomach or kidneys may put such a huge strain on her system it simply breaks down.

The possibility of developing toxemia is one of the chief reasons why modern women go to a doctor all through their pregnancies instead of waiting to call him, as Grandma did, when labor pains started up. They go to have their weight and blood pressures constantly checked, and have someone bawl them out if they are jumping ahead too fast. They also go to establish a relationship with a doctor as a strong father-figure and find someone to lean on and talk over anxieties with, instead of trying to drown them by pie and cake.

The proof of this is, says Dr. Alexander Rosenthal, chief of Obstetrics at Long Island Jewish Hospital, is that at free city hospitals, where many of the women who are delivered are ignorant and have never gone to doctors, it is not unusual to have three patients in a row with serious toxemia. In private hospitals, there may be only one such patient in three years.

FEARS OF ACT II

On top of all this, Act II has its old wives' tales to combat and its special fears to overcome.

A common and deep-seated fear is the fear of the baby dying before it can get born, again maybe as "punishment" for some old guilt. This fear often leaps up when a vigorously kicking baby stops kicking for a day or two.

This fear wells up in most normal women, however, but in them it is mild and transitory. It is only abnormal when it persists to the obsessive state.

MYTHS OF ACT II

A common myth of Act II is: "It is dangerous to take an automobile ride; it will joggle the baby and maybe cause premature labor." This myth was dispelled by the experience of the thousands of war wives who had little choice but to travel all over the place to follow their husbands around. As already told, they travelled not only by car, but by bus, boat or plane, and the most careful research showed no higher percentage of premature labor than in the wives who stayed placidly at home. The worst such hectic travelling did was to make the women tired when the trips were long, or to get them too far from the doctors they were accustomed to.

Another old myth says: "Don't cross your legs lest it tangle the umbilical cord." (We'll see in a minute why it can't possibly do this.) The most widespread is: "Don't have dental work done, because the baby pulls calcium out of its mother's teeth, so she loses a tooth for each child." The American Dental Association did a survey in 1963, and found that as many as 68 per cent of all pregnant women still believed the tooth-loss myth. Nonsense, they answered. Good teeth stay good during pregnancy, and bad teeth stay bad unless fixed.

THE CURTAIN GOES DOWN

So the curtain goes down on Act II, with a few anxieties, but with most women feeling basically as serene as they have ever felt.

"I feel so completely self-confident, impregnable and happy, like an unbreakable fort," one woman put it. And a Spanish soprano, after singing at Milan's La Scala while six months pregnant, added this humorous note: "I have much less stage fright with baby in me, because I think of him and not the audience. I took care not to push my high notes, because too much diaphragm might bump him on the head. He was quiet while I was singing, but as soon as I stopped, he started to applaud with his feet."

THE DRIFTING DREAM

And always, always during Act II, women keep speaking of the dream of drifting—drifting lazily, unthinkingly as on a sunlit sea. So dreaming and drifting, drifting and dreaming, we ring down the curtain on our Act II mothers and flash to baby again.

ACT II, SCENE ONE

Act II starts off for baby with a burst and a leap. In Scene One, the fourth month, a baby's height leaps up to eight or ten inches, or half as tall as it will be at birth. Its weight also leaps up to where it becomes six times as heavy as it was before, or a total of about six ounces.

To do all this fast growing, a baby needs food, water and oxygen. It gets these from its mother through the umbilical cord with the help of the remarkable placenta.

THE PLACENTA'S MANY JOBS

The placenta is remarkable because it acts as the baby's lungs, liver and kidneys all in one. Acting as lungs, the placenta exchanges carbon dioxide the baby does not want, for oxygen it does. Acting as kidneys, the placenta pumps the baby's wastes out into the mother's blood so they can be eliminated by her kidneys. Acting as liver, the placenta's digestive juices break down the mother's food and make it acceptable to the baby in proper baby-food style. And, if this weren't enough, the placenta acts as a huge manufacturing plant. As a hormone-making plant, it produces some hormones that stop the mother's nausea, others that ready her breasts to give milk, and also something not yet understood that helps bring on labor and birth.

The placenta also makes substances called globulins. In addition to filtering out many harmful germs that might hurt the baby, these globu-

lins fight infections positively. While most of these anti-infectious globulins are designed to help the baby, the placenta doesn't neglect the
mother. It passes on some germ-fighters to her as well, so that pregnancy
in many ways becomes one of the healthiest times in a woman's life.

Indeed, a woman's biological efficiency is so stepped up at this time
that the baby is never a "parasite" in the sense that used to be believed.
The old belief that "the baby takes all"—all a woman's strength, all her
sustenance—is false. Granted, the baby does get its food, its minerals, its
vitamins, everything it needs for growth through its mother. But the baby
never "runs her out." Nature gives a woman so many reserves that even
women who are seriously undernourished and barely have enough to eat
for one, much less for two, have been known to give birth to seven- or
even nine-pound babies without being drained. *How* nature does this
is a mystery, but it does.

THE UMBILICAL CORD

If the placenta is one remarkable pregnancy arrangement, the
umbilical cord is another and the amniotic sac a third.

The umbilical cord is like a long, flexible wire or pipe that runs
between the placenta and the baby's navel. (*Umbilicus* is the Latin word
for "navel.") This flexible pipe is a two-way pipe. Blood flows through
it in one direction, in a special tubular compartment, carrying oxygen and
food which it extracts from a mother's blood to the baby. The baby's
blood also flows through it in the other direction, carrying waste-products
back from the baby to its mother.

But what is remarkable is that this back-and-forth carrying goes on
in a closed circuit. That is, the blood that does all the carrying is the
baby's own blood. It goes round and round but never leaves the baby's
system of blood vessels. In the placenta extension of these, it picks up
what it needs there and discharges what it doesn't need, goes back, leaves
in the baby what it acquired and picks up from the baby's tissues what is
not needed. Then it rushes back and through the placenta again, and so
on round and round. The blood of the baby and the blood of the mother
are thus basically separate and distinct. They never meet, so the baby
cannot be "tainted with its mother's blood"—another old and false belief.
The mother in this sense is little more than a box that carries the baby
around.

FORCE AND SPEED OF THE BLOOD

Another thing to marvel at is the force and speed with which the baby's blood travels round and round and back and forth through the umbilical cord. Pumped by the baby's own heart, it travels at the astonishing rate of four miles an hour, so that it makes the complete round trip through the cord in only thirty seconds. This great force and speed has the effect of keeping the cord distended, the way a garden hose that is full of water is distended, so that the cord resists knotting and tends to straighten itself out if it becomes tangled as the baby kicks and moves about. The cord, therefore, very rarely becomes a knotted or tangled cord, even during the stresses and complexities of birth (and certainly before that a woman can cross and uncross her legs as much as she pleases).

Still another advantage of the speed of the whole business is the fact that nutrients in the foods the mother eats are quickly transferred to the baby—they get through within a few hours at most. And if she takes a cocktail, it gets through quickly, too, though this doesn't seem to harm the baby. No unborn baby has ever been known to be an alcoholic, although if the mother happens to be under the influence of some strong sleep-producing drug when the baby is born, the young one might be a little sleepy, too.

ACT II, SCENE TWO

In Act II, Scene Two, or the fifth month of pregnancy, the baby leaps ahead some more.

Now it grows to be a whole foot long, and more than doubles its six-ounce weight of the month before. It also begins to grow hair on its head and eyebrows, while both girls and boys grow tiny pink nipples on their breasts.

In Scene Two, also, its heartbeat becomes louder, its skeleton harder and its muscles stronger, with the result its mother can feel those reassuring kicks.

(Interestingly, when babies sleep between kicks, each has a favorite position. Pictures taken in the womb show one baby sleeping with its chin curled down on its chest, another with its head thrown back, just as in later life they will have their favorite sleeping positions, too.)

When awake, our fifth-month baby not only kicks, but turns.

Buoyed up by the waters of the amniotic fluid, it flops around as an energetic swimmer does, flipping from side to side and somersaulting head over heels. That is why it means little if an X-ray shows a baby heels down instead of head down just before birth. Like as not, it may turn itself at the last moment.

Interestingly, too, a baby taking a nap in the womb can be awakened by sounds, or other vibrations. A researcher named Sontag held tuning forks against a mother's abdomen. Lo! the baby responded with a wakening kick. He also tapped the side of the tub while the mother was taking a bath; the baby responded with a kick again. And one of Dr. Hamilton's women reported that her baby kicked so hard while she was at the movies seeing a noisy Western she had to go home.

ACT II, SCENE THREE

During the sixth month, the baby grows to about fourteen inches in length and a weight of about one and a quarter pounds. It also acquires a new skill: it can open its eyes. Even more important, it can breathe for twenty-four hours on its own if born now as a "preemie," though the chances of survival after twenty-four hours of such extreme effort for such a young infant are still slim; very few six-month babies have been known to live.

THE AMNIOTIC SAC

The amniotic sac, or the third wonder-working pregnancy organ, is the sac that contains the waters in which the baby happily floats. The sac is thin, shiny, transparent, tough and elastic, as a good plastic bag. It is also beautiful; researchers remark on how it shimmers and shines.

A remarkable feature of the sac is that it grows as the baby grows, and is always tightly closed. The umbilical cord protrudes through an extension of the sac, which hugs the cord so tightly it remains watertight just the same.

Another remarkable feature is that while the sac is watertight, the water within it is not stagnant water. In fact, says Geraldine Flanagan, more than a third of the water is removed and replaced every hour. But just where this fluid comes from, and where it goes, no one knows.

The total amount of water in the sac also grows each month as the baby grows. It reaches a peak from the fifth to the seventh month, then reduces itself to make room for the bigger baby, and stays reduced until birth.

And while water within the amniotic sac protects the baby from bumps and jolts, that's not all the water does. It keeps the baby at all times at an even, constant, warm temperature. It also makes the baby comparatively weightless, as a swimmer is comparatively weightless when swimming under the waves. The researchers who took the series of pictures of babies in the womb that yielded much of our present information saw babies rolling over and over in the amniotic fluid, buoyed up by the supporting waters. Yet babies on dry land cannot roll over by themselves in their cribs for months after they are born.

A final wonderment is the thick coating of grease a baby wears while in the amniotic sac. Since a swimmer constantly underwater usually finds his skin getting sore, nature coats the unborn baby's skin with grease to prevent this. Sometimes this grease disappears before birth; sometimes it is still present and has to be washed off. The grease at birth is merely a reminder of the long days spent in the amniotic sea.

THE PEACEFUL LIFE

So during Act II the baby, like its mother, mainly drifts and dreams, dreams and drifts. The placenta breathes for it, the placenta filters for it and extracts of pre-digested food are rushed to it through the umbilical cord for it effortlessly to absorb. It has nothing to do but grow, swim, kick and roll over for the sheer exercise and fun of it, while all the time soothing, warm waters protect it and hug it close.

The California poet Robinson Jeffers tells of his nostalgic yearning to recapture this pre-natal, effortless peace:

> "We came from a purer place
> And a more perfect heaven. . . .
> The nine months are better than the ninety years."

✳✳✳ 29 Pregnancy: Act III

Act III starts with another dramatic change. With the big event of birth drawing near, the dreaminess goes. There is a turn back toward reality as placidity gives way to excitement or heightened fears.

The fears once more divide into fears for the baby and fears for oneself.

FEARS FOR THE BABY

Fears for the baby are summed up into one uneasy sentence: "Something may happen to the child."

Again these fears are based on old wives' tales, told by women to other women almost since time began.

Why do women frighten each other with these tales? Maybe it's because pregnancy is the one great event in some women's lives, and they have to make it bigger than it is; make themselves into heroines by declaring, "Look what I went through!" Maybe it's a matter of the old being jealous of the young, and getting back at them by insinuating "I'll take the wind out of your sails." Recently there was a hot newspaper debate in New York over whether pregnant women should work, or stay at home. Some readers wrote in to say: "Keep them at home; they look ugly." "Bosh," answered the anthropologist, Margaret Mead, "the writers who say this are merely jealous. Jealous that pregnant women are doing something they can't."

Or are the old wives' tales a holdover from times past, when no one understood anything about pregnancy, so that the women who told them were once frightened in the very same way? Or do they stem from the ancient teaching that hope is God's prerogative, and He may become angry when mortals express hope too freely, so that Jewish women for centuries have been taught to quickly say "Konuhorrah," meaning "I love the Lord," before expressing any kind of joyous expectations for a child?

In any event, here are some of the ancient tales women still whisper to other women during Act III:

"*It is bad luck to buy anything for the baby in advance.*" This is one of the most widespread. At least half of Dr. Eleanor Hamilton's patients had heard it. One expressed it this way: "My girl friend is giving me a crib, but I don't want it in the house before the baby comes. It's like having a pot of water all boiled up and you don't have the chicken yet." Nevertheless, most women are sensible enough not to be influenced by this superstition and go right ahead with their purchases and plans.

"Don't choose a pediatrician before going to the hospital. An obstetrician is all right, but not a baby doctor." This is similar to the first, and based on the same irrational kind of fear.

"Don't walk downstairs." This is probably meant to mean, "Try to avoid accidents." Though, oddly, the same women who caution other women this way don't say anything about walking upstairs!

On the subject of avoiding accidents, Dr. Guttmacher has this to say: "It is easy to appreciate a pregnant woman's special concern if she falls violently, or is badly shaken in an accident. Of course pregnancy does not lessen her (own) chance for injury. But external trauma rarely harms the unborn child. If there is no vaginal bleeding within an hour after the accident, it is almost an infallible rule that no damage has resulted to the pregnancy."

"Don't look at crosseyed people, ugly people, or eat strawberries. They will cause birthmarks." This fear goes back to the Biblical story of Jacob and the speckled and spotted kine, or even before, and is one of the hardest to face down. But it can be said unequivocally that research has proven it to be unfounded. We now know the child is completely formed early in pregnancy; that there is no connection between the nervous system of the baby and the nervous system of the mother once it has been formed; and that the blood of the mother is completely separate from the blood of the child.

Because of all this, a child carried to full term is very rarely imperfect. In fact, according to another authority, Dr. Nicholas Eastman of Baltimore, Maryland, if it is even carried beyond the second half of pregnancy, the chances are 200 to 1 it will be born without the slightest blemish of any kind.

As to birthmarks, the commonest is the so-called "strawberry mark," which is merely a collection of normal blood vessels somewhat larger and more closely grouped than ordinarily and which can be easily removed. Babies born in the section of Holland famous for having the ugliest people in the world, or in Polynesia famous for the most beautiful, can be born with this birthmark, yet their mothers may have never eaten a strawberry in their lives.

"Don't have sex-relations during pregnancy." This one is so important it deserves a few paragraphs all by itself.

For centuries people have preached against sex-relations during pregnancy. Ministers and priests used to preach against them on the grounds that sex is for the purpose of conception only. Timorous doctors have forbidden them on the grounds they might bring on a miscarriage.

Let's look a little closer.

According to Dr. Irving Fischer, there is no connection whatever between intercourse and miscarriage.

Intercourse is usually forbidden during the last six weeks, however, because at this late date the baby is getting ready to be born and intercourse may set off premature labor, which is different from early miscarriage. Where twins are involved, it may even set off premature labor during the last ten weeks, since premature labor is much more easily induced when the mother is carrying twins. Twins take up so much extra space in the uterus that when living conditions get too crowded, they often decide to move out. Obviously, this is true also with triplets or quads. Mrs. Dionne delivered her famous quintuplets way ahead of the expected time.

But before labor starts or is about to begin, sex-relations will not "shake the baby loose." Nor will they infect it unless germs are introduced into the vagina almost immediately before labor begins, and the woman's body does not have time to kill them off by natural defense.

THE WIFE DECIDES

As to religious sanction for intercourse during pregnancy, Protestant Bishop Joseph Hodges of Cambridge, Massachusetts, sums up the thought of most modern leaders when he says: "Intercourse in pregnancy, like intercourse at any other time, is not morally wrong when it is not physically wrong, since it makes for a greatly desired unity between husband and wife. Though here it is up to the wife to decide."

In 1950, two social scientists named Landis and Poffenberger did a study of several hundred married women to see how wives usually do decide. Fifty-eight per cent said pregnancy had no effect on their desire. 17 per cent said desire was increased, and 25 per cent slightly decreased, this decrease coming mainly during the last three months.

And Dr. Hamilton found no basic change except a slight all-over decrease. Moreover, if the relationship was satisfactory before, the women said they felt guilty over this slight decrease and tried not to show it. Thus their husbands were not pushed aside.

DO MEN NEED CONTINUOUS SEX?

But do men and women *need* continuous sex? What happens to them without it during the last six weeks of pregnancy, plus the six weeks after delivery when the cervix is healing, making a total of three months' abstinence in all? Do they actually suffer if there are no relations during these three months?

Dr. Milton Sapirstein believes that in the normal average man the sex-drive is so urgent, especially when he is young, that after he has become used to regular relations he misses them if he is deprived of them for a really long period of time. Three or four months, though, is not a really long period. Also, a husband misses regularly established relations with his wife more when he is young. Dr. Sapirstein accepts the Kinsey figures that a man's drive is at its peak at eighteen, then diminishes in a straight downward line to the age of eighty or beyond.

Yet his drive, even at its height, is never so strong a woman has to give in to his request for sex every time he asks for it. She does not have to fear he will be harmed in any way if, when the occasion is not right, she firmly says no.

The sex-drive in men is also extremely plastic or subject to being trained, and to spontaneous diminution as well. Men such as priests, who do not have sex-relations, can get used to doing without them altogether and not miss them after a while. In fact, it would be quite difficult for a man to resume or start relations after years of abstinence, as Luther did. Luther said he married after years of celibacy to "please his father, tease the Pope and spite the devil." But then, Luther was a most unusual man.

WOMEN DIFFERENT

Women are different. The sex-drive in women is far less localized and concrete. It is also a receptive drive rather than an active drive. Because of this, even women who have been used to regular relations can quite easily drop them, then start again years later as if they had never stopped. So certainly a few months of abstinence is not physically harmful to either men or women.

On the other hand, most husbands are not sexually repelled by their wives' expanding bigness. Sharon, of Dr. Hamilton's series, reported her husband joking: "Darling, you look just the same from behind as you always looked." And Esther said: "My husband wanted a baby even more than I did. He doesn't mind having me big; he is very excited about my body. It isn't a beautiful thing really, but it is to him. He makes fun of me sometimes, like when I first put on a flannel nightgown. I looked pretty funny, and we both shrieked with laughter. . . ." Rima declared, "His appreciation of beauty in pregnancy has been a source of great pleasure to me. Through his eyes I've even come to think of myself as beautiful. I don't care how big I am. I am wonderful because he thinks me so."

These are normal reactions of normal husbands and normal wives. They are an echo of the frank delight people have always had in the pregnant woman, portraying her in painting and sculpture as the giver of life.

DISCOMFORTS! DISCOMFORTS!

But sex or no sex, delight or love, or jokes and battles, there are still the physical discomforts of Act III.

If there has been backache before, there is probably more backache. If there has been constipation before, there is more constipation.

Doctors are at verbal swords' points over the cause of the constipation and backache. Some think it comes from nervous tension, others from "lightening." Lightening is the sinking down of the uterus, after it has travelled up, in preparation for birth. The head of the baby, which lies usually downward, forces it down. This happily relieves the shortness of breath and tendency toward faintness the upward travels may have caused but at the same time it causes added pressure on the back and rectum, with constipation and backache the result.

Still, lightening is always a most welcome sign, because it indicates the baby *is* lying head down, and also that its head is not too large to go through that particular pelvis. Oddly enough, lightening sometimes happens as early as the seventh month. The uterus travels down, back up, then down again.

Drs. Kroger and Freed suggest that, regardless of lightening, it is a good idea to have an X-ray picture taken during the last month. The X ray will show the mother the position in which the baby is lying, doubly assure her it is head down, and smaller than the pelvic outlet, and may picture, too, its ever wonder-causing miniature fingers and toes. Besides, it is the first photograph of her child, and by all means her husband should see it, too.

If an X ray is not possible, the next best thing is seeing the famous "Birth Atlas" pictures taken by Dr. R. L. Dickinson and shown at most maternity centers. Like the X ray, they point up the perfection of the birth process that nature has evolved over millions of years.

PAIN IN RIGHT SIDE

Another odd but disturbing problem of Act III is a persistent pain in the right side. Why the right only? Because sometimes, as the uterus grows, it does not grow symmetrically. Instead it "leans over" to the right and gives some pain. Why it should lean over, nobody knows, but as many as 80 per cent of women find it does.

REHEARSAL-CONTRACTIONS

Then, during Act III, there are the persistent contractions of the uterus. These are disturbing because they seem to be a sign that labor is setting in. But usually not. The uterus contracts as a preparation for labor from as early as the fifth week on, though it is only during Act III that the contractions are actually felt. But they are "mainly "rehearsal-contractions"—rehearsal for the great event of birth rather than the oncoming of the event itself.

The difference between rehearsal-contractions and the real thing is this: Rehearsal-contractions last only a few seconds, are weak, irregular and essentially painless. Labor-contractions are strong, come at regular intervals, last longer and include more pain. Regular intervals between contractions are usually the chief guide.

VAGINAL SECRETIONS

Increased vaginal secretion is always upsetting. Yet increased secretion is quite normal during Act III. This is true even to the extent of having to wear a pad. These secretions are due to the greatly stepped-up estrogen activity of Act III. Dr. Alan Guttmacher says bathing and the liberal use of a soft washcloth should take care of them and joins other modern doctors in stressing "no douching" unless specifically prescribed.

TOXEMIA

Toxemia, as mentioned in the previous chapter, can be deadly. Its chief symptoms are a swelling of the face or fingers that make a wedding-ring markedly tight, persistent headache and rapid weight gain. The home treatment is a sharp reduction of both food and salt, plus rest, which usually takes care of the situation and stops it from getting worse.

If there's one gift a thoughtful friend can give a pregnant woman it's a bathroom scale.

SHOWERS ONLY

Another bathroom thought; most doctors say no tub-baths during the last six weeks. Showers only. This is again for the purpose of avoiding possible infection. Dirty tub-water can go in and up; shower-water goes over and down.

HOW TO PICK A DOCTOR

I keep talking about doctors. Suppose a woman hasn't picked one yet? It's rarer and rarer these days, but it happens.

Here are some suggestions from other women on this: Shy away from the kind of doctor who says "Just let me do the worrying for you—that's what you're paying me for." Look for one who has the desire to listen, and let a woman talk herself out.

Pick a cordial, friendly man too. A man who will be a warm support during one of the great moments in a woman's life. Not one who is self-conscious either, or who doesn't bother to volunteer information.

Olga put it, "I think my doctor is self-conscious himself, and therefore unable to put me at ease."

And Frances said, "The nurse told me all the things he forgot."

But Elinor enthused, "He works fast, but he has a wonderful touch."

So Act III moves toward its climax—moves with the excitement of looking forward, and with some almost inescapable fear.

What is baby doing or thinking meantime?

BABY: ACT III

Baby is, as far as we know, not thinking at all. Baby is merely doing. Growing mainly. Growing like mad. In the seventh month baby puts on another whole pound, and puts on as much as four more pounds during the next six weeks.

It also grows the long hair it will be born with, and vigorously practices sucking by sucking on the handiest gadget—its thumb. Geraldine Flanagan tells of babies actually being born with calluses on their thumbs from sucking-practice in the womb.

It is during the eighth month that baby usually settles for the head-down position. By this time, it is usually so big it fits tightly into the womb, and since its head is the heaviest part of it, and the womb is distensible at the bottom, it fits in, head down, very nicely. It also stops turning around very much; it's too big now to do more than turn from side to side. Somersaults are out.

In the ninth month, it fits into its nest even more tightly, so tight indeed that its arms and legs make obvious bulges on its mother's abdomen. And a kick from a nine-month baby, says Mrs. Flanagan, has been known almost to knock a book off its mother's lap.

But growth isn't enough. During the seventh, eighth and ninth months Its Majesty also gets fat, as majesties are wont to do.

It hasn't been fat before. Perhaps that's one reason few "preemies" born around the end of the seventh month live: They haven't enough fat to keep them warm in the shifting temperature of the outside world. So they have to be kept in steadily heated incubators, and even at that may have difficulty in breathing or digesting.

Above all, preemies are extremely susceptible to infection.

This matter of immunity to infection is vital. There is always that first definition of normal—the ability to survive. And all kinds of germs never encountered in the safe shelter of the womb assail a baby the minute it is born. In order to survive, it must be able to fight these germs. It gets this ability to fight from its mother during the last three months.

During Act III, a baby in the womb acquires immunity to all the diseases its mother ever had. From the special materials of the placenta, and maybe also from the amniotic fluid it swallows, it acquires antibodies to all her past infections such as whooping cough, chicken-pox, mumps and the common cold. And it retains these antibodies for about another six months after birth, at which time it has acquired some immunities of its own—immunities which, if it's a girl, it will develop throughout its lifetime and in turn pass on to another child.

This matter of the acquisition of its mother's immunities during Act III is so important it answers another persistent myth—that an eight-month baby is worse off than a seven or a nine.

This tale started in the superstitious days when doctors were excluded from the birth-chamber, but astrologers were invited in for the special purpose of foretelling the baby's future at the exact moment of birth, according to numbers and stars. Now, seven and nine have always been considered lucky numbers, but not eight. So the foolish astrologers predicted an eight-month baby was unlucky, when actually an eight-month baby has a big head-start over a seven, and a nine-month baby has the biggest start of all.

THE BABY STOPS GROWING

During the last two weeks of its peaceful womb life, the baby suddenly reverses itself. It stops growing. It stops because nature doesn't want it to get too big; also because, as far as we know, the placental activity diminishes too, and this sets off the dramatic change in the mother's hormone balance that starts labor. For if the baby kept on growing at the rate it has for nine months, with one cell growing into two hundred million cells weighing six billion times as much as the original fertilized egg, a human being would be twenty feet tall when he got ready to vote, and his weight would be astronomical.

So, instead of the stage being set any longer for holding in, during the last two weeks it is changed by the scene-shifters, and set to let go.

In fact, these last two weeks are so unlike what has gone before, both for mother and for child, that they get a special few minutes all to themselves. They are Between the Acts, or Intermission.

✳✳✳ 30 Intermission

Every drama has an intermission—a time when the actors rest and the audience goes out, draws its breath and comes back for more.

Here the intermission is different. It is the time between two dramas —the drama of pregnancy and the drama of birth. It is different too because the woman is both audience and actor. During intermission she increases her strange but pleasant indifference to all the other affairs of life and builds up instead her own inner awareness to where she does almost nothing but listen to her body's sounds.

THE GREAT HOPES

Changes during pregnancy are gradual for the most part. In spite of its division into three acts, no change is so sudden it is felt—just like that!—on a specific day. But the changes of the last two weeks rise to a climax. Now the signals from within her body cry out loudly to a woman, voicing the greatest fears and the greatest hopes she has known.

The hopes center on the child, and now that it is so soon to become an outside reality, they assume extravagant shape. Every woman secretly feels she bears a future hero in her womb, particularly if it is her first-born.

THE GUESSING GAMES

It is at this point that the sex-guessing and name-guessing games rise to a climax, too.

Guessing the sex of the expected child, or, better yet, controlling the sex from the beginning are games that are as old as mankind. People have believed they could control the sex of the unborn child by conceiving it under the light of the moon, under the influence of certain stars, on certain days of the month or by praying to certain gods.

Pearl Buck tells of a missionary friend in China who had prayed to her God for a boy, then had five girls in a row and began to doubt her religion. And Dr. Irving Bunkin of New York tells of a rabbi who was impatiently walking up and down in the waiting-room while his first child was being born, praying all the while.

"Why are you praying at this time?" the doctor asked.

"I am praying for the health of my son," the rabbi replied.

"Why are you so sure it will be a son?"

"Because I inherited the secret of making sons from my sainted ancestors."

Needless to say, it was a girl.

Nor are the advance guesses of the woman or her own doctor much better as a rule. An absurd superstition says, "If you stick out more in front than behind, it's a boy." And the recently much-heralded saliva test hasn't turned out to be any better than listening to the fetal heartbeat. Both are unreliable, with nature delivering about 106 boys to every 100 girls willy-nilly, no matter what anyone says in advance.

Name-guessing, like sex-guessing, reveals the parents' wishes in a different way.

Here it is not only the immediate family virtues that are hoped for, but the virtues of famous figures in the sports world, or the dramatic, literary or historical worlds. These tend to be heroic figures with whom the parents once identified as children or adolescents themselves, with John F. for John F. Kennedy, Douglas for Douglas MacArthur, Gloria for Gloria Vanderbilt or Geraldine for Geraldine Chaplin having their day.

THE GREAT FEARS

Hope is always balanced by fear, especially in the great life-crises like pregnancy, and most especially in the climactic last few weeks.

Now the chief fears are for oneself. These run from the seemingly small fear of not getting one's figure back (but nothing is ever small to a woman) to the deep, ancient fear of death, with many between.

A rather curious "between" fear is the fear of immodesty. Women have been so conditioned against immodesty they whisper to each other that labor and delivery may be terrible because you have to strip and let strange doctors look at you. Others whisper that labor and delivery may be terribly embarrassing because the bag of waters may break unexpectedly and then you will feel as ashamed as you did when you were a little girl and wet your pants.

Another curious fear women have—and even more so, their husbands—is having a baby too small for pride. When a child was born to Cleopatra, the court artists craftily drew pictures showing it as of almost full adult size. How could a daughter of the Pharaohs have a baby who did not look royal or king-sized in every way?

As for the fear of not getting one's figure back, there is a modern story about a Brooklyn school-teacher named Helen.

Helen had been a most unhappy fat adolescent, but just before her marriage had managed to diet down to a joyous size 12, and was petrified lest she never get down again.

One day during her ninth month, Helen happened to see a lovely blue dress, size 12, in a store window. That dress haunted her; she wanted it almost as much as she wanted the baby; she couldn't wait for the first time when she'd be able to try it on.

The first moment after delivery she could, she dashed downtown. The dress was still there, and she got so excited when she found it fitted her that the salesgirl couldn't help but notice it.

"What's the matter?" asked the salesgirl. "Isn't that your regular size?"

"Oh, yes," Helen breathed. "But I never thought I'd make it again."

But no fear compares with the fear of death. This over-rides all other fears during the last two weeks in many women, even those women who say, "I'm not exactly afraid," but betray it with the quaver in their voice.

This fear was based on reality in the old days. Women did die in childbirth in droves, especially during the Middle Ages when most of the ancient knowledge had been lost, and there was no sanitation, no anesthesia, no one to officiate except ignorant midwives. The result was an appalling loss of life. At one point in eighteenth-century London, the figures reached a whopping 50 per cent. Today in the United States they have shrunk to so small a size they are almost negligible—less than 2/10 of 1 per cent. Yet the fear remains.

It remains, according to Dr. Helene Deutsch, because its roots lie deep in the woman herself. During pregnancy, a woman's moods swing sharply. She swings from a feeling of infinite enlargement, a belief she is the whole world, to a feeling of infinite shrinking, a belief she is nothing. The feeling of infinite enlargement gives rise to emotions of love, motherly pride and happiness, the shrinking to emotions of depression, shame, destruction and death. Dr. Deutsch says,

During pregnancy the woman feels more and more that she bears a real life in her womb, a life that would be helpless and lost without her devotion. The fact that by her own strength she will give birth to another creature who will face her as an independent being, the approaching duality in the still existing unity, is perhaps woman's most powerful optimistic experience. But the pessimistic aspect . . . arises from the same experience; severe anxieties cast a deep shadow and trouble the peace and harmony of pregnancy. They crystallize into two ideas; 'I shall die in childbirth' and 'I shall not have a child.' Whatever individual and universally human guilt feeling, vestiges of memories, threats and real motives feed these fears, one has the impression that something very deep and primitive lies at the bottom of them.

For, gratifying as the child will be after it has been born, there is still an unwillingness to give up the union. The inner voice objects; what it will be later in the outside world is not what it is now. What is now in me, with me, a part of myself, will be lost. It will be there, but as another human being, not myself—something that will breathe with other lungs, pulsate with another pulse. . . . Now it is still in me but . . . soon to be a world outside me.

To make it the being that is outside her, the pregnant woman must deliver the child from the depths of herself. . . . She loses not only it, but herself with it. This, I think, is at the bottom of that fear and foreboding of death that every pregnant woman has, and this turns the giving of life into the losing of life. . . .

For separation is death, and only when the mother's love again receives the child in the outside world are the specters of death banished.

Whatever the reason, fear is very real for many women. And it only adds insult to dismiss it as "all in the head." Of course it is in the head! But the mind or head influences the body just as the body influences the mind, so fear that starts in the head can become as paralyzing as nausea that starts in the body. It only makes matters worse to tell a woman simply to "laugh it off." It is heartless besides.

Dr. Irving Fischer adds something else to this discussion. He thinks the fear of death during pregnancy is very common, and stems from the fact the mother often identifies with the baby in its small confined space, thinks how she would feel in such a small space, panics and wants "out." But she forgets the baby does not feel confined; it is happy in its small space surrounded by its fluid cushion; it does not want to get out at all!

And all people agree on the value of talking out death-fears with a doctor, a nurse, one's mother or husband, or a close friend. Dr. Eleanor Hamilton tells of one woman in particular, who seemed to have the greatest fear of any of her patients. At her last interview during Intermission, Sharon suddenly exploded and told Dr. Hamilton with much emotion about guilt over genital play, plus guilt over a former abortion she had

had. Having exploded this way, and uttering several "words you cannot say"—"masturbation" and "abortion"—Sharon left the office visibly relieved, and that same afternoon went into a relaxed labor that had seemed impossible before.

CHILDBIRTH CLASSES

Another good way to help to make fears pass is to join a childbirth class. Indeed, many doctors feel this is the real value of the classes. The exercises are good, the learning how to breathe during delivery is good, but most important is the fact the women no longer feel alone.

And loneliness is a terrible thing during a new experience like pregnancy. It is so terrible that Dr. Helene Deutsch tells of a woman who simply couldn't carry a baby through without repeated miscarriages until a friend conceived at the same time she did. With the help and support of her friend, she was able to carry her baby full-term, both women delivering almost to the hour. Today women who join a class find the same invaluable support.

DISCOMFORTS AND PAINS

A discomfort can be worse than a pain. The discomforts or irritations of the last few weeks are the physical discomforts—the assorted aches and bothers that make many women so restless, so heavy, awkward and tired, so nervous and cranky they would give anything to have it over and done with soon.

"I'm getting fed up with pregnancy," says Kit. "I wish labor would hurry up, I'm so mad and blue today."

"I don't mind pain," says Hester. "But this waiting business gets me. Everybody has something to say. Some say I didn't figure right. Others say, 'Is something wrong?' If I weren't so sensitive, I'd tell them all to go jump in the lake. Now I just wish it would come."

BACKACHE

There is the discomfort of backache. Backache comes from two things. First, there's the full load in front that has to be balanced by extra pressure on the back. Second, there's the special chemical produced by the placenta, especially during the last few weeks, that has as

its job the relaxing of the pelvic joints in order to get them ready for delivery. Both change a woman's whole way of carrying herself and walking. Result? A pain in the back, and a sway like a sailor on shore leave.

Dr. Alan Guttmacher doesn't think a woman ordinarily needs a
maternity girdle during pregnancy, but at the end she may in order to
relieve that aching back. Massage also brings relief. But here, while Dr.
Guttmacher recommends the use of liniment, Dr. Nicholas Eastman disagrees. Dr. Nicholas Eastman says it's the massage alone that does the
trick, and plain salad oil to grease the massaging hand will do just as well
as expensive liniments.

LEG CRAMPS

There is the discomfort of leg cramps. These are different than the
backache because they happen at night. The woman wakes up with a
start and the calf-muscles of her leg are knotted into a painful, hard ball.
Disturbed circulation probably causes this common nuisance; firm
kneading of the ball relieves it.

SWOLLEN FEET AND ANKLES

There is the discomfort of swollen feet and ankles. The feet are
not only the lowest part of the body; they are geographically the farthest
away from the heart. About a third of the normal twenty-pound weight-
gain of pregnancy is water (the amniotic fluid, plus other fluids held in
the tissues). Since the feet are the lowest part, a good deal of the tissue-
fluids naturally sink there, especially after much standing, and most
especially at the end of a warm day. Putting the feet up obviously relieves some of this, as does the wearing of wide, larger shoes. When the
swelling extends to the face and fingers, it cannot be relieved this way,
but soaking of swollen fingers in ice-water does help, as well as the elimination of as much salt as possible from one's diet.

A FREQUENT NEED ''TO GO''

Both at the beginning and end of pregnancy, there may be frequent
need for urination. Some doctors advise no fluids after supper if urination interferes with sleep. Others add: When labor starts in earnest,
urinate every three hours, even when the urge is not felt. Urination re-

lieves the fullness of the bladder, which in turn permits the uterus to sink down farther to where it should be near the end.

NOSEBLEEDS

Nosebleeds are a rather odd but common nuisance of pregnancy. They come because of the increased blood supply and blood pressure. This edema, or *mucosa,* diminishes air passages, and it is more easily injured and causes heavy breathing as if with a perpetual cold, or it comes out as nosebleeds. But the trouble all goes away at delivery-time.

HEMORRHOIDS

Hemorrhoids (or "piles") are common among pregnant women, especially during those impatient last few weeks.

The cause? Pressure this time on the lower half of the body, causing protruding rectal veins, bleeding or itching. The remedy? Vaseline applied with the finger while sitting in a warm tub bath. Or if the warm baths don't bring relief, doing just the opposite: applying pads soaked in ice-water. Best yet, realizing that at delivery-time, as with the nosebleeds, even the most severe hemorrhoids will usually disappear.

INSOMNIA

During the first few weeks of pregnancy, a woman wants to sleep all the time. During the last few, she can hardly sleep at all. She's so big by now it is hard to find any comfortable position. Besides, the baby doesn't know night from day, so it kicks as vigorously at midnight as it does at noon.

Dr. Eastman advises using any and every old-time home remedy for inducing sleep before resorting to pills, and, above all, to remember that *any* position that is comfortable is to the good. The baby is secure in its little fortress; it cannot possibly be crushed.

And Dr. Earle Milliard Marsh of San Francisco adds: If a pregnant woman simply can't sleep at night, let her take frequent short naps during the day instead. Here Dr. Marsh comforts her by saying she should feel neither lazy nor indolent if she does sleep during the day. "As if any woman were lazy and indolent when she is doing the greatest of all creative jobs!" exclaims Dr. Marsh.

JOYFUL EXPECTANCY

With all of these discomforts—backache, insomnia, what have you —almost as many women go through Intermission time in a mood of joyful expectancy as of nervous impatience.

There was Flo, who said: "Now that I can measure time in weeks, I'm more willing to wait. It's near enough so I can afford to be calm about waiting. Also, I can begin to plan now beyond the time of the baby's birth."

And Nora: "I'm so eager for it to start now. I feel as if I were coming into my own—taking my rightful place as a mother among my friends."

TRUE OR FALSE?

One universal problem remains. When *does* labor start? How is a woman to know?

The situation is complicated by the false contractions.

The uterus, as I said, contracts and relaxes constantly. This contraction and relaxing has been going on for a long time, but it doesn't become really strong until the middle of pregnancy. Then it rises to attention in the form of rehearsal-contractions. (Doctors call these Braxton Hicks contractions, after the man who identified them.) These show up as a hard lump that can be felt in the lower abdomen, a lump that remains for about half a minute, then disappears and comes back a few minutes later—all without pain.

Since nothing is ever simple, in a few women these false or rehearsal-contractions include pain, especially during the last few weeks. This makes them hard to distinguish from true labor contractions.

One way to distinguish between true and false is to change position. If standing, lie down. If lying down, stand up and walk around. False contractions usually go away on changing position; true ones do not.

Another way is to look for a discharge that women call "show," meaning a show of pink thickish blood. This "show" is really a soft plug that has been sealing off the birth area from other parts of the body and keeping it as sterile as possible. False contractions never eject this plug. True ones may or may not.

Another way, suggests Dr. Guttmacher, is to take a teaspoonful of paregoric if the contractions start at night. If false, sleep will probably soon come. If true, the paregoric is so mild it will have no effect.

(There's a widespread tale that says more babies start to be born during the night than during the day. Not so. It's just that we notice things more at night, especially things that dramatically upset our accustomed routine, like a dash to the hospital in the middle of the night.)

A Nürnberg doctor, with characteristic German thoroughness, compiled statistics on the birth-hours of over a hundred thousand babies. He divided the day into four periods of six hours each, namely 6 A.M. to noon, noon to 6 P.M. 6 P.M. to midnight, and midnight to 6 A.M. Lo! his figures showed almost exactly the same number born during each period, or approximately twenty-five per cent.

It seems that Junior-to-be just can't tell time.

The best way to tell false from true contractions is to time the contractions carefully and note their intensity.

Dr. Guttmacher gives these checkpoints: True labor pains are unique in that they can be compared to a song. "Unlike other pains," he says, "they rise in slow crescendo, remain fortissimo for a brief period, and close in moderate diminuendo; or they are like a scale that makes a leisurely ascent to a high tone and is held aloft for a few beats before the several descending notes are sung."

True labor pains also come in rhythm. That is, at fixed intervals. They may start at fifteen minutes apart (timed by a watch), then get closer and closer to three or four minutes apart, while the total length of an individual pain goes from, say, half a minute at the beginning to a minute at the end. But they do not come hit-or-miss, as false pains may.

The true labor pains usually start in the small of the back and after a few hours travel toward the center of the abdomen. They do not start in the abdomen, as simple intestinal cramps may.

Finally, true labor pains have a complete rest between them. They are like a car engine that starts up, stops dead and starts again, with no vibrations between.

These distinctions are so important they are worth memorizing, if only to avoid the feeling of foolishness that comes from useless dashes to the hospital, only to be sent home to wait some more.

An almost positive proof that labor is to begin is a leaking of the bag of waters.

This may be a frank leak in the form of a burst, or a slow dripping.

In either event, Dr. Marsh stresses the fact it should be welcome, too, as the harm of a "dry labor," or a labor without the waters, is another of those false old tales. Actually, he says, if the bag does break in advance, it means that labor will be slightly shorter than when it does not.

Dr. Marsh also stresses the fact that true labor may be announced by any *one* of the three signs—show, leaking and true pains—or a *combination* of all three. And above all that, women should not worry for fear they may deliver in the taxicab on the way to the hospital once labor does start. It is so rare for them to do so that it always makes a feature story in the papers. "It is an age-old obstetrical observation, however," he adds, "that when a child is born in a taxicab or an ambulance at the front door of a hospital, it does phenomenally well, as does the mother."

One of the oldest questions of history is: When is true labor to be expected? How long *does* pregnancy normally last?

The usual answer is 280 days, meaning ten moon-months, or nine calendar months plus a few days. But this is so strictly average that it would almost be better if people had never heard the figure, because if a woman doesn't deliver on the 280th day she is apt to go into a tizzy and be sure something is wrong.

Actually, there's only about one chance in five of a woman delivering on or about the 280th day. Nature, it cannot be repeated often enough, is not a machine. A careful study of seventeen thousand women shows 54 per cent delivering before "D" day, and 42 per cent later, with many, many as much as two weeks off.

Another factor to be considered is that women seldom know the exact day on which they conceived. But even in 425 cases of artificial insemination, where a single injection of semen obviously took, so that the day was known, the average woman delivered at around 270 days, but the variation was so wide it ran from 231 to 329 days. Two hundred and thirty-one days, of course, means only about eight calendar months in the womb, while 329 means more than ten.

Premature labor is something else again. Premature labor is usually thought of as something starting as early as the seventh month, since before that it is called a miscarriage. Doctors will suggest everything in their power to prevent premature labor, including absolute bedrest and avoidance of severe emotional disturbances like violent quarrels with one's relatives on any score.

In *Gone With the Wind,* Scarlett loses her baby prematurely after a nasty fight with her husband and a fall down the stairs. Most doctors believe the fight more than the fall was the cause.

All doctors know that the earlier a baby is born, the less chance it has of staying alive. The figures run this way:

A child born at the end of the seventh month has a fifty-fifty chance of survival.

A child born at the end of the eighth has a 90 per cent chance of survival.

A child born around the end of the ninth month has a 99 per cent chance of survival.

And a child that stays in the womb longer than nine months is not, as far as we now know, particularly harmed.

Another way of looking at it is through birth-weight. A child born at the end of the seventh month usually weighs no more than about 3½ pounds. At that weight it is extremely difficult to keep it alive. Its lungs aren't developed enough to cope with the outside air, so it has great difficulty in breathing. Its digestive system isn't developed enough, so it has great difficulty in eating and passing stool. Its circulation is still poor, so it finds it hard to keep warm and even an incubator can't always do the job. It looks extremely red and wizened because fat has not yet been deposited under its skin.

Other things being equal, then, the longer a baby stays in the womb, up to or around that average 280 days, the better. This is the answer to the women who, during the last impatient weeks, beg their doctors to "do something." Modern doctors know a lot of things they can do. But except for good and sufficient reasons like the presence of toxemia, they usually don't.

IT COMES TO AN END

It's only a proverbial long lane that has no turning; even the longest periods in life come at last to an end.

One day our lady-in-waiting wakes up feeling strangely happy, and with a strong desire to "do something" herself. Her fatigue and lassitude are gone; she has the energy to clean up the whole house, or to add some last touches to the baby's nursery or crib.

This usually means that true labor is close at hand.

The energy is a signal from her hormones—those same hormones that come to her aid in her hours of need. During pregnancy her estrogenic, or stimulating, hormones continued to go up and up, not falling until about a week before delivery. Her thyroid, or "holding," hormones go up, too.

But most important now, her adrenal, or "special situation," hormones go up. They go up in particular during the last few months, when, according to Dr. Hamblen of Duke University, they rise to four times their non-pregnant amount. And during the very last days, or just before they are needed most, they go up still more.

They go up to give the woman a special burst of reserve energy— to help her meet the stresses of labor, and see her through her biggest job.

With their burst, Intermission Time is over and another three-act drama is ready to begin.

✳✳✳ 31 The Drama of Birth: Act I

Act I of childbirth starts with a huge sense of relief. Intermission is over. The time of delivery—literal delivery from the impatience of the last few weeks—is at hand. No matter what the next few days or hours may bring, the woman can at least do something about the situation, and she is eager to start.

LABOR BEGINS

Labor begins slowly, especially with first babies. Since it does begin slowly, even when the pains are coming regularly five or six minutes apart there is no particular reason to rush like mad to the hospital except for the nervous need for action felt by the woman herself. In fact, many doctors prefer keeping their patients at home as long as possible, because they know that they tend to time labor from the minute they enter the hospital. The longer they're there, the longer the whole birth job seems.

Still, it's hard to keep a woman at home once she is eager to go, so off she usually runs, her husband or a friend tagging excitedly along.

IN THE HOSPITAL

Once at the hospital (and 90 per cent of modern babies in places like the United States, at least, are delivered there), a woman is shaved, given an enema to empty the lower intestines, examined rectally and put to bed in a "labor room."

Why a rectal examination instead of a vaginal one? To understand this, you have to know what is happening during the various stages of labor. Here's what is happening during the first stage, or Act I.

THE FIRST STAGE

A woman's uterus, or womb, is shaped like an upside-down pastry bag or bottle, you will remember, with the widest part at the top and a small extension below, the cervix, that corresponds roughly to the neck of the bottle. Before pregnancy, the uterus is a comparatively large organ and the cervix much smaller—only about half an inch long and about three-quarters of an inch wide.

But here's the difference: During the nine months of pregnancy, the uterus stretches and grows tremendously, until there is room inside it for both a baby and the bag of waters. But the cervix stays tightly closed and at its original small size.

During the first stage of labor, the cervix has to stretch and open up. In a few hours, it has to open up in width from about three-quarters of an inch to four inches, or become five times wider than it was in order to let the baby's head and body press on down and through.

The uterus does this monumental opening-up job in rhythmic movements, a little at a time, the way a gate opens up that hasn't been opened before. Each contraction represents a movement.

The force behind the opening-up movements comes from the uterus. Just as the uterus contracts with force during menstruation, and sends out impulses that cause the unwanted lining to shed, so the uterus contracts during labor and sends out impulses to the cervix to open up. But labor contractions are much harder. That is why they sometimes cause pain.

Of course, some cervixes open up or dilate under the force of the contractions much more quickly than others. No two women are alike in this respect any more than in any other. Dr. Earle Milliard Marsh estimates it takes about twelve to fifteen hours in first labors, with a few women managing it much faster and some considerably more. Meanwhile, the labor nurses or a doctor do repeated examinations to find out how things are going. They do this through the rectum rather than through the vagina as a rule because rectal examinations are more sterile. It is exceedingly important not to infect the vagina in any way, since it is wide open to infection during this time. So the nurses usually insert their clean, gloved fingers into the rectum instead. They can feel the cervix and tell how much it has opened up this way, and they report their findings as "one finger's dilation, two fingers' dilation," and so on until a goal of a four-inch opening, which equals about five fingers, is reached. When this happens, Act I will be over.

Now the twelve to fifteen hours of Act I can seem like a long, long time, especially if one is alone and frightened by the new experience. So some modern hospitals permit husbands in the labor room, to act as companions or back-massagers. The reason there is pain in the back and massage is helpful there is that the baby does not travel straight down from the uterus toward the vagina, as might be expected. It travels toward the back first. So at the beginning the back gets the full force of the labor contractions, and husbands make excellent back-rubbers.

Of course, some women don't want their husbands there. They want their doctors instead and want them desperately for the reassurance the doctor's presence brings. But while most doctors can manage to drop by for a few minutes, it is hardly reasonable to expect a busy doctor to stay constantly with one patient for twelve to fifteen hours, unless that patient is a millionaire. (Consuelo Vanderbilt told how, when she was the Duchess of Marlboro, she paid her personal physician not only to stay with her the whole time she was in the labor room, but also to travel down from Scotland—at $5.00 per mile—to stand by for the full week before the baby was expected.)

"Why don't they feed you when you are in labor?" asks a California woman. "I always eat when I am nervous. But my friends say I won't get a thing."

Her friends are right. A woman in labor can seldom have much except clear broth or tea. The reasons for this are that a full stomach may slow up labor, especially during the second stage when the abdominal muscles must be as free as possible to push. Second, a full stomach may cause vomiting if anesthesia is needed to ease the pains. Labor is just what the word implies—hard work. There's a big job on hand. All the body's energies are needed for that job. Eating and digesting food can wait.

In spite of the enema, too, there may be a strong desire to move the bowels or urinate during labor. This is because, as I said, the baby does not travel in a straight line down and out. It travels first in the direction of the rectum or bladder. As its head strains against the rectum or bladder, the strain is felt as an urge to urinate or move the bowels, an urge that at times may seem uncontrollable.

Margaret was the placid type. During her labor, she said: "I keep thinking I'd feel better if I could move my bowels. But I suppose it would be much better if I could just have the baby instead."

NATURAL CHILDBIRTH

Pain brings us to the hotly debated subject of so-called natural childbirth. How much pain is natural? Is it all caused by tension and the fear something terrible may happen during labor, or that labor may never end?

The idea that almost all pain does come from fear and tension was first put forth by a big, red-headed, enthusiastic Scotchman named Dr. Grantly Dick Read, who published a book in 1933 called (in America) *Childbirth Without Fear.*

Dr. Read contended that labor was painful for civilized women mainly because they had been taught to be afraid. Primitive women, on the other hand, had not had such teaching. Therefore, he said, their labors were comparatively short and painless. If all women could return to the "natural" ways of primitive women, their labors would become easy too.

Dr. Read's book caught on and spread like the proverbial wildfire. Even those women who had never read it heard about it from friends or magazine articles, and declared bravely they were all for the idea. A questionnaire sent out by the maternity-clothes shop at Lane Bryant, New York, got an overwhelming number of yes answers to the question, "Are you going to go in for natural childbirth?"

Why did so many women answer this way? Partly because of the almost irresistible appeal of the word "nature." If we have intestinal troubles, we often think we can hurry up and solve them by running out and buying "nature foods." If we have foot troubles, we think the answer is a pair of "natural shoes." And if we're bored or overwhelmed by city living, "Back to nature!" we cry.

The trouble is, we rush without thinking the matter through. Going back to "natural foods" may be fine, if it doesn't include going back to fly-specked meat or unpasteurized milk. "Back to nature!" is a wonderful slogan, if it doesn't mean discarding the eyeglasses we need to see with, throwing away the artificial teeth we need to chew with or leaving home the arch-supports without which we can't walk, no matter what the shape of our shoes.

So with "natural childbirth." It's a wonderful idea—up to a point.

CONFIDENT BIRTH

There are a few women of every race and class who do seem to breeze through childbirth—the women who deliver in taxicabs on the way to the hospital, or at home before any kind of help arrives. But these are almost always women having second, third or fourth babies, a fact the wonder stories about them usually omit.

For it stands to reason that the first of any undertaking is harder than the second, that a cervix or other birth-organ, once stretched, tends to stretch that much more easily again. Though even this is not always true. Dr. Logan Clendening at one time wrote rhapsodically about hens: "The hen is able to extrude the fertilized egg from her body with no more discomfort than arises from the writing of a sonnet." But a little later, he had to modify this statement when he found that farmers' wives often had to grease their fingers and insert them into the hen's birth-canal to help a first egg get born.

To be sure, too, the general program advocated by Dr. Dick Read has value. For doctors, its value lies in continually reminding them of the dangers arising from using too *much* anesthesia—from routinely "knocking everyone out." For women, its value lies in the exercise, the advance trip to the hospital, and the comradeship of the childbirth classes, all of which help to dispel fear and build up confidence instead. Dr. Robert Hall of Columbia Presbyterian Hospital says education in advance can cut the need for anesthesia in half.

But this adds up to "confident childbirth"—more than it does to "natural childbirth," since it implies confidence in oneself to do the job when called upon, and confidence in one's doctor to give the best kind of skilled help.

Yet confidence in oneself means reasonable confidence, not perfect confidence, and no woman can expect more. No woman should feel she is a "failure" or a "sissy" if at the last minute, in spite of all her brave resolutions, she finds some of her self-confidence evaporating and cries for outside help.

Dr. Earle Marsh summed up "confident childbirth" very well when, in an article addressed to other doctors and published in a medical journal, he said:

I want to emphasize two points about our approach to labor. First, we are not talking about painless labor. We are talking about helping the patient to deliver as naturally as possible, and with as little loneliness and pain as possible. The great majority of our patients do have pain, but it is usually bearable pain because we are careful to provide them with adequate and appropriate medications and adequate relief from loneliness during labor. But we do not talk of painless labor to our patients any more than we would talk to them about painless life.

Second, there is no such thing as 'childbirth without fear' any more than there is such a thing as life without fear. But with help and reassurance, one can work through an awesome event rather reasonably. The concept of 'childbirth without fear' comes from Grantly Dick Read's book, which unfortunately was so titled by an American publisher. Originally the book bore the title, *Revelation in Childbirth,* which is something quite different.

To re-emphasize, there is no such thing, as a general rule, as labor without fear, apprehension, pain or anxiety, any more than there is life without some fear, apprehension, pain or anxiety.

The appropriate and conventional techniques of modern obstetrics are combined, then, with attempts on our part to offer what might be described as humanistic support . . . support that can help another human being through an important and difficult period—a period which often has many ramifications with other events in this human's life.

The last paragraph contains the crux of the matter: Humanistic support is, on the part of the doctor, a humanism that offers medication when needed, as well as encouragement when needed.

Dr. Marsh has also written a booklet for his patients. Here he describes labor as an "athletic contest"—a hard, tiring job involving a great deal of muscle activity and nervous strain; and if it is a first labor, possibly the hardest work a woman has ever done.

He then goes on to tell what feelings to expect: "During labor you will experience many new feelings. They will range from joy to doubt and fear. As they occur, express them to your doctor, the nurses and your husband. (They will be feeling them too.) But by all means, be yourself. We are all with you."

When the cervix is about 60 per cent opened, the doubts and fears about labor reach a climax. This happens because at the 60 per cent mark, a first may have gone on for so long that the woman feels trapped. She seems to be getting nowhere, yet she can neither get out, go forward or back. Meanwhile, her pains as well as her tensions mount.

It is at this point that Mona said: "That pain made my temperature rise. . . . Oh, I'm not happy! I'm not happy! I wish the baby would just come!"

Mabel moaned: "And to think this has been going on for generations! It doesn't seem possible! I've stopped thinking about the baby. It's just all pain now."

Beth tried to be cheerful, but the best she could manage was, "The little spaces between the pains are so nice."

Dr. Marsh says such reactions are expected and normal, and "only evidence that the seriousness of labor is creeping over a woman." He reassures her again that everything is going according to schedule, and that everything about labor, especially a first labor, is and must be slow. A cervix that has never opened before cannot open fast, nor is it safe now to try to hasten things even when a doctor knows how.

Above all, it is at this point that Dr. Marsh starts offering medicine to relieve a woman's pains.

WHAT KIND OF MEDICINE?

What kind of medicine? The answer is far from simple. Giving medicine during childbirth is exceedingly tricky—much more tricky than during an ordinary operation, for example. During an ordinary operation, there is only one objective—to put the patient into a deep, painless sleep and keep her there while the doctor does the work.

But during childbirth the woman is doing the work, not the doctor. He therefore has the difficult job of doling out just enough to relieve her distress, but not so much he stops the birth process. Also there is the baby to be considered. Some drugs given during labor pass through the placenta immediately and harm the baby. So the doctor has to juggle three considerations—not harm the baby, relieve the mother and keep the birth moving along.

There are five main kinds of birth medicine a doctor has to choose from.

First, there are the analgesics, like Demerol. Analgesics are pain-relievers. They take the edge off misery and reduce the anxiety, but they do not put one to sleep. Analgesics are usually given by mouth or hypodermic.

Second, there are the anesthetics, like ether. These do put one into a more or less prolonged sleep. They are inhaled through a mask.

Third, there are gases, like trilene. These are also inhaled through a mask, but their effects last only for a moment or two. Each whiff eases one individual pain.

Fourth, there are drugs, like cocaine or novocaine, that kill sensations locally—in the case of childbirth, from the waist down. When injected into the lower part of the body, these drugs let the woman stay fully awake and conscious, but the labor pains are not felt any more than one feels a tooth being pulled when novocaine has been injected into the gums.

Fifth, there are amnesics—drugs like scopolamine. These have the peculiar quality of causing amnesia, or erasing the memory of pain. (The woman forgets the pain she felt, and later declares, "Doctor, I didn't feel a thing!")

Sometimes only one of these is used, sometimes several—a different one at different stages of labor.

But it is impossible to tell in advance exactly which may be used, and when, since no two labors are alike. The best the most skilled doctor can do is to instruct his nurses to use those he has found from his experience to be the best during the first stage of labor when he will probably not be on the scene in person, then to go on from there himself, according to what develops during the second stage, when he most certainly will be on the scene.

IS MEDICINE MORAL?

Is the use of any medicine at all moral during childbirth? Or does it go against God's command? This still worries many women. It was answered by a Scotch doctor over a century ago.

On January 19, 1847, Dr. James Young Simpson of Edinburgh delivered the first baby in history while its mother was under anesthesia. Anesthesia had been discovered only a few years before, and at the beginning it was still used mainly during operations. But Dr. Simpson had the insight to believe it could be used in childbirth as well, so he used it to ease the final birth pains of one of his slum patients.

Not surprisingly, he was immediately jumped upon. Sermons were preached and pamphlets printed against him. Some clergymen called anesthesia "a decoy of Satan . . . that will rob God of the deep, earnest cries which arise in time of trouble, for help." Others hammered away at the theme that birth was the result of the "carnal sin" of sex-relations, that this sin fell especially heavily on women because of Eve who had been "man's original temptation," and that all women were cursed with childbirth "pain" as a result.

But Dr. Simpson was a student as well as a doctor. He answered his critics by recalling how there had been similar religious objections to advances in agriculture. Ministers had thundered against the introduction of agricultural machinery into England because, they insisted, man had been commanded to "till the ground by the sweat of his brow," and machinery reduced this sweat. In one parish, communion had even been refused to anyone using a winnowing machine, on the theory that "God had made the winds, and the winds alone were supposed to separate the wheat from the chaff."

From there, Simpson went on to point out that the Bible had been translated and retranslated so many times it was often impossible to take literally, since during the translation many of the original meanings of its words had been lost. The Hebrew word now translated as "sorrow" may very well have meant "work." Work or labor, which is exactly what childbirth is. "In sorrow shalt thou bring forth children," may have been simply predicting that work or labor—the hardest work a woman is ever called upon to do—but no more than that.

But his best argument was one from Genesis. Here he quoted the description of the first birth of all—the birth of Eve from Adam's rib: "And the Lord caused a deep sleep to come upon Adam, and in that sleep He brought forth Eve." A deep sleep, said Simpson, is the very best form of anesthesia. And God himself used it! He won the day.

He won it so well that a short time later, he was appointed one of Queen Victoria's personal physicians.

But this did not impress him half so much as what he had done.

Reporting to his brother in a letter on both events, Dr. Simpson wrote: "Flattery from the Queen is perhaps not common flattery, but I am far less interested in it than in having delivered a woman this week without any pain while inhaling sulphuric ether. I can think of naught else."

Queen Victoria evidently thought about it, too. A few years later, she agreed to the use of ether during the birth of her seventh child, whereupon it became popularly known as "the anesthesia of the Queen," becoming so well accepted it was used on some 40,000 women in Edinburgh alone during the next few years. When Simpson died, the people of Edinburgh were so grateful to him that all the shops in the city were closed so the whole town could turn out at his funeral. Sir Walter Scott humorously suggested that a suitable inscription for his tombstone would be a "wee naked bairn" with the motto underneath, "Does your mither know you're out?"

To clarify the matter more, Pope Pius XII added the weight of his great authority to the morality of using anesthesia during childbirth.

In a 1956 lecture to a group of Catholic midwives and obstetricians, Pope Pius said, "Christian charity has always and ever taken an interest in mothers, at the time of their confinement; it has tried and still tries today to render them efficacious assistance, in accordance with the state of advancement of science and technique. This could be applicable at the present time to the new discoveries. . . . Christian obstetrics can here incorporate into its principles and its methods all that is correct and justified. . . ."

In this way, the Pope gave his sanction to Catholic doctors to offer, and Catholic women to receive, whatever relief from labor pains they could.

MORE ON PAIN

But this still doesn't answer all the labor-pain questions. Another is: Since this pain accompanies a normal and healthy process, why is it there at all?

Practically every other pain we have is a warning of danger—a signal that something has gone wrong. Take the normal process of digesting. Ordinarily it is completely painless. We eat a good meal and digest it without giving the matter a thought. But let us eat something poisonous, or something that disagrees with us, and we get a pain as a warning to stop.

Or take the other normal processes, like walking or breathing. We take a walk as a rule or breathe without giving these a thought either. But let a walk exhaust us unduly, or breathing become difficult, and once more we get a pain as a warning to stop. Why, then, is labor pain different? Why does it come even though nothing has gone wrong? What are we being warned against?

The answer seems to be that we are being warned against giving birth in an unprotected place. Labor pain comes hard and sharp to remind us to retreat to a sheltered spot—sheltered for ourselves, sheltered for the baby. A spot safe from marauding enemies or hostile eyes. Just as primitive women retreated to the woods, to the secluded banks of a stream or to a special birth-hut where experienced old women stood by ready to help, so, too, we retreat to a hospital or to the privacy of our homes, and call upon a doctor or a trusted friend.

ANOTHER CLIMAX

We come back to the woman we left in the throes of her labor pains.

We left her at a climax-point where her cervix was about 60 per cent open. Soon she reaches another climax, when her cervix becomes 100 per cent open.

This 100 per cent climax is an even greater one than the first, for in order to go from 60 per cent to 100 per cent dilation, the uterus has to contract about fifteen times and these fifteen contractions are especially painful and strong.

At the height of these especially strong contractions, Dr. Marsh offers some more medication. He also offers the reassurance that the woman suffering them is *not* caught in a trap. Her uterus has more than enough power to open her cervix fully, given a little patience and time. And with the cervix fully opened, the long first stage of labor is over.

The woman will soon be transferred from the labor room to the delivery room, and the much shorter Act II of the birth drama will be ready to begin.

❋❋❋ 32 Birth: Act II

The first thing one notices about the delivery room is that it is quite different from the labor room. In the labor room, there are as a rule several patients; in the delivery room there is only one. In the labor room, the nurses wear their white nursing uniforms; in the delivery room they have added strange-looking masks. In the labor room, there is one bed or table for each woman; in the delivery room there is the delivery table with its leg-stirrups and hand-grasps, plus two other tables.

THE THREE TABLES

The story behind the three tables starts in the year 1772.

Before 1772, the most dread enemy of woman was childbed fever—a mysterious disease that brought chills and high fever to otherwise healthy young women within a few hours or a few days after delivery, and quickly carried them to their deaths. This fever had rarely been known in the Biblical or pastoral days, but during the Middle Ages it swept Europe in epidemic form for centuries.

Some years the epidemics were so violent that one out of every five women died. In 1772 they reached a still higher peak. In Lombardy, Italy, every woman who bore a child died—not one emerged alive from the delivery room.

This terrible state of affairs caught the attention of an English doctor, Dr. Charles White of Manchester. He was one of those new-fangled "man midwives" who had finally been admitted to the heretofore all-female labor rooms after King Louis XIV of France had set the precedent by calling in a man to attend his mistress, Louise de la Vallière.

The first thing Dr. White did was to investigate the conditions in as many labor rooms (or lying-in chambers, as they were then called) as he could. He was appalled at what he found—the foul air from the tightly shut windows, the heat made hotter by the open fires lit winter and summer, the dirty sheets, the women themselves in bed with all their heavy woolen clothes on (nightgowns were almost unheard of), the general filth on furniture and floor.

He was so appalled that in 1772 he published the first treatise ever written on childbed fever. Here from that treatise is his description of a typical delivery, and the fever that all too often followed it:

If the woman's pains are not strong enough, her friends are generally pouring into her large quantities of strong liquors, mixed with warm water; and if her pains be very strong, the same kind of remedy is made use of to support her. As soon as she is delivered . . . she is covered up close in bed with additional clothes, the curtains are drawn round the bed, and pinned together, every crevice in the windows and doors is stuffed close not excepting even the keyhole, the windows are guarded not only with shutters and curtains, but even with blankets the more effectually to keep out the fresh air, and the good woman is not suffered to put her arm, or even her nose, out of bed for fear of catching cold.

He goes on to tell how after delivery she is supplied again with strong, hot liquors to keep up her perspiring and confined to a horizontal position so that the lochia (the post-delivery vaginal discharge) is caught in the folds of her vagina, or simply permitted to run out onto the dirty sheets, there to grow putrid and stale. He continues,

In a few days after delivery the patient is perhaps seized with a shivering fit, and the nurse is surprised, as she protests she has not had the least waft of cold air. Still more clothes are heaped upon her, more spirituous liquors and hot spices are given her to throw off the cold fit, which most certainly increase the succeeding hot one. . . . Nor is it to be wondered at that conditions are even worse in hospitals where a number are crowded not only in one house but in one ward, where the disease is conveyed from one to another by the putrid miasma lodging in the curtains, bed-clothes and furniture.

But observing and recording all this was not enough for Dr. White. Even though he did not know the cause of childbed fever—he thought it had to do with those "putrid miasmas" in the air—he determined to do something about it. He ordered drastic changes to be made in the lying-in rooms of his patients.

One order was to give women in labor cool or tepid baths—a most startling order for his day because baths of any kind were considered almost as dangerous as fresh air. A second was to use clean or at least well-aired sheets. A third was to open the windows. A fourth was to have the patient sit up and get out of bed as soon as possible. And the last and possibly the most startling was to have the midwives wear clean clothing and wash their hands.

INDIGNATION OF THE MIDWIFE

These orders were met with angry indignation. The midwives rose up in arms. To understand why they were angry, we must go back to a little more history.

In early pastoral days, midwives were a blessing to the community. In those days, they were volunteer members of the group who sat by women in labor, washed them with water from nearby wells or streams, encouraged them, cheered them on, did whatever they knew or could for the sheer humanity of it. But after Christianity promoted the doctrine that giving birth was the result of "carnal sin" or the "temptations of the flesh," this attitude was changed. Now anything to do with labor or birth was looked upon as dirty and shameful. So for many centuries afterward, almost the only women willing to help in lying-in rooms were the lowest in the community—drunkards, prostitutes, bedraggled hags who took on the other dirty jobs that no one else would do.

These lowly women had neither education nor training, were not licensed or supervised in any way and ran from birth to birth for a few coins or a bottle of cheap liquor. They did not dream of stopping to put on clean clothes or wash their hands. Besides, water for washing was extremely hard to come by. With the crowding into the cities of the Middle Ages, gone were the nearby streams and wells. There was no water even in the houses of the very rich; it had to be caught and hoarded in rain-barrels, or bought from itinerant water-peddlers who came by once or twice a week and charged a very high price. In such a situation, even a princess could admit she washed her hands only once a week. Who then did a mere doctor think he was to order midwives to wash their hands several times a day, maybe when they couldn't get a cent more for the job? It was much easier to stick to the old ways.

They stuck to the old ways even when Dr. Alexander Gordon of Aberdeen, Scotland, came along a few years later with a better theory than the "bad air" theory. Childbed fever, he announced, was caused by germs.

Now germs were a new discovery—the microscope had recently been invented and men could actually see them. And even though Dr. Gordon had never seen the germs of this particular disease, he was convinced they were the clue to the mystery. Childbed fever, he announced, was a germ infection. A virulent infection which invaded the raw surfaces of a woman's genital tract while that genital tract was wide open during delivery and was carried from one woman to another by dirty hands.

But the midwives, male or female, did not believe Dr. Gordon any more than they had believed Dr. White. They still went along with the "bad air" or "putrid miasma" theory, even when other doctors confirmed Dr. Gordon's findings; when, for instance, doctors told a man midwife who did an autopsy in the morning on a woman who had just died of childbed fever, that afternoon carried the infected parts to show to students in his classroom and the same evening, without stopping to wash his hands or change his clothes, rushed to deliver another woman who promptly died, too. Also how the next morning, still in the same clothes, he delivered another woman who died as well, with three more of his patients dying the same week.

And they continued to disbelieve even when more evidence piled up. When a study was made in 1840 of a Manchester charity-hospital which regularly used twenty-six midwives, and it was found that during one month of that year nearly four hundred women had been delivered by twenty-five of the twenty-six, with all surviving and doing well, but another thirty had been delivered by the last midwife and of this group more than half had developed childbed fever and died.

"How can this be due to bad air?" asked the researchers who did the last study. "All these women breathed the same air. Why did only those delivered by the twenty-sixth midwife die if she was not a carrier of germs from unwashed hands?"

But again they were met with skepticism. If it wasn't bad air it was coincidence, the skeptics argued. The experience of one man midwife and one female midwife proved nothing. They continued to go into labor rooms as dirty as before, the epidemics continued to rage and deaths of women from childbed fever continued to be accepted as an inevitable thing.

THE BREAKTHROUGH

At last, however, there came a breakthrough. In 1844, Dr. Ignaz Semelweis appeared on the scene.

Dr. Semelweis was different. Drs. White and Gordon had been comparatively obscure doctors connected with comparatively obscure hospitals or with none at all. But Semelweis was a Hungarian with the imposing degree of Master of Midwivery, and he was appointed chief of the obstetrical division of Vienna's famous Lying-In Hospital. That hospital was the largest of its kind in the world, with students flooding to it for study and training in obstetrics from every quarter of the globe.

In addition, by a lucky accident, right after Dr. Semelweis received his appointment, his predecessor changed his mind about retirement, and decided to stay on for two years more. Dr. Semelweis, therefore, had no hard duties, nothing to do for two years but research and teach. And the project he chose to research and teach on was the haunting problem of childbed fever.

As he started, he was struck by a seemingly strange phenomenon. There were two wards in the Vienna Lying-In Hospital. In both, the patients were almost the same age and in the same state of health when they arrived. But for years the mortality from childbed fever ran three to four times as high in the first ward as in the second ward. During the year 1846, for example, the score ran 460 cases which were fatal in the first ward as against only 105 in the second ward. And so it had gone during all the time since the hospital had been founded many years before.

Indeed, the disparity in the death rate in the two wards was so striking that the whole city of Vienna knew about it, and the women who were assigned to the first ward—almost all of them poverty-stricken charity patients—would cry bitterly and give themselves up for lost. Some of them were so terrified, they even were tempted to run back to the dingy hovels in which they lived. But many of them were bearing illegitimate children, and there was a quirk in the law that said that an illegitimate child born in the hospital would become a ward of the state, but not if born at home. So, for the sake of the children they knew they could not support, they took the chance and stayed.

A CLUE

Semelweis pondered on all this and concluded that the difference in the record of the two wards had to be more than coincidence. It had to have some real basis. But what?

He searched further and found a clue:

The first ward—the one where most of the deaths occurred—had always been used as a training-center for male students seeking medical degrees. Since they were seeking degrees, doing autopsies was an important part of their training. They spent their mornings in the dissecting rooms doing these autopsies; afternoons they were encouraged to visit the ward as frequently as possible, examine the women in labor there and compare what they found in the living with what they had found in the dead.

But the second ward was reserved for the training of female midwives. Since they were not seeking degrees, they were not permitted in the dissecting rooms. They spent their time in the second ward, and nowhere else.

"The male students must be carrying the germs of childbed fever picked up in the dissecting rooms right into the genital tracts of their patients," Semelweis reasoned. "It's the same thing that happened in England, only on a much larger scale!" And he ordered the male students to wash their hands before entering the ward.

REBELLION

But people being what they are, and hating change as much as they do, the medical students rebelled. They would *not* stop and wash their hands. They were busy men. Anyway, women had always died of childbirth fever and probably always would.

Besides, the doubters argued back at Semelweis, maybe it was the bad air after all? Wearily, he answered that the air in the two wards was obviously the same. Then maybe it was because the deadly first ward was more crowded than the second? "No," he said. "If anything, the second ward has always been more crowded than the first." Maybe there was a difference in the food, or the method of washing the sheets? No, the food and the method of washing were identical. Maybe it was a punishment for the "loose and abandoned lives" led by the women of the first ward? No, no! There were the same number of "loose women" in one ward as in the other. Maybe, reversing themselves, it was due not to looseness but to the wounded modesty of the women in the first ward who had to undergo examinations by men instead of by female midwives? Hardly a sound medical theory, he replied. Maybe . . . maybe . . . ah! they finally had it! Maybe it was because the male students examined the women more roughly and more frequently, and so injured them in some way? Semelweis ordered a reduction in the frequency and roughness of the male examinations, but the death rate was not altered a bit.

AN ACCIDENT

Then came one of those accidents that no researcher could possibly predict.

A Professor Jacob Kolletschka was in charge of the autopsy room. One day while demonstrating to his students the condition of the organs of a woman who had just died of childbed fever, the dissecting knife he was using accidentally slipped and cut his finger. Soon the professor developed blood-poisoning with chills, fever and convulsions—all the symptoms the woman had shown before she died. He died, too. What is more, when he was autopsied, his organs looked almost exactly like hers.

Here at last was the irrefutable link in the chain. The professor had infected himself just as the students were infecting their patients, and with the same virulent, quick-acting germs.

DRASTIC ORDERS

In May, 1847, Semelweis shocked and surprised his students by issuing orders on cleanliness more drastic than anyone had ever dreamed of. Before examining or touching a patient, they were not merely to wash their hands, they were to scrub and soak them in a powerful antiseptic. That, and nothing less, would do.

This time the students had no choice but to obey. And it worked! The death rate in both wards fell so sharply that within a short time it was down from one woman in ten to one woman in a hundred. The "mysterious disease" was a mystery no more.

There is a statue to Semelweis in Vienna, and a street named after him. But his real monument lies in those three tables now standard in every hospital delivery room. The first is a large table on which are heaped sterile drapes for the laboring woman's legs, abdomen and buttocks, as well as sterile gowns, gloves, masks and towels for her doctor and nurses. (The masks are to catch random sneezes, and the gloves go on as a double protection over the scrubbed hands.) The second table is a smaller one with bottles of sterile fluids with which to wash the patient just prior to delivery. The third is the sterile delivery table itself.

And here sterile means *sterile*—immersed in live steam which is far hotter than boiling water and better than the best antiseptic, because in live steam no germ could possibly live.

Because of all this, the death rate from childbed fever in America today stands at the tiny figure of one in a thousand, or one-tenth of 1 per cent.

If women were choosing their own Saints, they might well choose Saint Semelweis for the blessing of cleanliness and Saint Simpson for the blessing of anesthesia. For these two men reversed the attitude of centuries toward the sufferings of women in childbirth, and so did more for women than almost any men who have ever lived.

ACT II IS ON

With the transfer onto the sterile delivery table, Act II is on.

Now several things start to happen one after the other. The baby starts to travel downward in the direction of the vaginal opening. The woman gets the desire to bear down or push.

The baby's moves are governed primarily by the ever stronger and more closely spaced contractions coming from the uterus. But the mother's pushes double the effect. An involuntary uterine contraction plus a voluntary mother's push make the baby inch slowly but surely along.

An odd fact in this moving is that the baby, guided by some ancient instinct, keeps on shifting its position while it travels downward. Dr. Robert L. Dickinson took some remarkable X-ray pictures of a baby's travels and discovered that it constantly shifts the position of its arms and legs, and rotates its head as well, in order to accommodate itself in the best possible way to the cramped conditions of the birth passage. Sometimes during this shifting and rotating, the baby's soft head becomes slightly flattened and pointed and emerges looking like a little football instead of round. But this means nothing. Within a short time, it will become properly round again.

Ninety-six per cent of all babies travel down the birth passage head first. The remaining tiny minority travel down feet first, in which event the delivery is called a "breach."

When the head reaches the vagina and starts to stretch the tissues enough to let it push through them, the great climax of delivery is reached—a climax of both pain and fear. An almost universal fear is that the vagina may burst during this intensive stretching—burst or rip or get torn to shreds. It will do none of these. If there is a really over-sized baby, there may be a small amount of tearing, but never a tearing to shreds. The vagina has had nine months of gradual preparation for its stretching job—nine months and millions of years of evolution. "So do not worry about this," Dr. Earle Marsh reassures his patients when they express this fear. "You are safe."

But since there is always a bare chance there may be an oversized baby, most doctors play doubly safe and at the moment of "crowning," or when the top of the baby's head appears, they make a small cut that enlarges the opening of the vagina. This cut is called an "episiotomy" and it is a simple straight cut that is painlessly sewed up again. The episiotomy hastens delivery and so reduces the wear and tear on the mother. It also avoids the possibility of a jagged tear that very occasionally may go through into the urinary opening and later cause a constant, uncontrollable dribble of urine.

For some reason, the "natural childbirth" enthusiasts are against an episiotomy. Most doctors believe they are wrong.

THE CLIMAX OF PAIN

The great climax of pain comes at the moment of crowning.

Some women find this pain bearable. "I felt immense, like a volcano that is ready to erupt," is the way a woman who found it bearable described it.

"Please stop the pain. It's coming worse. It's not bad—it's worse. Oh, awful pain," said another to whom it was not bearable at all.

The women who find it unbearable are usually offered sedation now even though they may not have had it before—either a whiff of gas with each contraction, a block that cuts off sensation or a quick-acting anesthesia that for a short time puts them to sleep.

Some women accept this sedation, some refuse it and decide to stay entirely conscious so that they may experience these last few moments of birth to the full. But whether they accept the sedation or not, it is a highly personal choice. Some women can stand a lot of pain, some can't, and it does not necessarily make one more heroic than the other. Nor does staying fully conscious make one more "maternal" or "love one's baby more."

THE WORST IS OVER

Once the baby's head has pushed through the vaginal opening, the worst is over. For the head is the largest part of the baby; the shoulders and legs are narrower, and they are born with little effort, giving the woman a sudden terrific feeling of relief.

Here's how a woman who was conscious during the last few moments described this feeling of relief: "I felt the baby's head coming through. . . . They told me it was out, and I felt as if I could do nothing more. And then the rest came out, and it was the most terrific release. . . . It happens so suddenly; it sort of slides out of you. After all the effort you put into it—that sudden sliding out!"

Another said: "You yell at the first. At the last you don't yell because it doesn't hurt any more. . . . It was a wonderful feeling, like a hot flush going through you, and then everything came out. . . . The funny thing is, the moment it was over I relaxed. I could hardly believe that only a half hour ago, I had been in such pain."

And a third, taking her first look at her newborn baby, said, "Well, she's worth it. There's no feeling in the world quite like it. I can't even seem to remember what I was screaming about." Then she added with a grin, "Just think, I'm somebody's mother!"

In a thoughtful delivery room, all activity stops for a few moments after the final act of birth. Doctor and nurses stand still and smile quietly behind their masks, in order to let the woman freely express herself.

Sometimes that expression is of pure ecstasy; sometimes it is a few quiet tears. But always doctors and nurses are awed by it. For they know that no matter how many times they witness a birth, they are seeing the greatest act of creation of which a human being is capable, a high-point of work and love that in a planned and wanted birth has no equal so the scene never gets hackneyed or stale. Also, they are quiet until the woman asks the inevitable question, "Is she all right? Is she normal?" To which the answer 95 times out of 100 is "yes!"

❋❋❋ 33 Birth: Act III

Act III of the birth drama is a short encore—the delivery of the placenta or after-birth. A few more contractions and the placenta is pulled away from the uterine lining and slides out looking "pink and purple and beautiful" to a doctor's eyes.

The placenta comes out because its job is done. But as it does so, it leaves an open, raw spot about eight inches wide at the place in the uterine lining where it had been attached. It is this spot which is so highly susceptible to infection, just as any spot in the body is susceptible to infection when it is open and raw. Germs introduced into the birth-canal at any time during delivery can hang around and attack this spot, giving rise to childbed fever, as we saw.

The spot heals in a few weeks. During those weeks, absolute cleanliness is still in order. That means no tub baths and no sexual intercourse. But after those weeks, the danger will have passed.

A CAESAREAN

A few more questions on birth that puzzle many women: "What about a Caesarean?" Since a Caesarean eliminates the long hours of labor, shouldn't a woman choose it as easier than a normal delivery if it's up to her?

The answer is no. A Caesarean is not easier but harder. It is also not as safe.

Caesareans (from the Latin word *caedere,* "to cut") were introduced in Roman days for only one reason—as a last resort to try to save the life of the baby when the mother was definitely dying or already dead. Under such circumstances, a hasty cut to open up the abdomen and uterus and lift out the baby seemed at least worth a try.

But no Caesareans were attempted on living women then. It is doubtful that Caesar himself was born that way, since his mother Aurelia is reported to have lived to a ripe old age and surgery in those days was exceedingly dangerous. With no anesthesia, no antiseptics and little surgical skill, doctors during the early and middle ages seldom entered the abdomen of a living woman either, since they knew that if she wasn't dying she soon might be, from the shock of the experience if from nothing else, and the prime rule of medicine has always been to do no deliberate harm. They therefore did not dare to take the chance.

But there is such a thing as the courage born of desperation, and this is what happened in the year 1500. In that year a Swiss woman by the name of Nufer had been in labor with her first child so long that thirteen midwives had tried to help her and given up. She was still alive but the child simply could not get born. At that point, her husband decided to intervene. He was not a doctor but a sow-gelder (meaning a man who makes his living by removing the sex-glands from pigs and cows to make their flesh more tender), and though he knew nothing of human anatomy he decided he *would* take the chance. He got out his sow-gelding instruments, said a short prayer and made the cut. Miraculously, it worked. The child was born and his wife survived to bear him many more children. But the procedure was still so dangerous that hardly more than a dozen Caesareans were reported during the next hundred years, and the first successful American operation didn't take place until 1794.

Today, of course, surgical knowledge and skill has vastly improved. Especially great progress has been made during the last twenty years. Jacqueline Kennedy had three children in a row by Caesarean. Nevertheless, Caesareans are not something to choose except for a sound medical reason, like an extremely narrow pelvis. An operation is still an operation, while a normal delivery is something for which evolution has been perfecting a woman's body for millions of years.

FORCEPS DELIVERY

What about a forceps, or "instrument," delivery? Here women have heard just the reverse of what they have heard about a Caesarean; that forceps are in some way harmful. But that is not true. Forceps can be of tremendous help in hastening or easing birth.

Forceps look like big sugar tongs, the hinged kind of tongs with which icemen used to grip and deliver ice. They consist of two wide, curved blades, each blade just wide enough and curved enough to fit a mother's pelvis without tearing it, and fit a baby's head without harming it. They are used either high up in the birth-canal, to turn a baby who is in the wrong position or who is not descending properly, or lower down, to help a baby's head get through during the last few minutes of birth when for some reason it cannot seem to get through alone. To do either of these jobs, the two blades are carefully inserted into the birth-canal one at a time, then locked together so that the baby is gently but firmly gripped and eased along.

In this way they may save the mother several exhausting hours of labor, and save the baby several equally exhausting hours of banging its head against an opening through which it cannot manage to pass.

The story of the discovery of the forceps reads like a detective story. Since the beginning of time, difficult or delayed births have been a terrific problem. People have always been frustrated beyond measure by labors that start and inexplicably stop, start and stop again. For centuries, as a result, they have tried to hasten matters by such things as jumping up and down on the woman's belly, fastening her to a ladder and shaking the ladder, even leaning her up against a tree and riding a horse hard toward her, then suddenly turning the horse aside just before it rode her down in order to "frighten the child out."

Obviously, none of these worked.

But in the early part of the seventeenth century, along came two French Huguenot brothers by the name of Chamberlen, who emigrated to England, and developed the forceps. Each of the brothers, for some odd reason, was named Peter, so for convenience sake they were called Peter I and Peter II. The two Peters were not doctors but man midwives, or barber-surgeons, yet their forceps were so successful they were called in to deliver the ladies of the court as well as the queen herself, and they became rich and famous beyond their hopes.

They became so rich and famous, indeed, they decided to do something unethical—keep their discovery to themselves, or, at most, members of their own family. Medical discoveries have traditionally been shared with the world, but Peter I and Peter II decided to share theirs with no one but their wives and Peter III, Peter II's son.

At least two of the three Peters would work together when called in for a difficult birth. They would drive to the house of a woman in labor in a splendid carriage, alight dramatically and take from the carriage a huge gilded box in which was hidden what they referred to only as The Secret. Pretending to struggle under its weight, they would carry this box directly into the lying-in room, blindfold the woman so she could not see what was in it after it was opened, chase out the relatives or other midwives who had summoned them, lock the doors and proceed with the delivery.

This kind of hocus-pocus went on with great success for many years until the original Peters were all wealthy old men and Peter III in turn had a son, who for a change was named Hugh.

Hugh Chamberlen followed the family profession of midwifery but decided to do something even more unethical than his father and grandfather had done—sell The Secret to a non-competing rival for a huge sum. The place he decided to sell it was Paris, and the man he decided to offer it to was François Mauriceau, the most famous obstetrician in Europe. So, with the gilded box in his trunk, in 1670 he set off across the Channel in high hopes.

Now Mauriceau, like everyone else, had had many difficult and frustrating cases to contend with, and on the morning Hugh Chamberlen arrived he happened by chance to have a particularly difficult one—a dwarf so badly twisted and deformed by rickets she had been in labor four days. When Hugh boasted he could, with his Secret, deliver in fifteen minutes any woman in the world, Mauriceau figured that if he could deliver this one he had something worth selling for fair, and agreed to let him try.

But for once Chamberlen had met his Waterloo. He struggled for three hours, during which he hardly stopped to catch his breath, but finally had to give up in defeat. The poor dwarf died of exhaustion the following day. Mauriceau didn't buy.

After that, Chamberlen went on to Holland where, a little while later, he was able to demonstrate the forceps successfully and sell it. But he duped the Dutch doctors at that. He gave them the pattern for only one blade, which was useless without the other, then quickly pocketed his money and skipped home.

In time, however, another Chamberlen let the complete Secret leak out free. He did it for the simple reason he had no son he could persuade to carry on and use it himself. But when it did leak out, it had been kept in the one family, occasionally hidden under a trap-door in the attic, for over a hundred years.

ANOTHER BLESSING

If the Chamberlens hadn't been such rogues, we might admit them to our gallery of Saints. For their forceps, constantly refined over the years, have turned out to be another of those blessings that have reduced women's suffering beyond our power to compute.

And as a final argument against any lingering doubt that they may hurt babies, a study of 500 teenagers—76 per cent of whom had been born without forceps and 4 per cent with—was done by a team of researchers in 1941. The results showed little difference in intelligence or behavior. If anything, the ones helped by forceps had the edge.

✳✳✳ 34 Readjustment Time

The days and weeks following childbirth have always been days of reactions from the great experience that used to be called the confinement, or lying-in time. Today confinement and lying-in have an old-fashioned sound and are seldom used. But we still know that the rest and recuperation they imply are necessary, since during this time a woman's whole body and mind must readjust to the state of not being pregnant again —readjust after each birth the same way as after the first. A better name, therefore, is readjustment time.

PURIFICATION

Readjustment has always traditionally started with some kind of purification rite. Just as a woman was unclean or untouchable during menstruation, so too was she unclean or untouchable after childbirth, until she had been purified. In the days when water in the home was hard to come by, she was purified by being ceremoniously bathed in a nearby stream. If no stream was handy, she was bathed in an indoor pool, or at the very best sprinkled with holy water. In ancient Persia, fire was used instead of water; a woman who had just been delivered was made to lie naked for an entire month before an open fire, kept roaring day and night by her husband or other relatives, slowly being turned round and round like a roast on a spit.

Today the actual lying-in or resting period usually is spent in a hospital, and seldom lasts more than a week. During that week, nurses bring the cleansing waters to her, and the husband's job consists mainly in comforting her and bragging about his child.

THE LYING-IN WEEK

During the first lying-in or adjustment week, several things may happen to the new mother:

One is an intense and painful feeling that women describe simply as "longings." This longing is different from the food longings of pregnancy. It is an emotional longing, a longing to see and touch the new baby constantly. The separation from it is unbearable. Every cry down the hall, every sound from the nursery, is interpreted as trouble that cannot be borne unless she rights it herself. What is happening is that the physical umbilical cord connecting mother and child has been cut, but not the psychic umbilical cord. She is longing for the original pregnancy union when the child was safe within her, and it is a painful struggle to give this union up.

Accompanying this psychic pain may be a strange, shaking chill that comes on several hours after delivery, no one knows why. This chill lasts only for a short while, then goes away.

Other strange and unexpected pains may be a series of sharp uterine pains called after-pains. These are in reality tapering-off pains, as if the uterus could not stop its strong contractions all at once, but had to gradually taper off.

Not so painful, but also unexpected, is some vaginal bleeding or spotting, called the lochia. The lochia is again a tapering-off phenomenon —the throwing off of a few extra shreds of uterine lining that still need to be shed.

But the most upsetting experience of the first week is a period of weeping or depression, commonly known as the "baby blues." These blues may last for a few hours or a few days, and are all the more upsetting because they come after the elation of delivery. They are far more common than the emotional longing since many women have them and there are many reasons why.

A SUDDEN HORMONE CHANGE

The first reason for the baby blues is the sudden hormone change.

During pregnancy, you remember, there was an almost complete change in the woman's hormone system. Her pituitary stopped functioning in its usual manner, and her placenta took over the job of making most of the stimulating sex hormones her ovaries used to make. The placenta also took over the job of making many of the stimulating hormones, such as cortisone and ACTH, her adrenals used to make. But now the placenta has been suddenly withdrawn, and its stimulating hormones have been withdrawn, too. It takes about a week for a readjustment to be made, a week in which the pituitary gets back into the saddle and starts sending out "go" messages to her ovaries and adrenals to make their hormones as they did before she got pregnant.

During this readjustment week, there may be much fatigue. During this week, there may be a feeling of lowness and a marked tendency to weep until her hormonal seesaw gets back to swinging in its usual way.

EMOTIONAL CHANGES

But hormones never tell the whole story. There are also other reasons for the baby blues. The strongest is a curious feeling of letdown, or "emotional lag."

Right after giving birth, most women feel extremely heroic. They have finished a tremendous task, and they know it. But a few days later, when they figure they should still be feeling heroic, they no longer do. The hospital routine frustrates them. The stitches from their episiotomy are beginning to hurt. Worst of all, they don't feel what they think they should feel toward the new baby. They are not consumed with longing to see it. If anything, they take a good look at the little wiggly thing they have been waiting nine months for, dreamed such beautiful dreams about and say to themselves, "Is *this* what I produced? Is this *all* I had in me?" And somehow it doesn't seem enough. And since it doesn't seem enough, they don't feel the great rush of Madonna-like mother love they expected they would feel. Instead, they feel empty, lost, let down. And because they feel blue instead of joyful, they become guilty, and because they become guilty they get afraid they'll never be up to the job of raising the child. And because they are anxious and afraid, they become weepy and depressed.

This emotional lag, most doctors feel, is the main reason for the post-delivery depression. Yet unless it is exaggerated or lasting, it is a normal state of affairs. Some women do experience a terrific flow of mother love almost as soon as the child is born—even those who didn't particularly want it. This is well expressed in the novel *The Garrick Year*. Both the wife Emma and her young actor-husband David had dreaded having a child. In fact, the last two months before it was born, they were so miserable they hardly spoke to each other. Yet as soon as their daughter came, Emma describes her feelings this way: "Somehow, after she was born—and this is a common story—things improved out of all recognition. We changed. I can see it now; it was as simple as that. We changed. What I had dreaded as the blight of my life turned out to be one of its greatest joys. David, too, reacted overwhelmingly strongly to the child, and in the shock of our mutual surprise at this state of affairs we fell once more into each other's arms."

Other women don't react this quickly and happily. Mother love may be the basic factor in human survival. Human infancy lasts so long, and so much of human knowledge has to be learned, that continued care and teaching by a father and mother—especially a mother—is indispensable. This is probably how human marriage started—to provide survival-security to children. We who read this book are alive today mainly because we had parents who gave us care and security, and the generations who come after us will survive because we will give them the same. But that doesn't say that all women can begin giving it without a longer or shorter period of emotional lag. A period in which the baby has time to start becoming an individual in his own right instead of the fantasy-child it was in the womb. A period in which a woman can discover how good it is to be intensely needed. A period in which she can remember for the hundredth time that normal does not mean perfect, and become more charitable both to the infant's shortcomings and her own.

HORMONES AGAIN

Also, hormones play another part here. On the second or third day after delivery, a new hormone, prolactin, begins to be produced in a woman's body in full force. This prolactin is the milk-giving hormone; but it also does other things. The laboratory test for one unit of prolactin is an amount that, injected into an immature male pigeon, will be enough to make him sit as a female sits on a batch of eggs a male would otherwise ignore. So prolactin greatly increases a woman's motherly feelings as well as forming the production of milk. It increases this feeling still more if she breast-feeds her baby, since breast-feeding keeps up the prolactin supply.

WITCHES' MILK AND MYSTERIOUS BLOOD

Meanwhile, until the prolactin does come in full force, other things puzzle her and give her concern. Here are some of them.

Why do both boy and girl babies often have hard, swollen breasts at birth—swollen even to the point of secreting a little milk known as "witches' milk" (because for centuries it was thought to have mysterious properties since no one knew its cause)? The answer, prolactin again. Prolactin is made in small amounts even before birth, and passes through the placenta to the baby where it stimulates its breasts to give milk, too.

But in the baby the stimulation doesn't last; it goes away after about a week, the hard, swollen breasts subside, and the "witches' milk," if any, disappears.

Why do girl babies often have swollen genitals that sometimes give off a reddish discharge, or even a little actual blood? More hormone stimulation. The estrogens that flood the mother's body during pregnancy also go through the placenta in small amounts, affecting a girl baby's genitals in particular. The result may be a swelling and a few drops of blood that also soon go away.

Why do newborn babies get proud parents upset when they lose some of their original birth weight for a few days, no matter how much they're fed? This is a normal weight loss due to the stress of the big job of getting born. The babies will soon pick up and gain the weight back.

Why does a baby's head often look pointed like a little football instead of round, or have a definite lopsided lump on one side? This is the result of the compression while travelling down the birth-canal. Nature has made a baby's head deliberately soft and pliable so that it can stand the compression as it twists and turns and travels, yet not be harmed. Birth is a strenuous business for a baby, but its birth-cry after the job is done, remember, is not a cry of rage or pain. The cry is merely a reflex act by means of which it opens its mouth wide and takes in some air quickly. Its head will soon become properly round, and its cry will turn into a smile.

Why do a newborn baby's eyes sometimes roll about so wildly? This comes from lack of nerve coordination. When its nerves become better connected, its eyes will straighten out.

Most worrisome of all, why does a baby often breathe irregularly for a few minutes after birth, or even not breathe at all? This is because a baby's lungs don't always expand fully right away, so it breathes for a few minutes with half-expanded lungs, or does not breathe at all. But nature has provided for this contingency. A newborn, as you know, can survive a considerable period without breathing—much longer than an older child or an adult can.

TO NURSE OR NOT TO NURSE

Since history began, about 25 per cent of all women, records tell us, did not nurse their own babies for one reason or another, but got other women who had recently given birth to nurse for them.

Today the general figure of 25 per cent still stands. It is only in wealthy countries like America that things are different. In America, when the question of nursing comes up, about 65 per cent decide not to nurse, leaving only 35 per cent who at least try.

Why do two-thirds of American women choose not to nurse? San Francisco's Dr. Elmer Grossman thinks many factors are at work. The first, he believes, is pressure by the baby-feeding industry. Selling cow's milk to new mothers has become a big and profitable business on which the dairy industry has done much clever promotion. It is loath to give this business up and let mothers go back to their own milk, which is obviously free.

Next is pressure by the modern hospital. Almost all American babies are born in hospitals today, and it is much easier for the staff to shove a bottle into a baby's mouth when it is hungry than to pick it up and take it down the hall to its own mother. So many hospitals deliberately discourage it.

The next is discouragement by the woman's family. "Why should you bother when it will ruin your figure?" is the family's frequent refrain.

But the worst is the woman's own feeling of fear, or of inadequacy. Many women have been told by their husbands that their breasts are merely sex-symbols and, as such, belong exclusively to them. Others have been inhibited from childhood from touching any of the "private parts" of their bodies. One of Dr. Eleanor Hamilton's patients told her, "I remember a vague and terrible scene with my nurse over touching my genitals. I forget what happened, but henceforth I was scared stiff to touch myself anywhere, including my breasts to nurse."

Or if they find they can touch their breasts for nursing, there is the fear they won't succeed. Dr. Grossman thinks the chief deterrent here is the presence of a bossy mother or mother-in-law, or of an even bossier professional baby nurse who thinks she knows it all. If, as happened to another of Dr. Hamilton's patients, a domineering older woman stands by and keeps repeating, "You'll never do it! You'll never do it! Here, hand *me* that child!" the chances for success become almost nil.

Yet there are so many advantages to breast-feeding—advantages to the woman as well as to the baby—that the tide is beginning to turn.

The first advantage to the woman is pleasure. Deep, satisfying physical pleasure. There is a direct connection between the breast and the genitals, and during nursing the pleasure sensations in the genitals are sometimes akin to those of orgasm. The nipple is also an erogenous, or pleasure-giving zone and if you add to this the sensation when the baby reaches up and pats the breast while nursing, the pleasure can become intense.

Then there's the advantage of quicker involution of the uterus. It takes the uterus nine months to stretch from its original weight of two ounces to its full pregnancy weight of two pounds. But it takes only about six weeks to involute or shrink back. Dr. Nicholas Eastman calls this quick shrinking a "remarkable disappearing feat," and breast-feeding helps it shrink more quickly and more surely. Because of the direct connection between the breasts and the genitals, each pull of the baby causes a uterine contraction, and these contractions help speed up recovery and the flattening of the abdomen again. In this way, nursing, instead of ruining one's figure, helps get it back.

As for causing the breasts to droop, nursing doesn't do that either. The breasts do blow up during nursing, to be sure, but when it is over they shrink back to their former size unless the woman has allowed herself to get very fat all over. Then her breasts will droop from sheer weight. Heredity also plays a large part. In Bali, almost all women have small, upright breasts. In many parts of Africa, they do not. Anne Stevens, former director of the famed Maternity Center in New York, sums this up by declaring: "Take three women at random. Except for their nipples, I defy you to tell which has nursed and which has not."

Next comes the matter of breast-feeding and cancer. No one knows why, but many doctors believe breast-feeding does in some way seem to diminish the possibility of later breast-cancer. Maybe this is because the basic cycle of conception, pregnancy and delivery is not complete unless breast-feeding is added to it as a follow-through.

Then, breast-feeding seems to make a woman just plain "feel well." Other glands, like her thyroid and adrenals, are pepped up while she is nursing. If she manages to take some daytime naps to make up for her night-time disturbances, she should feel close to tops.

Finally, breast-feeding is of tremendous help in overcoming emotional lag. The experience of nursing is unique in the closeness it develops between mother and child as a result of the satisfaction of mutual needs. For not only does the baby need the mother and become grateful to her for being fed, but the mother needs the baby and becomes grateful to it for emptying her full breasts.

Such mutual gratitude, plus the psychic lift women get when they discover they can succeed at nursing after all, helps like nothing else to drive out the blues.

Nursing also gives the baby an increased immunity to disease.

A baby is born with immunity to almost all the diseases its mother is immune to, either because she's had them or been immunized against them. Polio is a notable example. If a mother has had polio herself, or polio-shots to immunize her, a newborn baby will not get polio either. This immunity is passed on to the baby during pregnancy, by way of the placenta, through antibodies against the disease formed in the mother's blood. But—and this is important—the immunities derived this way last for only about six months after birth. After this six-month head start, the baby must develop its own.

Breast-feeding appears to act as a booster to these original immunities. Helpful antibodies are still circulating in the mother's blood, and each time the baby sucks, some of these seem to be passed on through the milk.

Then there is the matter of cleanliness, or sterility.

Human milk is sweet, clean and sterile as it comes from the breast, just as cow's milk is sweet, clean and sterile as it comes from the cow. But cow's milk is subject to so much mixing, handling and time-delay before it reaches the baby that, even with the most modern methods of pasteurizing, some of this sterility may be lost. Mother's milk is subject to no handling and mixing, so clean and sweet it remains.

Next, human milk and formula milk are quite different in composition. Human milk contains a special kind of protein that formula milk does not, so fewer allergies develop in breast-fed babies. Also, human milk contains more calories to the ounce, so babies gain faster on smaller amounts. And the calcium in human milk is so superior that babies who are lucky enough to get it are less prone to the rickets that deform bones and teeth.

A study of 20,000 babies in the Chicago area, headed by pediatrician Dr. E. Robbins Kimball, confirms this. The breast-fed babies were found to have far fewer illnesses and allergies than the bottle-fed. Dr. Kimball also kept careful records of his own small patients over many years, and found he averaged only one house-call in two years to the homes of the breast-fed babies against one call every three or four months to the bottle-fed. Indeed, his mothers were so impressed with his findings that he persuaded almost 96 out of every 100 to try breast-feeding, a figure few gynecologists have bothered to attempt to match.

For when a well-known Long Island gynecologist, who did not encourage his mothers this way, was asked: "Why did the good Lord give
women breasts if they weren't supposed to use them?" and answered,
"Because the good Lord didn't know we were going to come up with
such fine formulas," the gynecologist was wrong. The good Lord still
knows what He's doing.

Of course, the trick to breast-feeding is getting started, and that
means getting started as soon as possible. Almost every woman finds milk
coming in her breasts two or three days after birth. Sucking brings this
milk out. Taking pills (usually enough estrogen or androgen to halt the
making of prolactin), or binding the breasts tightly, or merely not letting
the baby suck, dries this milk up.

It is because nursing must start as soon as possible that some doctors
even put the baby to the breast for a minute or two right in the delivery
room, as a sort of practice-session. Since a baby needs only water for its
first few days, because it has arrived with its own "packed lunch" to tide
it over, on the second or third day, when the mother's milk is ready, the
baby is ready for it, too.

Having started, the main obstacles to continuing are usually psychological. The mother must get over the notion she needs a special kind
of diet. Her usual diet, including plenty of liquids, will do as a rule. In
the old days, beer was thought to have some magical properties, and the
wet-nurses in England were paid merely with all the beer they could
drink. Today we think the chief value of beer lies in its relaxing qualities. Ordinary milk is just as good as beer—and much less fattening. Or
if one simply can't drink milk, as many adults can't, then its equivalent
in a daily small ration of cheese will do the trick.

More important than diet, the mother must somehow manage
peace and privacy while nursing, for excitement or fear can stop the
flow like nothing else. Farmers know this well. They know that if a
stranger walks into the barn, or a mouse scares a cow, the odds are strong
the milk will not come forth until Bessie has been soothed and quieted
down. For this reason, Dr. Eleanor Hamilton suggests that a woman
think of nursing-time as a "cocktail hour," and do all she can toward
enjoying that hour in peace.

She should also realize that no infant needs to be fed more often
than every two hours. "Demand feeding" is another of those unfortunate
terms. It does not mean feeding a baby every time it cries, since there
are a dozen reasons for a baby's crying, and hunger is only one of them.

"Demand" merely means on a reasonable schedule according to the individual baby rather than on the dot by the clock.

Above all, a woman must remember that nursing cannot be done as a duty. One can get pregnant from a sense of duty and, once it is well started, the pregnancy will carry on by itself. Nursing will not. The woman who grits her teeth and determines to nurse no matter how much she dislikes the idea, or feels it interferes with other things she must do, will either give the baby colic, or fail. Nursing should be done, agrees Dr. Grossman, only as long as a woman really enjoys it, whether it's for two days or two years.

But when she does enjoy it, it's a creative experience like no other except childbirth. A Los Angeles woman, after watching her daughter nurse her grand-daughter, said: "I saw a look on her face like nothing I had ever seen there before. It was more than love. It was ecstasy. She looked completely *lost*."

A final question that has been debated for ages: Does nursing act as a contraceptive? Is a woman who is breast-feeding safe from getting pregnant again? The answer is: Fairly safe, but not completely safe. Nursing *reduces* her chances of conceiving, but that is all.

One of the best-known modern studies of this was done by Drs. Mazer and Goldstein on 1200 nursing women. Fifty-five per cent started to menstruate during the first few months of nursing, while 45 per cent did not. And by the end of eight months, about 70 per cent were menstruating and 30 per cent were not.

Yet these figures do not tell the whole story: At the beginning of the nursing-period even those who did start to menstruate had many infertile periods. That is, the periods were not accompanied by ovulation, and without ovulation conception, of course, cannot take place. But as the nursing progressed toward the eight-month mark, which is about the time a baby's teeth start to come in so that nursing becomes uncomfortable and most women stop, more and more periods become fertile. Ovulation occurred quite frequently, and conception was possible again.

The reason for this is the stop-and-go arrangement of a woman's hormone system. When her pituitary is busy sending "go" messages to her breasts to make enough prolactin to produce milk, it is often stopped from sending messages that cause her uterus to menstruate or her ovaries to produce eggs. But as nursing tapers off and prolactin decreases, her pituitary gets fewer and fewer such "stop" messages, so it sends more and more "go" messages to her uterus and ovaries, until in due time her menstrual cycle is back in full form again.

But the human body is not a machine. No woman's system works perfectly or predictably. A woman never knows when her full cycle will return. Nursing is a better contraceptive than nothing, which women seem always to have more or less known. Dr. Erik Erikson tells of visiting an American Indian tribe not long ago and seeing a three-year-old boy eating a box of crackers and washing them down with good big drinks of his mother's milk. He was getting free milk and she, presumably, was hoping for something else. But the more modern woman will not want to rely on this kind of thing.

The hormone system is so delicate that many doctors believe she should not rely on the pills while nursing, for the pills may in turn interfere with her milk production. A diaphragm or other kind of contraceptive is in order until the nursing-period is through.

CONCEIVE AFTER ONLY SIX WEEKS

If a woman does not nurse at all, she may conceive again as soon as a few weeks after delivery. Without nursing, menstruation usually comes back six to eight weeks after delivery, and ovulation usually returns either before the first period or soon after, meaning that, if it comes back before, she can conceive even before she starts to menstruate again.

A few weeks after delivery is too quick for any woman to conceive, most doctors believe, no matter how much she wants more children. A leading medical text tells of a woman considered "biologically perfect," because she was 27 years old and had never menstruated. She had had her first child at fourteen, the result of an ovulation that preceded what would have been her first menstruation, and had immediately conceived after each delivery before she could start to menstruate again. Most women would say, "Heaven forbid!" to such a state of affairs.

Indeed, most women would say it so vehemently that Dr. Robert N. Rutherford reports that many of his patients who had enjoyed sex-relations before their first pregnancy abruptly lost their enjoyment afterward because they were so afraid of immediately getting pregnant again. The use of a reliable contraceptive is the only way to allay this fear and this contraceptive, to be effective, must be started even before the first

menstruation comes back since ovulation may precede it and permit conception to occur. If she is nursing, as I said, a diaphragm is temporarily
better than the pills since they may interfere with the flow of milk.

A LIFE CRISIS

But fear of a new conception or no fear, the days and weeks following a first childbirth are a crisis time in the lives of most women.

It is not easy to shift from being the more or less irresponsible child
of one's mother to becoming the very responsible mother of a child, and
the readjustment brings with it problems that may cause anxiety to the
point of panic, especially immediately after getting home from the
hospital.

How shall I bathe my child? How shall I handle it to dress and undress it? How often and what shall I feed it? How shall I interpret its
mysterious cries? Such questions are extremely insistent at the beginning
because, until it is a month old, almost no baby settles down to a smooth,
normal rhythm of having a need for something, crying to get it, feeling
gratified when it's been gotten and falling into a restful sleep. It does
not settle down because a baby has just undergone the great changes
birth involves, changes from living in darkness to living in light, from
living in a silent world to a world full of sound, from absorbing food
easily and constantly, without effort, to obtaining it hours apart, by work.

These changes involve a readjustment in its entire nervous system
—the nervous system which at birth is incomplete. And this readjustment may be so difficult it may take even longer than a month; it may
take two or three months, especially in first babies. For a first-time
mother's anxieties are so surely communicated to a first baby that it is as
hard to be a first baby as it is to be a first mother. Both may find it bewildering indeed.

Add super-cleanliness to the picture, and the task becomes still
harder.

A Chicago mother says she was so worried about cleanliness that
each time she prepared orange juice for her first baby she washed the
orange with soap, cut it with a knife sterilized in boiling water, lifted out
the knife with boiled tongs, then poured the juice into a sterile cup. She
also washed its diapers in three waters and rinsed them in five, feeding
the baby and changing her so often that sometimes she used forty diapers
a day. And the more of this she did, the punier and frailer her little girl

became. Naturally. How could a baby help but sense such anxiety surrounding it, and react by becoming tenser and more nervous itself?

EDUCATION AS A HELP

Here's where classes in education-for-childbirth are of help. They teach a new mother to relax, and realize her baby is not nearly as fragile a toy as it seems. In St. Vincent's Hospital in New York, for instance, they teach her that a bath is not necessary every day, since a baby perspires only on its forehead, which can easily be wiped off with a damp cloth. That daily bath is mainly a modern "magic" ritual that centuries of children managed very well without. They also tell her that heating up a baby's formula, if it is bottle-feeding, isn't necessary either, since a baby likes its milk just as well cold, and that keeping a baby bundled up day and night from head to toe is a waste of time and money since a baby whose skin is pink is producing its own warmth; it is only a baby with a purple skin who is asking for more coverings or clothes.

In fact, relaxing the mother by these and other devices is so important that even when a baby has colic, shown by the painful clenching of its little fists and the pulling up of its little legs an hour or so after eating, doctors now often sedate the mother instead of the child. For colic is usually caused by a nervous bowel-spasm, and a mother's nervousness is as catching as any germ. As she becomes calmer, the colic often disappears dramatically without the baby being treated in any way.

AN ASSISTANT MOTHER

But a new mother needs more than reassurance and relaxation. She needs help. Regular help in the form of some kind of assistant mother to tide her over the first readjustment weeks.

For the work a new mother has to do is tremendous. Dr. Robert Rutherford estimates that a new mother's work load increases as much as 40 per cent more than it was before the baby came for her first baby, and 20 per cent more for each later baby, since by now she has become more efficient. An assistant mother is therefore needed very much indeed.

In the old days, when families lived close to each other, this assistant mother was almost always the new mother's own mother. Today, with families so scattered, it is becoming harder and harder for the grand-

mother to be on the scene. Indeed, psychiatrists like Dr. Jane Pearce
think it's not a good idea for the grandmother to be there, even when
she can, if there are still unresolved conflicts between mother and
daughter. For there's nothing more tension-producing than a combination of an experienced grandmother and a new mother who's trying to
show how all-competent she's also suddenly become. The battle that may
follow can be shattering to all concerned, so it is far better in such cases
to postpone grandma's visit until things have settled down a bit. Meanwhile, it is wise to call in as an assistant an outsider with whom a new
mother does not feel compelled to compete.

But a new mother does desperately need an assistant of some kind.
Because here's another paradox: The more a new baby is dependent on
her, the more a new mother has strong dependency-needs of her own.
The more she wants to care for her child, the more she needs to be
taken care of, too. Theoretically, she should change right over from the
passivity of pregnancy to the activity of motherhood, but it just doesn't
work that way. There's another kind of emotional lag here—a lag in
which a new mother becomes, for a time, more dependent than ever on
some outside source to give her support.

The source she looks to most, of course, is her husband. When
we read of John Barrymore's not going to the hospital the night Dolores
Costello gave birth to their oldest son, but celebrating instead by getting
drunk with his cronies and staying drunk for days, we realize he was
deserting her in the deepest way a man can desert a woman. That's why
women with illegitimate children suffer even more keenly after delivery
than they did during pregnancy. So do war widows, or widows of any
kind; they are alone, with no man at hand to give them emotional
support.

A HUSBAND HITCH

Yet there's a hitch to looking toward one's husband. Even when he
is on the scene during this crucial time, he sometimes becomes so jealous
of the attention the new baby is getting—attention he formerly had all
to himself—that instead of coming forward with support, he withdraws
into a shell. Then there follows the common state of affairs known as
"the husband triangle" or "the husband blues," in which the husband
feels and acts like a third person who's been pushed out of the scene.

But there are two solutions to a triangle. One is to push the third person further out; the other is to pull him back in. A wise woman uses the second solution. No matter how harried she is, no matter how fatigued, she manages to spread her love around and draw her husband back in.

Here's where contraception is invaluable. Sex is the language of the body—a language that often speaks eloquently when nothing else can. If a man offers his wife sex at this time and she says "no" because she is afraid of another too-quick pregnancy, or because the prolactin she makes for a while now whether she nurses or not interferes with her production of sex hormones and so lessens her desire, he may interpret it as another rejection. And the more rejected he feels, the harder it is to pull him in. Young marriages often become exceedingly strained at this point for these reasons. It is no accident that the huge percentage of divorces occurs during the first five years of marriage, when a new baby, instead of drawing husband and wife closer together, flings them apart.

And divorce during the first five years is especially devastating. It is devastating for the baby, who needs a father as well as a mother if it is to develop basic trust in life—one father, not a confusing succession of fathers. It is devastating for the woman who, if she does find a new husband, will overestimate *him* for a short, exciting period, then meet up with the inevitable disillusionment when the excitement is over, leap maybe to another divorce and so go sadly on and on. It is devastating for society, which in time will have more and more problem-children on its hands from broken homes, more and more children who tend to divorce in turn.

For the propensity to divorce is contagious. The sociologist Dr. Judson T. Landis of the University of California carefully collected histories from 2000 of his students, including the histories of their parents and grandparents as well. He discovered that if neither set of grandparents had been divorced, only 15 per cent of their children had later divorced. If one set of grandparents had divorced, 24 per cent of their children had later divorced. But if both sets of grandparents had divorced, a whopping 38 per cent of their children had divorced, with all the misery and failure this implies.

A wise woman will do everything in her power to prevent this kind of thing. She will get as much outside help as she can afford during her readjustment time. She will pull her husband back as vigorously as she can into the triangle. She will make it a quadrangle and pull in her mother, too, as soon as she comfortably can. Above all, she will try powerfully to deny her panic and put on the best face she possibly can for herself, her friends—anyone who's looking. For she will realize that in a few weeks or months at most the crisis will be past. The baby's nervous system will settle down to a more predictable rhythm, while her nervous system will settle down, too, as she gains a measure of her ego-strength once more.

When this happens, confinement in its literal sense will be over. She will be ready to enter a new period, that of raising her child.

✳✳✳ 35 The Busy Years

The years of child-bearing and child-raising are the busy years, the years from about age 25 to 45. They are a time of great fulfillment, but a time of great sadness as well.

They are a time of great fulfillment because a woman needs desperately to be needed; needs this even more than a man. And no one needs her more than a small baby. As Dr. I. Newton Kugelmass says, "No living creature needs as much love as a newborn. He needs it to breathe easier, feed better, move more, feel securer, grow faster and thrive heartier. . . . Affection catalyzes all his body functions. In giving this affection, a woman becomes fulfilled."

That is why, when asked about the best years of their lives, most women unhesitatingly answer, "The busy years, of course. The time when my children were small." That is why, too, some women continually crave another baby—a new baby—in order to relive those best years over and over again.

THE TRAGEDY OF MOTHERHOOD

But the busy years are also sad ones because they bring inevitable conflicts. One conflict is between the child's desire to break the psychic umbilical cord and the mother's desire to keep it tied. Another is the conflict between her urge to sacrifice everything for her child, and her urge to hold back something of herself for herself.

Neither of these conflicts is ever fully solved. But there's a normal and an abnormal way of at least partly solving them.

THE NORMAL WAY

The normal way a woman resolves the conflict between the wish to keep her child tied to her and the child's wish to break away is to identify with him. To realize from the moment he is born that her union with him is only temporary, and, when he grows older, to enter as much as possible into his feelings, think his thoughts, dream his dreams, work actively toward the day when he will be relatively free.

THE ABNORMAL WAY

The abnormal way is to make her child identify with her. Not to dream his own dreams but to try to force him to dream hers, especially her unfulfilled dreams. If she is a frustrated actress, to dream that her son must become an actor. If she had little education, to insist that her daughter become a teacher. If she thinks she married badly, to make her child marry "well." This is the abnormal solution because it is not a way of showing love for her child, but merely an extreme self-love that expresses itself through her child.

Yet the more neurotic the woman, the more she behaves in this abnormal way. Then she becomes the typical "anxious mother" who, when her small son is playing happily away from her on the beach, starts bending him to her will by calling him back to her with a nervous cry every other minute with the excuse "he might go near the water and drown." Who later walks him to school every day, holding his hand firmly because "he might get into a fight with the other boys." Who, when he is twelve, is still giving him his bath because "otherwise he might not get his neck clean." And she would keep on with extremes, like bathing him well past puberty, if she weren't stopped by an intuitive dread of incest—a foreboding of danger for herself as well as for her boy—that eventually makes her stop.

WORSE WITH A GIRL

Yet if her child is a girl, some neurotic mothers do not stop at puberty. They may relinquish their sons but keep their daughters as close as ever. In fact, they may strengthen their authority over them and practically woo them during adolescence.

Dr. Helene Deutsch tells of a twenty-year-old girl who came to her as a patient suffering from severe anxiety state. She told how she was still sleeping in her mother's bed at her mother's insistence; even sucking her mother's fingers as a pacifier before falling asleep. And during the day she could not let her mother out of her sight either. If her mother went out for a short time, she felt compelled constantly to run to the window and look for her because "she might, for instance, have gotten run over." And the daughter herself scarcely dared venture out of the house. She had caught her mother's anxiety and become literally paralyzed with fright.

Yet when Dr. Deutsch discussed the matter with the mother, the mother had no conscious knowledge of what she was doing. She merely replied, "I slept in my mother's bed until I got married. And my mother slept in hers. What's wrong about that?"

The wrong is that, with girls so prone to anxiety anyway, she was piling up tragedy for her daughter and piling it up for herself as well. For such a mother is almost sure to become in time the "bitter old woman" who is constantly bemoaning the loss of her children's love.

As always, the abnormal points up the norm. The normal mother does not hold her daughter with such a strangling rein, nor does she feel jealous of her. Instead, she identifies her deepest problems and hurts. A mother in a Russian novel beautifully expressed this when she wrote to her daughter: "The icy winds of Grignan hurt me in your chest." In this way, Dr. Deutsch says, by feeling with her and wishing her only well, a normal mother overcomes her deep-rooted fear of loss.

COME BACK TO HER

For the "lost" children a mother frees eventually come back to her as friends, come back when they readjust their picture of her and tender memories again well up. The closely tied children never come back. They may send her flowers on Mother's Day, phone her at Christmas, even stay at home with her as dutiful sons or daughters, but they do all this as polite strangers at best. They simply haven't got the warmth to give her that she craves.

Says Dr. Deutsch, "A mother must not strive to achieve any other goals through her child but those of his existence. Otherwise, she runs the risk of failing in her purpose, and of being cheated of the experience of motherhood."

Dr. Margaret Strahl puts it a different way. "Foolish women," she says "keep the psychic cord tied so tight their children have no choice except to cut it with an ax. Wise women simply let the cord melt."

Not that it is easy to let it melt. No woman gives second birth to her children at adolescence with less pain and suffering than she had when she gave birth to them at first.

HOLD SOMETHING BACK

The second big problem a woman has to face during the busy years is how to hold back a little of herself for herself in preparation for the years to come. This is doubly important these days when a woman has a life-expectancy of close to 77 years. If you figure she marries in her early twenties, has her children by her thirties and lets them go in her forties, that means she has a full thirty more years of life left after they have gone. And thirty years of leftover life is a long time.

Before she can hold back something of herself for herself for these long later years, she must decide *what* she wants to hold back. She must face her identity-crisis again. In common language, she must "find herself." Find out what kind of woman she is, and what kind she wants to remain.

Answering these questions is not easy either. And they have always been more difficult for a woman than for a man.

A MAN'S PATH IS STRAIGHT, A WOMAN'S TWISTS

A man's path moves fairly straight along. A boy is brought up to be mainly one kind of person—active, dominant, successful. From childhood on, he is encouraged to that end.

A woman's path is not straight; it twists and weaves and breaks. A little girl is at first encouraged to be extremely passive and cuddly.

But soon her direction shifts and she turns from passive child to active tomboy in bluejeans. A few years of this and the path twists again at puberty, when she turns from active tomboy to comparatively passive female with menstrual waves she can't control. It breaks once more in her late teens when she turns from passive female to active secretary or vibrant partygoer. It breaks when she marries and turns to a comparatively passive, stay-at-home wife. It breaks again sharply at pregnancy when her body and emotions are hurled in new directions and she becomes extremely passive indeed. It turns back toward activity after delivery when her system readjusts. It wavers in most difficult directions as her children start to grow and she must juggle between two kinds of persons at once—a most active mother during the day, a receptive and responsive partner in bed at night. And it certainly breaks at menopause, or the changing years, when her hormone system readjusts all over again.

FATIGUE

As if this weren't enough, the busy years bring a tremendous amount of fatigue.

There's the sheer physical fatigue of caring for a house and one or more children—the endless washing and ironing and cleaning and cooking, the constant running after the infants and grabbing things out of their hands or mouths so they don't get hurt, the putting them to bed and waking them up and dressing them, the birthday parties given and attended, the shopping for clothes and eyeglasses and toys—all the repetitive chores that never seem to stop.

Then the physical fatigue is complicated by emotional fatigue. There's nothing as exhausting as strong emotions. Yet the busy young wife is strongly worried for fear bearing several children will ruin her figure or destroy her attractiveness to her husband. She may also be very jealous of her husband, who seems to be having such a good time all day at his job while she is "miserably tied down."

PUSHED AND PULLED

If this weren't enough, she has lately been kept in a state of constant turmoil by a group of women who have been pushing and pulling her around.

Hardly had the modern woman gotten the right to vote and feel self-respect because of it, plus the right to work and keep the money she got for that work, than the psychiatrist Dr. Marynia Farnham got after her, telling her this "feminist business" was making her into a sickly "lost sex" and that if she wanted to stay healthy and happy she should immediately go right back home, stay there and have four children at the very least. Then Simone de Beauvoir started to berate her, calling her a mere "second sex" for *wanting* to stay home, and urging her to feel extremely sorry for herself because, of all things, she had to menstruate—as if she could repeal natural laws developed over millions of years! And next Betty Friedan began shouting at her to become both a mother and not a mother, to stop being a victim of something vaguely called the "feminine mystique," or "the problem without a name," get out of the house fast after childbirth, dump her children onto a series of baby-sitters and demand a good job "just like a man."

Is there any wonder she is all confused at this point, hardly knowing who she is or what she wants to be?

BACK TO BEDROCK

To help her think these things through, let's go back to the basic definitions of normality. These are the ability to work and to love; to be more independent than dependent; to experience blue, or depressed, or "queer," periods but not indefinitely; and to gain not perfect happiness but a reasonable measure of happiness along life's way.

Now a woman has to do all this within the framework of her particular body and emotions. She cannot ignore her up-and-down hormonal or energy waves. She cannot ignore the long months of pregnancy and nursing, when her body is so large and awkward she has little choice but to be mainly passive and cared for. She cannot ignore her greater measure of inner awareness, given to her so that she can be aware of her menstrual and pregnancy changes, or her keener senses, given to her so that over the din of the worst traffic-noises she can hear her baby's cry.

She has to do all this, too, within the framework of her greater self-love, or narcissism, given to her so that she can dress up her body to attract and hold a mate who will *want* to support her while she is bearing their children or caring for them during the busy years. Finally, she has to do all this within the framework of the special kind of feminine masochism that helps her accept inevitable pain.

How in the light of this can she become "just like a man"? Dr. Kugelmass believes that for a woman to become "just like a man" is a catastrophe. For femininity (not at all the same thing as feminism) is the great catalyst, the essential mixing-agent that is at the heart of life. Femininity is the holder together of civilization, the conserver of warmth and forbearance that prevents us from cutting our collective throats. Men who have much warmth and forbearance usually get it through their women, or through their own female gifts. Thus, he says, if femininity fails, humanity fails, and all the king's men can never put it back together again.

The Italians, one of the most civilized people in the world, are a fine example of femininity holding the world together and of women who don't want to be "just like men." In his fascinating book about his countrymen, the journalist Luigi Barzini started by telling how the Italian male is famous for his extreme manliness, his pride, his jealousy, his strut down the street obviously the ruler of the roost. Women have been put on earth, proclaims this lordly creature, mainly to amuse him, and the more he beats them, like the more one beats eggs for a sponge cake, the more amusing they become.

But the truth of the matter is, M. Barzini goes on, this attitude is mostly show-off and nonsense. Certainly, he says, the Italian man is "the titular head of the household, but he is by no means the absolute monarch, and while the wife is officially a subordinate figure in charge of humbler duties, the centuries have taught her to make her husband forget how important she effectively is. She usually manages things in a subtle, almost imperceptible way; she assuages his feelings; she avoids open contrasts but generally has the last unspoken word. She keeps her place, of course. She would obviously lose her ascendancy if she forgot it. Her place may be the kitchen (in low-income families) the drawing-room and boudoir (for the more affluent) and for all, the double-bed at night. But whatever it is, it is a position of great power. Men run the country, but women run men."

Women have always run men this feminine way, at all times and all over the world. The bustling Orthodox Jewish mother, who held the family together while her husband and sons battled the world, did it in spite of the fact that she couldn't even sit in temple and worship beside her husband but had to remain in the balcony hidden by a special screen. The Chinese grandmother did it in spite of her bound feet.

INCONCLUSIVE SURVEYS

Such women, and other thinking women, have also always known that the so-called surveys about them are mainly either inconclusive or sheer nonsense. Many of the answers simply depend on the time when the survey was made. Was the woman menstruating at the moment, and therefore at a particularly low tide? Was she ovulating, and at a state of high tide? Pregnant, and in still a different state? Was she just over a fight with her husband and feeling unusually sorry for herself? Did she have a sick child and feel distraught? A recovered child, and feel blissfully content?

Since practically no surveyor ever asks such basic questions, no surveyor gets consistent answers. So we find Mrs. Friedan quoting surveys to make the point that most modern women are "trapped housewives" or in a constant state of despair, while at the same time *The Saturday Evening Post* is reporting on a survey done by the well-known pollster Dr. George Gallup, in which he quotes almost exactly the opposite results.

Dr. Gallup questioned over 2300 women, of whom 1800 were married and 500 were single. They were also women in all income brackets and of all degrees of education. A full 96 per cent of them said they were either extremely happy or fairly happy, and 88 per cent said they were either extremely satisfied or fairly satisfied with themselves as women, and with things as they were. Another large per cent of the married women reported motherhood was the "chief purpose in life" and childbirth "the most satisfying moment in their lives." Their chief complaints were the untidiness of their husbands or, humorously, the fact that about the only right still denied them was "the right to go to the man's john." Over and over again, on the positive side, the *Post* survey reported the feminine preoccupation with warmth, with one woman repeating, "Even my husband doesn't realize how warm I try to be."

STILL MORE FATIGUE

But let's say that some women, especially those who have worked before marriage, do want to go back to work soon after their children are born. Here they run smack into the problem of even bigger fatigue.

For no matter how many mechanical appliances they own, there are no substitutes for people. Someone—usually themselves—still has to buy the family groceries, cook the meals, supervise the children's homework, take them to the doctor and dentist. It can add up to a heavy load indeed. The psychiatrist Dr. Abram Kardiner says his working patients, whom he calls "spare-time mothers," are always telling him how the hours they spend nights and week-ends with their families are so much richer and more meaningful. But what he sees is different. He sees women so tired they can barely think straight, or women so overstimulated that his advice to them to try and get a few hours of extra sleep is useless because they are too tired to sleep, and before they know it find themselves resorting to more and more sleeping-pills. One husband described the endless fatigue that resulted by growling, "What we both need around here is a good wife."

Besides, there is the husband's resentment when his wife's job seems to take away his sense of status as the dominant male. Such a man often sarcastically refers to his wife as a "man-eater," all the more so when both are in the same line and compete actively with each other. It takes a rare husband like a Pierre Curie to compete actively with a Marie Curie and keep a happy household. Far more often, as in Hollywood marriages, fierce competition is the camel's back-breaking straw. The masseuse Sylvia of Hollywood tells how, the morning after the wedding of silent-screen stars Ina Claire and John Gilbert, she arrived to give Madame the daily massage that was never missed. She found the bride and groom sitting up in bed, screaming at each other. Some morning papers had announced the event as "Ina Claire Marries John Gilbert," others as "John Gilbert Marries Ina Claire." They were battling furiously over whose name should have come first in all the papers. Sylvia knew the union was doomed from the start.

Dr. William Menninger insists that great career success is often the cause of a woman's not becoming a wife in the first place. We hear so much about the "timid spinster," he says. We don't hear nearly enough about the super-successful "pushy spinster" whom men fear like the plague because she stuns them with sheer drive.

JEALOUS OF THE MAID

Another matter we don't hear much about is the working woman's jealousy of her own maid. Many a spare-time mother's abrupt dismissal of maids and sitters stems from her unspoken jealousy of the "other woman" who is home with her children all day long and seems to be diverting too much of their affection to herself. So she hires and fires a series of them, gets first one as meek and undemanding as possible, so meek she is afraid to discipline the children, then one as cold and strict as possible, so cold the children run wilder than ever in an attempt to outwit her, then another meek one followed by a strict one, ending up with havoc all around.

GUILT

But perhaps the biggest problem spare-time mothers have to face is the problem of guilt.

Guilt is a perennial burden to all of us, but it is the special burden of the woman who has been away from her children during their early years. If a beloved youngster gets something like polio that she could hardly have prevented if she had been on the scene every minute, she carries this burden heavily all her life. If a child becomes delinquent and she realizes it was partly her fault because she was not home enough to instill firm ethical values in him—something few nursemaids can do as well as herself even if they try, she carries the burden again. Someone has spoken of the "tragic finality of childhood." The working mother knows this finality better than most.

Dr. Kardiner says her guilt cannot possibly be estimated unless you sit in a psychiatrist's office, as he does, and listen to her trying to relieve herself of it. What makes it sadder is the fact that she has often been working as a means of groping toward a better sense of self-fulfillment, or of human dignity. The single woman gets this kind of dignity and fulfillment without guilt. The woman who assumes the triple role of mother, wife and businesswoman has a guilt problem often of enormous size.

Dr. Kardiner sums up by asking women to think through what they are mainly working for. A set of solid silver instead of plate? An electric carving knife instead of one that carves by hand? A shinier car? A fancier rug? "It is an exceptional character," he admits, "who is immune to the blandishments of convenience, luxury and small increments of pleasure." But these blandishments must be weighed against the fact that our high standard of living has brought more anxiety, more vigilance, and more pressures to keep up with the neighbors, rather than more happiness. What used to be a matter of free choice has become an obligation, and the constant struggle to provide the obligations like an expensive fur coat, two cars and a de luxe home adds up mainly to more fear and rage. The struggle for self-preservation becomes not the normal struggle to survive but merely the struggle to "get along."

HOME FOR TEN YEARS

The University of Chicago's Bruno Bettelheim suggests that one way out of the guilt-dilemma is for women to try and stay at home for at least the first ten years after their children are born. Then, if they feel they must, to seek an outside job as well. In this way, they can be full-time mothers during the important childhood years, and part-time mothers during the years their children need them less. This way they can also keep some of themselves for themselves, keep their "hands in" as it were, for the years when their children need them hardly at all.

This kind of job-postponement, says Dr. Bettelheim, may involve looking for a job like selling or nursing, where talent and initiative count, rather than a job that demands secretarial skill they may have lost from disuse. But it should make for greater contentment all around. Indeed, the proof it does make for more contentment lies in the fact that this is the solution a large number of married women are coming to by themselves. Also a large number of husbands seem to be able to take their wives' competition better as they grow older themselves.

Staying home for about ten years is also easier for a woman because she has a greater ability to identify with her husband than he has with her. A woman can gracefully take on the courtesy-title of Frau Doktor or Frau Avocat, as the German women do, and identify with her husband's professional life this way, whereas a courtesy Herr Doktor or Herr Avocat usually calls for an apology on the husband's part.

The one thing that may be difficult for a woman to do at any time is to accept money from her husband if it is doled out grudgingly, especially if she has made money on her own. Today it is harder than ever, since researchers at the Chase Manhattan Bank have come up with figures proving a wife is worth about $160 a week on the basis of her labors alone (44½ hours as a nursemaid at $1.25 an hour, six hours as a laundress at $1.90, thirteen hours as a cook at $2.50) concluding that even without overtime she earns as much as the average man.

But figuring her worth this way is foolish, too, because who can put price on her warmth and devotion? Besides, a woman *has* to do some amount of work for her own sake in order to release hostility, for without this release she can literally burn up.

Everybody continues to have some inner hostility throughout life, and we have more of it as we grow older, as we increasingly discover the world is not nearly the warm and comfortable place we at first imagined it to be. Some amount of frustration, rejection or insult continues to be the lot of us all.

Now hostility can be released by a woman in destructive aggression, using her favorite way of attacking with her mouth. She can give her husband or nearest child terrible tongue-lashings, screaming at them all day long. The trouble with this is that the screamed-at person becomes himself more hostile, and a non-stop battle follows with the husband or child, since they have more energy to scream with, usually winning.

The best way to get rid of pent-up anger, says Dr. William Menninger, is by work. Lashing out at things instead of people, by pushing a broom furiously across the floor, shaking a mop, swatting flies, rolling out pie crusts with a heavy rolling-pin. Or, if a woman for some reason can't do these, by taking a good long walk or going to the kind of play or movie that will let her have a good hard laugh or a good long cry.

A good cry is better than a good laugh, as Aristotle knew thousands of years ago when he spoke of a drama as a "tragic catharsis," or purge. His prescription for a drama is one in which there is a hero who is a little better than ourselves, but not so much better we cannot identify with him. Since he is better and does not deserve his fate, we feel mounting terror when he is beset by tragedy, and pity when he finally fails. Having experienced this pity and terror, we cry with it and leave the theater purged of our own piled-up emotions. So drama is more satisfying than comedy, since we come away from a drama cleansed of emotions too heavy to bear.

Luckily, crying is more approved of in women than men, so that women can indulge in it with less shame. The only caution here is that a mother should try, whenever possible, not to cry in front of her child. Any kind of breakdown by a parent is extremely upsetting to a child, especially in the early years when he tends to see his parents as all-powerful and all-wise. Breaking down and crying loudly means coming down to his level, which is something he neither wants nor understands.

I read an unforgettable short story some years ago about a poor, distracted cleaning woman. Her little nephew, who lived with her, was dying and she could not weep in front of him. It wasn't right for her to weep in her employer's house either, or on the street, and she did not have the money to go to a show. Yet she had to weep somewhere. She finally stumbled into a telephone booth, closed the door and cried herself out there.

But work off tension in some way like working or weeping we must, because otherwise it can turn back in on ourselves.

Tension can turn back in because anger, fear and sorrow call forth an extra supply of adrenal hormones—the hormones designed to ready us for fight or flight. When these hormones have been called forth, "angry blood" is circulating around surcharging our bodies with the energy needed to fight or run away. But since fleeing or fighting are often either unwise or impossible ways of working off this angry blood, we must do it by token fleeing or fighting instead. If we don't, it can back up and cause some of the tension-headaches women suffer from, the high blood pressure, the colitis, the stomach trouble. The popular descriptions of something that makes us angry, "That burns me up!" or "That gives me a pain in my stomach!" are quite literally true.

SAD HOTEL WOMEN

Because of this, there are no sadder women in the world than the rich women who live in luxury hotels. An occasional few pampered weeks in a hotel are fine. But women who live in one indefinitely with no housework to do, no cleaning, no cooking or creative job of any kind, dam up their natural outlets for hostility. This accounts for the eternal shopping sprees in which they dash from one store to another, buying clothes mainly to go out and buy other clothes. Or their savage gambling sprees, which build still more hostility, or their veritable bridge battles in which everyone bares his fangs.

Hotel women, even more than career women, are the great complainers about insomnia. Dr. William Menninger puts this into a memorable sentence when he says, "The trouble with doing nothing is that you cannot rest from it."

For the "career sickness" of the women in such high-powered jobs, who cannot turn off their intense competitive drives at night and sleep, is as nothing compared to the "uselessness sickness" of the idle women who perpetually kill time, and end up killing themselves.

RELIGION AS A TENSION-RELEASER

Of course there are other tension-releasers, in addition to work, available to women. Among these are clubs, knitting and handwork of all kinds, social games of bridge, canasta or golf. Above all, there are religion and sex.

Women make up the larger part of the worshippers of many congregations because women are prime believers in the values that conserve life. Having brought forth life, they must do everything in their power to conserve it, and have faith in a God who will help them do so. After all, it was the Roman Emperor Constantine's mother, not Constantine himself, who embraced Christianity first.

Women also make up the larger part of the worshippers because they need to establish a relationship with someone like a minister, rabbi or priest with whom they can sit and talk things out. For talk is a form of ventilation that releases tension in a most important way. Talking acts like ventilating a musty room; after it, the air feels good again. Talking with a friend is good, but talking with a minister, priest or rabbi is much better because such men are trained to do a special kind of listening, and are sworn, moreover, not to tell.

CREATIVITY AND SEX

Then there is sex as a tension-releaser.

Erik Erikson calls the chief purpose of sex the sense of generativity. Most people use the simpler terms "parenthood," or "creativity." During the busy years, creativity reaches a peak.

After the long years, in which the other senses that make for health and normality have been developed—the sense of basic trust, or independence of will, of initiative, of industry, of identity and intimacy—there comes this seventh sense of creativity. The desire to blend one's life with one's chosen partner and create a child that is the fruit of that blend. When this creation does not take place, or a substitute creation like writing a novel or painting a picture or doing old-fashioned "good works," the opposite is felt—a sense of stagnation. Life for stagnant women becomes merely a holding-operation, a day-to-day dawdle, a wasting of hours. As Erikson says, "Individuals who do not develop generativity often begin to indulge themselves as their own one and only child."

Yet aside from creativity, sex still releases married partners. For the sex-act has that prize as in the box of crackerjacks; it gives pleasure, while it possibly creates a child, and it also drains off anger and rage. It drains off anger, as he puts it, "not in the discharge of sex products in the sense of Kinsey's 'outlets,' but in heterosexual mutuality, an over-all discharge of tension from the whole body . . . [that] in some way appeases the potential rages caused by the daily evidences of the oppositeness of male and female, of fact and fancy, of love and hate, of work and play."

Thus, through the miracle of the sex-act, a woman complements a man as she was intended to do. She does not worry about being inferior or superior, but is content with being a complement or balance, as a hook complements an eye. And as she does so, she relaxes and releases some of her tensions along with his, as each both gives and receives. For as he gives of his sperm, she gives of her receptiveness and her egg. As she receives his caresses, he receives her assurance of his potency. And she continues to do this, as at the beginning of their marriage, without need for "the book," or mechanical tricks.

Above all, she does not begin to look for this release outside of marriage, since doing that usually leads to deep trouble. For few women can indulge in casual sex, as many men can do. Few women can divorce sex from love. So an affair may become a serious matter to a woman while it remains merely a playful interlude to a man.

The highly advertised Valentinos and Casanovas are not the Great Lovers that women expect them to be either, says Dr. William Menninger. The Great Lovers are the Gandhis, the Helen Kellers, the Schweitzers, who truly and lastingly give of themselves. "So said Jesus Christ," says Dr. Menninger. "So said Freud."

For a misconception of Freud's teaching is that sex is a cure-all for neuroses. But Freud never said that. Freud traced many neuroses to childish misconceptions about sex, but he never prescribed sex-relations to *cure* neuroses, especially relations frowned upon by society. For Freud was one of the most moral of men, and knew what great harm such relations can do. Dr. Emy Metzger tells of patients reporting sex-relations two and three times a day, yet remaining as neurotic and "empty" as before, because they were relations without warmth or love.

And Dr. Menninger adds that extra-marital relations almost invariably lead to unhappiness because, no matter how much a woman tries to conceal them, her husband senses the truth if only because of the subtle increase in her hostility toward him. Then he, in turn, increases his hostility toward her, and the marriage becomes a shambles. A married woman plus a Great Lover plus a husband thus add up to less happiness, not more.

LESS HOSTILITY IN WOMEN

With all this, there is not nearly as much hostility acted out by women, in the form of destructively aggressive acts, as there is in men.

The psychologist, Dr. Arnold Buss of the University of Pittsburgh, tells of experiments in which two groups of college students, one male and one female, were deliberately frustrated and insulted in a variety of ways. The women did not get nearly as angry, or act out their aggressions nearly as violently as did the men.

This ability to stand frustration better is one reason for women's greater survivability; one reason far fewer women become alcoholics and murderers, or commit suicide. For alcoholism, murder and suicide are the height of destructive aggression, turned both outward against society and inward against the self. The alcoholic turns against himself by falling down and injuring himself; committing a partial suicide with the little death of "passing out." He turns against the world by being irresponsible and antisocial, by smashing up the house, or running someone down with his car.

The suicide moves against himself by killing himself; against the world by saying in effect, "Now I'll be dead and you'll be sorry"; by getting revenge and heaping guilt on the people around them no matter how little they were at fault. And the murderer acts violently against himself by making the rest of his life a nightmare and an evasion, from his conscience if from nothing else.

When women resort to murder or suicide, they do it as a rule by pills or poison—again, ways of aggressively using the mouth. In spite of the tired old jokes about women's hair-pulling matches, how many people have actually seen one of those? Or, with the tiny exception of the Amazons, heard of women indulging in the mass slaughter men call war?

So we find another paradox: Women's sex hormones during the busy years keep their inner tides moving up and down, up and down, so that they can seldom remain on an even keel. Yet, emotionally, women do not swing to the extremes that men do. They are able to tolerate frustration more easily, keep their destructive aggressions under better control and stay closer to the stable norm.

NOT PERFECT OR IDEAL

Yet that norm does not mean perfect or ideal or fully adjusted, and was never meant to. During the busy years, a thoughtful woman looks about her and realizes that no one alive is perfect or ideal or fully adjusted, as she may have dreamed in childhood. They are merely reasonably perfect, reasonably ideal, reasonably adjusted, and that is all she can expect of anybody, including herself.

As the University of Texas psychologist Dr. Robert F. Peck says, we all lead lives including much quiet desperation, as Thoreau long ago knew. In Dr. Peck's words: "Most of us know the chaos of bewilderment, the tempest of unreasoning passion, the whine of years-long unhappiness, the tremendous sorrow of engulfing tragedy. Nobody escapes. Yet most of us 'make out' or 'get by,' and we do it without sinking into self-pity for the total love, total status, total pleasure we cannot possibly have.

"What is it to be normal?" Dr. Peck asks. "It is to be unreasonable with your spouse or children several times a week, yet try in a fumbling, half-inept but sincere way to make it up. It is to spend money foolishly, then work hard to stretch what's left till payday. It is to work hard all your life, say, with a railroad, always wishing you'd finished school and gone into teaching or law, yet proud of your 25 years of service. . . . It is to marry in haste, divorce in haste and marry five years later to a person you love all your life."

It is to realize that a husband does not spend all his days twiddling his thumbs at an easy, pleasant job while his wife is miserably tied down; that a man is as much tied down as any woman—to production schedules, sales quotas, domineering bosses, deadlines, plus the responsibility for his family's support.

It is to remember that taking on responsibility is an indispensable part of maturity for everybody, and so to do cheerfully and without undue self-pity what have been called "the chores of life."

It is to keep on trying to answer the insistent question, "Who am I?" but also the equally insistent, "What do you—and you and you—mean to me?" and so to keep on learning better and better how to love your neighbor as yourself.

It is to remember that Freud did not say normal was the ability to love *or* work, but to love *and* work. Love and work, work and love, and enjoy loving and working as one does.

Finally, it is to have the ability to come to terms with life's inevitable disappointments, even life's great tragedies, yet still maintain the hope that there will be some measure of happiness and fulfillment ahead.

✳✳✳ 36 Backaches, Face-Lifts and Such

A woman's body keeps changing in many ways during the busy years. Each change brings its problems, and each change calls for a change in her self-image.

Here are some things that may happen to her during the twenties, thirties and forties, and worry her when they do.

BACKACHES AND NECK ACHES

First, there are the extremely common and puzzling backaches—aches at the bottom of her spine, or aches in her neck near the top. These are puzzling because she seems to have been "doing nothing hard" all day—mainly sitting down sewing or reading or standing still ironing. Why should her back and neck ache from these?

They ache because she hasn't been sitting or standing properly, and her backbone has gotten out of whack.

The spine or backbone consists of a series of squarish blocks of bone with small, flexible spaces between. These bony blocks run fairly straight up and down, except at the top and bottom of the spine where they make

S curves. The top S curves forward where the neck joins the head; the bottom S curves backward toward the buttocks.

When these top and bottom curves are at a minimum, there is little strain. When they are exaggerated, with the exaggeration most likely to take place in the lower curve, there is a lot. During pregnancy a woman gets into the habit of walking with her buttocks thrust back to balance her front load. During other times, high heels thrust her trunk forward and her buttocks back. The result? Low back pain from an exaggerated S.

Doctors say that one way of counteracting the rear-end jutting out, usually called swayback or lordosis, is to stand at the ironing-board or kitchen sink with one leg raised on a stool, the way a barfly stands at a bar. This helps pull the buttocks forward to where they belong. Also to sleep on one's side, since this pulls the buttocks forward again. And to sew or read whenever possible with one leg crossed over the other, or on a footstool.

To counter the tendency to exaggerate the S curve at the top by pushing the head too far forward, they suggest sitting in an armchair for sewing or reading whenever possible, since this lets the arms rest and better supports the shoulders and back and keeps them straight.

VARICOSE VEINS

Varicose veins come from the extra load put on the legs during pregnancy, or during times of other sudden weight-gain. The legs are the furthest away from the heart. It therefore takes longer for the blood to be pumped to the legs, and their blood-circulation is comparatively poor. During any time of weight-gain, when the heart is under a special load, blood accumulates in the legs and tends to stay there, forming the thickened veins.

There are injections to relieve really bad veins, or, in extreme cases, operations. Fortunately, there are much better operations today than there used to be.

EYEGLASSES

A real upset comes to a woman when she suddenly finds she needs eyeglasses when she never needed them before.

This is because the eyes harden and become far-sighted almost on the stroke of forty, so that almost every woman has to get glasses at that time to correct this condition for near work. In the days when women didn't live to the age of forty, or in countries where they didn't read, they could be eyeglass-free to the end of their days. Still, there's that consoling thought about glasses: they do hide the wrinkles around one's eyes that time also brings. "A girl's face at sixteen is the face she was born with," says an old proverb. "A woman's face at forty is the face she has made for herself." A face with thought-wrinkles is a human face. But it's good at times to be able to hide the wrinkles too.

FACE-LIFTS

Some women are seriously concerned with the matter of face-lifts to "turn time back." This might be a good idea except that face-lifts don't turn time back for long. Three to five years is the average, and after several lifts it may be reduced to one year. For the skin is a very elastic tissue; if it weren't, no woman could ever grow fat and have her skin shrink back after losing weight. But as the years go by, the sex-hormones that nourish the skin start to wane, it loses some of this elasticity. Then it starts to act like a worn rubber-band. You can stretch it, but only so far before it will break or snap back. A face-lift is therefore quite different from a nose operation. In a face-lift, the entire delicate skin of the face is manipulated, mauled and stretched, and it doesn't stay stretched for long.

A friend tells of a famous, aging movie actress she happened to sit next to during a preview of her latest picture. On the screen, the actress's face looked youthful indeed. But pictures are released about six months after they are taken, and her face had evidently been lifted just before the shooting, for the contrast between the woman on the screen and the one in the audience was startling. The one in the audience looked tired and old, with her face fallen again and especially huge bags under her eyes from too much tampering.

The friend saw the same actress later in another picture. This time her face had been pulled taut again—so taut it looked like a death-mask. The masklike face, plus the jerky movements of a woman trying to dance in a way she no longer could, were so disturbing that my friend had to walk out.

Other women have been known to have their faces lifted to where they were no longer recognizable. My friend also tells of seeing another famous actress on TV. Her face had been so pulled and manipulated that if she hadn't been introduced by name she wouldn't have known her. Before, she had looked friendly and warm; now she had the face of a tense, hard woman who did not dare to smile for fear her skin might crack.

Yet many women still get their faces lifted over and over, though the cost is astronomical. Plastic surgeons consider facial operations strictly as luxuries unless they are necessary to repair damage from disease or accidents, and charge whatever they think the traffic will bear. A well-known Park Avenue surgeon admitted to me in the course of this research, "If I can make a woman who thinks she's unmarriageable marriageable, or help an actress get a new contract, is five or ten thousand dollars too much? Or fifteen hundred at the very least for an hour or two of my work?" "No, doctor," I politely murmured and fled.

But perhaps the most expensive part of face-lifting is the emotional expense—the continuous postponement of something we eventually have to meet. We all have to meet the fact of aging; indeed, we start to age as soon as we are born. If we all stayed young forever, or never died, the earth would soon become so cluttered there would be no room. The Romans knew this when they inscribed at the entrance to a cemetery, "Come and join the majority," indicating the necessity for everyone of the last long sleep.

But women are great rationalizers. They use all kinds of arguments to persuade themselves that what they *want* to do, they *have* to do. So one woman tells herself she has to lift her face for the sake of her job, though she is a crack writer and has been hired for her brains, not her looks. Another tells herself she has to do it to appear young to her children, though children feel much more secure with a mother who is obviously mature rather than with an equal or a pal. They have plenty of pals.

Finally, there is the matter of comfort. No matter how much a face operation may temporarily change a woman for what seems like the better, there is always the chance she may be much more comfortable if she stays as she is. The poet Walter de la Mare expressed this when he told of a friend, "He liked his face. There was an understanding between him and it. They had been through so much storm and stress together they were like old friends who did not want to part."

TO DYE OR NOT TO DYE

Women use the same arguments they use in favor of face-lifting, in favor of dyeing their hair when it starts to turn grey. They need dyed hair to keep their job, or to look young for their families. It has a familiar ring.

Now there is nothing wrong in changing the color of one's hair. But too few women realize that their skin color has changed as their hair has faded; that as their sex-hormones have waned, their skin has lost some of its rosy hue, and that soft-colored hair was meant to go with their new coloring as flaming red, brassy blond or shoe-blacking black never was. They forget that fiery red, bright blond or inky black hair actually makes a pale face paler by contrast, and since aging hands can't be altered, a dye-job on the head makes hands look older by contrast, too.

The vaudevillian Fanny Ward of a generation ago may have made herself a pot of money by appearing "forever young" through dye-jobs and face-lifts, but she did it from a distance behind the protection of footlights and by being photographed through a thick layer of camera-veils. From close up, with her wrinkled hands and unnatural face, she looked like a parody of youth. Women in the eighteenth century were smarter. They used white wigs or powdered their hair instead of dyeing it, knowing that white or grey softens the contours and flatters the face as the years go by.

Besides, as the sex-hormones wane, the hair, like the skin, becomes drier and more resistant to dye, so stronger and stronger chemicals are constantly needed to do the job. As a result, dyed hair often begins to look like a straw mattress no matter what kind of shampoo or "conditioner" is used. Appealing feminine warmth has then gone with the wind.

Admittedly, it takes courage for a woman to stop dyeing her hair if she has been doing it for years. Habit is strong. But once she has made the break and weathered the few weeks it takes to get used to any new look, it is surprising how much easier it becomes.

A LOST LITTLE GIRL

Most important, accepting a changed face and hair color as she gets older makes a woman less of a lost little girl in an adult world.

One of the hardest things about growing up is getting to feel one is no longer such a lost little girl. No longer a timid child, a shy adolescent or a hesitant bride, but a mature woman able to look the world straight in the eye.

Dr. Jane Pearce says many women stay lost because as children they built a strong security-system around themselves, like a moat around a castle. This security-system, she says, tells them, "This far you can go and no further, or you will provoke your parents beyond tolerance." As they grow, they continue to build this security-system, strengthening the restrictive mold in which their parents seemed to cast them and develop a persistent low image of themselves as inept, inadequate and unattractive, the kind of image many five-year-olds have. This low image progressively cuts them off from adult awareness and adult functioning. They give up the satisfaction of real needs in return for still more security and status, as the original prohibitions that once surrounded them limit them more and more. So they continue to think in fear, "I couldn't do that," or "Mother wouldn't have approved of that," or "What will the neighbors say?" and they pay so much attention to externals there is little left for internals, making them forget that the only security in life is the confidence to go on.

Every time a woman faces up to something, she develops more of this real kind of confidence. Every time she decides she still can grow, she gets more again. No man or woman ever becomes perfectly confident, to be sure. After John Lindsay put on his strenuous campaign for Mayor of New York, he told reporters he was so unsure of the outcome he "ran scared all the way." The point is, he ran. He didn't stay put and try to hold on blindly to what he had.

Did anyone ever need to convince Eleanor Roosevelt the way to become "secure" was to lift her face or dye her hair? Or Marie Curie, or Bess Truman? When Harry Truman was President, he passed a billboard one day advertising the play *Gentlemen Prefer Blondes*. "Hmm," he sniffed to the aide beside him. "Real gentlemen prefer grey."

SPECIAL CREAMS

The "over-35 creams" women fall for are another example of lack of self-confidence, and faith in foolish things. For except for medical ointments prescribed by doctors for definite conditions, the skin cannot absorb substances from the outside. So there are no special over-35 cosmetic creams, lotions or skin foods, no "queen-bee jellies" that will work magic for anybody except bees, no secret-formula "turtle creams" for anybody except turtles.

If a woman has a skin that needs improving, she can't get it from these any more than she can from mud-packs or milk-baths or drinking champagne out of silver slippers. She can only get it by feeding her skin like the rest of her body, from the inside, by eating more of the fresh fruits and vegetables that supply the vitamins and minerals she may lack, vitamins and minerals which in some mysterious way help her sex-hormones to function better, too. She can also help by cutting down on coffee, since coffee in abundance interferes with the absorption of vitamins, or by taking brisk walks that circulate her blood faster, or by taking specially prescribed hormones internally as replacement-medicine, though these are seldom needed until after the menopause.

There are no creams to rub on from the outside to enlarge her bosom either. Pregnancy will sometimes develop her breasts as a result of the vast quantity of hormones that feed all her tissues while she is carrying a child. But when pregnancy doesn't do this, it doesn't, as the actress Julie Harris concluded when she sighed, "If only I had a bosom, I could conquer the world!"

Of course, there are surgical operations that will enlarge small breasts by the insertion of artificial fillers. But few women are interested in going to this extreme since the operation leaves obvious scars, even though the foam-fillers that are now being used don't get as hard and tough as the older ones used to do.

BIRTH CONTROL VERSUS ABORTION

But the most pressing problem of the busy years is birth control— a problem even more pressing than in early marriage.

It is a little-known but startling fact that the majority of illegal abortions are performed, not on "wayward girls" as is generally supposed, but on married women in their thirties and early forties who already have three or four children, or the number most couples can decently educate, feed and clothe.

Abortions are also increasing in number. Dr. Harold Rosen of Johns Hopkins, author of an authoritative book on the subject, estimates there are now over a million and a half a year in the United States alone, and we may expect more. Dr. Rosen gives several reasons. First, he cites the thalidomide scare and the publicity given to the Sherry Finkbine case.

(Mrs. Finkbine had taken thalidomide, was frightened of the possible consequences, couldn't get an abortion in America and went to Sweden instead. She turned out to be right; her unborn child was deformed.) Second, he gives the German measles scare, the epidemic that started late in 1963 and is still sweeping some parts of the world, an epidemic which can also deform unborn children. Third, the fear expressed by many women that, if they have to bear another child when they already have so many, they will go mad.

TROUBLE IN THE LABOR ROOM

Madness aside (very few really do go mad) there is the matter of a woman's physical health. How many children are good for her health? Dr. John Rock answers, "Seldom more than the three or four most women want. The danger in childbirth drops with the second child, still more with the third and more with the fourth. But thereafter it begins to rise again. . . . The highest maternal death rates are in those areas where five or more children are the rule rather than the exception."

Also, says Dr. William Bickers, after three or four births the uterus often becomes so badly overstretched that it may cause serious trouble. "After three or four deliveries," he says, "we alert ourselves for trouble in the labor room. And we find it more frequently than not."

WOMEN OVER 35

How about women over 35? Is childbirth more dangerous or more difficult for them? Here age alone is not the determining factor. It depends on the number of children they have already had. If they've had more than three or four, the danger increases in the main for that very reason. Otherwise, with modern care and with the much better general condition of today's women, their firmer muscles and superior nutrition, a woman of 35 can do about as well as one ten years younger.

Recently Dr. Albert Highdon of Teaneck, New Jersey, did a study of 21,000 mothers in the still older age-group of forty or more. He found that, while they had longer labors with a first child than a similar group in their twenties had, and more need for Caesarean deliveries, the over-forty group still did well with good care. The older women, however, bore slightly more mongoloid children just as teenagers do. As many as 2 per cent were mongoloid as against 1½ per cent in the general population. "Mongolism for some reason seems to be more prevalent in the extremes of reproductive life," says Dr. Highdon. On the other hand, there were fewer miscarriages in the older group, something neither he nor his colleagues could explain. And other doctors have found that the children of older women, aside from the tiny number of mongoloids, tend to be brighter than other children.

SPACING OF CHILDREN

As to the spacing of children, two years apart is best, say most doctors, though Yale's Dr. Arnold Gesell disagrees and advises three. He believes it takes a child of three to accept a rival with a minimum of friction and that having babies one year apart, except for very special reasons, is much too frequent.

Queen Victoria also believed this. After she had borne four children in four years, and a total of nine children in twelve, she begged her daughters to learn how not to repeat her mistakes.

Between "the pills," rubber devices, spermicidal jellies, rhythm, and new means that are constantly being developed, today's woman does know how. She should use her knowledge well into her fifties, too. For while fertility tapers off sharply after 35, there is still the chance of one tiny ovum slipping through until about a year after menstruation has stopped.

FEWER HEADACHES AND TENSIONS

So between child-bearing, child-rearing and other productive activities, the busy years go by. Go by and bring their worries, but their compensations, too.

Among the compensations are fewer pre-menstrual headaches as well as less pre-menstrual tension. This good news is due to the fact that as fertility tapers off, there are not as many cycles that include ovulation, so a double hormonal wave is not built up during the second half of the month. And with no double wave there are far fewer tension days or tension-headaches of the special pre-menstrual kind.

Also, says Dr. A. E. Rakoff, there are fewer headaches and tension days during the busy years just because a woman *is* so busy. She is so busy concentrating on the pleasures of being a wife and mother instead of on the drawbacks that the good emotions drive away the bad.

Alexander Woollcott once sighed, "Why is it that almost every good thing in life turns out to be either immoral, illegal or fattening?"

Most women aren't half as worried by the temptations of the illegal or immoral as they are by the fattening. If only good food didn't pile up bad pounds, how much simpler everything would be! But food does, and the older we get, the more it does. One of life's inevitable disappointments is seeing our figures change even more quickly than our faces.

Here are some reasons for this sad state of affairs.

SPURTS DURING YOUTH, SLOWS DOWN LATER

Metabolism is the rate at which we burn food, and calories is the term for expressing the amount we burn. But metabolism and calorie-burning change with the years. The first big upward spurt in metabolism comes right after birth. Since the main purpose of eating is survival, during our first year we can and do eat and burn calories like mad. After that, there comes a temporary slowing down, until a second spurt reaches a peak around the age of ten when the tomboy activity is at its height. And there's another peak around fifteen when most girls are growing toward their greatest height. But after fifteen, the picture changes. Now there is a steady, inexorable and permanent slowing down.

George Washington University's Dr. Herbert Pollack, chairman of the Nutrition Committee of the American Heart Association, says this is how this slowing down works out:

At the age of fifteen, an active girl 5'2" tall weighing 125 pounds can utilize 1600 calories a day. In her twenties, she can utilize only 1370 calories a day. In her thirties, 1360 and by her sixties and seventies, she is way, way down.

This lessened utilization is due, for the most part, to a slowing down in activity. At fifteen, a girl is playing hard, swimming, dancing, batting a tennis ball and taking long hikes. By the time she is 25, she's slowed down to a stay-at-home housekeeper, a secretary or some other mainly sit-down job. By 35, she's a busier housekeeper, but she no longer wants to wash, sweep and scrub by hand. If she can possibly manage it, she's the proud possessor of an automatic washing machine, a vacuum cleaner, an electric broom and an electric dishwasher. By 45, she has acquired a car with automatic shift and power steering, and she seldom walks any place to which she can ride. A Stamford, New York, woman said it was good she had indoor plumbing instead of a privy, because otherwise she might find herself backing up her car to go to *that*.

Small wonder, then, if she continues to eat as much at 25, 35, or 45 as she did at 15, that her pounds mount up and her figure spreads.

MEMORY AND LOVE

Some women don't continue to eat as much. These women happily find their 25-, 35- or 45-year-old appetites adjusting to their 25-, 35- or 45-year-old burning abilities, feel content with lesser amounts and cheerfully go their way. But many women eat as much or more than they ever did. They do this because eating is far from simple. It is complicated by many things, including anxiety and the deprivation of love.

The baby eats mainly to survive. But soon more is added. Eating becomes a way of getting cuddled and being assured of love.

As a girl grows, her desire for love becomes stronger. At the minute the small girl can do for herself what her mother originally did for her—give herself love through food—she does. She gives it particularly on the occasions when a love-reward seems in order, like birthdays, holidays and graduations. What are these events without a celebrating cake she can devour down to the last delicious crumb?

ANXIETY AND REVOLT

In adolescence, eating becomes still more complicated. It adds to love and survival the ingredients of belonging, anxiety and revolt. Many of the rich foods on which a teenager gorges make her so full she forgets to be afraid. Others she eats both because the crowd is eating them and because formerly they were forbidden as "indigestibles." The zesty pizza pies in the dorm at midnight, the bacon-and-onion sandwiches over an open fire, the gooey double fudge sundaes with marshmallow and nuts: these are doubly alluring because for the first time in her life she has the power to eat what she pleases, and she indulges it to the hilt. So adolescence becomes the pinnacle of eating pleasure, with survival, love, belonging, anxiety and revolt all mixed in with it, as the teenager lives and loves almost literally from hand to mouth.

HABITS AND COMPLEXITIES

By the time a woman is grown, these ingredients have so added up that eating has become incredibly complex. A baby may know pretty accurately when it is hungry, what to eat and how much. An adult knows far less. Especially when the old feelings connected with food well up, an adult may find herself turning to ways of satisfying them that have nothing to do with real needs.

There was Eleanor, for instance, who always felt her littler and cuter sister got all the attention in the family. In her twenties, whenever her sister had a date and she didn't, Eleanor ate so much she ran straight up to 175 pounds. She stayed there until she got engaged herself, whereupon she got the self-confidence to reduce.

Oldest children often keep the habit of eating from jealousy or insecurity. So do musicians and actors after a performance, particularly when they're not sure they've done well. When Maria Callas was a young and struggling singer, she used to eat a whole pound of heavy cheese at a sitting. When she became successful, she was able to stop.

Great weight-gain is also common after the death of a beloved relative or friend, and the poor notoriously eat more than the rich. The poor eat because more expensive forms of entertainment are not readily available to them, so every holiday calls for a feast. They also eat from fear— fear that they "don't know where their next meal is coming from," forgetting that they do know; or from the old fear of tuberculosis, forgetting that tuberculosis has long since been practically conquered by drugs. Many people just eat in general to "keep up their strength," forgetting that unnecessary food actually taxes the strength by all the extra work it gives the body to do.

As to eating for revolt, one of the surest ways to get a woman long past adolescence to continue to eat for revolt is to have a doctor or member of her family force a diet on her. Then, like the drunkard who hides a fifth of whiskey in the toilet-cabinet because his wife wants him to sober up, she'll hide chocolate bars under her pillow or clean up everything in the refrigerator from sheer spite. This determination to eat or not eat is the basis, too, for much of the griping about hospital food. Hospital authorities usually buy the best obtainable, but the patient feels she is a prisoner and she didn't choose it, so she refuses to enjoy it no matter how much they try. Then when she gets out after an operation or after childbirth, she eats twice what she needs, for revolt as well as for other reasons. Marjorie, a St. Louis woman who gained forty pounds this way after an operation, defended herself with the old adage: "You always gain weight after an operation." But it isn't that you *have* to. It's just that you so often do.

DESIRE FOR LOVE

Probably the biggest factor in overeating is a continuation of the desire to buy one's self more love. Women who feel unloved often do their extra eating in restaurants, where waiters whom they tip generously hover about them and the proprietor beams as he observes the huge check. A 52-year-old woman who habitually ate in restaurants said she fancied herself a queen at such moments, surrounded by her grateful court. She also admitted to Drs. Kroger and Freed she still indulged in genital play several times a day, though married, because such play "gratified her without the need of involving or requiring anyone else." She was thus extremely infantile and self-indulgent on both counts.

Then there was the famous and beautiful actress Maxine Elliott. Speaking about Maxine in her autobiography, Elsa Maxwell says, "It didn't seem fair for so much brains and beauty to be wrapped up in one woman." But Elsa goes on to tell how Maxine disappeared from the stage at the height of her fame and Elsa found her in her Riviera villa sitting by the side of her pool, enormously fat and eating non-stop. It seems that Maxine had fallen in love with a young Australian tennis player many years her junior, and when he suddenly died she started to eat as compulsively as a chain-smoker smokes. Though her doctor warned her it would kill her—and it did—she couldn't let go. But we must never forget the fact of self-aggression. Perhaps this is what she wanted to do.

The singer Judy Garland goes on eating-binges when she is unhappy, too, ordering huge hotel meals sent up to her room at 3 A.M. when she can't sleep. Her weight goes up and down so violently she seems like a lost little girl in an adult world.

SCARE OFF HUSBANDS

Such compulsive eating is, of course, abnormal, for men as well as women. The most common reason for getting fat during the busy years is still the habit of continuing to eat as much as we did when young.

But there are two special reasons that apply to women only. The first is, to deliberately make oneself unattractive. Dr. A. E. Rakoff says that in the old days when reliable birth-control methods were not available, some women had such a fear of intercourse leading to unwanted pregnancy they met this by making themselves unattractive to their husbands, getting fatter and fatter as the years went by. It probably worked this way especially, he says, in Victorian England, where older women became very stout like the queen. Their obesity propelled their husbands into not "bothering them" or into the arms of other women while they pretended to look the other way.

The second women-only reason is the compulsion to eat up the leftovers in the kitchen while doing the dishes. Women will take an odd roll, a scrap of meat, an end of piecrust neither they nor anyone else wanted at the table, and swallow it with the excuse, "I can't bear to throw anything out." Instead, they throw it in. They're acting with that automatic hand-to-mouth reaction again. Yet they keep on doing this for years, then wail in astonishment, "How can I have gotten so fat when I eat like a bird?"

SOME MORE ARITHMETIC

Here's how they've done it:

A pound of body fat, according to Dr. Herbert Pollack, equals about 3500 calories. One soft roll, or eight potato chips, or half a cup of prune juice, equals about 100 calories. Let them eat just that extra hundred calories a day above their needs, and at the end of a year they have eaten 365 times a hundred, or 36,500 extra calories, adding up to ten extra pounds. Since there's nothing to do with these ten pounds but store them, unless they are worked off, they are ten pounds heavier. Keep it up for five years, and they are fifty pounds ahead.

More than this, says Dr. Rachmeil Levine, researcher at New York's Flower and Fifth Avenue Hospitals, for every pound of weight a woman gains, she gains another three-quarters of a pound of water held by the fat in the body. Keep on doing this—the thought is staggering!

Luckily, however, there's something that steps in and partly stops the up-and-up process. This is the fact that metabolism is dependent, among other things, on the square feet of body surface. A big or tall body with a big surface can burn up more than a small one, regardless of age or work. A big body is in some ways like a robber baron; its cells demand a lot of tribute. It therefore takes extra calories just to carry a big body around. So if one is really very fat or very tall, one can eat more than a small person and not gain as fast. It also works the other way around. When a large woman goes on a diet, she usually complains at first that she is constantly hungry. But once she becomes smaller, her body is not so insistent; it becomes satisfied with less.

A few more happy facts:

Three approximately equal meals a day are less fattening than two small meals and one large—say just coffee for breakfast, a sandwich for lunch and a traditional "good dinner." Experiments were done with rats divided into two groups called The Nibblers and The Gobblers. The Nibblers got three or more meals of nearly equal size. The Gobblers got tiny breakfasts and tiny lunches, leaving them so hungry they gobbled up their big dinners. Each group got exactly the same calories; the only difference was the way in which they were divided. The Gobblers gained more. Similar experiments were done with women, with the same results. Gobbling women gained more, too.

There's more to gobbling than eating big dinners, though. There's the matter of how fast anything is eaten. Many women afraid of gaining weight get into the habit of bolting whatever they eat because they are guilty about eating it in the first place, and swallowing it down fast somehow seems to get it out of sight and mind. Unfortunately, this only makes the situation worse. Now they feel guilty about their bad shape.

Dr. William Kroger sums up with this advice to women who want to keep their figures during the busy years: "Cut down on all food as you get older. But don't cut out your favorite foods altogether because living should be enjoyable, and eating is an important part of it. In the main, however, eat slowly of delicate things divided into nearly-equal meals."

And Dr. Arthur Grollman adds another "don't." "Don't put your trust in reducing medicines like thyroid pills. They are neither effective nor safe. If thyroid did a job, there wouldn't be any fat doctors around."

Other men add: "Don't put your energy into calisthenics or exercise-machines. Since these are usually used alone, nobody keeps up with them for more than a few weeks; they are too boring. Put your energy into competitive activities like golf, or growing better roses than your neighbor, instead. Competitive activities give you more than a workout. They give you companionship, and some of the love and attention you crave when you win."

As for steam-cabinets, all one loses in them is water. And when water only is lost, the body quickly rebalances itself and the water comes right back. Nice, passive alluring massage? Massage does increase heat-production a little, which in turn increases metabolism a little but that's all. It's the masseur who does the hard work who achieves the real weight loss.

It's most important, too, to get over the popular notion that one needs sugar for quick energy. Certainly sugar releases energy quickly, but then so does all food. Sugar releases it maybe fifteen seconds faster, at best, and the only person in whom these fifteen seconds might be crucial is a soldier actually ready to faint on a forced march, or a diabetic ready to go into a coma from too much insulin. But few of us are soldiers or diabetics. We are ordinarily tired people, and for us a cracker or a chunk of cheese will supply whatever quick energy we need.

In fact, things like crackers or cheese will do it even better. For concentrated sweets, like a candy bar at mid-afternoon or jam on the morning toast, send the blood sugar up so high that a reaction sets in, and a few hours later the blood sugar sinks down to abnormally low, so that the person who grabbed at them may soon find herself actually more tired or hungry than before.

Some people, of course, insist they constantly "crave" sugar, and this proves they need it. It doesn't. In unspoiled babies, food-cravings may be trusted. In adults, eating has become so overlaid with habit they can't.

The craving for sugar is mainly due to the fact that one remembers sweets with such pleasant memory from the time when they were special treats. But a person who got spicy hot dogs or salty dill pickles as youthful treats can crave dill pickles or hot dogs, and it doesn't prove she "needs" them, either. Besides, there were thousands of years when refined sugar as we know it today was unknown, and people enjoyed the natural fruit-sugars and honey instead. Yet they survived and stayed energetic. They also only got these natural sugars rarely, at certain seasons of the year. Can you imagine the Biblical Sarah "needing" fudge-bars so she could go about her labors, when the only memories she had were of fruits or honey a few times a year?

But all life is a going forward and a pulling back. So some women who remember sugar may still want to slip back occasionally into the happy delirium of childhood with such things as a mile-high lemon pie or a shimmering coconut layer-cake. But they should understand these sweets for what they are as one gets older—special, rare treats for special celebrations, not super-quick energy foods.

Surprisingly, some women find they actually lose their taste for sweets as they get older. As their metabolism slows down and their chemistry changes, their sugar-craving, if it ever existed, naturally fades away. These women are fortunate because a calorie-allowance is like money in your pocket; you can spend only so much. With sweets eliminated, one can buy more of the delicious meats, fishes, salads and plain cheeses that are true body-restorers. They can also buy a little more delicious butter, because of the pleasant fact that women's hormones seem to protect their arteries from clogging with cholesterol from fats like butter the way men's get clogged.

SOME WEIGHT TABLES

Here are some up-to-date tables on desirable weights according to height, compiled by the Metropolitan Life Insurance Company. As you study them, notice as always that normal has wide variations, and that different weights are given for different size frames, since a woman with big bones and wide hips has more place to tuck pounds in than a woman with tiny bones. Notice, too, that age does not count after 25 since an adolescent often tends to be too fat or too thin, but a woman should settle down by 25 and then stay the same until extreme old age.

Desirable Weights After Age 25

	Small Frame	Medium Frame	Large Frame
4' 10"	92-98	96-107	104-119
11"	94-101	98-110	106-122
5' 0"	96-104	101-113	109-125
1"	99-107	104-116	112-128
2"	102-110	107-119	115-131
3"	105-113	110-122	118-134
4"	108-116	113-126	121-138
5"	111-119	116-130	125-142
6"	114-123	120-135	129-146
7"	118-127	124-139	133-150
8"	122-131	128-143	137-154
9"	126-135	132-147	141-158
10"	130-140	136-151	145-163
11"	134-144	140-155	149-168
6' 0"	138-148	144-159	153-173

Desirable weights, of course, don't take into account fat distribution, the baffling problem of why some women seem to have all their bulges on their thighs and others around their waists. The only answer to this is, they just do. Usually their mothers and grandmothers did before them; the fat in their families simply tends to accumulate in that place. Experiments have been done in which a chunk of tissue from a woman's fat thighs was transposed into the back of one of her hands. The back of that hand soon got fat while the other did not. That's why "spot reducing" does no good unless one reduces all over; the bulges tend to come right back.

WHEN NOT TO REDUCE

With all this talk of reducing, there are times not to even try.

One time not to try, says Dr. Hilde Bruch, now of New York's Columbia Presbyterian Hospital, is during a time of extreme emotional tension, such as a period of mourning or when a member of the family is very ill. You can't go by the weight tables at such a time, and if a woman diets to the point where she finds she's always cranky or can't work, she is doing neither herself nor anyone else any good.

"We hear much about the self-indulgence and lack of will power of people who overeat," says Dr. Bruch. "It is rarely recognized that dieting may also be a kind of self-indulgence, a selfish preoccupation with appearance that may breed characteristics that make the dieter unbearable to those around her." Dieting to this point is another form of neurosis—an "all or nothing" attitude that makes the person end up with the loss of love she doesn't really want.

That's also the trouble with crash diets. They are so meager they amount to "nothing" in the long run, so almost no one ever sticks to them unless she lets a doctor lock her up in a hospital of her own accord. Surveys have shown that 65 per cent of women who go on crash diets promptly get off them, and at the end of a short time are back where they were before. They have merely wasted their enthusiasm, if they haven't done themselves more serious harm.

SOME MAY WANT TO STAY PLUMP

With all this, some women may just plain prefer to get plump or stay plump during the busy years. As their problems mount, a thick, solid body may seem a defense against the world. They don't care about the fact that 85 per cent of diabetics are overweight, and that if a woman gets diabetes after forty she probably won't need insulin at all if she gets down to her normal weight, or that gall bladder, foot trouble, arthritis and heart trouble are far more frequent in the overweight, as well as such unexpected things as cancer of the uterus. Some women don't care about these things; they would rather take a chance as they are. The effort involved in developing the amount of self-control it would take to break all the heavy hand-to-mouth habits they have built up through the years would be, they decide, too much. They feel rather like the teacher who sweated and strained to keep herself down until she was about to retire, then heaved a big sigh and announced, "Now I can go somewhere and spread in peace."

Besides, they know that some men *like* plump women, especially as they age and get plumper themselves. Some men think a plump wife is warmer and more comfortable to live with, more inviting, round and sexually attractive. "Men like sizable breasts and comfortable hips in their loving women," said the writer John McPartland. "Such ample women tend to help develop the abilities of the male." He used a wonderful word to describe the scarecrows who pose for fashion pictures. He called them "humanoids," mechanical robots on which to hang clothes, but devoid of human charms.

Other men like plump women as they get older because they're plain jealous. Caruso was like this. The great singer married late, and on his first trip away from home he wrote to his beloved bride Dorothy in his fractured English, "I hope you will get very fatty, so other men won't look at you." She didn't get fatty but that's what he would have liked.

✳✳✳ 38 Another Rung of the Ladder

The hardest disappointment for a woman to accept as the years go by is not the change in her face or figure, but the change of the menopause. The change that causes her once mighty menstrual tides to dwindle until they completely disappear.

Doctors call the time when they stop "the climacteric," meaning a climb up a rung in a ladder. For that's what the menopause is—another rung up life's ladder she must climb. And it's a difficult climb because for a long time she's been enjoying a period of comparative calm. But now comes a change that may shake her to her depths.

THE GREATEST PARADOX

For this is the greatest feminine paradox of all: unwelcome as menstruation may have been when it first arrived; rail at it as she may have, calling it a "pest" or "the curse," it is even more difficult to see it go. For its going marks the passing of time and the departure of fertility. And while that fertility may never have been used, while she may have never even tried to become pregnant, she still likes to think, "I could if I would." With the menopause she has to face it: she no longer can. Face, too, the curious fact that she is the only mammal to whom this happens. No other female animal lives beyond its power to reproduce.

HALF OF HER LIFE AHEAD

Women didn't always have to face it. When Christ was born, the average woman at birth expected to live only to the age of 25. That's one reason old people were so much venerated and talked about with wonder; they were the exception instead of the rule. The Bible gave three score and ten years of life as an ideal rather than a fact.

A woman didn't expect to do better than 25 for the next fourteen centuries either. It took until around the year 1400 for her life-expectancy to creep up to thirty, and another four and a half centuries for it to rise to forty. Between the terrible mortality from childhood diseases and epidemics like the plague, around the year 1850, an expectancy of forty was doing very well indeed. Queen Victoria told of a friend who in that year lost five children in one month from typhoid fever.

But then things started to improve fast. By 1900 a woman's expectancy shot up to 48 years, and between 1900 and now, with much cleaner food, warmer houses, better immunization against epidemics and childhood diseases, and vastly better childbirth care, it has leaped up to the astonishing figure of almost eighty years. For the first time in history, practically every woman can expect to live through to her menopause and beyond. Indeed, at the time of her menopause, around the age of fifty, she can expect to have almost a full thirty more years ahead of her, or close to half of her total life-span.

PUBERTY IN REVERSE

Yet with almost half of her life ahead of her, she not only ceases to menstruate around fifty, with 35 to 55 as the normal range, she sometimes also has upsetting sensations that shake her to the core.

These sensations are caused by a dramatic rearrangement of her hormone system, a rearrangement that is not like the rearrangement of pregnancy but like that of puberty in reverse. The menopause is therefore not "*the* change of life," as it has so often been called, but *another* change. Another change among the many that have already come to her and the many still to come. I therefore call the menopause merely "the changing years."

Let's go back again and see what her hormone-arrangement is at puberty, so we can better understand her rearrangement during the changing years.

THE SYSTEM AT PUBERTY

At puberty, a girl's hormones are tremendously on the increase, as her gland system starts to work like a huge telephone exchange. Her central or chief operator is her pituitary gland, and her sex-glands are the branch stations that receive "go" messages from her pituitary by way of her blood stream, telling them to get busy and start her menstrual periods. Her ovaries also send back messages through her blood stream to her pituitary telling when to stop. Her thyroid and adrenals are also receiving "go" messages from her pituitary, and sending back messages telling it when to stop.

At puberty, too, her telephone system is new and working creakily. This stop-and-go arrangement is far from smooth at first. There are times when her pituitary sends a "go" message to her sex-glands and they do not answer, so that a period, or several periods in a row, are skipped. There are times when the messages to and from her thyroid and adrenals are erratic, too, and she feels jumpy and nervous as a result. In fact, it takes several years for things to be worked out so that her periods come along regularly and eggs are released fairly regularly, too.

THE SYSTEM AT MENOPAUSE

But now, around the age of fifty, comes the end-point of this system. Now a woman's sex hormones begin to decrease instead of increase, her periods taper off, her ovaries send out fewer and fewer eggs and, in time, no eggs at all. This is because nature does not seem to want a woman around fifty to continue to produce children; doesn't want her to because, while she still might be able to bear them, she almost certainly won't easily be able to start the long haul of bringing them up. (Since a man has much less to do with bringing up children, nature lets men like Charlie Chaplin continue merrily to produce them in his seventies. A child-bearing wife of seventy would be in a sad state.)

So around fifty a woman, of necessity, begins to lose her fertility completely and this change comes as creakily, or even more creakily, than fertility began. It is spread out over several years and occasionally as long as ten years, since every great life-change comes slowly, and the changes that come to a grown woman come more slowly than to a racy young girl.

It is also a more erratic change because for years she has been on a kind of hormone plateau. Her pituitary during maturity developed a smooth and pleasant working-arrangement with her sex-glands, adrenals and thyroid, and now when that arrangement becomes drastically altered, her pituitary is puzzled. When her sex-glands, in particular, start to fail to respond to its calls, her pituitary doesn't accept the situation gracefully at first. It is not used to being disobeyed and it gets frantic. Instead of sending fewer and fewer messages to her sex-glands, it sends them more. Or it sends more messages to the other glands on the "party line"—her thyroid and adrenals—trying to get them to ring the sex-glands and wake them up. The whole process becomes so disturbed that for a while the whole telephone system becomes "out of order" for fair.

The menopause can be summed up this way: It is a period of years during which a woman's hormone system, that started up creakily in puberty and settled down quite smoothly during the busy years, dramatically jerks toward a halt, with her pituitary frantically sending out more and more messages to a pair of ovaries that increasingly fail to respond. And because the system becomes jerky, her balance-scale trembles more violently than ever, and she sometimes gets strange sensations as a result.

Here are these strange sensations. No woman gets all of them, and some women get none of them. But being the creatures of great inner awareness they are, the women who do get them are extremely conscious of them, and more frightened of them than they should be.

HOT FLUSHES, OR FLASHES

Take your choice on what you call them, the hot flushes, or flashes, are the most famous because they are the most obvious. Even women who haven't ever had them have seen them: the sudden reddening of the face and neck, the perspiration coming out on the upper lip, the quick reach for something to use as a fan, or the opening of a coat that wasn't open before. No one quite knows what causes the flushes. The best theory is that, since the various glands send their messages to each other by way of the blood stream, when the gland-system is acting up, the blood flow acts up, too. The blood flows in jerks and spasms instead of steadily. A spasm causes a rush of blood to the face and body that lasts an average of thirty seconds, and occasionally a few minutes or more.

The flushes come not only during the day but also during the night, and can be so bad they wake a woman time and again and drench her gown with sweat. But they are mainly nuisances and nothing more. With a doctor's help, they can soon be brought under good control.

HEADACHES AND NECK PAINS

Then there are the headaches. Rather strangely, a few women, instead of losing their headaches during their changing years, get worse ones. The headaches may be so bad they think they're "brain pains," and are sure these pains mean that the story is true, that the menopause makes you go suddenly out of your mind. It's not true. The rare woman who loses her mind now has been getting ready to lose it for a long time.

The menopausal headaches are mostly nervous tension headaches, and the same tension may cause pains to radiate down the back of her neck as well. But if a woman realizes they do come from nervous tension, and maybe gets some medicine to relieve the tension, she won't build them up into something worse than they are.

CHEST PAINS

Another menopausal pain is a chest pain around the heart, frightening because women seldom get pains around the heart.

These chest pains come from the estrogen deficiency; young girls with estrogen deficiency get similar pains. When hormones are taken to offset the deficiency, the chest pains usually disappear.

A SIGHING BREATH

Some women during the changing years sigh so loudly, deeply and often, they seem to be Tragedy Queens.

Why do they sigh like this, their families wonder? Is it from a general sense of sadness? A desire to call attention to their troubles? Or hormone deficiency once more? Probably all three, but sigh they do. Dr. David Scherf of New York's Flower and Fifth Avenue Hospitals believes the sighs are similar in origin to the chest pains. He gives hormones, and most of the sighs disappear.

TINGLING, ITCHING, AND A DESIRE TO URINATE

The list of strange sensations during the menopause seems endless. Add a tingling of the skin "like pins and needles," a most annoying itch around the genitals and a constant desire to urinate.

The constant desire to urinate is also caused by the waning of the sex-hormones, which for some reason irritates the bladder. And since the estrogens are prime skin-softeners and nourishers, it is their waning that causes the skin to tingle from dryness. The skin becomes particularly dry around the vagina, so dry that the vagina may become harder, its opening tighter and the whole genital region sensitive to the point of pain. This vaginal sensitivity may be very frightening to a woman who thinks any vaginal change means she has "caught something bad." All she has caught in this instance is a case of menopause, and of sex-hormones going down.

INSOMNIA AND FORGETTING

Insomnia is hardly a pain. Neither is forgetting. Yet when a woman suddenly can't remember where she put the sewing basket she used only yesterday, or bolts upright from a sound sleep as if something has struck her, the horrible thought returns, "Am I losing my mind?"

Forgetting and insomnia are also due mainly to her erratic blood flow during this time. A quick, unexpected rush of blood to her brain makes her bolt suddenly awake when she would otherwise rest quietly; a quick withdrawal of blood makes her temporarily forget what she would otherwise remember with ease.

DEPRESSION, IRRITABILITY AND FATIGUE

Probably the most upsetting of the new sensations are the depressions, the irritability, the states of terrible fatigue. The calmest woman may find herself jumping at street-noises she hardly noticed, shouting at her family when she did not shout before. The gayest woman may find herself unaccountably depressed and weepy and the most energetic may feel the kind of fatigue that makes her want to run to a bed and throw herself down.

Such women must remember that before each menstrual period, when sex-hormones were low, states of depression, irritability and fatigue were quite common, too, though they were comparatively mild and passed so quickly she scarcely noticed them. Now with sex hormones that are getting constantly lower and lower, these states can last much longer and become hard to disregard.

So a depression may last for weeks instead of days, and energy may suddenly evaporate in the middle of the morning. But when that happens, she is mainly suffering "the menopause blues."

CHANGING MENSTRUAL PATTERNS

As if all this weren't enough, the menopause makes the average woman quite confused over when she's going to have her next menstrual period, what kind of period it will be, or if she will ever have another again. For she may have a light period followed by a heavy period, then no periods for a few months, then a few light or heavy ones in a row. Or she may gradually taper off, or even just stop cold.

Doctors say all these menstrual patterns are normal during the menopause, however. The only abnormal patterns are a long row of heavy periods without any light ones between.

These abnormal patterns should be looked into because they may indicate trouble—the most common being drastic changes in the endometrium that brings fibroids. Fibroids indeed are common during the menopause, though as the sex hormones continue to wane and the blood supply to the uterus is progressively lessened, they often shrink of their own accord. Still, they may not shrink, and a hysterectomy may be in order. But if a hysterectomy is suggested to remove them, sober and conscientious doctors suggest they be carefully watched for a while before surgery is decided on, since a hysterectomy is hardly something to have simply because the operation at the moment happens to be in style.

If the fibroids do not shrink and an operation must be done, moreover, sober doctors say that if a woman is 45 or under, it is important to try and save her ovaries. Some surgeons like to take out ovaries on general principles while doing a hysterectomy, but there's a big difference between a simple hysterectomy for fibroids, or removal of the uterus only, and a hysterectomy plus a double ovariectomy, or removal of the uterus and both ovaries as well. For the uterus does not make any hormones, so the removal of only the uterus does not throw a woman into a "surgical menopause," meaning a removal of practically all her sex hormones overnight. A removal of both ovaries does. And with the child-bearing period past, the uterus serves little purpose, but the ovaries definitely do. Left in, the ovaries may continue to secrete small amounts of hormones for as long as fifteen years, or just enough to be a crucial factor between a drastic change, full of trouble, and a slow change, with little or none. So unless a woman is over 45, or the situation is more complicated than just fibrosis, even a fraction of ovaries should be saved if it's at all possible.

TIDE-OVER OR LONG TERM?

Among the most blessed of all the medical discoveries ever made for women are anesthesia for childbirth, the birth-control pills, and the pills that replace some of the sex hormones that women lose during the changing years. The replacement pills came into full bloom around the 1930's, when estrogen and the other hormones were discovered and made, and since a popular one is yellow and oval, women sometimes affectionately refer to them as "pumpkin seeds."

Until recently doctors have been sharply divided on the way to use them. Should they be given only as temporary medicine, to tide a woman over the worst of the discomforts a withdrawal of her own sex-hormones may bring? Or should they be used indefinitely almost to the end of her days? A large number of doctors have now swung over to the indefinite side. They reason that replacement hormones should be given over the long term, just as insulin is given over the long term for diabetes or digitalis for heart trouble. Since the menopause often results in an indefinite hormone-deficiency state, they argue that this deficiency should be indefinitely made up.

(The menopause is a deficiency state, however, not a deficiency disease. A disease is something that happens to only a few people; a disease also means that something in the body has gone wrong. The menopause happens to every woman, and nothing has "gone wrong" in the same sense of the words.)

"THEY'RE THE FOUNTAIN OF YOUTH!"

Women being the enthusiastic creatures they are, hearing of the replacement pills they have rapturously cried: "They are pills to keep you young! A female Fountain of Youth has been found at last!"

Alas, the women are wrong. The replacement pills are not pills to keep you young. They are pills designed for a specific purpose, and to do certain specific jobs. These jobs are to quiet the over-riding pituitary, and so to lessen the fatigue, counter the depression, reduce the flushes and relieve as many as possible of the menopausal discomforts that bewilder and distress. And these they do in a most blessed way.

SOME PREVENTIVE JOBS

They are also designed hopefully to do some preventive jobs, such as stopping the calcium from being drawn from a woman's bones. Estrogen favors the laying down of calcium in the bones, so when her sex hormones dwindle, there is apt to be calcium loss. As a result, her bones may become thinner, more porous and brittle, and a condition called "osteoporosis," (from *osteo* meaning "bone" and *porosis* meaning "porous") may develop, especially in the bones at the top and bottom of her spine.

If her bones become thinner at the top of her spine, her head will tend to jut forward more than it did before, causing the unattractive "dowager's hump." If her bones become brittle at the bottom of her spine, low back pain may result, or eventually a broken hip. Broken hips, says the orthopedic surgeon Dr. Howard Rosen of New York's Hospital for Joint Diseases, are almost eight times as common in older women as in older men, mainly because women start to lose their sex-hormones and the calcium in their bones much earlier than men do. "Old women do not fall and break their hips," explains Dr. Rosen. "They break their hips because they fall. And they fall because their hip-bones have become disjointed from long-term estrogen loss. They can fall while walking slowly across a room; they can slide out of a comfortable chair and fall. Yet the hip-trouble has always come first."

But estrogen and calcium loss are not the only factors in broken hips and "dowager's hump," says Dr. Rosen. Women are more prone to suffer broken hips because their pelvises are wider and differently jointed than men's. They are also more apt to develop dowager's hump because their heavy breasts tend to pull their heads forward as their spines weaken. And women tend to shrink more than men do because there are about 25 flexible disks between the long blocks that make up the spine, and these disks also tend to lose some of their fluids and grow smaller with calcium loss. Let each of these 25 disks get even a tiny bit smaller, and the result is an average loss of one to two inches in height, while a very tall woman may lose even more. Add to this the pull of gravity that pulls a woman still further forward as she ages, and the "little old woman" is on her way.

Taking estrogen can slow down the shrinking process, says Dr. Rosen, but it cannot stop it altogether. Nor can it cure it once it has taken place.

Nor can taking estrogen stop women from getting some of the other troubles they suffer after the menopause, such as joint pains and distortions in their fingers, for here not only calcium but unknown factors are involved. Nor can taking estrogen stop their leg-bones from becoming weaker and lighter so that their arches drop and their feet spread, making them need wider and more comfortable shoes. Again, it may slow them down but not stop them altogether.

Yet since many doctors are convinced that estrogen is of at least *some* help in minimizing these processes, men like Boston's Dr. John Rock, Detroit's Dr. F. P. Rhoades and Brooklyn's Dr. Henry S. Acken, Jr. do give it indefinitely as replacement medicine, even up to the age of ninety or more. But other doctors do not. Philadelphia's Dr. A. E. Rakoff, author of one of the most widely accepted medical texts on hormones, is among those who do not. Dr. Rakoff believes in giving his patients estrogen only for the few months or years of the actual change-over time, if they are suffering from the menopausal flashes and the rest. Then he takes them off it because he says he is not convinced from his research that estrogen is the only, or even the most important, hormone involved in aging, and is not at all sure what, if any, preventive jobs it can do.

Besides, women also get obviously older from age twenty to fifty while they still have plenty of sex hormones. If loss of estrogen or progesterone were the sole answer to the aging problem, and taking them would "keep them young forever," why would this be true?

TESTS FIRST

In any event, almost all doctors agree that the replacement pills should not be started while a woman is still menstruating. For menstruation proves she still has a full quota of her own sex hormones, and it is silly or asking for trouble to take more, since the extra amount may lazy up her own ovaries or upset her cycle long before the time it would normally become upset. They also agree they should on no account be started until careful tests and examinations are made to make sure dwindling hormones are the cause of any symptoms she may have.

For that's one of the difficult things about the changing years—the fact that practically every new and strange symptom a woman suffers from may be due to something else instead. Her chest pains may be due to really serious heart trouble. Her erratic blood flow may be due to serious high blood pressure. Any and every one of her discomforts may be merely masquerading as menopausal symptoms, and only a skilled physician can tell which is which.

Dr. Henry S. Acken, Jr., chairman of the Public Education Committee of the American College of Obstetricians, is very positive on this point. "Estrogen replacement pills," says Dr. Acken, "should never be given until a careful history and careful examinations are made. These include a complete physical exam, a gynecological exam, a Pap smear for the detection of genital cancer and a test called a Maturation Index, which tells quite accurately how much of her own estrogen a woman still has. If she has enough of her own, or if there are other contraindications, the pills should on no account be started because then they will either do her no good or do her real harm."

Also, he says, once a woman is taking the pills, she should have all these tests and exams repeated at least once a year, and the dosage adjusted and readjusted according to her individual needs. For some women's hormones dwindle at a much slower rate than others, and no one can guess in advance what that rate will be. It has nothing to do with how fast or slow her mother's dwindled. It has nothing to do with whether she considers herself "weak" or "strong." Like each pregnancy, it is one of those unpredictable and personal things.

It is so personal, says Dr. Acken, that as many as 35 per cent of all women are lucky enough never to have *any* menopausal symptoms or trouble, because their sex-hormones dwindle so slowly they continue to make enough to protect them for quite a time.

The hormones the lucky women continue to make may be either estrogens made by their ovaries, or extra estrogens made by their adrenals. For in some women, as their ovarian sex-hormones decrease, their adrenal sex-hormones miraculously increase and partly offset their ovarian loss. These women have a change that is so smooth they give it hardly any attention. It is merely "another change," in the best sense of the words.

In addition to those who have no symptoms or trouble, the Chicago psychiatrist Dr. Therese Benedek says that as many as 85 per cent of all women sail through the changing years with so little trouble there is no interruption in their daily routine. And in the ones who do have trouble, she believes the menopause is seldom the sole cause of their complaints.

For husband problems and child problems reach a climax at this time, too. Sons and daughters marry, and mothers get into a dither over whom they marry. Husbands get restless at their jobs, and wonder if there's still time to switch, and wives get sympathetically restless and wonder with them. With a whole slew of complexities that can hurl women all at once into a state almost of "battle fatigue," how can the menopause alone be blamed for their jitters, or the disturbance of their accustomed peace of mind?

WRINKLES AND FACE CREAMS

Then there are the cosmetic problems of the changing years. A woman's face as well as genitals may start to dry and wrinkle quite noticeably now, and she can't help but be upset over this too. She may not be quite as upset as Gertrude Lawrence was when she took the part of the faded mother in the movie made from Tennessee Williams's *The Glass Menagerie* and insisted her script-writers add flashback scenes that were not in the original merely to show her as a girl "in full bloom," but upset she is sure to be.

For the waning of the sex hormones not only causes a woman's face to become drier and more prone to wrinkles; it also makes it bruise more easily. It also thins the much-wanted hair on her head while it thickens the unwanted hair under her chin. More unwanted hair makes its debut now because, as her estrogens, or female sex hormones, fall, her androgens, or male hormones, remain at their same level, so the balance between them shifts and there are proportionately more androgens than there were before. Yet taking more estrogens will not get rid of this unwanted hair; only electrolysis will. As for the special hormone-creams so widely advertised to "erase the wrinkles," here's what an unbiased researcher found:

Dr. Howard T. Behrman, a member of the Council of Cosmetics of the American Medical Association, recently devised and reported on what is called a "double blind" test. Twenty-seven women volunteers, all between the age of 35 and 65, but most of them in the menopause, were asked to rub the two sides of their faces each day for several months with creams. The right side was to be rubbed with a plain, cheap cold cream, the left side with one of the expensive hormone-creams. The creams were simply marked with a code number so the women had no idea which cream was which, and couldn't let enthusiasm run away with them. The doctor conducting the test didn't know which cream was which either, so he couldn't get overenthusiastic or prejudiced, either. Thus both women and doctors were "blind."

At the end of six weeks, and again at the end of three months, Dr. Behrman carefully examined both sides of the women's faces; he also took large, clear photographs they could look at themselves. But neither he nor they could see any difference whatever in the two sides, except that in a few instances *both* sides had improved. This was probably because some of the women had very dry faces to begin with and had never used any kind of cream before, so the simple act of rubbing any kind of lubricating substance had helped soften them a bit.

AGING TISSUES

But if hormone creams don't help, don't hormone pills taken internally beautify her face, or "turn time back and make her young again?" Unfortunately, very little, says Dr. Rakoff, unless you look at her face under a microscope. For much as women may hate the words "aging tissues," aging tissues are what they are beginning to have around fifty.

And not only do different women age at different rates, no part of their body ages at the same rate. In some parts, like the face, breasts and neck, the regeneration or regrowth impulse rapidly disappears. In others, like the vagina, it persists. So the replacement pills can markedly improve a woman's vaginal tissues while at the same time they are doing almost nothing for her breasts or face.

Yet improving her vaginal tissues is in some ways much more important than improving her face. For when a wife's face gradually changes, her husband gets so used to the change he hardly notices it. If she stays animated and warm, his eyes play a delightful trick on him and he still sees her as the radiant bride she once was. Besides, if he does notice a change in her face, it is no reflection on him. If her vagina changes, it is.

For while a normal man in no sense has a "male menopause" comparable to a woman's, he does have a crisis of confidence around fifty. Almost universally, his confidence in himself is shaken by his arrival at the half-century mark, and stays shaken for several years. If during this difficult time, his marital relations obviously suffer too, his super-sensitivity on the subject makes this seem like the last straw. A dry or shrinking vagina whose cause he does not understand, but which is almost sure to disrupt their long-established harmony because relations have become distasteful, if not actually painful, to her for this reason, may make him guiltily conclude the fault is partly his. And since few husbands and wives talk as frankly about such matters to each other as they should, a subtle rift can start between them, and grow and grow.

If for no other reason, hormone pills that will soothe, soften and relax the vagina should be discussed with a woman's doctor now.

THE CANCER QUESTION

If the words "aging tissues" are disliked, the word "cancer" is dreaded. Do the hormone pills cause breast or genital cancer? This is the most nagging question of all because if they do, no matter how helpful they are otherwise, they must be ruled out.

The frightening idea that they do cause cancer got around some time ago when some experimental mice were injected with huge doses of estrogen and developed breast cancer as a result. But what most people didn't stop to realize was that the mice were of a special strain bred to be cancer-prone. Also that relating animal experiments to human beings may produce grossly misleading reports, especially in the field of hormone research.

Since that time, literally hundreds of experiments have been done that have not borne out the original mouse experiment. Chicago's Dr. M. Edward Davis has been giving estrogens for 25 years to women who needed them because they had had their ovaries removed early in life by necessity, and has not had a single case of genital cancer develop as a result. Even more to the point, millions of women have been taking the birth-control pills which are similar in composition to the replacement pills, and cancer has in some instances actually decreased.

The American University of Beirut's Dr. William Bickers sums this up when he says: "Estrogen is no more cancer-producing than a charcoal-broiled steak." And the noted gynecologist Dr. Howard F. Taylor of the Columbia Presbyterian Medical Center adds: "It has been my practice, when a woman asks, 'Will hormones give me cancer?' to reply, 'Madam, take the estrogen and give up your cigarettes. You will be happier, and the cancer risk is immeasurably less."

But—and this is a vital "but"—while estrogens do not *cause* cancer, they can make a cancer already present grow. No one knows the cause of cancer, but we do know that cancer-cells are wild cells that multiply like mad. And since sex hormones stimulate a woman's breasts and genitals so markedly, if she already has a breast or genital cancer she does not know about and takes more hormones, they can stimulate it to where it will grow even more quickly than it otherwise would. This is one reason for repeated exams and tests while taking the replacement pills to rule out cancer or other trouble that may have independently started, which the pills could make immeasurably worse.

TO BLEED OR NOT TO BLEED

Next to the question of cancer comes the question of bleeding. Does a woman want to continue to bleed, or have menstrual periods, once her menopause is past? For the pills can be taken in two ways, one likely to cause bleeding and the other not.

To understand why this is so, another review is in order.

Menstruation is really "withdrawal bleeding." During the first part of the menstrual month, under the influence of estrogen, the lining of the uterus is thickened and built up. During the second part of the month, under the combined influence of estrogen and progesterone, the lining is further developed. Then, at the end of the month, both hormones are suddenly withdrawn, the lining is shed and bleeding occurs. Knowing this, doctors can often regulate irregular menstruation, or produce bleeding at will, by giving estrogen and progesterone on certain days and withholding or withdrawing them on others. They are also sometimes able to induce periods in the rare woman who never started to menstruate at all. They can also do the same thing after the menopause by giving sex hormones for a certain number of days to build up the uterine lining, then withholding them for a few days to make token periods without ovulation result.

This is what some doctors are now doing, notably Brooklyn's Dr. Robert E. Wilson. For a psychological lift, Dr. Wilson says, he is creating token periods in his older women who want them, if not every month then by a still more complicated schedule every other month, and he continues to create such periods until around the age of 75, when they become obviously ridiculous.

Other men, like Seattle's Dr. Robert N. Rutherford or Macon, Georgia's Dr. Gordon W. Jackson, do not believe in doing this. They say most of their patients are not the least bit interested in having periods after the menopause for any reason, nor do they want the bother of remembering on which days to take pills and on which days to skip them. In fact, these doctors say, when they ask their patients about having more periods, most of them answer with a fervent "God forbid!" So they give the pills without interruption, usually one every day of the month, and, while the women get other benefits, they no longer shed the lining or bleed.

NOTHING IS SIMPLE

But even taking one pill every day without interruption may still have its problems. No two women are alike. So one pill a day may cause bleeding in certain women because they happen to have a uterus that is unusually sensitive to sex hormones. The smallest dose may progressively build up enough lining so that it suddenly and unexpectedly sheds and causes bleeding of its own accord. And since sudden, unexpected bleeding is also a cancer sign, these women often have to be rushed to a hospital for a D and C to make sure the bleeding is from hormone-stimulation and nothing else. If this weren't enough, there is the ever-present question of weight-gain.

As a woman gets older and her sex hormones wane, her entire body often gets drier and thinner even without eating less, simply because estrogens are water-retaining hormones. With fewer estrogens, she has less water to store and make her puffed. But if she starts taking estrogens again some of this water may promptly come back, astonishing her no end when she steps on the scale and discovers her weight has gone up. The answer to this is that she must take still another kind of pill to eliminate the excess water.

It adds up to the far from simple fact that, while the menopausal pills are indeed a blessing for the women who need them to ease them up this particular rung of life's ladder, and while they may also help do certain preventive jobs, they are hardly Fountain of Youth stuff for all women to gulp at will in the sure hope they will keep them "feminine forever," or make them bounce around eternally and impossibly young.

✳✳✳ 39 The Sheltering Years

This is the final paradox: Women are able to accept age better than men because of the very "narcissism" for which they have been so often criticized.

Narcissism derives from the Greek legend of the young Narcissus who accidentally saw his own beautiful image reflected in the waters of a pool and became so enamored of that image he remained transfixed and gazing at himself forever. But the point of the story is that it was a youth, not a maiden, who did this. Also, it was a fixed image with which he became enamored, not a changing image. Narcissus could never have borne seeing himself grow old.

A MAN'S POWER-IMAGE

A woman can bear seeing this more easily because a man's concept of himself is concerned primarily with power. All his life his power has been steadily increasing until in maturity it reaches a peak—power to

drive a car at breakneak speed, to handle dangerous tools, to fight off enemies, to win his way to money and position, to eat and drink what he
pleases and to pay the check with a nonchalant air.

When any of this power goes, or even diminishes, he is rocked back
on his heels. And around the age of sixty some of it invariably begins
to go. From now on, he knows, he will no longer be able to handle
dangerous tools with quite so much dexterity, drive a car quite so fast,
knock down an enemy so easily or eat and drink his fill. Worse, his
financial power may be about to diminish markedly, too. The chair he
sat in with such authority will in all likelihood soon go to another,
while forced retirement reduces his income to half or less.

But a woman has never had such a strong power-image. So when
her body weakens, or her salary lessens, it is not such a stunning blow.

More, a woman almost never retires in the same sense a man does,
to watching games when before he played them, to sitting around the
house wondering what to do between breakfast and lunch or lunch and
dinner except to read the paper or wander down the block to meet a
few old cronies and reminisce about the past.

A woman still can make the breakfast and dinner she eats, tidy up
the house, sew clothes for her grandchildren or new curtains for the
living-room, continue to do a dozen pleasant jobs much as she did before.

So in spite of her gradual accumulation of wrinkles, her graying
hair, the shrinking that makes her lose height no matter how many
hormones she takes; in spite of the occasional leg-cramps due to more
erratic blood flow to and from her legs, the shrinkage of her mouth
tissues so that the bridgework becomes loose that formerly was tight;
in spite of any and every cosmetic change, she never feels as licked as
a man does. She knows she can still radiate with the glow of contentment or self-respect, a glow that gives her the unconventional charm
of a Helen Hayes who retains her "gift of joy," or an Eleanor Roosevelt
who kept gifts of such courage and vitality to the end that her ungainly
body was barcly noticed because her radiant soul shone through.

THE MIND IS DURABLE

A woman, as she ages, keeps relearning, too, that her body does not
age at the same rate all over. Her digestion may be poorer, her gall
bladder less efficient in processing fats and her bowels more sluggish, but
her mind is the most durable of all.

The late Dr. Edward Steiglitz, a great authority on aging, in 1948 gave a memorable address at the New York Academy of Medicine, which he called "On Being Old Too Young." In it, he kept repeating that it's a lot of nonsense about old dogs not being able to learn new tricks. This silly story, he said, had been spread around and perpetuated by three kinds of people: the lazy old, the jealous young who wanted to inflate their own egos at the expense of their elders, and the lazy teachers of the old who forgot that in order to teach an old dog effectively one has to know more than the dog.

Dr. Steiglitz insisted that the so-called "impairment of memory" of older people was due not only to changes in the brain but to inattention and lack of interest in new faces, new places, new ideas. "It is surprising how well the aged remember when they are truly interested in what they are hearing, reading or seeing," he said. "Memory continues with use and depreciates with disuse . . . like so many other skills."

Actually, Dr. Steiglitz said, memory, if anything, tends to become more accurate with age, if a little slower. He quoted an experiment done by Professor Carl Camp at the University of Michigan with two groups of men, one aged 35 to 45 and one 65 to 76, in which Professor Camp had each group memorize a nonsense paragraph and repeat it back. The older men took longer to do the memorizing, but their accuracy was higher than that of the younger men.

The old fool, he summed up his address by saying, was mainly the young fool grown older. "Experience is profitable only if we learn not to repeat our mistakes. The child learns to walk by falling down; the old person can grow wiser only if he continues to have the courage to experience and conquer fear."

Because of all this, because the mind, if used, continues to be useful in the later years, when a woman finds she can no longer work eight hours a day, she can work four. When she cannot work four, she can work three, two or one. Until she becomes very old indeed, she seldom gets to the point where she cannot work at all. And her few hours of skilled work may even earn her as much satisfaction or pay.

They tell this story about the great engineer, Charles Steinmetz. Steinmetz, well along in years, was one of the chiefs at the General Electric laboratory in Schenectady. A rival company had built a huge dynamo that had cost a tremendous amount of money and effort but somehow had a flaw in it. None of their men could make it go. In desperation, they borrowed Steinmetz from G.E. The tiny hunchback came over, asked merely to borrow a ladder and a hammer, then proceeded to climb up and all over the dynamo, giving it a few taps with the hammer and listening intently. Then he announced, "The trouble is here," and left.

His whole performance had taken less than an hour, yet for this he sent them a bill for $10,000. Though he had solved the problem, when the rival company received the bill they protested its size and asked for an explanation. Steinmetz replied, "For my hour's time, I am charging you one dollar. The other $9,999 is for my experience in knowing where to look."

ABNORMAL DEPENDENCE

If a woman thinks she can't work at all—not even an hour or two a day—there is usually something psychologically wrong with her. She is exhibiting an abnormal amount of helplessness or dependence on others—helplessness that may be a form of hostility since its object is to compel others to feel sorrier for her than they rightfully should.

Dr. Alvin Goldfarb, consultant to the Hebrew Home for the Aged in New York, points out that an abnormally dependent woman of this kind often keeps complaining to him endlessly about how much her children neglect her, how they never come to see her, send her gifts, remember her birthdays. The list of complaints goes on and on. But when he investigates, he finds that the very woman who is complaining the loudest is usually getting the most attention from her children, not the least. She is a bottomless pit when it comes to attention; no amount could possibly satisfy her exorbitant demands. On the other hand, the more independent and self-respecting a woman continues to be, the more she appreciates the reasonable amount of attention she does get, and the less she tries to make her children feel guilty when they are doing their best.

WORK MAKES TIME FLY

But there is another reason a normal woman will want to continue to work as many hours a day as she can: this is that work makes time fly instead of crawl.

A great complaint of many older people is that their days seem endless, that time hangs heavily on their hands. It is only the empty days that hang heavily, not the full. And with their children grown and gone, women can have more days than ever that seem empty unless they are filled with work. But it must be more than "busy work"; it must be meaningful work to be truly satisfying. Continuing to keep house within four walls is good up to a point. But now the outside world is calling her more loudly than ever, calling for the special feminine qualities of warmth and motherliness for the larger work that is never done—the fighting for better food, better medicine, better schooling, better living conditions that make for human dignity for the poor and oppressed of the earth everywhere.

For humanity has crept forward not only on the shoulders of the Einsteins, the Darwins and the Galileos, but on the Florence Nightingales, the Margaret Sangers, the Marie Curies, the Harriet Beecher Stowes, who gave of their strength and compassion to the very last.

LOOKING AHEAD

And if a woman does not feel she has the education to do the work of a Curie or a Sanger, she can still do other kinds of work. Especially creative work that keeps her looking ahead. Planting a garden that keeps her looking ahead to a new season to see if those zinnias or phlox will grow into flowers she can be proud of. Developing a skill like making ceramics or painting that keeps her looking ahead to see if she will be able to make more beautiful ceramics or paint lovelier pictures next year. Doing creative community work like volunteering to shelter a group of retarded children or planning a club program for the local hospital, that will keep her looking ahead to see if the children and hospital will improve. For only by constantly looking ahead instead of back can she keep the essential spirit of youth that will win her more praise than all the hormones on the shelves.

FEAR OF LONELINESS

Doing creative community work also dispels the other bugaboo of older people—loneliness. As a woman's children grow up and perhaps move to distant cities, as her best friends or her husband perhaps dies, loneliness becomes a genuine problem. And the only way to conquer loneliness is to get out among new people; make new friends to replace those who have gone.

"I wake up every morning as full of enthusiasm for the day as a little girl on Christmas," Elsa Maxwell once said. Elsa at seventy still had this determination to get out and make new friends. So did the Metropolitan Opera singer Marjorie Lawrence who, stricken with polio so that she could no longer appear on the stage, began to conduct an opera workshop at Southern Illinois University from her wheelchair. Both of these women may have been technically "alone." But they were not lonely, nor could they be.

One way not to try to solve loneliness is for a woman to move in with her grown children. At least, not to do this on impulse without stopping to think the matter through.

Many women, suddenly bereaved, lose their judgment, hastily sell off their homes and all their possessions and move in with their married children, to regret the step later enormously. After a while they begin to miss their once-familiar surroundings—the armchair in which they used to sit so comfortably, the dresser inherited from Aunt Sarah, the hundred and one homely little mementoes that brought back moments of pleasure through the years.

Worse, they find that a household made up of two generations of adults seldom pans out unless a great deal of advance preparation has gone into the plan. Who will use the living-room for personal guests, and when? Who will decide what food should be served, and at what time? Who will stay home and baby-sit on which night? Who will be final arbiter on how to bring up the grandchildren when grandmother has a firm set of opinions on the subject and daughter a totally different one?

Grandchildren can be a source of tremendous comfort to an older woman. They can be like the grass over which she throws her sheltering shade, sheltering them from the harsh winds and scaring sun much as a tree shelters the earth. She can also find joy in teaching them her values, handing down the wisdom she has learned—wisdom that keeps not only her family but her culture survivable and able to advance. She can do all this with a minimum of responsibility for the chores of their upbringing and a maximum of the pleasure their companionship brings.

But grandchildren can also be the cause of much fatigue in too-close quarters. For this reason, a better solution to the where-to-live problem, researchers have found, is for a woman to keep her own home as long as possible, have a small place a few blocks or even a few miles away from her family, and do as much visiting back and forth as is helpful and pleasant for them all. But they warn against deciding to huddle in an Old Ladies' Home with just other women if it is at all avoidable, because in order to keep vital and feminine every woman needs to talk to a man at least once a day.

SEX IN OLD AGE

If a woman's husband is still alive and they wish to do more than talk—if they wish to continue sex-relations—this should cause no guilt-feelings no matter how old they are. For sex has a value far beyond procreation; it has a social and cohesive value between two married lovers. So while sex in the later years may not contain the excitement it once did, nor drain off as much hostility since there is less to be drained, it can still be a great comfort. It can be a ceremonial renewal of the faithful pact of their original marriage vows, that brings comfort to both as these vows are joyously renewed again and again.

EATING ALONE

Then there's the matter of eating alone.

If a woman does find herself alone, this usually means eating alone. And often a woman who eats alone gets bored with cooking and lets herself slip into the coffee-and-cake habit or the buns-and-tea routine. This can hurt her no end. For coffee and cake may be filling and easy, but the calories they supply are in the main what doctors call "empty calories." They have almost none of the proteins and vitamins older women so badly need.

Proteins like those in meat, cheese, fish or eggs are badly needed to keep on replacing worn body cells. Vitamins like those in fruits or vegetables are badly needed since older people become less efficient in extracting the vitamins from the food they do eat.

Older people also need tastier food. They may need less, but they should enjoy it as much as they can. Yet the taste-buds of an older person are not nearly as keen as those of a young person, and even less if artificial dentures cover the roof or the lower part of the mouth where the taste-buds mainly are. So the ancient idea that a diet of tasteless "pap" was the only diet suitable for older people only succeeded in making them miserable, and was all wrong besides.

To be sure, a soft diet may be more or less necessary for a woman who has so few teeth she can barely chew. But even then she can enjoy things like zesty cheese omelets, chopped meats, or the puréed fruits and vegetables like those found in so-called "baby foods." If these last are seasoned up a little, they will give her far more enjoyment and do far more for her than just mushy cereal, buns and tea.

A FEW VICES

Dr. Russell Cecil, another authority on aging, even suggests that older people develop a few "vices" solely for the sake of pleasure. Vices like a relaxing drink before dinner, or an occasional pleasure jaunt they think they can't afford. Vices like more frequent trips to the beauty-parlor, since regular trips to the beauty-parlor can do wonders for the self-love all women need to the end of their days.

Freud believed that love of self is a "psychic cosmetic that keeps one young." When asked if a certain woman was attractive, he is said to have replied, "She thinks she is, so she seems that way."

For continuing to love oneself and have a few vices contribute greatly to human happiness, and a reasonable amount of happiness is important too.

The pioneer women who went West in the covered wagons knew this. Many of them are still alive and in their nineties, and the magazine *American Heritage* recently interviewed them to see what they remembered of their cross-country trek. "It was wonderful! Wonderful!" they replied. "All those seas of grass, and hardly a dish to wash!"

Of course they had suffered hardships, but they had deliberately chosen to dwell on their happy memories. And this deliberate dwelling on happiness had helped them to keep sanely alive.

A SENSE OF INTEGRITY

So a woman approaches the last stage of her journey. And as she does, Erik H. Erikson adds a final sense she must develop if she is to keep normal. He adds to the sense of basic trust and all the others the indispensable sense of integrity that is the opposite of a sense of despair. This sense of integrity he describes as conveying "some sense of world-order and spiritual sense no matter how dearly paid for. It is the acceptance of one's one and only life cycle as something that had to be and that, by necessity, permitted of no substitutions. It thus means a new, a different love of one's parents. It is a comradeship with the ordering ways of distant times and different pursuits as expressed in the simple products and sayings of such times and pursuits. Although aware of the relativity of all the various life styles that have given meaning to human dignity, the possessor of integrity is ready to defend the dignity of his own life style against all physical and economic threats. For he knows that an individual life is the accidental coincidence of but one life cycle with but one segment of history and that for him all human integrity stands or falls with the one style of integrity of which he partakes.

"For healthy children will not fear life if their parents have integrity enough not to fear death."

This was expressed in another way by two old women during the Montgomery, Alabama, strike when Negroes chose to walk to and from their hard day's work rather than ride on segregated buses they considered degrading. "I am not walking for myself only, but for my children and grandchildren," one old woman said. The other said, "My feet are hurting, but my soul's at peace."

So, too, if a woman works and loves to the end to the extent of her ability; if she finds some measure of pride and happiness along the way—pride and happiness she can bequeath to her children and grandchildren so that they can truly honor her memory—she can say in all sincerity, "My feet are hurting, but my soul's at peace."

❋❋❋ Doctors Who Have Helped Me

Henry S. Acken, Jr., M.D., FACS, FACOG, Consultant in Obstetrics and Gynecology, Methodist Hosital, Brooklyn, New York

Frank Adair, M.D., Emeritus Attending Surgeon, Memorial Sloan-Kettering Cancer Center, New York City

William Bickers, M.D., Chairman and Professor of Obstetrics, American University, Beirut, Lebanon

Earl D. Bond, M.D., The Institute, Pennsylvania Hospital, Philadelphia, Pennsylvania

James C. Doyle, M.D., FACS, Gynecological Surgeon, San Francisco, California

Milton Edgerton, M.D., Professor of Plastic Surgery, Johns Hopkins University, Baltimore, Maryland

Joseph Fletcher, D.D., Episcopal Theological School, Cambridge, Massachusetts

Roswell Gallagher, M.D., Chief, Adolescent Unit, Children's Hospital, Boston, Massachusetts

Bernard Glueck, M.D., Director of Research, Institute of Living, Hartford, Connecticut

Arthur Grollman, M.D., Professor of Experimental Medicine, University of Texas, Austin, Texas

Erlmer R. Grossman, M.D., Berkeley Pediatric Group, Berkeley, California

Alan Guttmacher, M.D., President, Planned Parenthood, Visiting Professor, Albert Einstein Medical School, New York City

Albert L. Highdon, M.D., FACS, Gynecological Surgeon, Teaneck, New Jersey

Irene Josselyn, M.D., Child Psychiatrist, Phoenix, Arizona

Abram Kardiner, M.D., Chief, Payne Whitney Psychiatric Clinic, Columbia Presbyterian Medical Center, New York City

I. Newton Kugelmass, M.D., former Research Assistant in Pediatrics, Yale University, New Haven, Connecticut

John La Farge, S.J., Editor, *America* (National Catholic Weekly), New York City

Rachmeil Levine, M.D., Chief, Endocrinology Research, Flower-Fifth Avenue Hospital, New York City

William Malamud, M.D., Senior Consultant, Research Foundation, National Foundation for Mental Health, New York City

Earle Milliard Marsh, M.D., Assistant Professor of Obstetrics and Gynecology, University of California Medical School, San Francisco, California

John S. Miller, M.D., Assistant Professor, Obstetrics and Gynecology, University of California, San Francisco, California

Mrs. Marian Genniaria Morris, Psychiatric Social Worker, The Children's Hospital of Philadelphia, Philadelphia, Pennsylvania

Jane Pearce, M.D., Harry Stack Sullivan Institute, New York City

Robert F. Peck, M.D., Chief, Personality Research Center, University of Texas, Austin, Texas

A. E. Rakoff, M.D., Professor of Endocrinology, Jefferson Medical School, Philadelphia, Pennsylvania

Howard Rosen, M.D., FACS, Orthopedic Surgeon, Hospital for Joint Diseases, New York City

Alexander H. Rosenthal, M.D., Chief of Obstetrics and Gynecology, The Long Island Jewish Hospital, New Hyde Park, Long Island, New York

Arthur Roth, M.D., Founder and former Director, The Teenage Clinic, Oakland, California

Robert N. Rutherford, M.D., Executive Editor, *Pacific Medicine and Surgery*, Seattle, Washington

Nevitt Sanford, Ph.D., Director, Institute of Human Relations, Stanford University, Stanford, California

Milton Sapirstein, M.D., Neuropsychiatrist, Mt. Sinai Hospital, New York City

Leon H. Saul, M.D., Professor of Clinical Psychology, University of Pennsylvania Medical School, Philadelphia, Pennsylvania

Donald R. Threlfall, M.D., Pala Medical Center, San Jose, California

Jules E. Vandow, M.D., Associate Clinical Professor of Dermatology, New York University Postgraduate Medical Center, New York City

E. Lee Vincent, Ph.D., Professor of Human Development, Chatham College, Pittsburgh, Pennsylvania

William L. Webb, Jr., M.D., Psychiatric Consultant, Plastic Surgery Service, The Henry Phipps Psychiatric Clinic, Baltimore, Maryland

Edward T. Wilkes, M.D., Associate Clinical Professor of Pediatrics, New York University Medical School, New York City

GRATEFUL ACKNOWLEDGMENT IS GIVEN TO THE FOLLOWING FOR
PERMISSION TO QUOTE COPYRIGHTED MATERIAL:

Alfred A. Knopf, Inc., for "The Happy Family" by John Levy, 1962

Dr. Leo Kanner for "Do Behavioral Symptoms Indicate Psychopathology?" 1960

Life Magazine, for the article on subteens, and the article on Marilyn Monroe "Fame
    May Go By and * * So Long, I've Had You," copyright by Time, Inc., 1962

Eleanor Hamilton, Ph.D., for her unpublished doctoral thesis, "The Emotional Aspects
    of Pregnancy."

Norma Millay Ellis, for the poem "God's World," from Collected Poems, Harper and
    Row, copyright, 1913 and 1940 by Edna St. Vincent Millay, and the poem
    "Souvenir," from Collected Poems, Harper and Row, copyright 1923 and 1951
    by Edna St. Vincent Millay

W. W. Norton and Co. for "Childhood and Society" by Erik H. Erikson, 1950, and
    "The Emotional Problems of Living" by Gerald H. Pearson and O. Spurgeon
    English, 1945

The American Academy of General Practice, for the article "Confident Childbirth"
    by Dr. Earle Milliard Marsh, 1951

Dr. Helene Deutsch and Grune and Stratton for "The Psychology of Women" by Dr.
    Helene Deutsch, 1944

The Metropolitan Life Insurance Co. for material from their Statistical Bulletin

Harper and Row, for "Her Infinite Variety" by Morton Hunt

The Bruce Publishing Co., for "Fundamental Marriage Counselling" by Dr. John
    Cavanagh

The Irving Berlin Music Corporation, for lyrics from the song "Somebody Is Coming
    to My House" (formerly "Someone Is Coming to My House") copyright 1913,
    renewed 1940.

Random House, for "Paradoxes of Everyday Life" by Dr. Milton H. Sapirstein, 1955,
    and "Shadows on the Grass" by Isak Dinesen

Atheneum Publishers, for "The Italians" by Luigi Barzini, Copyright 1964 by Luigi
    Barzini

❊❊❊ Books and Articles That Have Helped Me

FOR GENERAL BACKGROUND

Deutsch, Helene   The Psychology of Women, Grune and Stratton, 1944
Kardiner, Abram   Sex and Morality, Bobbs Merrill, 1954
Weiss and English   Psychosomatic Medicine, W. B. Saunders, 1943
Benedek, Therese   Psychosexual Function in Women, Ronald Press, 1952
Farber, Mustachi and Wilson, editors, Man and Civilization, McGraw-Hill, 1965
Schilder, Paul Ferdinand   The Image and Appearance of the Human Body, Paul, Truber and French (London), 1935
Kinsey, Alfred H.   Sexual Behavior in the Human Female, W. B. Saunders, 1953
Buonaparte, Marie   Female Sexuality, International Universities Press, 1953
Strecker, Edward A.   Basic Psychiatry, Random House, 1952
Reik, Theodore   Sex in Man and Woman, The Noonday Press, 1960
Journal of the American Medical Society, April 26, 1958. "Why Do Females Live Longer?"

INFANCY AND CHILDHOOD

Hurlock, Elizabeth   Childhood Development, McGraw-Hill, 1955
English and Pearson   The Emotional Problems of Living, W. W. Norton, 1955
Erikson, Erik   Childhood and Society, W. W. Norton, 1950
Balint, Alice   The Early Years of Life, Basic Books, 1954
Pearce and Newton   The Conditions of Human Growth, Citadel Press, 1963
Smith, Clement A.   The Physiology of the Newborn Infant, Charles C. Thomas, 1951
Gesell, Arnold   Infant and Child in the Culture of Today, Harper, 1943
Carmichael, Leonard (editor)   Manual of Child Psychology, John Wiley, 1954
Schauffler, Goodrich C.   Pediatric Gynecology, Year Book Pub. Co., 1942
Davis, Clara   The Self-Selection of Diet Experiment—The Ohio State Medical Journal, August, 1938
Lees, Hannah   The Word You Cannot Say, Today's Health, Feb., 1955
Bakwin, Harry   Masturbation in Infants, The Journal of Pediatrics, May, 1952
Bruch, Hilde   Obesity in Childhood, American Journal of Diseases of Children, Volumes 58 and 59
Redl, Fritz   Pre-adolescents, What Makes Them Tick? The Child Study Association of America
Talbot, N. B.   Obesity in Children, Medical Clinics of North America, 1945

PUBERTY

Grollman, Arthur A.   Essentials of Endocrinology, Lippincott, 1954
Paschkis, Rakoff & Cantarow   Clinical Endocrinology, Hoeber, 1958
Maisel, Albert Q.   The Hormone Quest, Random House, 1965
Bruch, Hilde   Obesity in Relation to Puberty, Journal of Pediatrics, 1941
Benedek, Therese   Insight and Personality Adjustments, Ronald Press, 1946

ADOLESCENCE

Gallagher and Harris   Emotional Problems of Adolescence, Oxford University Press, 1958
Roth, Arthur   The Teenage Years, Doubleday, 1960
Montague, Ashley   Adolescent Sterility, C. C. Thomas, 1946
Farnham, Marynia   The Adolescent, Harper and Row, 1951
Hurlock, Elizabeth   Adolescent Development, McGraw-Hill, 1951
Blaine and McArthur (editors)   Emotional Problems of the Student, Appleton-Century Crofts, 1961
Jersild, Arthur   Psychology of Adolescence, Macmillan, 1957
Baruch, Dorothy   New Ways in Sex Education, McGraw-Hill, 1953
Josselyn, Irene   The Happy Child, Random House, 1955
Josselyn, Irene   The Adolescent and His World, Family Service Assn., 1952
Sulzberger, Marion B.   What Is the Best Way to Treat Acne in the Adolescent? Current Medical Digest, Jan., 1953
Edgerton, Jacobson and Meyer   Surgical-Psychiatric Study of Patients Seeking Plastic (Cosmetic) Surgery, British Journal of Plastic Surgery, July, 1960
Meyer, Jacobson, Edgerton and Cantor   Motivational Patterns in Patients Seeking Elective Plastic Surgery, Psychosomatic Medicine, May-June, 1960
Aufricht, Gustave   Philosophy of Cosmetic Surgery, Plastic and Reconstructive Surgery, Nov., 1957
Novak, Emil   Gynecological Problems of Adolescence, Journal of the American Medical Society, Vol. 117, 1941
Sanford, Nevitt   Personality Development During the College Years, Journal of Social Issues, Vol. 12, 1956
Bond, Earl   The Student Council Study, American Journal of Psychiatry, Vol. 109, 1952
Cavanagh, John   Fundamental Marriage Counselling, Bruce Publishing Co., 1956
Dickinson, Robert Latou   Tampons as Menstrual Guards, The Journal of the American Medical Association, Vol. 128, 1945
Blewett, E. K.   Severe Dysmenorrhea and Its Treatment by the Suppression of Ovulation, Medical Record and Annals, Sept., 1949
Haus, Goldzier and Hamblen   Dysmenorrhea and Ovulation, American Journal of Obstetrics and Gynecology, Nov., 1947
Chadwick, Mary   Women's Periodicity, Noel Douglas (London), 1933
Maisel, Albert Q.   The Hormone Quest, Random House, 1965
Balint, Alice   Psychology of Menstruation, Psychoanalytic Quarterly, May, 1937
Benedek, Therese   Insight and Personality Adjustment, Ronald Press, 1946
Bickers, William   Menstrual Distress, Charles C. Thomas, 1957
Flugel, John Carl   The Psychology of Clothes, International Psychoanalytical Library, 1930

EARLY MARRIAGE AND SEX

Levy and Munroe   The Happy Family, Alfred A. Knopf, 1962
Ellis, Havelock   Studies in the Psychology of Sex, Random House, 1928
Frantzblau, Abraham   The Road to Sexual Maturity, Simon and Schuster, 1954
Merrill, Frances E.   Courtship and Marriage, Sloan Associates, 1949
Sapirstein, Milton H. and Alis De Sola   Paradoxes of Everyday Life, Random House, 1955
Reik, Theodore   The Need to be Loved, Farrar, Strauss, 1963
Turner, E. S.   A History of Courting, Dutton, 1955
Hunt, Morton   The Natural History of Love, Dutton, 1955
Rock, John, and Loth, David   Voluntary Parenthood, Random House, 1949
Guttmacher, Alan   Babies by Choice or Chance, Doubleday, 1959
Pincus, Rock, Garcia, Rice-Wray, Paniagua and Rodriguez   Fertility Control with Oral Medication, American Journal of Obstetrics, June, 1958
Masters, William H.   The Sexual Response Cycle of the Human Female, Western Journal of Surgery, Obstetrics and Gynecology, Jan.-Feb., 1960
Masters and Johnson   Human Sexual Response, Little, Brown, 1966
Klein, Viola   The Feminine Character, International Universities Press, 1949

PREGNANCY AND BIRTH

Graham, Harvey   Eternal Eve, Doubleday, 1951
Marsh, Earle Milliard   Confident Childbirth, General Practitioner, Dec., 1951
Guttmacher, Alan   Pregnancy and Birth, Viking Press, 1957
Flanagan, Geraldine Lux   The First Nine Months of Birth, Simon and Schuster, 1962
Patten, Bradley Merrill   Human Embryology, Blakiston, 1953
Hamilton, Eleanor   Emotional Aspects of Pregnancy, unpublished doctoral thesis
Hall, Robert E.   Nine Months Reading, Doubleday, 1960
Hilliard, Marion   Women and Fatigue, Doubleday, 1960
Rosen, Harold E.   Therapeutic Abortion, Julian Press, 1954
Greenhill, Jacob Pearl   Principles and Practice of Obstetrics, Saunders, 1951
Eastman, Nicholas H.   Expectant Motherhood, Little, Brown, 1943
Dick-Read, Grantly   Childbirth Without Fear, Harper, 1959
Doyle, James   Handbook of Obstetrics and Gynecology, Lange Medical Publishers, 1954
Menninger Clinic Bulletin   Contraception, Jan., 1943, also Sept., 1953
Eastman, Nicholas J.   editorial on abortion, Obstetrics and Gynecology, 1953
Menninger Clinic Bulletin   Emotional Factors in Pregnancy, Jan., 1943
Kroger and Freed   Psychosomatic Gynecology, Saunders, 1951
Alexander, A.   Psychosomatic Medicine, Norton, 1950
Benedek, Therese   Nursing and Pregnancy, American Journal of Orthopsychiatry, Vol. 19, 1945
Horney, Karen   Eating During Pregnancy, American Journal of Psychoanalysis, 1954
Davidson, Harold A.   The Psychosomatic Aspects of Educated Childbirth, New York State Journal of Medecine, Nov., 1953
Bickers, William   Patterns of Uterine Motility in Relation to Spermigration, Fertility and Sterility, 1951
Doyle, James C.   Vaginal Infections and Their Management, The Urologic and Cutaneous Review, Vol. 55, No. 10, 1951

MATURITY

Saul, Leon H.   Emotional Maturity, Lippincott, 1947
Buss, Arnold   The Psychology of Aggression, John Wiley, 1961
Menninger, Karl   The Vital Balance, Viking, 1963
Wolff, Harold G.   Headaches and Other Head Pains, Oxford, 1963
Bruch, Hilde   When Not to Diet, Colliers, February 5, 1954
Reider, N.   The Concept of Normality, Psychoanalytic Quarterly, June, 1950
Erikson, Erik H.   Identity and the Life Cycle, Psychological Issues, Vol. 1, No. 1, 1959
Saul and Wenar   Early Influences on Development and Disorders of Personality, Psycho-analytic Quarterly, Vol. 34, 1965
Pollack, Herbert   Obesity and Heart Disease   American Heart Association, Jan., 1957
Gray, Madeline   The Changing Years, Doubleday, 1957
Gallup and Hill   The American Woman, Saturday Evening Post, Dec. 22, 1962
Acken, Henry S., Jr.   The Menopause, Its Meaning and Management, The New England Obstetrical and Gynecological Society, Vol. 18, 1964
Saul and Pulver   The Concept of Emotional Maturity, Comprehensive Psychiatry, Feb., 1965
Alexander, Franz   Emotional Maturity, Bulletin, Illinois Society for Mental Hygiene, Nov., 1948
Jackson, Gordon   The Management of the Menopausal Patient, Current Medical Digest, Jan., 1965
Shelton, E. Kost   The Use of Estrogen after the Menopause, Journal of the American Geriatrics Society, Oct., 1954
Rhoades, P. F.   The Menopause, a Deficiency Disease, Michigan Medicine, June, 1965
Wilson, Brevetti and Wilson   Specific Procedures for the Elimination of the Menopause, Western Journal of Surgery, Obstetrics and Gynecology, May, 1963
Bergler and Kroger   Kinsey's Myth of Female Sexuality, Grune and Stratton, 1954
Masters, William H.   Sex Steriod Influence on the Aging Process, American Journal of Obstetrics and Gynecology, Oct., 1957
Frank, Lawrence   Live Long and Like It, Crozer Quarterly, Oct., 1947
Masters, William H.   Endrocrine Therapy in the Aging Individual, Obstetrics and Gynecology, July, 1956
Peck, Robert F.   What Is Normal? The Alcalde, January, 1961

❊❊❊ Index

A. Z. test, 233-234
abortion, 213, 215, 231-232, 251-253, 349-350
accidents, and pregnancy, 267
Acken, Dr. Henry S., Jr., 370, 371, 372
acne, 87, 150-154
Adair, Dr. Frank, 95-96
adolescence, 126-174; and acne, 150-154; and awareness, 128; and eating, 353; and exhaustion, 132
adrenal glands, 81, 235; function of, 85-86; hormones of, 88, 243, 256, 286, 312, 338, 363, 364, 372
after-birth, the (see placenta)
aggression, 7, 37-39, 68, 207; constructive, 37-38, 68, 148; destructive, 5, 37-38, 68, 337, 341-342
aging, 373-374, 377-385
allergies, 12, 19, 318
ambivalence, 128-129, 190
amnion, the, 247, 248, 252, 261-262, 264-265, 283-284; fluid of, 248-249, 264
androgens, 88, 106; and acne, 87, 150-151, 153-154; and sex-drive, 87; and unwanted hair, 159, 373 (see also sex-hormones)
anesthesia, 290-295, 304-305
anger, 36-39, 148; expressions of, 37-38; releasing, 337 (See also tension)
anorexia nervosa, 60-61, 172-173
anxiety, 52-53; and eating, 353; defenses against, 74-75; about "measuring up," 173-174; and mother and child, 322-323; oral release from, 43, 132-133, 172, 341; during puberty, 100;

in school, 69; about sex-relations, 172 (See also fears; tension)
appetite: and emotions, 63-65; increase in, 97-98, 258-259; loss of, 60 (See also eating; weight)
Arey, Dr. L. B., 119
arthritis, and pregnancy, 243
Ascheim, Herman, 233
Astor, Mary, 132-134
Aufricht, Dr. Gustave, 155
awareness, 12, 36; during adolescence, 128; kinds of, 98-99, 238; during pregnancy, 238, 275, 331

baby, development of (see embryo; fetus; infancy)
"baby blues," 312-313
backaches, 343-344; during pregnancy, 256, 270, 279-280
Barclay, Dorothy, 32
Baruch, Dorothy, 172
Barzini, Luigi, 332
Bashkirtseff, Marie, 139, 143-144, 147
bathing, and menstruation, 116
beauty, the, 202-207
Beauvoir, Simone de, 78, 331
bed-wetting, 39, 42, 46, 48
Behrman, Dr. Howard T., 373
Bender, Dr. Lauretta, 48
Benedek, Dr. Therese, 111-112, 228-229, 372
Bergman, Dr. Elizabeth, 66
Berry, Dr. Paul C., 179
Berthold, Arnold Adolf, 81-82, 83
Bettelheim, Dr. Bruno, 336
Bickers, Dr. William, 125, 350, 375

Binger, Dr. Carl, 132
birth, process of (*see* childbirth)
birth-control, 211-218, 349-351 (*See also* contraceptives)
birth-cry, the, 10, 315
birth statistics, 6-7, 55, 245
birthmarks, 267
births: multiple, 113, 268; premature, 264, 273, 284-285
body: changes in, 1, 91-101, 146, 343-349, 352-353; image, 18-24; obsession with, 93-94, 98-100, 147, 149-174
bowels, control of, 29-32
breast-feeding, 314, 315-322
breasts: and the adolescent, 157-158; changes in, 1, 91, 93-96, 232, 235-236; enlarging, 349
breathing, in babies, 10-11, 18-19, 315
Brown-Sequard, Charles Edouard, 82-83
Bruch, Dr. Hilde, 62-65, 360
bunions, 164-165
Bunkin, Dr. Irving, 275-276
Buss, Dr. Arnold, 341

Caesarean delivery, 307-308
calcium, 87, 369-370
calories, 168-170, 352-353, 356-357, 383
Camp, Professor Carl, 379
cancer: and birth-control pills, 217; and breast-feeding, 317; fears of, 95; and heredity, 243; and hormone pills, 374-375; and overweight, 361
Carter, Richard, 166
castrates, 81-82, 87
Cavanagh, Dr. John R., 124-125
Cecil, Dr. Russell, 384
celibacy, 200, 269
cervix, 221, 287-288, 290, 292, 296; fluid of, 221, 229
Chadwick, Mary, 104
Chamberlens, the, 309-310
change of life (*see* menopause)

childbed fever, 297-304, 307
childbirth, 286-310; and anesthesia, 290-295, 304-305; Caesarean, 307-308; classes in, 279, 290, 323; confinement after, 311-326; death in, 276-279, 297-304; delivery in, 2, 304-310; and depression, 312-313; early impressions of, 77-79; labor in (*see* labor); and medications, 291-296, 305; natural, 289-292; for older women, 350-351; pain of, accepting, 118; premature, 264, 273, 284-285
chromosomes, 243-244
Clendening, Dr. Logan, 290
clitoris, 15, 54
clothes, fads in, 146
Colette, 384
colic, 320, 323
conception, 108, 218-230; breast-feeding and, 320-322; complexity of, 219-223; defective, 251-252; difficulties of, 218-219, 223-229; fears of, 119-120, 211, 226, 356 (*See also* pregnancy; contraceptives)
Condom, Dr. Charles, 212
confidence (*see* self-confidence)
confinement, after childbirth, 311-326
conflicts, with parents, 29-33, 36-39, 130-136, 326-329
conscience, 26, 41, 134
constipation, 32, 238, 270
contact lenses, 163
contraceptives, 113, 114, 125, 211-218, 325, 351; and cancer, 374-375; and infertility, 218
contractions, 271, 282-283 (*see* labor)
corpus luteum, 108
courtship, 190, 192, 208, 209
cramps, 112, 114-117, 120
creams, hormone, 348-349, 373
creativity, 51, 68, 139, 339-340, 381-382
crushes, 139-143, 148
crying: at birth, 10, 315; importance of, 24; as tension-release, 337-338
curiosity, a life force, 34-36, 73

dating, 100, 122, 148, 205
Davis, Dr. Clara, 56-58
Davis, Kingsley, 22-23
Davis, Dr. M. Edward, 375
daydreaming, 74, 134, 145-148
death, fears of, in pregnancy, 276-279
death wishes, 40-41, 238-239
decision-making, in adolescence, 131
delinquency, 148
delivery room, the, 297-304
dependency: after childbirth, 324; in old age, 380; during pregnancy, 239, 257-258
depression: after childbirth, 312-313; in menopause, 367
destructiveness, 37-38, 68, 337, 341
Deutsch, Helene, 76, 102, 120, 144, 149, 186, 198-199, 224-225, 226, 229, 239, 252, 277-278, 279, 328
diaphragms, 125, 212, 214
diabetes, and pregnancy, 243
diaries, 143-144, 148
Dickinson, Dr. Robert Latou, 123-124, 271, 304
dieting, 356-360; children and, 66-67 (See also eating; weight)
Dinesen, Isak, 180
diseases: congenital, statistics of, 245-246; immunity to, 273-274, 318; and the placenta, 241-243; proneness to, 179; resitance to, 7, 19
disillusionment, in marriage, 208-211, 230
divorce, 325
Doderlein's bacillus, 93
douches, 124, 214, 257, 271
dream loves, 184-186
dreams (see daydreaming)
drugs, 116; and the placenta, 241, 242, 243 (See also medications)
dyeing hair, 161-162, 347

Eastman, Dr. Nicholas, 267, 280, 281, 317

eating: in adolescence, 168-173; and emotions, 55-67 passim, 169-170, 353-356; fads in, 95, 145-146; in infancy, 19, 352, 353 (see also breast-feeding); and living alone, 383; and menstruation, 121-122; in old age, 383-384; and pregnancy, 258-259; problems with, 55-67, 352-361 (See also weight)
Eberlein, Dr. Walter, 62
Edgerton, Dr. Milton, 155-156
education, for women, 177-183
eggs (ova): number of, at birth, 17, 107; and progesterones, 215, 216; ripening of, 86, 93, 107; travels of, 108, 221-223, 246-247
electrolysis, 159-160, 256, 373
Ellis, Havelock, 102, 166, 197
Elliott, Maxine, 355
embryo, development of, 246-250
emissions, nocturnal, 193, 195
emotions: and acne, 154; and androgens, 153-154; and appetite, 63-65; after childbirth, 311-326; and eating, 55-67 passim, 169-170, 353-356; and hormone reactions, 228-229; and the menstrual cycle, 110-112, 117, 119-120, 122; and the miscarriages, 252-253; and premature labor, 284-285; and sterility, 225-229; tides of, 1, 4, 106, 110-112
energy, 18, 73-74, 80, 186; burst of, in adolescence, 129-130
English, Dr. O. Spurgeon, 30-31, 40, 42, 50, 51-52, 59, 142
episiotomy, 305, 313
Erikson, Erik H., 24, 25, 33, 41, 45, 321, 339-340, 384
escapism, 132-134 (see fantasy-life)
estrogens: and acne, 150, 151, 153; and aging, 368-377; and calcium, 369-370; deficiency of, 366; and emotional tides, 110-112; function of, 86-87, 107-108, 114-115, 150, 151, 234-235; and nausea, 237, 240; and

pregnancy, 234-235, 237, 271, 285-286, 315; replacing, 113, 368-372

examinations, internal, 113, 232-233; during labor, 288

exhaustion, in adolescence, 132

expectations, exaggerated and irrational, 202-205, 209; parental, 39, 47-48, 132-136

eyeglasses, 163, 344-345

eye-hunger, 19-21

eyesight, 12, 344-345

face lifting, 345-346

fairy tales, 127-128

Fallopian tubes, 15, 18, 108, 220, 221, 222

Fallopius, Gabriello, 18, 212

fantasy-life, 127-128, 137-148 *passim*, 183-186, 193-194 (*see* daydreaming)

Farnham, Dr. Marynia, 153, 331

father, as love object, 138-139

fatigue, 132, 330, 333-334, 367

fear: at birth, 12-13, 15; of boys, 100; of conception, 119-120, 211, 225-226, 356; growth of, 38-41; during labor, 289-296; of loneliness, 183, 188, 381-383; of male genitals, 142; in pregnancy, 260, 266-268, 276-279; and sterility, 225-226

feet, problems with, 164-168, 280

female versus male, 178 (*see* sexes . . .)

femininity, 331-332; acceptance of, 52, 99, 126; badge of, 126; developing, 90-101; maintaining, 383; rebellion against, 122

fertility, 229; attitude of men toward, 223; clinics for, 213, 215; departure of, 351, 362, 364; development of, 113; maximum time of, 114, 219; and nervousness, 224, 225 (*See also* ovulation; sterility)

fertilization, 108, 222-223 (*see also* conception)

fetus: determining sex of, 275-276; development of, 250; 261-265, 273-274 (*See also* embryo)

fibroids, 368

figure (*see* body)

Fischer, Dr. Irving, 79, 125, 228, 257-258, 268, 278

Flanagan, Geraldine, 248, 249, 264, 273

flashes, hot, 365

food and feeding (*see* eating; breast-feeding; weight)

forceps, use & discovery of, 308-310

Franzblau, Dr. Abram, 78

Freed, Dr. Herbert, 237, 259, 270, 355

Freud, Dr. Sigmund, 5, 340, 343, 384

Friedan, Betty, 331, 333

friendships, 74-77, 139-140

frigidity, 52, 194-195, 199

frog test, for pregnancy, 233

Fromm, Dr. Erich, 132, 137, 184

frustration: against others, 36-39; and teething, 24-25; tolerance of, 341, 342; and weaning, 25-26, 33 (*See also* anxiety; tension)

Gallup, Dr. George, 333

Garland, Judy, 170, 355

genes, 243-246, 247

genital play, 49-54, 192, 193, 195, 229; and acne, 153-154; sex-desire and, 51-52; and tampons, 124-125

genitals, 155-156; and breasts, 316-317; development of, 87, 250; fear of, 142; handling of, 125, 316 (*see also* genital play); male, 219-220; in newborns, 315; undeveloped, 215 (*See also* clitoris; penis; vagina)

germ-cells, 243 (*See also* eggs; sperm)

German measles (rubella), 241-242, 350

Gesell, Dr. Arnold, 28, 44, 47, 55, 351

Gibson, Dr. Eleanor, 13

glands: adrenal (*see* adrenal); milk, 235; pituitary (*see* pituitary); sebaceous, 150; sex (*see* sex glands); sweat, 158, 159; thyroid (*see* thyroid)

glasses (*see* eyeglasses)

globulins, 261-262

Glueck, Dr. Bernard, 54

Goldfarb, Dr. Alvin, 380

Gordon, Dr. Alexander, 299-300

grasping reflex, 14, 20, 28

Grollman, Dr. Arthur, 357

Gross, Dr. Frank M., Jr., 105

Grossman, Dr. Elmer, 316, 320

growth: in adolescence, 126-174; of the embryo, 246-250; of the fetus (*see* fetus); food for, 55-67; in infancy, 18-26; of the newborn, 3-18; patterns of, 48; during puberty, 95-98; as stress, 48, 94-95; unevenness of, 97

guilt: and death wishes, 40-41; and food, 65; and parental conflicts, 130-136; of the part-time mother, 335-338; and sterility, 225-226

Guttmacher, Dr. Alan, 221, 222, 233, 251-252, 267, 271, 280, 282-283

hair: curling, 160-161; dyeing, 161-163, 347; and sex-hormones, 347, 373; unwanted, 157, 159-160, 373

Hall, Dr. Robert, 290

Hamblen, Dr. E. C., 115-116, 120, 286

Hamilton, Dr. Eleanor, 238, 264, 266-267, 268-269, 270, 278, 316, 319

Harding, Dr. Esther, 185, 186

headaches, in menopause, 365

heartburn, & pregnancy, 238, 255-256

Hecht, Ben, 182, 184

height, 96-97, 173

hemorrhoids, 281

heredity, 96, 242-246

heroes & heroines, 140-144, 148, 184-185

Hicks, Braxton, 282

Highdon, Dr. Albert, 350-351

hips, broken, 369-370

Hodges, Bishop Joseph, 268

homosexuality, 140

honeymoon, the, 195

Hooker, Davenport, 249, 250

hormone creams, 348-349, 373

Hormone Quest, The (Maisel), 215

hormones: adrenal (*see* adrenal glands); and the placenta, 261-262, 273-274; prolactin, 314-315, 320, 325; sex (*see* sex-hormones); thyroid, 84-85, 87, 286

hospitalism, 24

hostility, 37-41; against parents, 75, 103-104, 131-132; releasing, 337-343 (*See also* aggression; tension)

hunger: definition of, 63-64; in infancy, 19-20 (*See also* eating)

Hunt, Morton, 177-179

Hurlock, Dr. Elizabeth, 11

hymen, the, 16, 53-54, 123-124

hysterectomy, 16, 368

identification, 72-73, 91, 327-328

identity, sense of, 90-91, 162-163, 175, 188-189, 329-332

idols, 139-144 (*See also* heroes . . .)

imagination, 39-40; and foods, 58-59 (*See also* daydreaming; fantasy-life)

inadequacy, sense of, 27-28, 76

independence, developing, 26-33

infancy, 18-26

infantilism, 75, 226, 257-258

infection: in childbirth (*see* childbed fever); immunity to, 273-274 (*See also* diseases)

infertility, 218-230

initiative, development of, 34-36

insatiability, of men, 194-195

insemination, artificial, 224-225, 284

insomnia, 281, 339, 366-367

integrity: body, 29-30, 142; ego, 384-385

intelligence, 177-182

intercourse, sexual (*see* sex-relations)

invasion, dislike of, 118, 142

irritability, 367

Jackson, Dr. Gordon W., 376

Jacobson, Dr. Wayne, 155

jealousy, 28, 324-326

Jeffers, Robinson, 265

Jersild, Professor Arthur, 170

Josselyn, Dr. Irene, 99, 131
Juliana, Queen of the Netherlands, 241

Kanner, Dr. Leo, 46-47
Kardiner, Dr. Abram, 49, 334, 335
Karelitz, Dr. I., 44
Karnaky, Dr. K. J., 125
Kennedy, Jacqueline, 308
Kimball, Dr. E. Robbins, 318
Kinsey Report, the, 194, 219, 269
Kleegman, Dr. Sophia, 224
Kolletschka, Professor Jacob, 303
Kroger, Dr. William, 237, 259, 270, 355, 357
Kugelmass, Dr. I. Newton, 99, 172, 326, 332
Kupperman, Dr. Herbert, 107

labor, 282-296, 304-306; and eating, 288-289; false, 282-283; and hormones, 274; premature, 268, 284-285; and rehearsal-contractions, 271 (See also childbirth)
Landis, Dr. Judson T., 325
Landis, Professor Paul, 173
Lapidus, Dr. Paul W., 164
Lawrence, Gertrude, 372
Lawrence, Marjorie, 382
legs, problems with, 168, 238, 280, 378
leucorrhea, 256-257
Levine, Dr. Rachmeil, 356
Levy, Dr. John, 73, 188, 199-201, 209-210
life-expectancy (see survivability)
lochia, 298, 312
logic, capacity for, 178-179
loneliness: fear of, 183-184, 188, 381-382; of pregnancy, 279
lordosis, 97, 344
love: descriptions of, 183-184; development of, 34-41; falling in, 183-187, 208; of father, 138-139; of girl friends, 139-140; of heroes & heroines, 140-144; mother, 313-314, 326-329; of music & nature, 139; and the newborn, 326; of self (see self-love);

sexual (see sex-relations); of suffering, 139, 147, 186-187
love-play, 201-202
lying-in, after childbirth, 311-314

McAlister, Sir Norman, 242
Maisel, Albert Q., 215
male versus female, 178 (See sexes . . .)
malnutrition, 121-122, 231
marriage: adjusting to, 195-196; and the beautiful woman, 202-207; disillusionment in, 208-211, 230; early, 188-190; and security needs, 239, 314; yearning for, 187-190 (See also sex-relations)
marriage manuals, 196-197, 202
Marsh, Dr. Earle Milliard, 281, 287, 291-292, 305
masochism, feminine, 117-118, 331 (See also suffering, attraction to)
masturbation (see genital play)
Maturation Index, 371
maturing, early and late, 173-174
Mauriceau, François, 309-310
Maxwell, Elsa, 382
Mead, Margaret, 266
medications, & childbirth, 290-296, 305
memory, 366-367, 379
Menkin, Miriam, 216
Menninger, Dr. Karl, 27
Menninger, Dr. William, 334, 337, 338, 340-341
menopause, 114, 330, 349, 361-377
menstruation, 101-126; absence of, 121-122; and acne, 150-151; and bathing, 116; beginning of, 94, 96-97, 101-104; blood of, 104-106, 109-110, 159; and breast-feeding, 320, 321-322; and caloric intake, 169; and cramps, 114-118, 120; definitions of normal, 120-121; emotions and, 122, 230-231; estrogens and, 87, 107-109, 114-115, 151; malnutrition and, 121-122, 231; and menopause, 367-368, 375-376 (See also menopause); and nerves, 119-121;

odors and, 109, 159; and perma-nents, 161; and pregnancy, 230-232, 247; and psychological well-being, 216, 376; stress and, 231; synthetic hormones and, 216, 371; tampons and, 16, 122-125; and the uterus, 17
mental abilities, 177-182
metabolism, 352, 356-359
Metzger, Dr. Emy, 116, 341
Meyer, Dr. Eugene, 155
midwives, 298-300, 302, 309
milk, human, 318
Millay, Edna St. Vincent, 139, 210
Milton, Dr. G. Alexander, 178
miscarriage, 251-253, 268, 351
modesty, 35
mongolism, 350-351
monogamy, need for, 225
Monroe, Marilyn, 129-130
Montague, Dr. Ashley, 113
morning sickness, 232, 236-240, 259
mother: conflict with, 29-33, 37, 326-329; devaluation of, 75, 130-132, 134; a magical being, 71-73, 77-79; spare-time, 333-336
mother love, 313-314, 326-329
motherhood, 1, 7, 311-343; and mar-tyrdom, 5, 99; spare-time, 333-336
mouse test, for pregnancy, 233-234, 235
mouth, the: and body integrity, 29; as pleasure & release organ, 43, 132-133, 172, 341; sensitivity of, 19-20
music, love of, 139

nail-biting, 46, 48, 99
napkins, sanitary, 122-125
narcissism, 149, 331, 377 (See also self-love)
nature, love of, 139
nausea (see morning sickness)
nerve cells, 18-19; at birth, 9, 14, 315
nerves: and eating, 172-173; and fer-tility, 224, 225; interaction with hor-mones, 225; role of, in menstrual cycle, 119-121; and intercourse, 196

nervous habits, 38-39, 99
neuroses, 132, 134, 340-341
New, Dr. Maria, 96
newborn, the, 2-18, 314-315, 322-323
normality, 1; definitions of, 5, 6, 47-48, 120-121, 331, 342-343; descriptions of, 46-48; meaning, at birth, 3-6; tests of, at birth, 13-14
nose worry, 154-157
nosebleeds, in pregnancy, 281
nursing (see breast-feeding)
nutrition, and menstruation, 121-122

obesity, 61-67, 122 (See also weight)
odors, body, 158-159
opiates, 116
organs of reproduction, female, 15-18 (See genitals; ovaries; uterus, etc.)
orgasm, 192-198; in youngsters, 53
ova (see eggs)
ovaries, 15, 93, 107; description of, 17; and the pituitary, 88, 91, 106-109, 215, 234-235; prenatal, 250; and sex-hormones, 16, 17, 86, 91, 106-109, 234-235, 240, 368
ovulation, 107-110, 121, 221, 351; breast-feeding and, 320-322; cause of cramps, 114-115; inducing, 113-114; and middle pain, 118-119; and hormones, 215, 216-218, 228, 234, 235

pain: at birth, 10, 12-13, 14-15; chest, 366, 371; after childbirth, 312; en-joyment of, 117-118, 147; impor-tance of, 12-13; and labor, 288-296, 304-306; middle, 118-119 (See also suffering)
parental bonds, 71-73, 130-136, 138-139
parental expectations, 39, 47-48, 133-136
Parmalee, Dr. A. H., 13-14
passivity, 31, 45, 72, 136, 329-330; in pregnancy, 254-255
Patten, Bradley A., 244-245

Pearce, Dr. Jane, 36, 189-190, 324, 348
Pearson, Dr. Gerald H., 30-31, 40, 42, 50, 51-52, 59
Peck, Dr. Robert F., 342
pelvis, 75, 97, 370
penis, 15, 40, 219; "loss" of, 40, 50-51
permanent waving, 161
permissiveness, 131
personality strength, 128-129, 136
perspiration, 158-159
pets, need for, 70
Pincus, Dr. Gregory, 213-215
pituitary gland, 81, 94, 97, 215; after childbirth, 312, 320-321; function of, 88-90, 91, 96; and the menstrual cycle, 106-109, 363-364; and pregnancy, 234-235, 312
placenta, the, 248; delivery of, 306-307; function of, 240-243, 261-262, 265, 279-280, 312
Planned Parenthood Federation, 214
plastic surgery, 155-157
playmates, 69; imaginary, 39-40
plumpness, 360-361
Pollack, Dr. Herbert, 352, 356
Potter, Dr. Edith L., 251, 252, 253
power, 73-74, 80 (See also energy)
praise, need for, 69, 138, 381
pregnancy, 230-286; and accidents, 267; acne and, 153; arthritis and, 243; and backache, 256, 270, 279-280, 344; bathing in, 272; bleeding in, 247, 253, 267; breasts and, 232, 233, 235-236; compulsive, 255; and compulsive eating, 258-259; and constipation, 238, 270; and contractions, 271, 282-283 (see also labor); discomforts of, 236-238, 255-259, 270-272, 279-281; diseases & drugs in, 241-243; and a doctor's care, 259, 272; and douching, 257, 271; a dreamlike state, 254-255, 260; false, 231-232; fears & worries in, 260, 266-268, 276-279; feeling life in, 254, 263-264; and hemorrhoids, 281; hormones of, 215, 234-236, 256,

271, 312; hysterical, 231; and awareness, 238, 275, 331; and insomnia, 281; and intercourse, 268-270; and leg cramps, 238, 280; length of, 284-285; loneliness of, 279; and nausea, 232, 236-240, 259; and nosebleeds, 281; passivity in, 254-255; preventing (see contraceptives); "proof positive," 254; and sex-desire, 268-269; signs of, 230-238, 254; and teeth, 260; tests for, 233-235; and toxemia, 259, 272, 285; tubal, 223; and urination, 232, 235, 280-281 (See also abortion; childbirth; conception; labor)
pride, manly, 180-181, 193, 195, 332
progesterone, 110, 113; function of, 86, 108, 110-111, 115, 215, 240, 375-376; and pregnancy, 234-235, 240; synthetic, 117, 215-217; and water-retention, 110-111 (See also estrogens; sex-hormones)
prolactin, 314-315, 320, 325
puberty, 62, 90-101; and acne, 150-154; and anxiety, 90-100; growth-spurt of, 169; and hormones, 87, 363; phyical changes of, 17, 91-98; precocious, 96; and the thyroid, 85
"pushiness," 180-181, 334

quarrels, lovers', 190-191

rabbit test, for pregnancy, 233, 235
Rakoff, Dr. A. E., 103, 351, 356, 370, 373
Read, Dr. Grantly Dick, 289, 290, 291
reading jags, 70
readjustment time, after childbirth, 311-326
receptiveness, 196, 202, 207 (See also passivity)
rectum, the: and body integrity, 29-30
reducing, 66-67, 356-361 (See also eating; weight)
reflexes: grasping, 14, 20, 28; startle, 13-14 (See also sucking)

religion, as therapy, 229, 339
replacement pills, 349, 368-377
reproductive system, 7 (*See* genitals; glands; ovaries, *etc.*) retreat, age of, 100-101
Rhoades, Dr. F. P., 370
Rhodes, Dr. Andrew J., 242
rhythm method, of birth-control, 214
rhythms, 127, 139; as tension-release, 43, 44, 51
Rice-Wray, Dr. Edris, 217
Rock, Dr. John, 213, 215-216, 223-224, 228, 231, 350, 370
roles, female, in history, 175-177, 181
Roosenburg, Henriette, 121
Roosevelt, Eleanor, 4, 348, 378
Rosen, Dr. Harold, 349-350, 369-370
Rosenthal, Dr. Alexander, 259
Roth, Dr. Arthur, 168, 171, 174
rubella (German measles), 241-242, 350
Rubin Test, 223, 225
Rutherford, Dr. Robert N., 111, 113, 237-238, 321, 323, 376

Sanford, Nevitt, 188
Sanger, Margaret, 213-214, 381
Sapirstein, Dr. Milton, 192, 197, 202-207, 269
Saul, Dr. Leon H., 5, 117, 187
Schauffler, Dr. Goodrich C., 54, 95
Scherf, Dr. David, 366
Schumann, Dr. Edward, 83
scrotum, 219-220
sebum, 150
secretiveness, 140
security-system, 348
self-confidence, 26-31; in adolescence, 138; in childbirth, 290-291; in older men, 374, 377-378
self-discovery, 18-24, 50 (*See also* identity; self-image)
self-image: changes in, 98-101, 343; development of, 18-24, 50, 98-101; importance of, 22-23; of men, 377-378; and nose surgery, 156-157 (*See also* identity)
self-love, 23, 137-138, 149, 331, 384; the beauty and, 206-207; and eating, 169, 259, 355; extremes of, 327, 355
Selye, Dr. Hans, 86
Semelweis, Dr. Ignaz, 300-304
Senn, Dr. Milton E. J., 47, 121
senses, keenness of, 12, 15, 21, 36, **331**, 383-384 (*See also* awareness)
sex-desire (or drive), 200-202, 229; after childbirth, 325; and genital play, 51-52; loss of, 121; in pregnancy, 268-269; and hormones, 87
sex glands, 80-84, 86-88, 97, 119, 158, 363-364
sex-hormones, 52, 76, 86-88, 215, 312-313; and acne, 87, 150-151, 153-154; and adrenals, 88; and aggression, 37-38; and attraction to males, 138; deficiency of, 366, 368-369; and energy, 73-74, 80-84, 86-87; and hair, 159, 161, 347; male, 37-38, 80-83, 87-88, 159; and menopause, 364-377; and menstruation, 106-117, 320-321; and ovaries (*see* ovaries); and permanents, 161; of pregnancy, 215, 234-236, 271, 312; at puberty, 91-99, 363; and skin, 345, 346; synthetic, 89, 215-218, 349, 268-377 (*See also* androgens; estrogens; progesterone)
sex organs, female, 15-18 (*See* genitals; ovaries; uterus, *etc.*)
sex-relations: and acne, 153-154; adjusting to, 195-196; after childbirth, 307, 321-322, 324-326; desire for (*see* sex-desire); disorders in, 199-200; extra-marital, 340-341; frequency of, 200, 219, 224; interest in, peaks of, 194; as language of the body, 325; man's role in, 180-181, 193, 196, 197-199; before marriage, 192-194; and miscarriage, 268; need for, 269, 339-341; and neuroses, 340-341; in old age, 383; peculiari-

ties in, 201-202; as pleasure, 51, 118, 193; and pregnancy, 268-270; preparation for, 31, 141-148, 192 (*see also* genital play); and pre-teens, 76-79; starvation of, 136; and tension-release, 339-341; woman's role in, 181, 196, 197-199

sexes, differences in, 12, 32, 36, 106, 142; acne, 154; aggression & hostility, 5, 37-38, 148, 174, 341-342; attraction to suffering, 186-187; fears, 38-39; food needs, 56, 85; glands, 80-90; as lovers, 184, 191-207 *passim*; mental abilities, 177-179; observing, 35, 40, 50-51, 142; passivity, 31, 45, 72, 136, 329-330; sex-interest, 194; pelvises, 370; psychosexual development, 138-139; self-images, 377-378; senses, 12, 36, 331; shrinking, 370; survivability, 5-9, 179-180, 341-342

shame, 26-33

shrinking, 370, 378

Simpson, Dr. James Young, 294-295, 304

skin: concern with, 149-154; drying of, 372-374; elasticity of, 345; excitation of, 198-199; nourishment of, 348-349; sensitivity of, 12, 19, 238

sleepiness, & pregnancy, 232, 235, 281

Smith, Dr. Clement A., 10

Sontag, L. W., 264

soul-mates, 185-186

speech (*see* talking)

sperm cells, 108; hazards of, 219-224

Spock, Dr. Benjamin, 42, 51

startle reflex, 13-14

Steiglitz, Dr. Edward, 379, 383

Steinmetz, Charles, 379-380

sterility, 80-82, 218-230; emotional, 225-229; and fevers, 219-220; and progesterone, 216

sterilization, 245-246

Stone, Drs. Abraham and Hannah, 213-214

Strahl, Dr. Margaret, 329

Streeter, Dr. George, 251

strength: personality, 128-129, 136 (*See also* survivability)

stretch marks, 256

stress: growth as, 48, 94-95; menstruation and, 231; and sex-relations, 196 (*See also* tension)

stuttering, 39

sucking: at birth, 3, 11, 15; prenatal, 273; thumb, 42-45, 46, 48, 51, 273

suffering: acceptance of, 118, 331; attraction to, 77-78, 139, 147, 186-187

sugar, cravings for, 358-359

Sulzberger, Dr. Marian, 151-152

surgery, 229, 368; plastic, 155-157

survivability, 38, 244-245, 273; of females, 5-18, 179-180, 341-342, 362-363; of "preemies," 273-274, 285

talking, a tension-release, 36-37, 339

tampons, 16, 122-125

taste, sense of, 11, 12, 15, 383-384

Taylor, Dr. Howard F., 375

teenagers (*see* adolescence)

teeth, and pregnancy, 260

teething, 24-25, 33, 44

tension: in labor, 289-296; and newborns, 322-323; pre-menstrual, 111, 351; releasing, 36-51 *passim*, 74-75, 131-132, 338, 339-343

Terman, Dr. Lewis, 37-39, 148

testes, 80-83, 219-220

testosterone, 37-38

thalidomide, 241, 349-350

Thompson, Dorothy, 202

thumb-sucking, 42-45, 46, 48, 51, 273

thyroid gland, 81, 97-98, 363-364; deficiency in, 61-62, 66, 84; function of, 84-85; hormones of, 84, 87, 286

tomboyism, 70-74, 98, 170, 352

touch, sense of, 11, 12, 21

touch-hunger, 19-21

toxemia, 259, 272, 285

training, toilet, 29-32

trichomonas, 257

trust, 24-26, 33, 45

tubes (*see* Fallopian tubes)
Tyler, Dr. Edward T., 216-217

umbilical cord, 250, 262-263, 264; tangling, 10, 260, 263
urination, frequency of, 232, 235, 280-281, 366
uterus (womb), 15; at birth, 17; cells of, 111; changes in, with growth, 92-93; changes in, with pregnancy, 233, 237-238, 240, 254, 271, 287, 350; and conception, 108; and contractions, 271, 282; description of, 16-17; and nausea, 237-238; inefficiency of, 115; involution of, 317; lining of, 86, 107-109, 114-115, 223, 234, 247, 306, 375-376; and the placenta, 240-241; and pregnancy discomforts, 256, 271 (*see also* labor); during puberty, 95-96; tipped, 116-117

vagina: acidity of, 93, 220, 257; aging tissues in, 374; at birth, 15; and body integrity, 29; changes in, 233, 366; discharges from, 93, 233, 256-257, 271, 298, 312; fluids of, 111; insensitivity of, 124, 125
varicose veins, 256, 344

venereal disease, 212, 218
Victoria, Queen of England, 294-295, 351
virginity, 16, 53-54, 123-124

walking, learning, 28-29
Wall, Dr. Richard, 13
water, retention of, 87, 110-111, 377
weaning, 25-26, 33
weight: at birth, 3-4, 55, 285, 315; charts for, 171, 359; and pregnancy, 258-259; in puberty, 97-98; reducing, 66-67, 356-361; variations in, 171, 354, 359-361; worries over, 168-170, 352-361 (*See also* eating)
White, Dr. Charles, 297-300
Whitman, Walt, 101, 246
wiggling, 75
Wilkins, Dr. Lawson, 171
Wilson, Dr. Robert E., 376
withdrawal, 47, 137-138
womb (*see* uterus)
work: habits of, 139; and love, 5, 331, 343; as tension-release, 337, 338

X ray, 270-271; and acne, 151-152

Zondek, Bernard, 233